Corvette 1968–1982
Restoration Guide
2nd Edition

By Richard Prince

motorbooks

Dedication

For my mother, whose love and wisdom permeates all that I do.

First published in 2011 by Motorbooks, an imprint of Quarto Publishing Group USA Inc., 400 First Avenue North, Suite 400, Minneapolis, MN 55401 USA

Motorbooks titles are also available at discounts in bulk quantity for industrial or sales-promotional use. For details write to Special Sales Manager at Quarto Publishing Group USA Inc., 400 First Avenue North, Suite 400, Minneapolis, MN 55401 USA.

To find out more about our books, visit us online at www.motorbooks.com.

ISBN-13: 978-0-7603-4057-8

Editor: Peg Goldstein and Zack Miller
Creative Director: Michele Lanci-Altomare
Design Managers: Brenda Canales, James Kegley, Brad Spinger, and Kim Winscher
Layout by: Chris Fayers

Printed in China

On the front cover: Beautifully restored 1971 Corvette.

Inset: Chevrolet's mighty 454 big block.

On the title page and back cover: 1978 Indianapolis 500 pace car replica.

Contents

Acknowledgments 4

Preface 4

Introduction 5

CHAPTER 1   **1968–1969** 8

CHAPTER 2   **1970–1972** 50

CHAPTER 3   **1973–1977** 93

CHAPTER 4   **1978–1982** 151

Appendices 202

Index 223

Acknowledgments

I wish to thank the following people for their generous assistance in creating this book: Jack Corso, Jack DiMaggio, Stephen Gansky, Bill Hermanek, Gus Lucas, Chris Mazzilli, Bill Mehrkens, Debbie Padawer, Stan Rivera, Mark Rudnick, Joel Shapiro, Jon Shapiro, Steven Sharpe, Louis and Kelly Sitar, Kevin Smith, Michael Vaccarelli, and Dave Weber, along with his staff at Collision Unlimited. I would also like to thank the National Corvette Restorers Society for the invaluable work its members and leaders have done in gathering, preserving, and disseminating a wealth of information about the Corvettes we all love so much. And last but certainly not least, I offer a sincere thank-you to the men and woman at General Motors, who have labored long and hard to make Corvette the pride of America and, without qualification, the best sports car in the world.

Preface

This book is intended to provide restorers of 1968–1982 Corvettes with the technical information needed to return these cars to the exact configurations they were in at the time of final delivery by Chevrolet Motor Division. This is not a how-to manual, however. Rather, it is a compendium of information about how the cars were originally built, including available options, exterior and interior colors and materials, correct components and their respective factory finishes, part numbers, casting numbers, date codes, and the like. The book will not tell you how to do a restoration procedure, but it will tell you where and how to read original part numbers and date codes, what parts your restoration procedures should be done with, and how those parts should look when you are finished.

Owing to the explosive popularity of the 1968–1982 models, an ever-expanding body of published information is available to assist the restorer. To obtain the greatest benefit from this restoration guide, it should be used in conjunction with some of these other valuable resources. Among them are Chevrolet's chassis service, chassis overhaul, and shop manuals. These provide detailed instructions, diagrams, and specifications for component service, repair, and overhaul.

Though it does not provide how-to instructions per se, another invaluable companion to this restoration guide is Chevrolet's *Corvette Assembly Instruction Manual,* available for each year of production. Each manual is an exact reprint of the assembly instructions that production line workers used to build the cars. Each manual contains hundreds of exploded drawings showing how virtually every part of a Corvette goes together.

These materials, as well as many others, are readily available from any major Corvette restoration parts supplier. They complement this restoration guide perfectly in that they will show you how to do many of the procedures commonly performed during a comprehensive restoration.

Introduction

In January 1953, 30,000 fortunate individuals had the privilege of walking into the grand ballroom of New York's Waldorf-Astoria Hotel to view the GM Motorama. Reflecting the postwar feelings of American invincibility and unparalleled ingenuity, this extravaganza was designed to showcase the company's creative talent in ways that would leave a lasting impression. At a cost in excess of five million 1953 dollars, the Motorama was the epitome of showmanship and marketing genius. Incredibly ornate displays, beautiful women, and elaborate stage productions orchestrated by the best choreographers and dancers Broadway had to offer certainly contributed to the desired effect, but it was the cars that really stirred people's emotions.

This was the golden era of the dream cars, fantastically styled and engineered vehicles designed to demonstrate the company's prowess while at the same time thrilling spectators. Among the more notable dream machines, which included the LeSabre and Buick XP-300, there was one car that really stood out from the others. Called Corvette, this little white two-seater sports car, perched on a revolving turntable in front of a panoramic image of the Manhattan skyline, was the sensation of the 1953 Motorama. Public reaction was so strong, in fact, that GM decided to actually put the car into production, something that had never before been done with a dream car.

In June 1953, a scant six months after it made its debut on the Waldorf-Astoria stage, production of the Corvette began on a pilot assembly line in an old, empty customer delivery building on Van Slyke Avenue in Flint, Michigan. By year's end, only 300 of the cars were built, though plans were underway to increase production capacity substantially for the following year. But unfortunately, the public's reaction, which was so hot at the Motorama, had cooled considerably when the cars came to market, and by the end of 1954, as many as ⅓ of that year's 3,640 Corvettes remained unsold.

What was it that caused this apparent turnaround in the public's attitude? Quality control problems, mediocre performance emanating from the car's six-cylinder/two-speed automatic Powerglide combination, as well as a relatively high cost in spite of the use of many passenger car components utilized to keep cost down, certainly all played a role. Perhaps the most important factor, however, was

inadequate marketing. In 1953, Chevrolet was the largest division of the largest automobile manufacturer in the world. It had a well-deserved reputation for building economical and reliable transportation for the masses. The decision makers at Chevy, who were more accustomed to producing hundreds of thousands of ordinary passenger cars per year, knew virtually nothing about selling low-volume, largely handmade sports cars to a few thousand devoted enthusiasts.

As a result of poor sales performance and mounting losses, the Corvette "experiment" came perilously close to ending as quickly as it had begun. But to their everlasting credit, a small, intensely dedicated group of individuals within Chevrolet simply would not allow this to happen. They recognized and systematically addressed the car's shortcomings and turned an apparent loser into a sure-fire winner. The year 1955 saw the introduction of the legendary small-block V-8 and, at the end of the year, a manual three-speed transmission. In 1956, Corvette marked the beginning of its racing legacy, and the following year brought such high-performance options as fuel injection, a heavy-duty brake and suspension package, and four-speed manual transmission.

With the introduction of the awesome Sting Ray in 1963, the Corvette's reputation for world-class performance was upheld with features such as independent rear suspension, fuel injection, racing brakes and suspension, and Posi-Traction rear axle. In addition, 1963 marked the beginning of the car's development as a true GT machine. Options like air conditioning, power steering and brakes, and leather seat covers gave buyers great latitude in equipping their cars just as they wanted them.

By 1968, when the sensational third generation Corvette was introduced, the car had really reached maturity. Four-wheel disc brakes and four-wheel independent suspension were standard. Buyers had a choice of no less than seven different engines, five different transmissions, and a wide variety of performance options. By simply checking off the correct boxes on the order form, a race-ready Corvette could be ordered directly from Chevrolet. And for those more interested in luxurious motoring, a bevy of grand touring and luxury features were also available. Corvettes equipped with full power, air conditioning, leather seats, AM-FM stereo, and all the other comfort and convenience features were perfect long-distance cruisers.

Third-generation Corvettes, commonly referred to as Stingrays or Sharks, remained in production until 1982, longer than any other Corvette model. In their 15 years of production, more than 542,861 Stingrays were built, a staggering number when you consider the marque's near demise for lack of interest 20 years earlier.

The period between 1968 and 1982 was a fascinating and tumultuous time in the automotive industry. The beginning of this stretch marked the end of the golden era of Detroit muscle machines. Appropriately equipped Corvettes, such as those sporting the potent L88 or exotic ZL1 option packages, were the undisputed kings of the muscle car epoch. As the 1960s turned into the 1970s, unrestrained power and speed fell victim to increasingly stringent insurance industry demands, governmental regulations, and market considerations. Research and development dollars that had previously been directed toward enhancing performance were now targeted at meeting fuel economy, exhaust emissions, and safety requirements. As a result, all cars, including Corvettes, got heavier, clumsier looking, more expensive, and slower. But Corvette, unlike many other cars, weathered the storm with dignity and managed to emerge from this rather gloomy era with its character and place in history still intact.

As the 1970s came to a close and the 1980s dawned, a transformation in the automobile building business began to emerge. Science had finally caught up with the mandates from Washington and elsewhere and was on the brink of surging ahead. Through the application of very sophisticated computer technology, superior manufacturing techniques and materials, and high-tech electronics, Corvettes met all of the safety, emissions, and economy demands imposed upon them and were performing admirably at the same time.

In the nearly two decades since their production came to an end, collector interest in third-generation Corvettes has grown steadily. The sheer number of cars produced as well as the great variety of offerings during the Stingray's 15-year model run, including incredibly high horsepower big-blocks, efficient and powerful computer-directed small-blocks, convertibles, and special offerings such as the 1978 Indy Pace Car Replicas and 1982 Collector Editions, mean there is something of interest for just about everyone.

In addition to the selection and variety of third-generation Corvettes available, collector interest in these cars has also been generated as a result of their recognition by the major Corvette show organizations, most notably Bloomington Gold and the National Corvette Restorers Society. Recognition has fostered interest in showing the cars at the highest levels, and this in turn has encouraged their restoration. In the great free market tradition, the resultant demand for correct restoration parts has induced manufacturers and suppliers to make available just about anything needed for the restoration of a Shark Corvette.

Concurrent with the emergence and maturation of the Shark restoration hobby is a need for increasingly detailed and accurate information about the cars. To succeed at the highest levels of judging, realize the maximum economic return from the investment in restoration, and, for many people, derive the greatest feelings of accomplishment and happiness from their efforts, an intensely detailed and factory correct restoration is essential.

This book is intended to provide restorers of 1968–1982 Corvettes with the technical information needed to return these cars to the same exact configuration they were in at the time of final delivery by Chevrolet Motor Division. This is not, however, a how-to manual. Rather, it is a compendium of information about how the cars were originally built, including available options and their permissible combinations, exterior and interior colors and materials, correct components and their respective factory finishes, part numbers, casting numbers, date codes, and the like. It will not tell you how to do a restoration procedure, but it will tell you what parts the procedure should be done with and how they should look when you are finished.

As you utilize the information contained herein while traversing the road to restoration, you will experience the full range of human emotions. At one end of the spectrum is the pain of scraped knuckles and the depression that inevitably results from feelings that your car will never go back together again. At the other end, and of far greater importance, are the intense feelings of accomplishment derived from a job well done and the unmitigated delight you will take in the finished product.

As you travel the road to restoration, experiencing the agony of a thousand small setbacks and the ecstasy of a million small victories, I urge you to remember one thing above all else: Your Corvette, and, in fact, all of the Corvettes in all the world, are not worth your use of one finger on one hand, your eyesight, or your life. Automotive repair and restoration is an inherently dangerous pursuit. However, by consistently practicing safe habits, you can reduce the probability of injury to an absolute minimum. In an automotive shop, 99 percent of safety is the result of using common sense and overcoming the lazy tendencies inherent in all of us. Do not, under any circumstances, fail to use goggles, a breathing mask, hearing protection, and all the other proper safety gear necessary for the task you are performing and the tools you are employing.

If you have any doubt concerning your personal safety, consult an applicable shop manual and seek professional advice. Remember, regardless of how much you love your Corvette and how special it is and how important it is to complete what you are doing as quickly as possible, it is still just a car. And a car is just a conglomeration of metal, plastic, rubber, and glass that together is not worth one single cell in your body.

After personal safety, the second-most-important thing for practitioners of the restoration art is to have fun. General Motors has always built Corvettes to realize a profit for its shareholders. That is the purpose of GM's and every other corporation's existence. In contrast, the magnificent men and women within Chevrolet who transformed what would have been little more than a footnote in automotive history into a respected and beloved automotive icon the world over had something even more important than corporate profits in mind. They had feelings of excitement and passion in their hearts, for they knew they were creating far more than just another car. The Corvette transcends mere transportation, and the people who built it recognized it as an expression of the American ideal, the near perfect melding of art and science, the creation of a legacy that would endure long after they were forgotten. For these people, the Corvette was far more than the source of their livelihood; it was also a major source of joy in their lives.

As you delve into the restoration hobby, you too will feel what the car's creators felt, for you too will be playing a role in preserving and perpetuating the Corvette legend. It is my sincere hope that you find the information in this book useful and that it plays a role in enhancing your enjoyment of the Corvette restoration hobby.

Chapter 1
1968–1969

1968–1969 EXTERIOR
Body Fiberglass

The first year for what is now commonly called the shark body style was 1968. With the exception of the door skins, which differ due to the different door opening mechanisms, 1968 and 1969 body panels are functionally interchangeable. There are, however, various minor differences between some 1968 body parts and their 1969 counterparts. For example, the rear lower filler panel differs in that '68s have rectangular backup lamps mounted in them and 1969s do not. Another example is the top surround panel, which was strengthened in 1969 with the enlargement of the lip in the front corners adjacent to the hood opening.

All 1968 and 1969 body panels are made from press-molded fiberglass. The panels are smooth on both sides and are very dark gray in color.

Body Paint

All 1968 and 1969 cars were painted with acrylic lacquer. Factory paint is generally smooth and shiny, though some orange peel is clearly evident throughout. Roughness and poor coverage are fairly typical along the very bottom edges of body panels and in less conspicuous areas such as edges of the wiper door, inside the front fender vents, in the door jambs, and on the headlamp bezels. The factory did not use clear coat, even with metallic colors. Because clear coat was not used, metallics might be slightly mottled or blotchy.

Front Bumpers

Front bumpers are chrome plated and held to the car with semi-gloss, black-painted steel brackets. Cadmium-plated hex-head bolts are used to retain the bumper to the brackets, and cadmium and/or black oxide hex-head bolts hold the brackets to the chassis. The most commonly seen head markings on original bolts are "TR," "TRW," "RSC," "SCC," and "M." These head markings represent the respective bolt manufacturers.

Unpainted or silver-cadmium-plated shims are sometimes used between the front outer bumper mounts and the body.

Front Grille Area and Parking Lamps

The front grille assembly is made from three pieces of black molded plastic, each with horizontal slats. The grilles remain all black for 1968 and for 1969 cars assembled through

For 1968 the Corvette got a completely redesigned exterior and interior, but the underlying chassis was largely unchanged.

This unrestored 1968 is one of 2,473 Corvettes painted International Blue that year.

Corvettes from 1968 were plagued with a number of problems, including poor body panel fit and paint finish, particularly early in production. Today that is irrelevant to collectors, who covet original, unrestored examples like this one.

approximately January 1969. Grilles in cars assembled after approximately January 1969 are black, with the front edge of each horizontal slat painted silver. Some 1968s and early 1969s have grilles with a black top bar and silver-edged lower bars, and some cars have all-black outer grilles and a center grille with silver edges.

In 1968 two black Phillips-head screws in each of the outer grilles hold them on. One is above and one is below the turn signal light on each side. These screws go into brackets that are riveted to the car's body. In 1969 the holes for these screws are present in the grilles, but the screws are not used. Instead, the 1969 grilles are held in place by the turn signal lamp mounting bolts.

In 1968 and 1969, the front turn signal lamps get clear plastic lenses with amber bulbs. A very light gray gasket seals the lens to the housing. The lenses are held by chrome Phillips-head screws that have special knurled shanks. A fiber optic cable is inserted into the top of each parking light housing.

Rectangular side marker lamps are used at all four corners in 1968 and 1969. The lamp housings, which can be seen only from behind the body panels, are made from white plastic. Very light gray gaskets seal the lenses to the lamp housings.

In 1968 front side marker lamps have clear lenses with amber bulbs. In 1969 the lamps have amber lenses and clear bulbs. For both years, the rear side marker lamp lenses are red. Front and rear side marker lamp lenses are trimmed with stainless steel, and all lenses contain a cast-in date indicating the year the lens was first utilized.

Front License Plate Bracket

All 1968 and 1969 front license plate brackets are painted semi-gloss black and are held on by two cadmium-plated hex-head bolts. A small rubber bumper is inserted in a hole

Vacuum-actuated headlamp doors, a fiber optic light monitoring system, three-speed automatic transmission, and removable T-tops for the coupe model were some of the features introduced in 1968.

toward the bottom center, and two white plastic nuts insert into square holes in the upper corners.

A small brown paper bag marked "LICENSE ATTACHING" on one side, "REAR PLATE PARTS" on the other, and "UNIT NUMBER 3875313" along the top came in the car originally. In it were four large, cadmium-plated, slotted pan-head screws for the front and rear license plates. All cars also came with two stainless-steel license plate frames sealed in plastic bags and placed in the luggage area. Original frames have stainless rivets, while service replacements have silver cadmium-plated rivets.

Front Headlamps and Headlamp Bezels

All four headlamp bulbs in 1968 and 1969 were made by Guide and feature a Guide T-3 logo in the glass. All bulbs have a centered triangle with "T-3" surrounded by vertical bars.

Headlamp bezels are die-cast aluminum, not fiberglass as in later cars, and painted body color. Paint on the bezels is usually not as shiny or smooth as it is on the body.

Three different headlamp door sizes were used in 1968. The earliest design was the smallest, and the two successive designs were each about ¼ inch larger.

Cars from 1968 do not have any headlight washer nozzles or nozzle holes in the bezels. Those from 1969 have two chrome-plated headlamp washer nozzles in each bezel. Both nozzles are pointed at the middle of the low-beam (outer) bulb, one from above and one from below.

A semi-gloss black plastic shield is behind each front grille to shield the headlamps from view when the light assemblies

On all 1968s and 1969s manufactured through approximately January 1969, the leading edge of the front grille was painted silver. Later grilles were all black. Some cars have a mix of early and late grilles, for example, with black outer grilles and silver edges on the center grille behind the license plate.

are in the down position. The shields are each held to the body by three self-tapping, black phosphate, Phillips pan-head screws with integral flat washers. Beginning in approximately May 1969, a slightly smaller shield was utilized.

A cadmium dichromate-plated vacuum actuator is mounted behind each headlamp assembly. Original actuators have a ¼-inch-diameter hose connection tube that extends about 9/16 inch from the actuator body before its 90-degree bend. Replacement actuators have a 5/16-inch-diameter tube that extends about 3/8 inch from the body before turning 90 degrees. A translucent red ink marking is normally found on each actuator adjacent to the tube. A red-striped hose connects to the back of each actuator, and a green-striped hose connects to the front.

Front Fenders

All 1968 and 1969 front fenders are functionally interchangeable. Three of the four fender vents are functional and help remove hot air from the engine compartment. The fourth vent is blocked and painted semi-gloss black. In most black cars, the blocked vent is painted body color and not semi-gloss black. Front fender louver trim molding is optional for 1969s but not for '68s. The chrome and metallic-silver-painted louver trim moldings are each held by two chrome-plated Phillips-head screws.

In 1969 both front fenders have an emblem reading "Stingray" above their louvers. Cars from 1968 did not have these emblems.

The 1969 Stingray emblems are chrome, with the thin stepped edge surrounding each letter painted black. Emblems are held onto the body by an adhesive strip, and each has three long studs used for positioning only, and therefore they do not get nuts. Original emblems feature an "i" without a dot. Later replacements have a small groove cut into the "i" to simulate the dot. Some later replacements also have a thick black plastic adhesive clearly visible behind the emblem.

Hood

All 1968 and 1969 cars originally equipped with a small-block engine have a low-profile hood with a single wind split down the middle. There are no emblems, decals, or other markings on these hoods.

Hoods on all cars equipped with a 427 engine (except optional L88 and ZL1 engines) have a raised area with twin simulated vents in the center for added engine compartment clearance. The leading edge of each simulated vent has a piece

The Corvette Stingray body styling was quite radical when introduced in 1968. The design was very well received by the buying public, and it helped propel Corvette sales to a new record of 28,566 units in 1968.

The high-dome hood with 427 emblems was used in 1968–1969. This car is one of 1,932 '68s equipped with an optional L68 427/400 engine.

Big-block-equipped cars came with a special hood. It had a "power bulge" that gave added clearance for the air cleaner. All such hoods came with "427" emblems on either side of the bulge.

of cast-metal trim. It is chrome except on the inside, which is painted semi-gloss black.

L88- and ZL1-equipped cars utilize a special hood with a higher bulge than the hood on other 427-powered cars. These have a functional cold air induction feature that directs outside air to the carburetor from the base of the windshield.

All 427-equipped cars, including L88s and ZL1s, have a 427 emblem on each side of the hood bulge. The emblems are comprised of three separate numerals, which are chrome plated with black-painted recesses.

Windshield Vent Grille, Wiper Door, and Wipers

The windshield vent grille is painted body color and is retained by black-oxide, recessed Phillips flathead screws with fine threads. The area beneath the vent grille is painted semi-gloss black.

The windshield wiper door, like the vent grille, is painted body color. A stainless-steel trim strip is on the rear edge of the wiper door. The strip is painted body color except for an unpainted, polished bead that runs adjacent to the windshield. The strip is attached to the wiper door with hidden clips in 1968 and small round-head pins that look like rivets in 1969.

Body-color fender trim that extends the look of the wiper door molding is mounted to the top of each fender with a black Phillips oval-head screw at the inboard end. The shape of this small piece of trim is different in 1968 and 1969, causing it to touch or nearly touch the stainless-steel windshield pillar trim in 1968 and mount about $5/16$ inch away from the trim in 1969.

Wiper arms and blade holders are dull black in color, and each holder says "TRICO" on one end. Wiper blade inserts are 16 inches long and also say "TRICO." They have various patent numbers molded in and two raised ribs below the writing.

Windshield Washers

In 1968 two flat, black metal tubes are welded to L-shaped brackets. The brackets in turn are attached to the underside of the windshield vent grille with a hex-head screw in very early cars and a Phillips-head screw thereafter.

Most 1969 Corvettes assembled through approximately December 1968 use the same washer nozzles as 1968 cars. Those 1969s assembled after approximately December 1968 have a different configuration. In these cars, the two short lengths of flat black tubing are each welded to a metal block screwed to the body at the base of the windshield.

Late 1969s have yet another washer nozzle configuration. In these cars a length of metal tubing is welded to a small tab at the end of each wiper arm and is further retained to the arm by three or four black plastic clips.

Windshield, Door Glass, and Back Glass

All 1968 and 1969 Corvette windshields were manufactured by Libby Owens Ford (LOF) utilizing Safety Plate glass. The LOF logo, SAFETY PLATE, and a two-letter manufacturing date code are etched into the lower right side of the windshield. In the date code, one letter represents the month and the other denotes the year. There is no discernible pattern to the letter usage, so you must refer to the glass date codes in Appendix R.

"ASI" is written in the upper right portion of the windshield. The letters are white and sandwiched between the laminates of glass, not etched into the surface like the LOF logo and date code.

Both side windows are made from LOF Safety Flo-Lite glass, which has the manufacturer's logo and a two-letter date code etched in, just like the windshield. If the glass is tinted, the words "Soft-Ray" or "Soft-Ray Tinted" are also etched in. In addition, the words "Astro Ventilation" are present in white silk-screened letters in the lower forward corner of each window. The word "Astro" is a continuous script with no breaks, and the lines are very crisp. The "Astro" script in some reproduction glass has breaks and blurred edges.

Back windows in 1968 and 1969 coupes, like the windshields and side glass, have the LOF logo and manufacturing date code etched in.

Door Mirror, Handles, and Locks

All 1968 and 1969 Corvettes have one chrome-plated outside rearview mirror mounted on the driver's door. A mounting base is held to the door by two screws. The mirror goes over the base and is held on by a black-oxide Allen-head screw. A thin gasket goes between the base and door and is visible when the mirror is installed.

The mirrors on early 1968s were mounted about six inches farther forward than they were on later '68s and on '69s. This change occurred in approximately March 1968.

The mirror's head is rectangular and measures $3\frac{7}{8}$ inches high by $5\frac{3}{8}$ inches wide. The glass is coded with the manufacturer's symbol and a date code. Mirrors supplied by Donnelly Mirror, Inc. include "DMI" in the code, and those supplied by Ajax Mirror include "AX." For example, the code

All 1968–1969 Corvettes came with a side mirror on the driver's door only. Original mirror heads measure $5\frac{3}{8}$ inches wide by $3\frac{7}{8}$ inches high. Cars built prior to approximately March 1968 had the mirror installed close to the front edge of the door, as shown here. After approximately March 1968, the mirror was installed about 6 inches farther back.

in a Donnelly mirror manufactured in April 1968 would read "4-DMI-8," while the code for an Ajax mirror manufactured in February 1969 would read "2-AX-69."

All 1968 door handles consist of a spring-loaded press-flap grab and a push-button release. The door lock is incorporated into the push-button release, which sits in a recess molded into the fiberglass door skin.

In all 1969s, the door release mechanism is incorporated into the spring-loaded press-flap grab. The door locks in '69s, which are positioned below the door handles, feature polished stainless-steel bezels. Original bezels are retained to the cylinders by means of a continuous crimp around the entire circumference. Incorrect replacement locks may have bezels retained by four tangs. A thin black rubber gasket is visible between the lock and door.

On original 1968 and 1969 press-flap handles, the spring action is provided by a coil spring on the hinge shaft. A butterfly spring covering a coil spring is incorrect. When the flap is depressed, the spring is visible. A thin black rubber gasket is visible between the handle and door.

A 1968 door release button and lock assembly. The spring-loaded press flap on top of the door serves only as a grab bar in 1968. In 1969 it functions as both a grab bar and a door latch release.

Side Rocker Molding and Optional Side Exhaust

Side rocker molding for all 1968 and 1969 Corvettes is comprised of two sections. The larger piece is fiberglass painted semi-gloss black. The smaller piece is brushed aluminum that is polished along the top and painted semi-gloss black along the bottom. The smaller piece goes on top of the larger one, and seven black oxide Phillips oval-head screws pass through both to attach them to the body. In addition, the larger piece has two mounting tabs on the bottom underside toward the front. Two black oxide Phillips fillister-head screws pass through these into J nuts affixed to the lower edge of the body.

Side-mounted exhaust was an option for 1969 cars only and was first available in December 1968. The pipe covers replace the standard rocker molding. The side pipe covers are made from chrome-plated metal with a fiberglass insulator bonded to the inside. The covers have horizontal ridges in the middle. The covers are painted semi-gloss black between the ridges and along the top edge. Six black oxide Phillips oval-head screws retain each cover to the car's body.

Side exhaust cars did not have exhaust tip cutouts in the rear valance or an exhaust pipe hangar at the middle chassis crossmember. Front side fenders, the fronts of the rear wheel wells, and the bottoms of the rear quarter panels were trimmed to make clearance for the side exhaust. Also, side exhaust cars got insulation between the outer chassis rails and body.

Radio Antenna

A radio was still an option for Corvettes in 1968 and 1969, and approximately 1,400 cars were built without one during the two years. On those cars, no radio antenna was installed, but on all others, a 31-inch fixed-height antenna was mounted on the driver-side rear deck.

A black plastic gasket goes between the antenna base and the car's body. The base is also made of black plastic beneath a chrome bezel. The base, along with the portion of the antenna assembly beneath the body, is retained by a chrome cap, with two flat areas for a wrench to grab.

Original fuel door and nose panel crossed-flag emblems have a black square in the upper left corner of the checkered flag, as shown in this 1968 example.

In 1968, masts thread into the base, while 1969 masts sit in an additional black insulator and are held by a metal collar with two flat areas for tightening. For both 1968 and 1969 antennas, the mast ball is .300 inch in diameter, not .250 inch as seen on some later replacements.

Rear Deck Vent Grilles and Gas Fill Door

Two vent grilles are installed on the rear deck behind the back window or behind the convertible top deck on convertibles. The vent grilles are painted body color and are each retained by four black oxide Phillips flathead screws. The lips in the body the grilles sit on and the vent channel below are sprayed with flat black paint, with varying degrees of coverage.

Gas lid doors are painted body color and feature a chrome and painted crossed-flag emblem. For 1968s assembled through approximately late April 1968, spin rivets retain the emblem. For the remainder of 1968, either these same rivets or chrome-plated acorn nuts are utilized. For all of 1969, acorn nuts are used.

For 1968s assembled through approximately late April 1968, four spin rivets hold the gas door to its hinge. Starting in May 1968, the rivets were replaced with four Phillips fillister-head screws. These screws are normally chrome plated, but some are black. For the remainder of 1968 models, either spin rivets or screws are utilized. For all of 1969, screws are utilized.

In both 1968 and 1969, a latch that is part of the hinge assembly holds the door in the open position. A tab peened to the underside of the door inserts into a receptacle in the gas door bezel to hold the door closed. The receptacle is formed from two spring-loaded pieces of white nylon.

For both 1968 and 1969, the polished gas door bezel is held to the body with chrome-plated Phillips oval-head screws. In both years, there are no rubber bumpers to cushion the door when it is closed.

All 1968 and 1969 Corvettes came with a twist-on gas cap, not a locking cap. The locking caps, which are usually flat

All 1968–1969 Corvettes came with two-piece rocker moldings. The lower part is fiberglass painted semi-gloss black. The upper section is polished aluminum with a black-painted accent area along the top edge. This is an unrestored 1968. The reddish brown showing through the black is the underlying primer, evidencing that very little paint was sprayed onto this rocker when it was new.

All 1968s made prior to approximately May 1968 had this kind of fuel door. The door's lid and crossed-flag emblem were retained with spin rivets. Most later 1968 and all 1969 doors and emblems were held in place with acorn nuts.

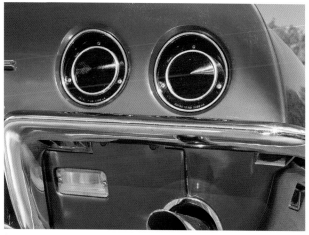

All four taillamp lenses were identical in 1968. A separate backup lamp was in the rear valance panel. The 1968 taillamp and backup lamp lenses were dated "1968." Early 1969 outer taillamp lenses may be dated "1968," while all others were dated "1969."

and chrome plated, were dealer installed or aftermarket. All correct caps are silver cadmium plated and have only the word "VENTED" stamped in. Later caps have additional words, such as "SEALED" and "OPEN SLOWLY CAUTION," stamped into them.

For 1968 and 1969, the gas cap has a handle for twisting it on and off. The handle is attached by two ears that are bent over and spot welded onto the cap. On original caps, the ears face down when the word "VENTED" is upright.

A black rubber boot surrounds the gas filler neck in both years. The boot has a plastic nipple facing the rear of the car, and a rubber drain hose attaches to it. The hose, which has a metal spring inside to prevent it from collapsing, runs down behind the gas tank and exits the body through a hole adjacent to one of the rear bumper braces. A black plastic tie wrap holds the hose to the bumper brace.

Rear Fascia, Tail Lamps, Bumpers, and Related Parts

The rear fascia has "CORVETTE" spelled out in eight individual letters centered between the taillamps. Each letter is chrome plated, with silver paint in its recessed face.

An audio alarm was optional beginning in May 1968. All cars so equipped have a lock cylinder switch on the rear body panel, between the tail lamps and above "CORVETTE." All 1968s and 1969s use an open-style lock cylinder that does not have a spring-loaded face-plate and a crimped-over bezel like the door lock cylinders. No gasket is used between the alarm lock cylinder and body.

The recessed area of the body where the rear license plate mounts is covered by a chrome-plated, die-cast surround trim. A lamp assembly mounts at the top of the recess behind the rear body panel and illuminates the rear license plate. A fiber optic cable inserts into the license lamp housing. A black rubber bumper is inserted into the rear valance panel centered toward the lower edge of the license plate. Two white, plastic

push nuts for the license plate retaining screws insert into square cutouts in the rear body panel.

All 1968s utilize four rear lamps, each with a red, conical lens. Three chrome-plated Phillips-head screws retain the lenses.

All 1968s have a rectangular backup lamp assembly mounted beneath each rear bumper. Each lamp has a clear lens held by two chrome Phillips-head screws. A black rubber gasket seals each lens to its housing.

All 1969s utilize four rear lamps, but the lenses on the two inner lamps are different than in 1968. The two outer ones utilize red, conical lenses that function as taillamps, stop lamps, and turn signals. The two inner ones utilize red lenses with clear plastic centers that function as backup lamps. These are conical shaped, with concentric grooves on the inside.

Rear bumpers are chrome plated and are attached to the body with brackets painted semi-gloss black. As with the front bumpers, cadmium-plated hex-head bolts retain the bumpers to the brackets, and cadmium and/or black-oxide-plated hex-head bolts hold the brackets to the chassis.

The rear valance panel is painted body color but often shows poor paint quality, including runs or sparse coverage

Rear side marker lamp lenses were red with the date molded in.

along the bottom edge. It is retained to the body by four cadmium-plated, indented hex-head bolts. The two outer ones utilize integral washers, while the two inners have separate flat washers.

Cars equipped with optional side exhaust do not have the exhaust tip cutouts in the rear valence panel or rear quarter panels. Cars with undercar exhaust have rounded cutouts in the body. The cutouts are trimmed with chromed die-cast bezels that are round in shape but with open bottoms. The bezels are retained by chrome Phillips oval-head screws.

Convertible Tops

Convertible tops are made from vinyl with a woven pattern. They were available in white, tan, or black, regardless of exterior body color. The front header roll and tack strip cover are also vinyl but have a grained rather than a woven pattern. Two small stainless-steel trim pieces cover the ends of the tack strip. The trim pieces are flared around their perimeter and attach with one small, bright Phillips flathead screw. The back window is clear vinyl and is heat sealed, not sewn, to the inside of the top.

The convertible top back window contains a manufacturer's logo, manufacturing date, and the words "VINYLITE, TRADE MARK, AS-6" and "DO NOT RUB DRY WASH WITH WATER SOAKED CLOTH" heat stamped in the driver-side lower corner. The date code is normally three or four numbers, with the first one or two representing the month and the second two representing the year. For example, a convertible top manufactured in April 1968 would have a date code of "468."

A paper "caution" label is sewn into the top in the driver-side corner below the heat-stamped logo and date in the window. The label reads:

WARNING
DEALER — DO NOT REMOVE
FOR CARE OF REAR WINDOW
AND TOP MATERIAL
SEE BOOKLET
"HOW TO OPERATE FOLDING TOP"

The convertible buyer could choose either a soft top or a hardtop, or both for an extra cost. The hardtop is painted body color unless it is vinyl covered. All vinyl-covered hardtops are black. Beginning in approximately December 1968, stainless-steel tips were installed on the lower rear points of the top to protect them from damage.

In 1968 and most of 1969, hardtops mount at seven points. Two studs pass through the latches on the rear deck that the convertible top's pins normally go into. These studs are secured underneath the deck panel with L-shaped brackets and nuts. A chrome-plated hex-head bolt passes through a chrome-plated bracket in each lower rear corner of the top and threads into a nut inserted in the body. Three

latches along the front header secure the top to brackets on the windshield header. In late 1969, an additional mounting bolt was added to the rear of the top beneath the middle of the window. The bolt passes through a ferrule in the deck and is secured with a nut.

The hardtop rear window contains the LOF manufacturing logo and is date coded with two letters like the remainder of the body glass. The first letter represents the month of production, and the second represents the year of production. (Refer to Appendix R for glass date codes.)

Tires, Wheels, and Wheel Covers

Corvettes in 1968 and 1969 came with Goodyear, Firestone, or Uniroyal F70x15 bias-ply nylon cord tires. The standard tire for all three years was a blackwall. Whitewalls and redlines were optional both years. Raised-white-letter tires were available as an extra cost option beginning in approximately September 1969.

Whitewalls and redlines were either Firestone Super Sport Wide Ovals, Goodyear Speedway Wide Treads, or Uniroyal Tiger Paws. The Firestones have a ⅜-inch white stripe that is 1⅛ inches from the bead edge. The Goodyears have a ⁵⁄₁₆-inch white stripe that is 1 inch from the bead edge. The Uniroyals have a ⁵⁄₁₆-inch stripe that is 1⅜ inches from the bead edge.

Regardless of brand, the original tires have nine ribs on the tread. When fully inflated, Goodyear and Uniroyal tires have a tread width of 6½ inches, while Firestones have a tread width of 6¾ inches.

Raised-white-letter tires are believed to be Goodyears or Firestones, not Uniroyals. Goodyears say "Goodyear Wide Tread F70-15" in block letters. Firestones say "Firestone Wide O Oval" in block letters.

All 1968 and 1969 Corvettes were equipped with steel rally wheels. The front sides of rally wheels are Argent Silver. This color is predominantly silver but has a slight greenish hue. The back sides of the wheels are painted semi-flat black and always have silver overspray, since the front side was painted silver after the black was applied to the rear.

All wheels are stamped with a date code and size code on the front face. All 1968 Corvette wheels are 15 by 7 inches, as indicated by the stamped code "AG." All 1969 Corvette wheels are 15 by 8 inches, as indicated by the stamped code "AZ." The code is adjacent to the valve stem hole.

Also adjacent to the valve stem hole is the manufacturer's logo and date code stamping. One side of the hole is marked "K," which is believed to represent the wheel manufacturer, Kelsey Hayes. This is followed by a dash and a "1," which likely represents Chevrolet, though it may represent a specific wheel plant. Next comes another dash and either a "7," "8," or "9" to denote the last digit of the year of manufacture. This is followed by a space and one or two numbers to indicate the month of manufacture. On the other side of the valve stem hole are one or two more numbers that represent the day of manufacture.

Full metal wheel covers were optional in 1968–1969. When installed, each standard valve stem was fitted with the extension shown here. The manufacturer of the extensions was Schrader. That company's name, along with "24" and "U.S.A.," was molded into the end of each extension's outer section.

Slightly less than one-third of all 1968s came with this optional bright metal wheel cover. Chevrolet passenger cars used a similar cover, with a flat center section instead of the Corvette's protruding center section.

Stainless-steel trim rings and chrome center caps are standard for all cars. Original trim rings are held to the wheel by four steel clips. Center caps should read "Chevrolet Motor Division" in black-painted letters.

A full wheel cover was available as an extra cost option for all 1968 and 1969 Corvettes. Called option P01 in 1968 and PO2 in 1969, this cover has a stainless-steel outer rim and closely spaced radial fins that converge outward toward a protruding ornamental disc in the center. The disc is chrome around its edge, black in the middle, and contains the Corvette crossed-flag emblem. Other Chevrolet products use a similar wheel cover, but those have a flat center disc instead of the protruding disc utilized for Corvettes.

Wheels on cars equipped with standard trim rings and center caps utilize black rubber valve stems that measure approximately 1¼ inches long. These are fitted with caps that come to a point and have longitudinal ridges around the entire perimeter and the molded manufacturer's name, Dill.

Wheels on cars equipped with optional full wheel covers have extensions threaded onto the standard valve stems. The extensions have white inner shafts that are visible because they are not fitted with caps. The name of the manufacturer, Schrader, is molded into the ends.

To ease the balancing process, wheels are sometimes marked with a tiny weld drop or paint dot at their highest points. This mark is lined up with an orange dot on the tire. Balance weights are the type that clamp onto the edge of the rim and are placed on the inside of the wheel only. Original balance weights usually have "OEM" molded into their faces. There is usually a small white or colored dot of paint on the tire adjacent to each balance weight.

All cars have a full-size spare tire and wheel that are identical to the other four tires and wheels. The spare wheel is not fitted with a wheel cover like the other four.

The spare tire and wheel are housed in a carrier bolted to the rear underbody area. The carrier is fiberglass with steel supports. The fiberglass is unpainted, and the steel support is painted semi-gloss black. The tire tub portion of the carrier has a fair amount of flat to semi-gloss black paint on its outside surface, applied during the blackout process. A lock covered by a black rubber boot goes over the spare tire carrier access bolt.

1968–1969 INTERIOR
Trim Tag

Interior trim color and material, as well as exterior body color and body assembly date, are stamped into an unpainted, stainless-steel plate attached to the driver's door hinge pillar by two aluminum pop rivets. This plate is commonly called a trim plate or trim tag.

Trim color and material are indicated in the plate by a three-number code. For example, in 1968 trim code "408" indicates a red interior with leather seat covers. Exterior body paint is likewise indicated by a three-number code stamped in the trim plate. For example, in 1969 code "980" indicates Riverside Gold. (Refer to Appendix T for paint and interior trim codes.)

The body build date is the date when the painted and partially assembled body reached the point on the assembly line where the trim plate was installed. The car's final assembly date is typically one to several days after the body build date. A letter indicating the month followed by two numbers indicating the day represents the body build date. The letter "A" was assigned to the first month of production, which was August 1967 for 1968 cars and August 1968 for 1969 cars. The second month of production was assigned the letter "B"

All 1968–1969 Corvettes came with a stainless-steel trim plate riveted to the driver-side door hinge pillar. The trim code shown is "414," which indicates that this car came with medium blue vinyl. The paint code "978" tells us the car was painted International Blue. The body build code in the upper right is "F22." The letter represents the month, with "A" denoting the first month of production, "B" the second month of production, and so on. The numbers represent the day of the month. Since 1968 production began in August 1967, "F" represents January, so this tag was stamped and attached to the body on January 22.

and so on. Therefore, a body assembled on August 6, 1967, would have "A06" stamped into the trim plate, and a body built on May 11, 1969, would have "J11" stamped into its plate. (Refer to Appendix S for body build date codes.)

Seats

Standard seat upholstery for 1968 cars is a combination of very slightly grained flat vinyl with Chevrolet's "basket-weave"

vinyl inserts sewn into the seat bottoms and backs. This same seat upholstery was likely used in some early 1969s and sporadically in later '69s that had black vinyl interiors. Standard seat upholstery for 1969 cars is a combination of very slightly grained flat vinyl with Chevrolet's "comfort-weave" vinyl inserts sewn into the seat bottoms and backs.

The difference between the basket-weave and comfort-weave inserts is the texture and pattern orientation. Basket-weave is somewhat coarser, and the pattern is in an over/under crisscross that resembles a woven basket. Regardless of which weave is used, all seats have vertical insert panels.

Leather seat covers were available as an extra cost option for all interior colors except gunmetal in 1968. Only the insert portions of the seat covers were leather, while outer, lower, and side panels were vinyl. Leather seat covers have vertical panels just like their vinyl counterparts. The leather inserts had a basket-weave pattern in 1968 but were smooth in 1969.

Each seat rests on two seat tracks, which allow for forward and rearward adjustment of the seat's position. The tracks are painted semi-gloss black in early 1968s and plated black phosphate in later '68s and all '69s. Each track is held to the floor by one black phosphate, indented hex-head bolt at either end, for a total of four per seat. The front bolts are covered by a cutaway flap of carpet while the rear bolts simply pass through the carpet.

An unrestored 1968 with a Medium Blue vinyl interior.

Correct 1969 seat upholstery. Headrests were a mandatory option in all 1969s built through January 1, 1969, and were standard in all cars built thereafter.

The seat adjust lever is painted semi-gloss black in early 1968s and plated black phosphate in later '68s and all '69s. All levers are fitted with a chrome ball screwed onto their ends.

Headrests were an extra cost option for all 1968 Corvettes. They were a mandatory option for all '69s assembled through approximately January 1969 and were standard equipment thereafter. All headrests are covered with a smooth, faintly patterned vinyl.

The seat backs are made of molded plastic and match the interior color. They are retained by two chrome-plated

This is an original seat in an unrestored 1968. Starting in mid-July 1968, the seat back release was positioned higher than seen here.

Phillips-head screws at the bottom. In 1968s assembled through approximately mid-November 1967, the seat back is released by means of a chrome-plated lever surrounded by a chrome-plated bezel positioned near the bottom of the seat. Those 1968s assembled after approximately mid-November 1967 do not have the bezel around the release lever.

In 1968s assembled after approximately early July, and in all 1969s, the seat release lever is positioned higher than it was previously.

In 1968 and 1969, the seat back position is adjustable. The adjustment mechanism on the seat back consists of a black plastic stop through approximately July 1969, after which an adjustable black rubber stop replaced the plastic one. The plastic or rubber stop contacted a pad on the seat bottom. The pad is silver-cadmium-plated metal on 1968s assembled through approximately mid-July 1968. The pads on 1968s assembled thereafter and on all '69s are made from black rubber.

Lap and Shoulder Belts

All 1968 and 1969 coupes were equipped with lap and shoulder belts, while convertibles came with standard lap belts and shoulder belts as an extra cost option. A company called Hamill manufactured all belts, and a tag bearing that name is sewn to them. Original tags were made from a thin, silklike woven material, while some reproductions and later GM tags are made from a thicker paperlike material. The tag indicates the date the belt was manufactured by an ink stamping, with a number representing the week of the year and another number representing the year. The meaning of the letter between the numbers is not known with certainty, but it may denote the day of the week or the manufacturing plant where the belt was made. For example, a stamping of "16 E 68" means the belt was made the 16th week of 1968.

Hamill manufactured most 1968–1969 Corvette seat belts. All belts had a label printed with manufacturing information, including a date code. The first two numbers of the date code represent the week of the year. The last two numbers are the final digits of the year. In this example, "50 E 67" translates to a manufacture date of the 50th week of 1967. The meaning of the letter "E" is not known.

In addition to the tag bearing the manufacturer's name and date code, other, smaller tags are sewn to the belts. All 1968s have tags sewn into both the male and female lap belts. These tags read, "THIS BELT CONFORMS TO SAE 14C FEDERAL MOTOR VEHICLE SAFETY STANDARDS HAMILL MODEL C11."

In 1968 another label is sewn into the male lap belt on the side opposite the label described above. This label reads "IMPORTANT, READ OWNER'S MANUAL, WEAR LAP BELT AT ALL TIMES, ADJUST LOW AND SNUG, EXTEND BELT COMPLETELY FROM ANY RETRAC-TOR, SHOULDER BELT MUST NOT BE USED WITHOUT LAP BELT."

In 1968 the shoulder harness also has two labels sewn in. In addition to the tag bearing the manufacturer's name and date code, a tag reads, "IMPORTANT, DO NOT USE WITHOUT A LAP BELT, LEAVE ENOUGH SLACK TO INSERT HAND WIDTH BETWEEN BELT AND CHEST, DO NOT USE IF LESS THAN 4 FEET 7 INCHES TALL, WHEN NOT IN USE SECURE SHOULDER BELTS IN RETAINERS."

In 1969 lap belts have a sewn-in label that reads "IMPORTANT, WEAR LAP BELT AT ALL TIMES, AD-JUST SNUGLY."

In 1969 shoulder belts have a sewn-in label that reads "IMPORTANT, ATTACH SHOULDER HARNESS SE-CURELY TO LAP BELTS, DO NOT USE IF LESS THAN 4 FEET 7 INCHES TALL, DO NOT USE WITHOUT A LAP BELT."

All belts are made from a three-row webbing material and are the same color as the carpet. The material used for lap belts is slightly thicker than that used for shoulder belts.

In 1968 inboard lap belts rest in a receptacle in the center console when not in use. In 1969 a chrome clip attached to the front of each seat bottom holds the outboard lap belts when they are not in use.

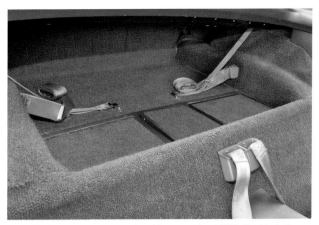

The original rear passenger compartment in an unrestored 1968. Shoulder belts were optional in all 1968–1969 convertibles, optional in coupes produced through the end of calendar year 1967, and standard in coupes beginning on January 1, 1968.

In 1968 the female lap belt latch is comprised of a stainless-steel housing fitted with a chrome-plated back. Release of the belt is accomplished by means of a square push-button adorned with the GM logo on the latch's front.

On some 1968s, the outboard (male) half of the lap belt passes through a grommet in the carpet, and in other '68s, the outboard belt has a retractor mechanism.

In 1969 the female lap belt latch is encased in semi-rigid plastic matched to the interior color. In early '69s, the female latch has a square plastic cover with a round release button adorned with the GM logo. In later '69s, the female latch is made from stainless steel with a brushed silver finish. In the center is a square black release button with a rigid metallic sticker that says "GM" in silver letters on a blue background.

The outboard (male) half of 1969 lap belts passes through a grommet in the carpet. A vinyl band around the belt holds excess webbing. Beginning in approximately November 1969, a stainless-steel clip attached to the front of each seat bottom held the outboard belts when not in use.

Door Panels and Door Hardware

All door panels are made from molded vinyl and match the interior color. Door panels in 1968s assembled through approximately April 1968 have an integral door pull molded in. In 1968s assembled after this date, a separate vinyl grab pull is added below the molded-in pull.

All 1969s have a separate, vertically mounted door pull anchored with a silver-cadmium-plated Phillips pan-head screw. The 1969 vertical pull is vinyl-covered steel matched to the interior color.

An insert is fastened to 1969 door panels. The insert is covered with the same comfort-weave-patterned vinyl as the seat upholstery.

In both 1968 and 1969 side windows, felts are fastened to the top edges of each door panel with heavy metal staples.

This is an original 1968 seat belt receiver.

An original door panel in an unrestored 1968. The recess in the lower portion of the upper protrusion served as the inside door pull. This style was used in 1968 Corvettes produced through approximately mid-March 1968. After that a different panel, with a separate door pull held by screws, was used.

Door panels are attached to doors by means of chrome Phillips oval-head screws that go through the face of each panel at the upper front and rear corners. These screws have a separate finishing washer.

Inside door release handles are chrome, with black paint in the knurled center area. A round black emblem glued to each handle features the crossed-flag logo. In early 1968s, the back of the door release lever is smooth. In later '68s it has two ridges, and in '69s it has four ridges.

The inside lock knob is chrome, with a black stripe painted in the center indent. There is a light beige plastic washer between the lock knob and door panel.

Those 1968 Corvettes equipped with standard manual windows have chrome-plated window cranks with plastic knobs that match the interior color. The 1969 models utilize chrome cranks with opaque or black plastic knobs. Unlike some later replacements, the knobs on original cranks are about one inch away from the door panel's surface. There is a light beige plastic washer between the window crank and door panel.

Door Jambs and Door Perimeters

The jamb and perimeter of each door are painted body color. Early 1968s are usually painted body color around the entire perimeter of each door. Later '68s and all '69s are painted body color around the entire perimeter, with the exception of the top front area, which is painted semi-gloss black.

The door striker, which is the large pin threaded into the door post, and its corresponding receiver in the door are both cadmium plated. The striker is a special indented hex-head bolt and should not have any body paint overspray.

The courtesy light pin switches and "door ajar" warning light/alarm system pin switches are cadmium plated and should not have any paint overspray. All pin switches have "SX," the manufacturer's logo, stamped into the head of the plunger.

A door jamb in an unrestored 1968. Note the sloppy application of yellow weather strip adhesive, which is very typical of factory configuration. Also note the unpainted striker latch screws and the brass door alignment wedge.

As with the pin switches, door strikers, and door striker receivers, door alignment blocks and door weather strips were added after the body was painted and should not have any body paint overspray. The main door weather stripping is two separate pieces and typically shows a gap in the center on the bottom of the door.

Early 1968 cars do not have water-deflecting strips attached to each doorpost near the "door ajar" warning light/alarm system pin switches. These strips are present in later '68s. They are unpainted black rubber pieces that are glued to the body.

All 1969 cars have plastic water-deflecting strips painted body color. The strips in early '69s are glued onto the body. In 1969s assembled after approximately mid-September 1969, the strips are pop riveted in place.

Door hinges, bolts, and return springs (there should be one spring in each top hinge) are painted body color in both 1968 and 1969.

The federal government required that all vehicles assembled after September 1, 1969, have a "vehicle certification label" glued toward the top of the rear portion of the driver's door. It contains the VIN, as well as the month and year the vehicle was produced. The label was placed on after the body was painted and therefore should not have any paint overspray.

Door sills are bright aluminum with black-painted ribs. Each sill is held on with four black phosphate Phillips oval-head screws.

Kick Panels, Quarter Trim Panels, Pedals, and Carpet

Kick panels beneath the dash, just forward of the doors, are molded plastic and are interior color. On air-conditioned cars, the passenger side panel was cut by hand for increased clearance, and the cut is frequently rough. One chrome Phillips oval-head screw in the forward, upper corner of each panel holds it in place. The panels have a bevy of small holes for the speakers that mount behind them. Speakers were mounted behind these panels in 1968 but not in 1969 cars. Some replacement kick panels have a slot in the speaker grille area. Others have a solid rectangular area in the middle of the speaker grille holes. Neither style is original for 1968 or 1969.

The quarter trim panels just rearward of the doors are vinyl-covered plastic in 1968 and molded plastic in 1969. For both years they match the interior color. They are each held in place by a piece of metal trim retained by four chrome Phillips oval-head screws. The quarter trim panels on coupes also have one chrome Phillips oval-head screw with a trim washer at the top.

For all 1968s and 1969s, accelerator, brake, and clutch pedals have black rubber pads with horizontal ribs and polished stainless-steel trim. The accelerator pedal measures 5⅝ inches high by 2 inches wide and does not taper like some later accelerators.

All 1968 and 1969 Corvettes are fitted with carpet made from an 80/20 loop pile molded material dyed to match interior color. Three rubber plugs in the driver's foot well and three more in the passenger's foot well help hold the carpet in place. The plugs pass through the carpet near its upper front edge and have the GM part number 3868790 molded into the top surface.

Carpet covers the bulkhead behind the seats. This carpet has an unfinished lower edge covered by the floor carpet. The floor carpet has stitched vinyl piping to finish the edge.

Rear storage compartment doors each have carpet under their frames. One piece of carpet covers the rear storage area floor and extends up the rear bulkhead. The edge at the top of the bulkhead is trimmed with sewn-on binding and is held in place by glue in 1968 through early 1969. Beginning in approximately April 1969, the top of the bulkhead carpet is retained by three rubber plugs. Separate pieces of untrimmed carpet cover the two wheelwells.

The front carpet has a molded-vinyl accelerator heel pad sewn into the corner of the driver's foot well adjacent to the

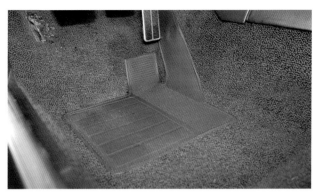

This is an original carpet heel pad in an unrestored 1968. The spacing of the ridges, particularly in the area beneath the accelerator pedal, is often different in reproduction heel pads.

accelerator pedal. Heel pads have horizontal ribs that extend to within ¼ inch of the top stitching holding the pad to the carpet. A very faint manufacturer's logo consisting of "IMCo" in an oval is found in original heel pads.

Carpeting in all 1968 and those 1969 Corvettes assembled through approximately mid-September does not have a dimmer switch pad. Carpet in '69s assembled after approximately mid-September 1969 may have a sewn-in, molded-vinyl dimmer switch pad.

Dash Pad and Dash Panels

Upper dash pads, as well as driver's and passenger's dash panels, are made of soft vinyl and match interior color. The two vertical panels are attached to the upper pad by means of six Phillips oval-head screws with conical washers. The screw heads are painted to match interior color, except in some cars with black interiors. In those cases, the screws are finished in black oxide plating.

Dash pads do not have white stitching across their tops, as is seen in 1970 and later cars. A hard plastic grille, in the interior color, is located in the defroster opening of the upper pad.

Corvettes from 1968 do not have a pocket storage area inset into the passenger-side dash panel. Instead, the panel is simply smooth.

A three-pocket storage area is inset into the passenger-side dash panel in 1969 Corvettes. The storage pocket assembly is made from vinyl and is the same color as the interior. The pockets each have two rows of horizontal stitching along their top edges. The two smaller, outboard pockets are retained to the larger one with a single chrome-plated snap. A spring-loaded retainer behind the dash holds the three-pocket assembly tight against the dash panel.

Interior Switches, Controls, and Related Parts

All 1968 and 1969s have a headlamp switch mounted in the upper left corner of the driver-side dash pad. For 1968s and 1969s assembled through approximately mid-December,

This is an original 1968/early 1969 headlamp switch knob and bezel. Those 1969s made after approximately November 1968 used a longer black grained knob with a chrome circle in the center.

the headlamp switch knob is made from smooth gloss black plastic and is relatively short. It has a white circle on the face and radial grooves around the circle.

In 1969s assembled after approximately mid-December 1969, headlamp knobs are made from grained gloss black plastic with a chrome disc in the center. This second design knob is about one inch longer than the first. A black plastic bezel behind the knob has the word "LIGHTS" in white letters.

All 1968 and 1969 Corvettes have air vents on both sides of the dash, toward the lower, outboard corner. The vent mechanisms are chrome spheres that rotate to change the direction of airflow. There is no mechanism for controlling the volume of air in 1968. In 1969 a chrome-plated push/pull knob next to each sphere controls the volume.

In 1968 only the ignition switch is located in the upper right driver-side dash panel. The switch is integrated into the steering column for 1969 and includes an antitheft column interlock feature.

A small black T-handle pull mechanism beneath the driver-side dash on the left side releases the hood latch. The handle is black, with the words "HOOD RELEASE" in white

painted block letters across its face. The hood release cable is in a spiral-wound metal sheathing.

A semi-gloss black bracket mounts the wiper door override switch, wiper arm override switch, and headlamp door override switch. Those 1968s assembled prior to approximately mid-January 1968 and not equipped with air conditioning have these controls mounted under the dash, between the steering column and center console. Those 1968 Corvettes assembled prior to approximately mid-January 1968 and equipped with air conditioning, all '68s assembled after approximately mid-January, and all '69s have these override controls mounted under the dash, directly beneath the steering column.

The trip odometer reset knob, which is mounted to the left of the override switches, has a grooved black rubber cover. The wiper door override switch has a large, round, shiny black knob with grooved edges. The wiper door override switch and headlamp door override switch are both vacuum switches that mount to either side of the wiper arm switch. The two vacuum switches have dull black plastic push/pull knobs.

Steering Wheel and Steering Column

All 1968 steering wheels have a simulated-wood rim made from plastic, molded to a brushed stainless-steel three-spoke center with a pattern of parallel lines extending from the center of the wheel to the outer rim. Steering wheels from 1968 are 16 inches in diameter.

A 1968 ignition switch and bezel. In 1969 the switch was incorporated into the steering column.

This original 1968 steering wheel is 16 inches in diameter, with a simulated wood rim and a two-piece stainless-steel center section. Some reproductions have a center section with all three spokes made from a single sheet of steel. Original 1966 and earlier Corvette steering wheels look similar to the 1968 wheel but have a center section crafted from a single piece of stainless steel.

The 1969 steering wheel has a black grained vinyl rim and is 15 inches in diameter.

All 1969 steering wheels are black, regardless of interior color. They have grained vinyl rims molded to a three-spoke stainless-steel hub. Each of the spokes has a brushed finish, with a pattern of parallel lines extending from the center of the wheel to the outer rim.

The standard steering columns and optional columns in 1968 and 1969 are painted whatever the interior color is, in a semi-gloss finish. With a telescopic column, the locking ring is painted the same color as the rest of the column.

The optional column in 1968 is telescopic but does not tilt. A thick locking ring below the steering wheel controls the telescoping function. Twisting the lever on the ring counterclockwise releases the locking mechanism and allows the column to telescope.

The optional column in 1969 is a combination tilt and telescoping unit. This tilt-telescoping column has a thick locking ring below the steering wheel to control the telescoping function. The ring is painted to match the rest of the column. Twisting the lever on the ring releases the locking mechanism and allows the column to telescope.

A lever similar to but shorter than the turn signal lever controls the tilt function of the optional steering column. This lever has a chrome-plated stem and smooth black plastic knob. It is located between the turn signal lever and dash and threads into its mount.

Most 1969 steering columns have a "caution" sticker on their left side. This sticker pertains to the ignition switch/column interlock mechanism. There are two versions of the sticker. The first, used on cars assembled through approximately July 1969, has a white background and reads "AS PART OF THE NEW LOCKING COLUMN FEATURE, IT IS NORMAL FOR THE MAST JACKET SHIFT BOWL TO ROTATE WHEN SHIFTING THE TRANSMISSION. HOWEVER DO NOT ATTEMPT TO ROTATE THE SHIFT BOWL BY ITSELF AS DAMAGE TO THE SHIFT LINKAGE WILL RESULT."

The second sticker, which was used on cars assembled in approximately July and August 1969, has a clear background and reads "THIS IS A ROTATING INTERLOCK—DO NOT MANIPULATE—DAMAGE MAY RESULT."

The steering column design was changed toward the end of 1969 production, eliminating the rotating mast jacket shift bowl. This eliminated the need for the "caution" sticker, so late production cars do not have it.

All columns have a four-way flasher switch mounted on the right side. All 1968 and 1969 standard columns, as well as all '68 telescopic columns, utilize a short switch with a one-piece chrome-plated knob, with black-painted, debossed letters in the head spelling the word "FLASHER."

Tilt-telescopic columns from 1969 are fitted with a flasher switch that is longer than the above-described switch. In addition, this switch differs in that its head is concave and has no writing in it.

All 1968–1969 horn buttons were made from grained metal painted to match the interior. The top left square in the checkered flag, adjacent to the pole, was white in cars built up to approximately December 1967 and black, as shown here, in cars built thereafter.

Both 1968 and 1969 Corvettes use the same turn signal lever. It is comprised of a chrome-plated shaft with a gloss black plastic end. The end has molded-in grooves parallel to the chrome shaft.

All 1968 and 1969 models use a textured metal horn button painted to match the interior. A crossed-flag emblem is in the center of the button. The upper right square in the flag is white in cars assembled through approximately January 1968. In later '68s and in '69s, this square is black.

Interior Windshield Moldings, Sun Visors, and Rearview Mirror

Three pieces of vinyl-covered molding matched to the interior color cover the inside of the windshield frame for all 1968 and 1969 Corvettes. The two side pieces are held on by plastic retainers attached to the reverse side. The plastic retainers are not visible when the moldings are installed. In addition, each side molding has one chrome Phillips-head screw retaining it at the top. Very early 1968s sometimes have two chrome-plated Phillips oval-head screws retaining each side piece of molding. The top piece of molding is retained by four chrome recess-head Phillips screws.

Sun visors utilized in 1968 cars are covered with padded soft vinyl with the same "Madrid" pattern as the vinyl covers on the optional headrests. Each sun visor is held to the windshield frame with chrome recess-head Phillips screws. The brackets mounting 1968 visors have ⅛-inch diameter holes and have a more pronounced offset, resulting in the visors mounting farther from the windshield frame.

Sun visors utilized in 1969 cars are covered with padded soft vinyl with the same comfort-weave pattern as the vinyl seat covers. Each sun visor is held to the windshield frame with chrome recess-head Phillips screws. The brackets mounting 1969 visors have ³⁄₁₆-inch diameter holes and have a less pronounced offset, resulting in the visors mounting closer to the windshield frame than they do in 1968.

Some 1969 Corvettes were originally equipped with a card describing the operation of the ignition lock and engine starting procedures. This card was wrapped around the driver-side sun visor.

All 1968 and 1969 Corvettes have an interior day/night rearview mirror mounted to the center of the upper windshield frame. The mirror is eight inches wide and is held to its mount with a slotted oval-head screw. A piece of trim covered with interior-color vinyl is mounted over the base of the mirror mount at the windshield frame. All interior mirrors have stainless-steel housings with gray rubber trim around the perimeter. A gray lever at the bottom center moves the mirror between its day and night position.

Instruments and Radio

The center console instrument cluster housing is cast metal painted semi-gloss black. In 1968s the painted surface is smooth, and in 1969 it is textured. In the upper left portion of the center console instrument cluster housing is a solid bar separating the seat belt warning light from the button below it. Later replacement housings don't have this bar. There is space for two more warning lights in the upper right portion of the housing. In 1968s assembled through approximately early March 1968, the additional squares say "DOOR AJAR" and "LOW FUEL." Some '68s assembled in this time frame have a square that says either "DOOR AJAR" or "LOW FUEL," with the other square left blank. In 1968 cars assembled after mid-March 1968, the upper right light reads "DOOR AJAR" and the lower reads "WIPER O'RIDE." In 1969 cars, the upper right light reads "DOOR AJAR" and the lower reads "HEAD LAMPS."

The windshield wiper/washer control switch is mounted above the center console instrument cluster housing. The switch knob is hard black plastic with the words "WASHER-PUSH" painted in block letters on its face. In cars assembled prior to mid-December 1967, the letters are light blue. In '68s assembled thereafter and in all '69s, the letters are white.

An original windshield wiper and washer switch assembly. Earlier 1968s, built prior to approximately late December 1967, used light blue letters on the washer pushbutton. Cars made thereafter used white letters.

The correct speedometer and tachometer for 1968–1969. The tachometer redline varied, depending on which engine the car was equipped with.

All gauges, including the speedometer and tachometer, have a semi-flat black background. All gauge needles are straight. With the exception of the needle for the optional speed warning, which is pale yellow, all gauge needles are red. Gauge numerals are slightly greenish white. Tachometer redlines vary according to the engine. The high-beam indicator light, which is in the speedometer face, is red in all cars and reads "BRIGHT."

All 1968 and 1969 Corvettes came standard without a radio. If the purchaser elected not to buy one of the optional radios, the car was delivered without one. For those cars not equipped with a radio, a block-off plate is fitted to the cutout where the radio would otherwise go. The block-off

An unrestored center stack in a 1968. The radio shown is a U69 AM/FM radio. The housing was smooth in 1968 and had a pebble-grain texture in 1969. In 1968s made through approximately early March 1968, the two square lamp openings in the upper right had some combination of "DOOR AJAR," "LOW FUEL," or a blank cover. After approximately mid-March 1968 through the end of 1968 production, the upper alarm lamp said "DOOR AJAR," and the lower said "WIPER O/RIDE." In 1969 the upper alarm said "DOOR AJAR," and the lower said "HEADLAMPS."

plate for both years is painted semi-gloss black. It has a flat face with a thin raised-chrome border around its perimeter near the edge.

As an extra cost option, one of two different Delco radios could be ordered. The first is an AM/FM push-button radio. The second is an AM/FM push-button radio with stereo reception. Both radios have a small slide bar above the dial that changes reception between AM and FM, and both have "Delco" written across the lens face in greenish-white script. The 1968 stereo radios have the word "STEREO" written in script, while 1969 stereo radios have the word "STEREO" in block letters.

All 1968 and 1969 stereo radios have an indicator light that comes on when FM stereo is being received. The light illuminates the word "STEREO" in green.

In 1968s assembled through approximately late May 1968, two different radio knobs are used interchangeably. The first knob is painted silver around its outer ring and has a concave face painted semi-gloss black. A raised rectangle in the face is painted silver.

The second 1968 radio knob is very similar to the first design, except the areas painted silver in the first design are chrome plated in the second. The second knob is used exclusively in '68s assembled after approximately early June 1968.

Radio knobs used in 1969 Corvettes are shiny black plastic with convex faces and a chrome-plated ring around the perimeter. Beneath the main radio knobs on all 1968s and 1969s is a secondary control ring, which is chrome plated. The one on the left controls tone, and the one on the right, which is functional only on stereo-equipped cars, controls balance. The left secondary control ring always has a tab, and the right one has a tab only for stereo.

Center Console, Shifter, and Park Brake

All 1968 and 1969 center consoles are made from molded vinyl in the same color as the interior and do not have stitching along the top edges. Park brake lever consoles are made from rigid molded plastic and also match interior color.

Radio access side panels at the forward sides of the center console are interior color. In 1968 these are held in place by clips on the back. In 1969 they are each retained by two chrome-plated Phillips-head screws.

The shifter surround insert in the top of the center console is painted semi-gloss black both years. In 1968 it is smooth, and in 1969 it has a pebble-grain texture. Four black-oxide-plated Phillips oval-head screws retain the insert.

In 1969s engine specifications are debossed into a rectangular insert below the lower fiber optic indicators. The specifications stamped into the insert include horsepower, torque, compression ratio, and engine displacement.

No 1968s have the above-described engine data plate. Instead, they have a crossed-flag emblem in the area below the lower fiber optic indicators.

The 1969 center console area. Note correct radio knobs and the shifter knob, which is black chrome.

Details of the rear of the shifter console top plate, showing fiber optic indicators and the crossed-flag emblem in an unrestored 1968.

This heater control assembly is correct for 1968 only. All 1968s and those 1969s without air conditioning use a switch with three speed positions. Those 1969s with air conditioning have a four-position switch.

In manual transmission–equipped cars, the shift pattern is indicated next to the shifter. The shift pattern area is semi-gloss black, and the letters and numbers are chrome, as is a border around the pattern. The shifter boot for all 1968 and 1969 manual transmission cars is made from black rubber. In 1968s the boot has a single bellows and in 1969 it has a double bellows. Manual shifters for all years have a chrome shaft and threaded-on ball. In 1968 this ball is silver chrome plated, and in 1969 it is plated with black chrome. Four-speed shifters for both years have a T-handle integral to the shaft to control the reverse lockout. Three-speed manual shifters do not have a T-handle.

On Corvettes equipped with automatic transmission, the shift pattern is also next to the shifter. Chrome letters are used to indicate shifter position. Rather than a boot, automatic transmission shifters are surrounded by a two-piece gloss-black plastic seal that slides back and forth as the shifter is moved. Automatic shifters for all 1968s and 1969s have a chrome shaft topped by a black plastic ball, with a chrome spring-loaded button in the top.

Heater/air conditioning control assemblies used in 1968 and 1969 differ slightly from one another. For example, in 1968 the left thumbwheel indicator positions for non-air-conditioned cars read, "OFF," "AIR," and "DE-ICE." The right indicator positions read, "COLD" and "HOT." In 1969 the left indicator positions read "OFF," "AIR," "DE-FOG," and "DE-ICE." The 1969 right indicator positions read, "L" and "H."

Both styles of control assembly utilize green letters and a separate fan switch plate inset into the larger assembly. A chrome lever sets fan speed. Fan switches in all 1968 cars and non-air-conditioned 1969 cars have three positions in addition to "off." All air-conditioned 1969 cars use a switch with four positions in addition to "off."

Whether the car is equipped with air conditioning or not, its control assembly employs two large black plastic rotary thumbwheels on either side. The left thumbwheel controls temperature, and the right thumbwheel controls the system setting.

All non-air-conditioned cars have two fresh-air vent controls on the center console. In all 1968s and those 1969s assembled through approximately January 1969, the controls are sliding levers with chrome-plated rectangular knobs. The faces of the knobs are painted semi-gloss black and have raised-chrome block letters reading "OPEN" and "VENT."

Those 1969s assembled after approximately January 1969 use a different type of fresh-air vent control. This second design has a smooth, shiny, black plastic ball with a flat area mounted to a black oxide metal arm. On their flat faces, the balls say "CLOSE" in white painted letters and have a white arrow.

All 1968s and 1969s have an ashtray set into the center console insert next to the heater/air conditioning control assembly. The ashtray door is semi-gloss black and slides back and forth with slight resistance. The ashtray is chrome plated and can be removed for cleaning.

All cars are equipped with a cigarette lighter. The lighter uses a shiny black plastic knob with a white circle and white concentric grooves in its face. Each lighter has "63 CASCO 12V" stamped in its element.

On 1968 and 1969 Corvettes equipped with the optional rear window defogger, a control switch is mounted on the left trim panel forward of the center console. The switch uses a large, round, chrome-plated knob.

All 1968 and 1969 Corvettes have a park brake lever mounted between the seats. The lever's handle is made from hard, shiny black plastic, with a crosshatch pattern to enhance grip. Chrome trim separates the black plastic grips in all cars, with the possible exception of some very early '68s. A release

All 1968–1969 Corvettes came with three storage compartments behind the seats. The 1968 driver- and passenger-side compartment lids are made from pressboard material and are either painted flat black or left natural brown, as shown here. The center lid is flat black or brown pressboard or black plastic. In 1969 all three lids are pressboard painted flat black or left natural brown. Cars not equipped with optional Posi-Traction were not supposed to get the limited-slip differential "caution" decal but sometimes did anyway.

button on the top of the lever is also made from hard, shiny black plastic. The slotted opening in the park brake lever console is covered by a rippled black plastic cover that slides along with the movement of the lever.

Rear Storage Compartments and Their Contents, Batteries, and Rear Window Storage Trays

All 1968 and 1969 Corvettes feature three enclosed storage compartments behind the seats. These have lids covered with carpet that matches the interior carpet. In 1968 the driver- and passenger-side lids are made from brown pressboard material that's either painted flat black or unpainted. In 1968 the center compartment lid is pressboard painted flat black or unpainted, or black ribbed plastic. In 1969 all three doors are pressboard and either unpainted or painted flat black.

Stickers for tire pressure, jacking instructions, and the limited-slip differential are on the underside of the passenger-side compartment lid. Limited slip was an option in 1968 and 1969, so some cars are not equipped with it. Nonetheless, most cars still received the limited-slip differential sticker under the passenger compartment lid.

Each lid is surrounded by a molded plastic border that is painted to match interior color. The entire assembly of all three lids is also surrounded by a color-matched molded plastic border.

Each lid is hinged and latches with a spring-loaded mechanism. Each lid has a chrome button to release its latch. Starting with 1969s assembled after approximately mid-January 1969, a vinyl hoop was added to each door to help pull it open. The vinyl hoop is stitched together and is the

An original 1968 park brake console with recesses for seat belts. The 1969 console did not have the recesses. Original consoles were made from hard vinyl, while some reproductions were made from hard plastic.

same color as the interior. It is retained to the lid by a chrome Phillips-head machine screw secured with a ⅜-inch nut on the underside of the lid.

Each molded plastic border is held to its lid by chrome flathead Phillips screws. Each lid is held to its hinge by black oxide round-head Phillips screws fitted with integral black oxide flat washers. Each hinge is held to the compartment surround by rivets. The whole assembly is held to the body by black oxide, silver cadmium, or chrome-plated flathead Phillips screws.

The center compartment is fitted with a locking chrome release button. The same key operates the storage compartment lid lock and the spare tire compartment lock, but a different key operates the antitheft alarm switch on those cars equipped with the optional antitheft burglar alarm.

The compartment directly behind the driver's seat holds the vehicle's battery. It has a thin foam seal around the perimeter of the door opening to help keep battery fumes from entering the passenger compartment. This seal is not one continuous piece of foam but instead has a seam where the two ends of the strip meet.

Beginning with those 1968s assembled after approximately mid-January 1968, aluminum-foil-backed fiberglass matting is used for insulation in the two large storage compartments. Use of this insulation continues in 1969.

All 1968 Corvettes and those 1969s assembled through approximately mid-June 1969 use a top-post model R59S Delco battery. Small-block-engine-equipped 1969s assembled after mid-June 1969 use a model R79S side-terminal battery. Big-block-engine-equipped 1969s assembled after mid-June 1969 use a model R79W side-terminal battery. In either case, the side terminals face toward the front of the car when the battery is correctly installed.

All batteries used in 1968 and 1969 have six cells covered by two plastic caps, each covering three cells. Each cap has three Delco split circle logos molded into its top. The split circles are painted dark orange. A black rubber vent hose runs from each cap through a hole in the underbody.

Battery cables for all 1968s and those 1969s assembled through approximately mid-June 1969 are the Delco spring-ring design. A gray felt washer impregnated with an anticorrosive chemical is found beneath the positive terminal end on the positive battery post.

All 1969s assembled after approximately mid-June 1969 have side-terminal battery cables. This cable has red positive ends and black negative ends, each with a raised Delco split circle logo. Both terminals are fastened to the battery with a ⁷⁄₁₆-inch hex-head bolt.

The passenger-side storage compartment contains a removable insert. The insert, which is like a squared-off bucket, is made from grayish black fiberboard and measures 6¼ inches deep. For 1968 and 1969 convertibles only, the fiberboard insert contains a ½-inch open-ended wrench for installation and removal of the hardtop.

All 1968s and those 1969s assembled through approximately early June 1969 left the factory with a Delco R59S battery. The example shown is the currently available reproduction. Later 1969s got a Delco R79S side-post battery. Note the foil-backed fiberglass insulation behind the battery. This insulation was added to driver- and passenger-side storage compartments beginning in approximately January 1968.

Also inside the fiberboard insert is an off-white cotton pouch with a yellow drawstring. The drawstring is held on by an encasement stitched with red thread. The pouch contains four silver washers and four oblong gray phosphate shims, used to adjust the seat backs to the occupants' preferred positions.

In addition to the hardtop wrench and seat hardware pouch, the storage insert holds a number of other items. A small white paper envelope with the "GM mark of excellence" logo and instructions printed in black letters contains the car's keys and the key knockouts. A small brown paper envelope contains license plate screws. "LICENSE SCREWS" is written in black ink on the outside of this envelope. Another small brown paper envelope is included with Corvettes equipped with optional P02 deluxe wheel covers. This envelope contains four extensions for the valve stems.

The final item in the storage insert is the owner's packet. In 1968 this packet is contained in a clear vinyl envelope with a yellow hex-head key and "DON'T INVITE CAR THEFT!" printed in blue on the outside. A part number, 3955549, is printed on the outside of this envelope. Included in the envelope are an owner's manual, warranty folder, Protect-O-Plate, air pollution control system information booklet, trim ring installation instruction card, override control instruction sheet, and radio instruction sheet if the car is equipped with a radio.

In 1969 the owner's packet is contained in a clear vinyl envelope with a yellow rectangular head key and "DON'T INVITE CAR THEFT!" printed in blue on the outside. A part number, 3950779, is printed on the outside of this envelope. Included in the envelope are an owner's manual, warranty folder, Protect-O-Plate, consumer information booklet, trim ring installation instruction card, and radio instruction sheet if the car is equipped with a radio.

Two different owner's manuals are used in 1969. The first edition is found in cars assembled through approximately early February 1969. The second edition is found in cars assembled thereafter.

The fiberboard insert in the passenger-side rear storage compartment lifts out to reveal additional storage area beneath. A jack and jack handle are mounted to the bottom of the compartment (to the car's floor panel), with a black spring that latches onto a black hook riveted to the floor.

Jacks from 1968 and 1969 differ in the size of their bases. All 1968 and some early 1969 jacks have a six-by-four-inch base, while later 1969 jacks have a nine-by-five-inch base. All jacks are painted semi-gloss to gloss black and have the letter "A" stamped in their chassis contact pad. This letter is the logo for Auto Specialties Manufacturing, the company that made the jacks.

In addition to the manufacturer's logo, all or almost all jacks contain a date code stamping. The stamping is on the jack's large side arm and contains a number for the year followed by a letter for the month, with "A" representing January, "B" representing February, and so on. For example, the date code stamping for a jack manufactured in June 1968 would say "8 F."

All jack handles are painted semi-gloss black and include a pivoting, ¾-inch boxed hex wrench on the end for removing and installing lug nuts. A thick rubber ring is fitted around the hex wrench end to prevent rattling.

In addition to the jack and jack handle, electrical relays and a flasher unit are mounted in the area underneath the fiberboard insert on those cars equipped with the audio antitheft alarm system.

All 1968 and 1969 coupes have two storage bags to hold the T-tops when they are removed. Some cars have bags dyed to match interior color, while others have black bags regardless of interior color. Earlier cars for each year are more likely to have a color-matched bag. Later cars are more likely to have black bags.

All bags have a date code stamped in ink inside. Typical date stampings contain a month and year designation. For example, bags manufactured in October 1968 read "10-68." In addition to the date stamping, bags might also contain a logo stamping representing the manufacturer. The most common logo seen is "TEX."

All T-top storage bags have a flap that closes over the opening. Bags found in all 1968s and in those '69s assembled through approximately October 1969 utilize Velcro to hold the flap closed. Bags found in '69s assembled after approximately October 1969 use three chrome-plated snaps to hold the flap shut.

All 1968 and 1969 coupes have adjustable T-top hold-down straps. As with the T-top bags, early cars tend to have straps dyed to match interior color, and later cars tend to have black straps regardless of interior color. All coupes have two straps that attach to chrome-plated anchors. The anchors are fastened to the floor of the rear luggage area. The anchors are secured by chrome-plated Phillips oval-head screws. The adjustment clips on the straps have the manufacturer's logo stamped in. The strap manufacturer is the Irving Air Chute Company.

All 1968 and 1969 coupes have molded-vinyl trim mounted to the underside of the T-tops. The vinyl is the same color as the interior.

All 1968 and 1969 coupes have a rear window storage tray mounted above the rear luggage area. Trays in 1968s have a black, vinyl-coated spring clip to hold them up. Trays in '69s have a rectangular cast handle painted gloss black to hold them up. The cast handles contain the words "BACK WINDOW STORAGE" in raised-chrome block letters.

The rear window storage tray is made from black fiberboard. Each tray has nine slots and a metal strip riveted on toward the front of the car. In 1968 this metal strip is painted gloss black or left unpainted. In 1969 it is unpainted and polished to a high luster. The tray contains two riveted-on spring clips to hold the rear window securely.

Convertible Top Frames

For all 1968 and 1969 convertibles, top frames are painted semi-gloss black. A black fiberglass header panel is secured to the front underside of the top frame. Three chrome-plated latches secure the front top header to the windshield frame. Black rubber coats the latch levers, and each latch is accompanied by an adjustable tensioning bolt. In 1969 only the tensioning bolt is rubber tipped.

The convertible top frame's rear bow is secured to the body deck lid with two chrome-plated pins that insert into chrome-plated receptacles affixed to the body. Chrome Phillips oval-head screws hold the pins to the rear bow. In 1968 the pins are ¼ inch in diameter. In 1969 they are enlarged to ⁵⁄₁₆ inch.

The underside of the convertible top, including the top material itself and the pads, is always black, regardless of interior color.

The optional removable hardtop on those convertibles so equipped has a padded vinyl headliner, with the color matched to the interior. Front latches for the hardtop are chrome plated. Unlike the soft top, the levers on these latches are not rubber coated. The hardtop latches each have a tensioning bolt. As with the soft top, the tensioning bolts are rubber tipped in 1969 only.

All 1968 and most 1969 hardtops have two mounting studs in the rear. Very late '69s have a third mounting bolt in the center of the hardtop, beneath the rear window.

The underside of the convertible deck lid is painted body color. Deck lid release levers, release cables, and lock mechanisms were all mounted prior to painting and should therefore also be painted body color.

The latch receptacles mounted underneath the rear deck, which receive the pins in the rear bow of the convertible top, are black and not body color. The rods that control the receptacles are also black. Deck lid rubber bumpers are black, as are their brackets. The receptacles attached to the body that receive the convertible deck lid's front locating guides have white nylon bushings.

1968 AND 1969 MECHANICAL
Engine Blocks

Engine block casting numbers for all 1968 and 1969 engines are located on the top, rear, driver side of the block, on the flange that mates to the transmission bell housing. (Refer to Appendix F for engine block casting numbers.)

All Corvette engine blocks were produced with a casting number on top of the driver-side rear of the block, adjacent to where the bell housing mounts. The number shown here, "3916321," is correct for earlier 1968 427 engine blocks.

All 1968–1969 Corvette engines had a VIN derivative, assembly date, and suffix code stamped into a pad on the front passenger side of the block, immediately adjacent to where the water pump mounts. This 1968 stamping is from car number 194378S409643. The "T" tells us that the engine was produced at the V-8 engine plant in Tonawanda, New York. The date code "0111" indicates that it was assembled on January 11, 1968. The suffix code "IM" tells us that it is a 427/400 engine coupled to a manual transmission.

Engine block casting dates for all 1968 and 1969 small-blocks, and those 1969 big-blocks in cars assembled after approximately March 1969, are located on the top, rear, passenger side of the block, on the flange that mates to the transmission bell housing. The casting date for 1968 big-blocks, as well as 1969 big-blocks in cars assembled prior to approximately March 1969, is located on the passenger side of the block, adjacent to the engine mount area.

The engine block casting date for all blocks consists of a letter for the month, one or two numbers for the day, and one number for the year. For example, a block cast on June 17, 1968, would have a casting date of "F 17 8." As is typical of cast numbers (but not stamped-in numbers,) the letter "I" is used to denote the month of September.

All 1968 and 1969 engines contain two distinct stampings on a machined pad on the top of the passenger side between the cylinder head and water pump. One stamping is commonly referred to as the assembly stamping, and the other is commonly called the VIN derivative stamping.

The assembly stamping begins with a prefix letter to indicate the engine assembly plant. "V" indicates the Flint plant, where all small-blocks were assembled, and "T" designates the Tonawanda plant, where all big-blocks were assembled. Following the prefix letter are four numbers

indicating the month and day of assembly. After the numbers indicating the assembly date are three suffix letters denoting the particular engine. This suffix code is often referred to as the engine broadcast code or simply the engine code. (Refer to Appendix C for engine suffix codes.)

To illustrate what a typical engine assembly stamping looks like, consider the following 1968 combination: a base 327/300-horsepower engine built on May 5 and coupled to an automatic transmission. The assembly stamping for such an engine would read "V0505HO."

Most big-blocks have the assembly stamping on the outboard side of the pad and the VIN derivative stamping on the inboard side. Most small-block engines have their two stamp sequences reversed, with the assembly stamping on the inboard side and the VIN derivative stamping on the outboard side.

Always remember that the engine assembly date must come after the engine block casting date (you can't assemble an engine before the block is cast), and both the casting date and assembly date must precede the final assembly date of the car (you can't final assemble a car before the engine has been cast and assembled). The great majority of engines were cast and assembled a few weeks before the car's assembly date. Some engines, however, were cast and/or assembled months prior to installation in a car. Six months is generally accepted as the outer limit between an engine assembly or casting date and the final assembly date of the car.

The VIN derivative stamping, as the name implies, is a stamping containing a portion or a derivative of the car's vehicle identification number. For example, the VIN derivative stamping for the very first 1969 assembled would read "19S700001." The second car would read "19S700002" and so on.

All 1968 and 1969 engine blocks, with the exception of 1969 ZL1s, are cast iron painted Chevrolet Engine Orange. All 1969 ZL1 blocks are cast aluminum.

Some blocks were painted before exhaust manifolds were installed. Therefore coverage on the sides of the block behind the manifolds is good. Other blocks apparently had the exhaust manifolds installed when they were painted, and the manifolds got painted as well. The engine stamp pad was normally covered up when the engine was painted, so it normally appears unpainted.

Cylinder Heads

As with engine blocks, all 1968 and 1969 cylinder heads have both a casting number and a casting date. As with blocks and other cast parts, the cylinder head casting date typically has a letter to indicate the month, one or two numbers to indicate the day of the month, and one number to indicate the year. (Refer to Appendix G for cylinder head casting numbers.)

All 1968 and 1969 small-block engines utilize cast-iron cylinder heads. All big-block engines also utilize cast-iron heads, with the exception of the optional L88, L89, and ZL1, all of which have aluminum cylinder heads.

All cylinder heads and head bolts, with the exception of the aluminum heads, are painted Chevrolet Engine Orange. Aluminum heads remain unpainted, though they often have orange overspray around the bottom.

Intake Manifolds

All 1968 and 1969 small-block intake manifolds are cast iron, and all big-block manifolds are cast aluminum. As with engine blocks and cylinder heads, intake manifolds contain casting numbers and casting dates. As is typical of cast engine parts, the casting date consists of a letter designating the month, one or two numbers designating the day of the month, and a number denoting the year.

Casting numbers for all manifolds are on the top surface, as are casting dates for cast-iron manifolds. For aluminum manifolds, casting dates are on the underside and are therefore not visible when the manifold is installed on an engine. (Refer to Appendix H for intake manifold casting numbers.)

All 1968 Corvette intake manifolds have a machined opening at their forward edge for an oil fill tube. The 1969 intakes do not have this opening. In 1968 the oil fill tube and its cap are painted Chevrolet Engine Orange with all 327/300 engines. Some 327/350 engines have a chrome cap. The cap has a flat top with a central depression and a central rivet with "S" stamped in. The 427 oil fill cap is chrome plated and located in the valve cover. It has a large central depression with a central rivet with "S" stamped in. In 1969 the base engine cap is painted orange and has "ENGINE OIL FILL AC FC2" stamped in. Optional 327/350 engines and all 427s in 1969 used the same chrome-plated cap used in 1968.

All 1968 and those 1969 L88 and ZL1 engines made through at least April 1969 utilize a cast-iron thermostat housing. All other 1969s utilize a cast-aluminum housing. Housings on Chevrolet Engine Orange–painted intake manifolds are painted orange as well. Housings on aluminum

intakes are unpainted. No 1968 or 1969 thermostat housings have a hole for a temperature sending unit. Housings used on certain other Chevrolets and some replacement housings have a tapped hole. Later GM service replacements have a GM logo cast in the top, while originals have an alphanumeric code cast in.

Thermostat housings on big-block engines are fastened with two hex-head bolts. Housings on small-block engines are fastened with a tall hex-head bolt and a short double-sided stud with a hex in its center. Nothing attaches to the stud that sticks up on the short side of the housing.

With original 1968 and 1969 intake manifold side gaskets, but not with later GM replacements, semicircular tabs stick up between the runners for cylinders three and six and for the exhaust heat crossover passage. Also, original front and rear intake gaskets do not have side tabs for locating the gaskets on the block's rail, as do later replacements.

All intake manifolds are held on by ⁹⁄₁₆-inch hex-head bolts. The bolts do not get any type of washer.

Engine lifting brackets are attached to most 1968 and 1969 Corvettes. On small-blocks, one bracket is attached to the second intake manifold bolt from the front on the driver side. If the car has a manual transmission, the other bracket is attached to a bell housing bolt on the passenger side. If the car has an automatic transmission, there is no rear lifting bracket.

On all big-block engines, except those fitted with tri-power, the front lifting bracket is attached to the two front intake bolts on the driver side. Tri-power engines do not have a front lifting bracket. The rear lifting bracket on all big-block engines is attached to the rear of the passenger side cylinder head.

Regardless of engine size, if a lifting bracket is attached to a part painted Chevrolet Engine Orange, it is also painted that color. If it is attached to an unpainted aluminum part, it is left unpainted or painted silver.

All intake manifolds, including aluminum examples, were installed before engines were painted. Therefore, on those engines with cast-iron intakes, hold-down bolts, as well as any exposed portions of gaskets, are painted Chevrolet Engine Orange.

Aluminum intakes were crudely masked off prior to engines being painted. Therefore engines with aluminum intakes may have orange paint overspray on edges, bolts, and gaskets. If orange overspray was excessive, the factory sometimes sprayed the area along the edges of the manifold silver, resulting in silver overspray on bolts, gaskets, and sometimes even cylinder heads.

Distributor and Ignition Coil

All 1968 and 1969 Corvettes use a mechanical tach drive Delco Remy distributor. All distributors have a thin aluminum identification band secured around the housing, in a recess just above the distributor hold-down clamp.

The identification band is natural on one side and dyed pinkish red on the other. While the majority of cars have the dye on the outside of the band, some have it inside, making it difficult to see when the band is installed on the distributor.

The identification band has the words "DELCO REMY" stamped into it. This is followed by a seven-character part number and a date code. (Refer to Appendix K for distributor part numbers.)

The date code, which represents the day the distributor was assembled, consists of a number representing the year, a letter representing the month, and one or two numbers representing the day of the month. For 1968 and 1969 distributor date codes, the letter "A" represents January, "B" represents February, and so on. As is typical of stamped-in date codes, the letter "I" is skipped, so September is represented by "J." The date code on a distributor assembled on March 17, 1969, would read, "9 C 17," and one assembled November 21, 1968, would read "8 L 21."

While most distributors were made several weeks before the engine was assembled, it is entirely possible that several months separated the two. As with most other components, six months is the generally accepted maximum for all distributors, except those installed into L88s and ZL1s. Distributors for these engines may have assembly dates more than six months prior to the engine assembly date.

All 1968 and 1969 Corvettes utilize a distributor housing without a small hole opposite the tachometer drive gear. Later distributor housings, beginning in mid-1970, have this small hole and are therefore not correct for 1968 or 1969 cars.

Distributor housings are painted semi-gloss black and have one of several daubs of colored paint just below the distributor cap on the passenger side, toward the front of the car.

All distributors, including those for L88s and ZL1s, are fitted with a vacuum advance unit. Vacuum advances have a part number stamped into the bracket that mounts the vacuum canister to the distributor.

All 1968 and 1969 Corvettes, except those equipped with an L88 or ZL1, use a black Delco Remy distributor cap. In 1968 some original caps had "PATENT PENDING" or "PATENT 2769047" molded into the top. Original 1969 caps have been observed with the words "DELCO REMY PAT. PENDING R" or "DELCO REMY PATENT 2769047 R" molded into the top between the towers. Cars equipped with an L88 or ZL1 utilize a dark-brown Delco cap.

All 1968s and 1969s use a Delco Remy ignition coil. All coils are held by a silver-cadmium-plated, stamped-steel bracket. The coil is clamped into the bracket with a slotted round-head machine screw, and the bracket is held to the intake manifold by two hex-head bolts. If the car is equipped with a radio, a capacitor is held to the coil bracket with a clamp retained by a single screw.

Coils are painted gloss black and have the last three numbers of their Chevrolet part numbers embossed in the

Cars equipped with option K66, transistor ignition, have a pulse amplifier mounted to the front of the driver-side fender well. Original amplifiers have the part number stamped into the base, while service replacements have it stamped into the housing. For 1968 the part number is 1115005, and for 1969 it is 1115438.

housing from the inside out, so they are raised up. (Refer to Appendix L for coil numbers and applications.)

In addition to the final three numbers of the part number, some ignition coils (coils 270 and 263) also have "B-R" embossed in their cases. Coils utilized with the optional transistor ignition system have a red, black, and silver foil sticker that reads "Delco Remy Ignition Coil for Transistor Ignition."

Transistor ignition was a required option with L71s, L88s, L89s, and ZL1s. It was optional on other engines.

Transistor ignition includes a different distributor, a special wire harness, a different ignition coil, and a pulse amplification box. The amplification box is mounted to the driver-side front inner wheelwell. It is visible if you look between the driver-side front inner wheelwell and the driver-side front corner of the body with the hood in the raised position.

The correct 1968 pulse amplification box has a plug to receive a mating plug in the transistor ignition wire harness. The correct 1969 amplification box has a three-wire pigtail coming out of it and terminating in a plug connector. The plug connector is mated with a corresponding plug connector in the transistor ignition harness.

Original 1968 and 1969 pulse amplification boxes have a part number stamped into the base. For 1968 the part number is 1115005, and for 1969 it is 1115438. Later boxes sometimes have the part number stamped into the amplifier's housing rather than its base.

Ignition Shielding

All 1968 and 1969 Corvettes equipped with a radio are outfitted with ignition shielding. All pieces of shielding are plated with flash chrome. Its quality and appearance are not very good.

All small-block and big-block cars have a two-section main ignition shield. It consists of a surround that completely encapsulates the distributor and coil, and a lid for the surround.

The surround for 1968s and 1969s assembled through approximately spring 1969 is held together by three spot welds. Later '69s have two small Phillips-head screws at the seam, in addition to the spot welds.

A translucent white plastic shield is held to the underside of the top lid by four plastic rivets. Three chrome-plated wing bolts retain the lid to the surround. The main shield, or top shield as it is sometimes called, attaches to support brackets with two chrome wing bolts on each side. The support brackets are painted Chevrolet Engine Orange and attach to the intake manifold bolts.

Small-blocks have a vertical ignition shield on each side of the main shield. The vertical shields encase the ignition wires. These vertical shields are not used on big-blocks. All small-blocks also use a pair of boomerang or V-shaped sections of chrome-plated shielding to encapsulate the spark plug wires. The boomerang shielding runs from the bottom of the vertical shields to the area beneath the spark plugs.

All small-blocks have four silver-cadmium-plated spark plug heat shields, each covering two plugs. Each shield is fastened to the cylinder block with a single indented hex-head bolt. The bolts pass through brackets attached to the heat shields. The brackets, like the shields, are cadmium plated.

Small-blocks also have four chrome-plated spark plug ignition shields. The spark plug shields are retained to brackets with chrome-plated wing bolts. The brackets have "FPM" stamped in to represent the manufacturer. Later, incorrect GM replacement brackets have "CNI" stamped in.

Small-block cars not originally equipped with a radio still have the two main shield support brackets on the back of the intake manifold and the cadmium-plated spark plug heat shields. They do not have any of the chrome shielding.

Instead of spark plug wire and spark plug shields like small-blocks, big-blocks have special spark plug wires covered with braided stainless-steel wire. Toward the end of each wire, the braid ends in a hoop that fastens to valve cover bolts to provide a ground. The hoops on the right side attach in pairs to the forward-most bolt and the third bolt back. On the left side they attach to the second and fourth bolts back.

Big-block cars not originally equipped with a radio do not have the main shield support brackets or braided steel spark plug wires.

Spark Plug Wires

All 1968 and 1969 Corvettes, except those equipped with an L88 or ZL1 engine, use black spark plug wires manufactured by Packard Electric. Wires for L88s and ZL1s are made by Packard Electric but are brown in color.

All wires are ink stamped every few inches with "Packard T V R Suppression" and a date code. The date code indicates the quarter and the year of manufacture. For example, wires labeled "2Q-69" were made in the second quarter of 1969.

Wires for small-block engines have black boots with 90-degree bends at the spark plug end and straight black boots at the distributor end.

On those 1968 and 1969 big-blocks equipped with a radio, wires have gray boots with 135-degree bends at the spark plug ends and black boots with 90-degree bends at the distributor ends. On those big-blocks not equipped with a radio, the wires are the same, except the boots are straight at the distributor ends.

Carburetors and Choke

All 1968 and 1969 Corvettes are carbureted. Original carburetors come from either Rochester, Holley, or Carter. Carter was at times contracted to manufacture Rochester Quadrajet carburetors for General Motors, so the Carter-built Quadrajets are almost identical to the Rochester-built ones. Carter-built Quadrajets are identified as being manufactured by Carter and use Carter's system of date coding rather than Rochester's system. (Refer to Appendix J for 1968 and 1969 carburetor numbers.)

Rochester-built Quadrajets contain an alphanumeric sequence stamped into a flat, vertical area of the main body on the rear of the driver side. Either the full seven-digit GM part number or the final five digits of the part number are stamped in. Several letters, which identify the specific plant where the carburetor was made, may be stamped here as well. Finally, four numbers denoting the date of manufacture are also stamped into this area.

Rochester utilized the Julian calendar for date coding its carburetors. With this system of dating, the first three numbers represent the day of the year, and the final number is the last digit of the specific year. For example, the Julian date code for a carburetor made on January 1, 1968, would read, "0018." The first three digits, 001, represent the first day of the year. The final digit, 8, represents 1968.

Julian calendar dating can be tricky because of the extra day in a leap year. For example, the Julian date code for a carburetor made on December 31, 1968, would read, "3668," since 1968 was a leap year.

Carter-built Quadrajets don't use a Julian calendar coding system. Instead, they use a single letter and a single number. The letter denotes the month, with "A" indicating January, "B" indicating February, and so on. The letter "I" is not used, so September is represented by "J."

The number in the date code for Carter-built Quadrajets is the last digit for the year of manufacture. For example, a date code of "C8" indicates that the carburetor was made in March 1968.

Holley carburetors have three distinct stampings on the front driver side of the air horn. The top stamping is the

All factory-installed 1968–1969 Holley carburetors contain a seven-digit GM part number, a Holley part number, and a manufacturing date code stamped on the front of the air horn. The first character of the date code is the final digit of the year, the second character is a number or letter representing the month, and the third character is a number denoting the week of the month. In the example shown, "7A1" represents the first week of November 1967.

seven-digit GM part number, which may be followed by one or two letters.

Below the GM part number is the Holley list number. The list number corresponds to Holley's part number. This stamping says "LIST," followed by four numbers and then an additional number, letter, or combination of numbers and letters.

Below the Holley list number is the date code. Holley date codes in 1968 and 1969 utilize three characters. The first is a number representing the last digit of the year, the second is either a number or a letter representing the month of production, and the third is a number representing the week of production.

For the month of production, numbers 1 through 9 denote January through September, "O" denotes October, "A" denotes November, and "B" denotes December.

A Holley carburetor manufactured on April 3, 1969, would have a date code of "941," with "9" representing 1969, "4" representing April, and "1" representing the first week of April, which includes April 3.

All 1968 and 1969 carburetors are plated gold dichromate. Rochester carburetors tend to be darker and more uniform in color than Holleys.

All engines equipped with a single carburetor use a single accelerator return spring. It is black phosphate plated and mounts from the primary shaft bell crank to the accelerator cable mount.

Accelerator return spring usage varies on those engines equipped with tri-power. Earlier cars appear to utilize a single spring attached to the center carburetor throttle lever and the linkage clip to the front carburetor. A second, smaller spring was later added. This second spring was attached to the bottom of the center carburetor throttle lever and the bracket holding the accelerator cable. Later 1969 tri-power

cars appear to have only the second, smaller spring and not the first.

All 1968 and 1969 Corvettes, except those equipped with an L88 or ZL1 engine, utilize a mechanical carburetor choke controlled by a thermostatic coil. The coil is mounted in a recess on the passenger side of the intake manifold and is covered by a cadmium-plated steel housing. A rod links the coil to the choke linkage on the carburetor. L88 and ZL1 carburetors did not have a choke.

Air Cleaner

L88 and ZL1 engines utilize a unique air cleaner arrangement. A base painted gloss black rests on the carburetor, with a thin gasket between the two. A dark gray foam ring sits in the outer lip of the base. A 5½-inch diameter circular metal screen sits in a recess in the inner lip of the base. A small, semi-gloss painted lid goes over the metal screen and is retained by a silver-cadmium-plated wing nut.

The remainder of the L88 and ZL1 air cleaner system is housed in the hood. The underside of the hood has a unique fiberglass housing bonded on. A foam and metal air cleaner element resides in the underhood fiberglass housing. When the hood is shut, the foam ring in the outer lip of the air cleaner base seals against the underhood housing. Fresh air is drawn in from the base of the windshield, travels through the underhood housing, passes through the air cleaner element and small metal screen, and enters the carburetor.

All 1968 and 1969 Corvettes not equipped with an L88 or ZL1 use an open element air cleaner assembly. The assembly is comprised of a base painted gloss black, an element, and a chrome lid. The base has a fitting for a breather tube that connects to the right-side valve cover. The center mounting hole in original lids was punched downward, not drilled, and the edge of the hole was rolled over and crimped back. This is visible on the underside.

All single-carburetor engines use an air cleaner with a 14-inch diameter chrome-plated lid. Tri-power engines have chrome-plated triangular lids. All lids have red and silver foil decals identifying engine displacement and horsepower rating. In addition, all lids have service instructions and the replacement filter part number silk-screened on the underside.

Original air filter elements have "BEST WAY TO PROTECT YOUR ENGINE—REPLACE WITH TYPE A 212 CW" silk-screened in white around the horizontal lip. Furthermore, original elements, unlike later replacements, have a fine wire screen around the outside. Most replacements use a noticeably heavier wire. Earlier cars probably utilize an element with the wire screen in a diagonal pattern. Later cars probably use an element with the wire screen in a horizontal pattern. With a horizontal pattern, the wire forms rectangles, with the longer measurement running vertical when the element is installed.

Valve Covers

All 1968 and 1969 base engines are fitted with stamped-steel valve covers painted Chevrolet Engine Orange. A raised area spans their width, but they do not have "Chevrolet" stamped in like earlier covers do. They are held on with hex-head bolts and metal tabs that are also painted orange. Original valve covers have more rounded corners than later replacements. Also, original covers do not have spark plug wire brackets or oil drip rails welded to them.

A PCV valve inserts into a rubber grommet in the driver-side valve cover. A hose connects the PCV valve to the carburetor. The intake for the PCV system is in the passenger-side valve cover.

Covers for 1968 do not have an oil fill, since 1968 intake manifolds have an oil fill tube pressed in. Covers for 1969 have a steel twist-on oil fill cap in the driver-side valve cover. The oil cap is painted orange on base engines and has "S" (for Stant, the manufacturer) stamped into the rivet in the center.

In 1968 the optional L79 327/350 engine is equipped with the same stamped-steel valve cover as base engines, except it is chrome plated instead of painted.

In 1969 the optional L46 350/350 engine is equipped with natural-finish cast-aluminum valve covers. These covers have seven ribs running from end to end on top. Both the driver- and passenger-side covers have holes for the PCV system, and the driver side has a hole for the oil fill. The oil fill cap is the same as the one used for base engines, except it is chrome plated. The passenger-side cover has a rigid black disc with a crossed-flag emblem in a circle glued in the spot where the oil fill cap is located on the other cover. As with the painted steel covers, a vent hose connects the passenger-side valve cover to the air cleaner base, and a PCV valve is in the driver-side valve cover. Aluminum valve covers are retained by silver-cadmium-plated, indented hex-head bolts.

All 1968 and 1969 big-block valve covers are plated with low-quality chrome. They all have internal drippers spot welded on, and the spot welds show as irregular indents on the outside of the cover. A foil decal reading "Tonawanda #1 Team" is on the top of the passenger-side cover toward the front. A twist-on, chrome-plated oil fill cap is located on the passenger-side cover.

A number of changes were made in big-block valve cover design in 1968 and 1969. The first covers are the same as those used on 1967 big-block Corvettes. The passenger- and driver-side covers each have two welded-on brackets to hold plastic spark plug wire looms and two clips on the intake side of the cover to hold wires. The rear of the driver-side cover has a large depression to clear the power brake booster. This cover is used on cars with both power and nonpower brakes.

A second big-block valve cover came into use in approximately January 1968. With this design, the L-shaped bracket for the forward spark plug wire loom on the passenger side is moved back, so it is no longer centered between the cover ends. Instead, it just about lines up with the cover's breather hose opening. The deep depression in the rear of the driver-side cover is eliminated, and a much smaller depression is substituted. Finally, the two welded-on clips on the intake side of the cover are replaced with a single clip centered on the bottom of the exhaust side.

In approximately July 1969, another change in big valve covers appeared. The rearmost welded-on spark plug wire loom bracket on the driver side is moved forward about two inches. This change places it forward of the rear intake manifold bolt rather than rearward of it.

A final change is incorporated beginning in approximately December 1969. The small clearance depression first seen in approximately January 1968 is eliminated.

Exhaust Manifolds

All 1968 and 1969 exhaust manifolds are cast iron. The casting number is normally on the side facing away from the engine, and a casting date is normally on the side facing toward the engine. (Refer to Appendix I for exhaust manifold casting numbers.)

Small-block exhaust manifold casting dates normally include a letter denoting the month and one or two numbers denoting the day of the month. Big-block exhaust manifolds normally include a letter denoting the month, one or two numbers denoting the day of the month, and one or two numbers denoting the year.

Small-block exhaust manifolds were not yet installed when engines were originally painted, so they show no signs of overspray. Big-block manifolds may or may not have Chevrolet Engine Orange overspray.

No 1968 or 1969 exhaust manifolds use a gasket where they mount to the cylinder head.

Small-block manifolds use $\frac{7}{16}$-inch hex-head bolts with two concentric rings on their heads. The front two bolts and rear two bolts on both sides of the engine have French locks, with one of the two tabs bent over. In addition, the same front and rear bolts on each side have thick, flat washers between the French lock and manifold. However, if the exhaust manifold bolt also retains a bracket (such as an air-conditioning bracket), the flat washer is usually not used.

Bolts holding big-block manifolds on have been observed with three different kinds of heads. The most prevalent has two concentric rings, like small-block manifold bolts. A second design, with an integral washer, a recessed hex-head, and "A" (the manufacturer's logo) in the center of the head, is also utilized. A third variety is a simple hex head with no markings at all.

No 1968 or 1969 big-block exhaust manifolds have French locks or any type of washers used with the bolts.

Starter Motor

All 1968 and 1969 Corvettes have a Delco Remy starter motor. Automatic transmission–equipped cars utilize starters with aluminum noses, while starters for manual transmission–equipped cars have cast-iron noses. The only exceptions are '69s equipped with big-blocks and automatics, which have cast-iron starter noses.

On 1968 starter motors, field coils, as well as the solenoid, are retained by slotted-head screws. On 1969 starter motors, field coils, as well as the solenoid, are retained by Phillips-head screws. Motor housings and both aluminum and cast-iron noses are painted semi-gloss black.

The starter's part number and assembly date are stamped into the side of the motor housing. The date code contains a number representing the last digit of the year and a letter denoting the month, with "A" representing January, "B" representing February, and so on. As is typical of stamped-in date codes, the letter "I" is skipped, so September is represented by "J." One or two numbers indicating the day follow the letter denoting the month. For example, a date code of "9B14" indicates that the starter was made on February 14, 1969. (Refer to Appendix N for starter motor part numbers.)

Starter solenoids have a black Bakelite cover for the electrical connections. Solenoid housings may be painted semi-gloss black or silver cadmium plated.

A black-phosphate-plated spring clip clamps around the starter solenoid in all cars. A protrusion on top of this clip holds the starter motor wires away from the engine and exhaust system.

All cars use a stamped-steel brace to support the forward end (the end facing the front of the car when the starter is installed). The brace mounts to a stud on the starter's end plate and to a threaded boss in the engine block. The brace is painted semi-gloss black.

Late 1968s and all 1969s have a heat shield to protect the starter motor. Small-block engines are fitted with rectangular shields, while big-blocks get larger, irregularly shaped shields. Small-block shields are painted semi-gloss black, and big-block shields are plated with poor-quality flash chrome. Heat shields attach to the solenoid screws with barrel nuts.

Oil Filter

All 1968 and 1969 engines, including small- and big-blocks, utilize AC Delco spin-on oil filters. Original filters are white with a red AC logo, blue circumferential stripes, and blue lettering reading "FULL FLOW" and "TYPE PF-25." It is likely but not certain that some original filters had "BEST WAY TO PROTECT YOUR ENGINE—REPLACE WITH AC TYPE PF25" embossed on the bottom. Later replacement GM filters are painted dark blue, with a sticker bearing the AC and GM logos.

Alternator and Voltage Regulator

All engines are fitted with a Delco Remy alternator mounted on the driver side. Alternator housings are made from cast aluminum and are not painted or coated with anything.

All alternators had a part number, amp rating, and assembly date code stamped in the front portion of the housing near the mount boss. In cars equipped with power steering and a 427 engine, the alternator was mounted sideways, as shown here, making it somewhat difficult to read the stampings. This is a 1968 alternator. It does not have cooling fins on the back of the housing as seen in 1969.

The front half of the housing has the unit's part number, amperage rating, and assembly date code stamped in. The date code contains a number for the year and a letter for the month, with "A" representing January, "B" representing February, and so on. As is typical of stamped-in date codes, the letter "I" is skipped, so September is represented by "J." The letter denoting the month is followed by one or two numbers for the day. For example, an alternator stamped "8F17" was assembled June 17, 1968.

The alternator pulley on all L88s, L89s, ZL1s, and L71s is machined from solid material and is silver cadmium plated. While this high-performance pulley is randomly seen on other engines, most other applications used a zinc-plated, stamped-steel pulley.

The lower alternator bracket on 1968 and 1969 small-blocks is stamped steel painted Chevrolet Engine Orange. The upper brace is stamped steel painted semi-gloss black.

The lower alternator bracket on all 1968 and 1969 big-blocks without power steering is cast and painted semi-gloss black. The lower bracket for big-block cars equipped with power steering is stamped steel painted semi-gloss black. The upper brace for all big-block engines is stamped steel painted semi-gloss black.

External voltage regulators are utilized in 1968 only. In 1969 the regulator is integral to the alternator.

The 1968 external voltage regulator is mounted on the left inner wheelwell adjacent to the alternator. "DELCO REMY" is stamped into the gloss black regulator cover from the inside, so the letters are raised up. "DELCO" and "REMY" are not lined up on original covers but are on later replacements.

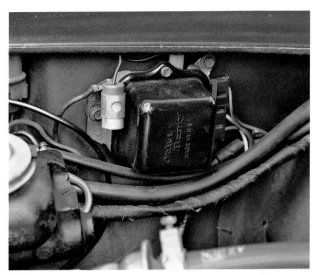

An external voltage regulator was used in 1968 but not in 1969, when Corvettes got alternators with internal regulators. This is an original 1968 regulator, distinguished from later service replacements by the positioning of the "Delco Remy" stamping in the cover. In originals "Remy" is below "Delco," as shown. In replacements "Remy" is next to "Delco." Also, originals have part number "1119515" stamped into the base, while replacements have part number "1119519" stamped in. Radio-equipped 1968s got the capacitor shown. It has the number "086" on the downward-facing end, and the cream-colored plastic connector on the end of its wire is correct. Later service replacement capacitors had a clear plastic connector.

The regulator cover is secured to the base with two silver-cadmium-plated hex-head bolts. Bolts on cars assembled through approximately November 1968 have slots in their heads. Bolts used in cars assembled thereafter do not have slots.

The voltage regulator base is zinc plated and has a part number and date code stamped in. The part number for original 1968 regulators is 1119515. Later service replacements are stamped with part number 1119519. The date code contains a single number denoting the year and a letter indicating the month. The letter "I" is not used, so "J" represents September.

Power Steering Pump and Fuel Pump

Small-block 1968 and 1969 cars equipped with power steering use a power steering pump painted semi-gloss black, with a neck that is the same diameter from top to bottom. The necks on big-block pumps, in contrast, widen toward the bottom.

Two different power steering pump caps are used in 1968 and 1969. The first, used in 1968 through mid-1969, is stamped steel and says, "CHECK OIL HOT, USE AUTOMATIC TRANSMISSION FLUID TYPE A" on top. The second design is black plastic and says, "FILL TO PROPER LEVEL, USE APPROVED FLUID" on top.

Small-block cars usually use a semi-gloss black, stamped-steel pulley for the power steering pump. All big-block–equipped cars use an open spoke, cast pulley for the power

steering pump. Cast pulleys are painted semi-gloss black or are black phosphate plated.

All 1968 and 1969 power steering pumps, regardless of engine, use a semi-gloss painted, stamped-steel support bracket.

All 1968 and 1969 Corvettes use an AC brand mechanical fuel pump that's natural dull silver in color. The pumps have "AC" cast into the top or side of the upper housing and a five-character part number stamped into the underside of the mounting flange. In 1968 small-blocks use pump number 6440568, L88s use 6440482, and other 427s use 6440659. In 1969 small-blocks use pump number 6440658, L88s use 6440718, and other 427s use 6440659.

Only those 1968 and 1969 Corvettes equipped with a Rochester carburetor utilize an external fuel filter. When so equipped, the filter is a metal body design manufactured by AC. It is silver colored, with an AC logo and "GF432" silk-screened on in red ink.

The filter is located on the front right side of the engine above the fuel pump. It is held by a silver-cadmium-plated stamped-steel bracket. The bracket is secured to the pivot for the air injection reactor (AIR) pump. Two steel lines come out of the top of the filter. The larger of the two is the fuel feed to the carburetor, and the smaller is the fuel return line to the tank. The fuel return line has a short length of rubber hose connecting it to the chassis fuel return line. In 1968 small tower clamps secure the hose, and in 1969 spring clamps hold it.

Water Pump, Engine Fan, and Fan Clutch

All 1968 and 1969 small-blocks use casting-number 3782608 water pumps. This pump's snout does not have reinforcing ribs, and the top of the pump housing does not have a boss for a bypass hose fitting.

All 1968 and 1969 big-block engines use casting-number 385624 water pumps. All big-block pumps utilize a bypass hose connected to a fitting on top of the pump housing. The bypass hose has a ¾-inch inside diameter and a molded 90-degree bend. It connects to a fitting in the front of the intake manifold and is secured at both ends by SAE type-D screw-type clamps. The clamps are stamped "10."

All solid lifter engines utilize a deep-groove water pump pulley, while pulleys on hydraulic lifter engines have a shallower groove. Most water pump pulleys are painted semi-gloss black, though some originals have a black phosphate finish.

All 1968 and 1969 Corvettes use a thermostatically controlled, viscous coupled fan clutch. The thermostatic control is via a rectangular bimetal strip on the front face of the clutch. The front face remains unpainted, but the remainder is sometimes seen with dull aluminum paint.

Original clutches usually have a date code stamped in the flange that goes against the water pump pulley. The code contains one or two numbers indicating the month, one or

All 1968–1969 Corvettes came with a viscous drive fan clutch. As shown here, the clutch was mounted to the water pump with bolts and split-ring lock washers in 1968 through the spring of 1969. After that the clutch was mounted with studs, nuts, and split-ring lock washers, not bolts. The shaft and mounting flange were typically painted silver. An inspection mark, which is most often yellow, is sometimes seen on the mounting flange. A green mark is often seen on the clutch's fins. A date code and manufacturer's logo were stamped into the edge of the mounting flange. This example was made on April 8, 1968. "SC" represents the manufacturer, Schwitzer Corporation.

two numbers indicating the day, and two numbers denoting the last two digits of the year. Thus a clutch manufactured on May 11, 1969, would be stamped "5 11 69." The date code stamping is often followed by "SC," which represents the manufacturer, Sweitzer Clutch.

On all 1968 and those 1969 cars assembled through approximately April 1969, fan clutches (as well as water pump pulleys) are retained by silver-cadmium-plated grade-eight hex-head bolts. These bolts are frequently seen with "AP," "RSC," or "WB" head markings. Each bolt gets a split-ring lock washer.

Fan clutches in 1969 cars assembled after approximately April 1969 are retained by studs and nuts that thread into the water pump's front hub. Regardless of whether bolts or studs are utilized to retain the fan clutch and water pump pulleys, the clutch hub has holes, not slots.

All 1968 and 1969 Corvettes use a cooling fan painted gloss black and mounted to the fan clutch. Cars equipped with air conditioning usually use a seven-blade fan with a part number and date code stamped into the edge of one or more blades. The date code contains a letter for the month, with "A" designating January, "B" designating February, and so on. As is typical of stamped-in date codes the letter "I" is skipped, so September is represented by "J." Following the letter indicating the month are two numbers to denote the year.

Small-block air-conditioned cars use a seven-blade fan that is essentially flat along the outer edge of each blade. In contrast, the ends of blades on big-block air-conditioned cars are irregularly shaped and come to an off-center point.

Cars not equipped with air conditioning use a five-blade fan. Five-blade fans do not have a part number or date code stamped in.

A minority of air-conditioned cars have a five-blade fan instead of the more commonly seen seven-blade unit. The five-blade fan differs from those seen in non-air-conditioned cars in that its blades are pitched at a more severe angle.

Radiator, Hoses, and Related Parts

Corvettes from 1968 and 1969 use either a copper or aluminum radiator, depending on the engine and transmission choice and whether the car is equipped with air conditioning.

Aluminum radiators have a part number and date code stamped into the top left side. The date code consists of two numbers to denote the year and a letter to indicate the month, with "A" representing January, "B" representing February, and so on. To the right of the stamping is a rectangular foil sticker printed "HARRISON," which is the manufacturer. Aluminum radiators are painted semi-gloss to gloss black.

Those 1968 and 1969 Corvettes equipped with L88 engines utilize a unique aluminum radiator. It resembles the aluminum radiator used in other Corvettes but is slightly larger. Also, its top neck is long and curved instead of short and straight.

Copper radiators were also manufactured by Harrison and have that name debossed in the passenger-side radiator tank. In addition, a stamped-steel tag containing a two-letter broadcast code and a part number is attached to the passenger side of copper radiators. As with aluminum, the copper radiators are painted semi-gloss to gloss black.

The lower radiator support area in unrestored 1968. Note the foam seals between the radiator support and the front cross member, and the rubber seals stapled to the front cross member. Body color overspray and varying degrees of blackout paint coverage are typically seen in this area.

Corvettes in 1968–1969 got either a copper or aluminum radiator, depending on the engine and transmission choice and whether the car was equipped with air conditioning. Small-block cars with an aluminum radiator got steel fan shrouds. Some very early 1968s with copper radiators also got steel shrouds, but all other cars with copper radiators got black fiberglass shrouds. Note the rubber seal stapled to the top of the radiator support, original-style tower clamps on the radiator hose, and varied surface finishes in this unrestored 1968.

Those 1969 Corvettes equipped with an L88 coupled to an automatic transmission utilize a fiberglass shroud. No other L88- (or ZL1-) equipped cars use a fan shroud.

Most 1968 and 1969 cars with copper radiators use an unpainted black or very dark gray two-piece plastic shroud with a bolt-on extension on the bottom. Very early 1968 cars fitted with copper radiators are sometimes seen with semi-gloss painted steel fan shrouds.

All cars fitted with aluminum radiators, except L88s and ZL1s, as noted above, use a semi-gloss painted, stamped-steel shroud.

In 1968 a strip of rubber is utilized to seal the top of the radiator support to the hood. In 1969 a thick, black foam rubber seal replaces the rubber flap. In both years, black foam rubber strips seal the shroud to the radiator.

Those 1968 and 1969 small-blocks without air conditioning use an aluminum radiator expansion tank. Small-blocks with air conditioning do not have expansion tanks. The only big-block to get an expansion tank in 1968

All 1968–1969 cars with a copper radiator or brass expansion tank used this RC-15 cap. The top of the cap was plated silver cadmium, but the rivet holding the cap's parts together was unplated brass, as shown in this original 1968 example.

is the L88, and that tank is aluminum. In 1969, 427/390, 427/400, 427/430, and 427/435 engine cars all use an aluminum expansion tank. Those 427/390 and 427/400 cars with air conditioning use a brass expansion tank.

Aluminum tanks are unpainted and have the Harrison logo debossed in the side. The 1968 and 1969 aluminum expansion tanks differ from earlier ones in that earlier ones have one outlet on the bottom and 1968 and 1969 units have two outlets.

In addition to the Harrison logo, the part number 3016340, "FILL 1/2 WHEN COLD," and a manufacturing date code are embossed in the face of aluminum tanks. The date code contains two numbers to denote the year and a letter to indicate the month, with "A" representing January, "B" representing February, and so on.

Brass expansion tanks are longer and thinner than their aluminum counterparts. They are approximately 3 inches in diameter and 20 inches long. A thin brass tag with "Harrison," a part number, and a date code stamped in is soldered to the side of the tank. The whole tank is painted gloss black.

Cars that don't have an expansion tank use an RC-15 radiator cap rated at 15 psi installed directly on the radiator. Cars with a brass expansion tank use the same cap installed on the tank. Cars with an aluminum expansion tank use an RC-26 cap, also rated at 15 psi, installed on the tank.

Both the RC-15 and RC-26 caps have the AC logo and the words "TURN TIGHT" and "REMOVE SLOWLY" stamped in them. On the RC-15 cap, "RC-15" and "15#" are stamped inside of a stamped circle. On the RC-26 cap "RC-26" and "15#" are stamped, but not inside a circle.

All radiator and heater hoses are molded black rubber. Stamped on radiator hoses in white ink are a part number, the GM logo, and several letters that are believed to be manufacturer's codes. In addition, there is usually a blue line running the length of the hose.

Heater hoses usually contain a GM logo in white ink. They sometimes have "DL" or "U" stamped on them also. Most original hoses are smooth (not textured) and have three or four thin ridges running lengthwise.

All 1968 and those 1969 Corvettes assembled through approximately September 1969 use tower-style clamps made by the Wittek Manufacturing Company. These clamps have a galvanized finish and contain the size, the words "WITTEK MFG. CO. CHICAGO U.S.A.," and a date code stamped into the band. The first number of the date code denotes the quarter, and the following two numbers indicate the year.

Those 1969 cars assembled after approximately September 1969 use SURE-TITE stainless-steel worm drive clamps for the radiator hoses. All applications use size-28 clamps, except air-conditioned big-blocks, which use size 32 on the lower hose only. Original clamps have "SURE-TITE" in italics stamped along the circumference of the band. In addition, "WITTEK MFG. CO. CHI. U.S.A." is stamped into the worm screw's housing.

All cars use tower-style clamps for the heater hoses. The ⅝-inch heater hoses use 1¹⁄₁₆-inch clamps. This clamp has a galvanized finish and contains the size, the words "WITTEK MFG. CO. CHICAGO U.S.A.," and a date code stamped into the band. The first number of the date code denotes the quarter, and the following two numbers indicate the year.

The ¾-inch heater hose uses 1¼-inch clamps. These clamps have a cadmium-dichromate finish that results in a translucent goldish tint as opposed to the smaller clamps' dull silver color. The larger 1¼-inch clamps contain the manufacturer's logo and size designation but do not have a date code. Instead, they have "DCM" stamped into the band.

Brake Master Cylinder and Related Components

All 1968 and 1969 Corvette master cylinders are manufactured by Delco and contain a casting number and the Delco split circle logo on the inboard side. Non-power-assist master cylinders are casting number 5455509, and power-assist masters are casting number 5480346.

In addition to the casting number, each master contains a two-letter application code stamped into a flat, machined boss on the top front of the unit. Most cars with power-assist brakes have "PG" stamped into the master cylinder. Most without power assist have "DC" stamped in. There is also normally a date code stamped into the flat surface adjacent to where the front brake line threads in. The entire master cylinder is semi-gloss black, except for machined areas, which are natural.

All masters contain two bleeder screws above the brake line ports and two steel wire bails that hold the cover on. A small vinyl sticker with two letters is folded around one of the bail wires. This sticker is white with red letters, which are "TG" for power brake cars and "YA" for manual brake cars.

All master cylinders use a stamped-steel, cadmium-dichromate-plated cover fitted with a rubber gasket. The cover has two domes that are not connected by a small ridge

Original master cylinder and power brake booster in an unrestored 1968. The master cylinder cover is correct for 1968 and most of 1969. Later 1969 covers have "USE DELCO SAE J 1703 BRAKE FLUID" stamped into the forward dome. A paper label with the "TG" broadcast code is correct for power brake master cylinders. The circular paint daub on the booster is an inspection mark. The original spring clamp securing the vacuum hose to the plastic fitting in front of booster has squared tangs, while replacements have rounded tangs.

as in later units. "SERVICE WITH DELCO PARTS" is stamped into one dome, while "USE DELCO SAE J 1703 BRAKE FLUID" or "SERVICE WITH SAE J 1703 BRAKE FLUID" is stamped into the other dome.

Power brake boosters, on cars so equipped, are painted gloss black and frequently have a spot of yellow or white paint somewhere. The paint is thought to be an inspection mark or an application code.

Some boosters have a Julian date code stamped on top opposite the vacuum valve. The code contains a number corresponding to the final digit of the year and three numbers denoting the day of the year. For example, a booster stamped "9134" was manufactured on the 134th day of 1969.

Air Conditioning and Heating System Components

All 1968 and 1969 Corvettes equipped with air conditioning utilize a model A-6 Frigidaire compressor. Compressors are painted semi-gloss black and have a green, black, and silver foil sticker on top of the housing. The sticker contains a date code and model number.

The date code normally consists of two numbers for the month, two numbers for the day, and one number corresponding to the last digit of the year. The final number indicates the shift during which the unit was assembled.

For all 1968 small- and big-block-equipped cars, and some 1969 small-block cars assembled through approximately November 1968, the model number is 5910645. For some early 1969 and all later 1969 small-blocks, the model number is 5910741. For all 1969 big-block-equipped cars, the model number is 5910740.

Driver-side engine compartment details in an unrestored 1968. The correct power brake master cylinder has the casting number of "5480346," wiring and vacuum hose routing, and the original ribbed and marked AIR pump hose with tower-style clamp.

The air-conditioning system for all cars includes a POA valve assembly that is natural aluminum in color. The thermostatic expansion valve, the tubing crimped onto the ends of the hoses, and the manifold block that connects the hoses to the back of the compressor are also unpainted.

An unpainted, dark gray fiberglass housing covers the evaporator. There is a Harrison foil sticker on the housing, as well as a fan relay. The relay has a cover painted gloss black with "DELCO REMY" stamped in from the inside. The relay mounts by means of a silver-cadmium-plated bracket that has "881" stamped in.

Those 1968 and 1969 Corvettes with air conditioning have a vacuum-actuated valve spliced into the heater hose. Tower-style clamps are used to retain the heater hose to the valve. When the air conditioning is on, this valve shuts off the flow of engine coolant to the heater core.

The blower motors for both air-conditioned and non-air-conditioned cars are painted gloss black. Motors on air-conditioned cars have a rubber tube that extends from the motor housing to the evaporator housing. Motors on non-air-conditioned cars do not have this tube. Motors have a part number and date code stamped into their mounting flanges, as well as the words "DELCO REMY DAYTON OHIO USA." The date code contains one or two numbers to denote the month and two numbers to indicate the year.

Air conditioning was available as an extra cost option on all cars except those equipped with an L88, L89, L71, or ZL1 engine.

Windshield Wiper Door Mechanism, Wiper Motor, and Related Components

All 1968 and 1969 Corvettes have a vacuum-actuated wiper door. The door is moved up and down by a vacuum motor mounted on the upper right side of the firewall. In all 1968 Corvettes, as well as early 1969 cars, the vacuum actuator is cylindrical. Later '69s use an actuator that resembles two pie tins joined together. All vacuum actuators are cadmium dichromate plated.

The vacuum motor is controlled by a cadmium-dichromate-plated vacuum valve. The body of the valve has two ridges extending into the depressed center. Later replacement valves have only one ridge.

In 1968 to mid-1969 cars, the valve is mounted on the rear of the right, front inner wheelwell housing. In those cars assembled after mid-1969, it is on the upper left side of the firewall near the emissions sticker. As with the vacuum motor, the valve is plated cadmium dichromate.

All 1968 and 1969 Corvettes utilize wiper motors that are die-cast natural silver in color. A black plastic cover goes over the wiper motor.

In 1969 only, the wiper motor has a sticker indicating the unit's part number and date code. All motors are part number 5044731. The date code utilizes the Julian calendar, with three numbers for the day of the year and a single number

All 1968 and early 1969 Corvettes used this vacuum actuator to open and close the wiper door. Starting in approximately March 1969, the actuator body was made from two tapered sections instead of this single cylindrical section. The rubber boot covering the actuator arm shown here, with three bellows in the middle and straight ends, is correct for 1968 and most of 1969. Late in 1969, the boot had an additional bellows on either end.

representing the last digit of the year. (Refer to Appendix P for wiper motor part numbers.)

The washer pump utilized for 1968 has three ports. A three-port pump is again used in 1969, but with the addition of a valve containing an additional two ports. The two extra ports are for the headlamp washer system.

For 1968 and 1969 Corvettes without air conditioning, the windshield-washer-fluid reservoir is mounted on the rear of the passenger-side inner wheelwell housing. The reservoir is rigid black plastic and has marks indicating fluid level.

All air-conditioned cars use a flexible plastic bag to hold washer fluid. The front of the bag is clear, and the rear is very dark gray. For 1968s this bag is mounted on the passenger side front inner wheelwell housing. For 1969s it mounts on the lower driver-side firewall.

All 1968 windshield wiper motors were fitted with a three-port pump, as shown. In 1969 an additional valve, with two more ports, was added to the motor assembly. The two additional ports directed washer fluid to the headlamp nozzles.

An original air injection reactor pump in an unrestored 1968 427 Corvette. The pressure relief valve on top of the pump housing is correct for 1968 and early 1969.

An original tower-type hose clamp in an unrestored 1968. Reproduction clamps are usually made from thinner-gauge material.

Air Injection Reactor System and Other Emissions Components

Air injection reactors (AIRs) are installed in all 1968 and 1969 Corvettes, including L88s and ZL1s. The AIR system includes black-cadmium-plated tubes (they tend to be black on small-blocks and brownish on big-blocks) that thread into each of the four runners on both exhaust manifolds. Therefore, all AIR-equipped cars have four holes drilled and tapped into each manifold.

The AIR pump body is die-cast aluminum and natural in color. A rough-textured sand-cast plate painted semi-gloss black covers the back of the pump.

All pumps contain a centrifugal filter (the piece that looks like a fan) behind the pulley. It is made from opaque white plastic and has squared-off fins. A white filter with rounded-off fins or a black plastic filter is not correct.

Small-block engines use a steel spacer between the front pump pulley and the centrifugal filter. Big-blocks do not use a spacer. The spacer is unplated or silver cadmium plated, and the pulley is gray phosphate plated or painted semi-gloss black.

Pulleys used on all small-blocks in 1968, and the base engine in 1969, have part number "3917234" stamped in. Pulleys found on 1969 L46 engines have part number "3932458" stamped in. AIR pumps on all 1968 and 1969 big-block engines use a pulley with part number "3925522" stamped in.

Most pumps are date coded, though the date can be difficult to see with the pump installed. It is stamped into a boss on the rear underside of the body. The sequence may begin with a letter to indicate the assembly plant or specific line. Then one or three numbers indicate the day of the year on the Julian calendar. Earlier dates (prior to the 100th day) might start with two zeros or might not. For example, a pump assembled on the fifth day of the year might be stamped "005" or simply "5." A fourth (or second) number follows to denote

the last digit of the year. This is followed by a number indicating the shift and a letter indicating the model of the pump.

The lower pump bracket is painted Chevrolet Engine Orange, and the upper bracket is semi-gloss black. For small-blocks, the lower bracket is cast and contains the number "3923214." For big-blocks, the lower bracket is stamped steel.

The diverter valve body is natural in color, while the diaphragm cover and check valves are cadmium dichromate. The diaphragm cover has a round sticker printed with a two-letter broadcast code. The diverter valve muffler is plated gray phosphate. The diverter valve part number is stamped into the valve below the muffler. Check valves have a part number stamped into their center ridges.

Hoses connecting the various parts of the AIR system are molded black, and hose clamps are tower style. Clamps have a galvanized finish and contain the size, the words "WITTEK MFG. CO. CHICAGO U.S.A.," and a date code stamped into the band. The first number of the date code denotes the quarter, and the following two numbers indicate the year.

All 1968 and 1969 Corvettes have a PCV valve located in the left-side valve cover. The valve has a part number stamped into it. For those engines equipped with a Holley carburetor, the PCV valve is part number CV746C. For those equipped with a Rochester carburetor, it is number CV736C.

All 1968 and 1969 Corvettes equipped with automatic transmission or air conditioning have an anti-diesel/fast idle solenoid mounted with a bracket to the front of the carburetor. The bracket is cadmium dichromate plated. The solenoid housing is silver cadmium plated and has a white sticker that reads "CAUTION NEVER USE TO SET IDLE SEE SERVICE MANUAL FOR ADJUSTMENT" in red letters.

On non-air-conditioned cars equipped with an automatic transmission, a pinkish wire runs along the driver-side valve cover and plugs into the solenoid. The wire is secured by clips attached to the valve cover.

Early in 1968, the emissions decal was glued to the top of the radiator on the driver side. Later it was placed on the driver-side firewall, behind the master cylinder and adjacent to the hood latch pin. This original example is in an unrestored 1968 assembled in January 1968. Note how rough the firewall surface is, with fiberglass strands clearly visible through the blackout paint.

On air-conditioned cars, a single green wire in a black fabriclike protective tube comes out of the air-conditioning compressor harness and plugs into the solenoid.

All 1968 and 1969 Corvettes have what is commonly called an emissions label glued in the engine compartment. On early 1968 cars, it is found on top of the radiator on the driver side. On later '68s and all '69s, it is glued to the left upper area of the firewall. The labels are white and contain engine tune-up specifications, as well as information about the emission control systems installed in the car.

Engine Compartment Brackets, Latches, Wiring, and Related Components

The firewall, underside of the hood, and engine compartment side of the inner wheelwells are painted semi-gloss black. The wheel sides of the front and rear inner wheelwells are also painted semi-gloss black, though coverage is usually sparse. In addition, the rear areas of the wheel sides normally have some undercoating.

Some 1969 Corvettes have a section of very dark gray insulation fastened to the forward underside of the hood. It is held in place with glue and three black discs that lock onto pins imbedded in the hood. This insulation is seen more frequently in cars equipped with big-block engines, though there appears to be no consistency in its use.

All 1968 and 1969 big-blocks have a small oil pressure line bracket on the left side of the engine block. In 1968 a steel tube goes from the block fitting to a junction at this bracket. Another steel tube continues up to the oil pressure gauge.

In 1969 a steel tube extends from the block fitting up to a junction on the bracket. A black plastic tube continues up to the oil pressure gauge.

All 1968 and 1969 small-blocks utilize black plastic tubing that goes directly from the engine block fitting to the oil pressure gauge. The plastic line has tiny white lettering and is fastened at both ends with brass fittings.

Engine compartment wiring harnesses and vacuum hoses are bundled together in a circle. Vacuum hoses are fastened to each other with pieces of nonadhesive black plastic tape used as ties. The electrical harnesses and vacuum hoses are held to each other with black plastic tie wraps.

All vacuum hose is color-coded with an ink stripe that runs the length of the hose. Larger hoses have a green, red, or yellow stripe, while smaller hoses usually have a white stripe.

The original engine compartment in a 1968 equipped with an optional L68 427/400 engine.

The hood was mounted to the body when it went through the paint process, so hood hinges normally show body color overspray, as well as black from the engine compartment blackout spray.

All cars have a horn relay mounted to the inner wheelwell. The relays have a zinc-plated cover with "DELCO REMY" and four letters stamped in from the inside out. The cover sits on a white plastic base for 1968 models and on a black plastic base for 1969 models.

A silver-cadmium-plated metal bracket attached to the horn relay mounts it to the left-side inner wheelwell housing. The bracket has "12V" and the last three digits of the relay's part number stamped in it. The part number is 1115862 in 1968 and those 1969s made through approximately late November 1968, and 1151115890 in 1969s made thereafter. In 1968 through early 1969, the stamping is therefore "862," and in later 1969s it is "890."

All 1968 and 1969 Corvettes have two horns, a high and a low note. The high note is part number 9000246, and it mounts on the passenger side. The low note is part number 9000245, and it mounts on the driver side.

Horns have the last three digits of the part number and a manufacturing date code stamped into flat areas near the sound opening. The date code contains a number denoting the year, a letter denoting the month (with "A" representing January, "B" representing February, and so on), and another number indicating the week. So a horn stamped "8B2" was made the second week of February 1968. Each horn is spot welded to a mounting bracket, and the whole assembly is painted semi-gloss black. (Refer to Appendix O for horn relay and horn numbers.)

Hood hinges are silver cadmium plated and usually have both body color and underhood black overspray. Hinges are usually fastened by black-phosphate-plated, indented hex-head bolts.

The hood support for 1968 and 1969 is silver cadmium plated and has two sections that telescope together as the hood is lowered. Early 1968s utilize two bolts to secure the bottom of the support to the inner wheelwell housing. Later '68s and all '69s use a third bolt that passes through the fender's drip rail.

The hood latches are black phosphate plated and mount with black-phosphate-plated hardware. The driver-side male latch has the hood release cable, attached with a brass barrel cable stop that utilizes a hex bolt to lock the stop to the cable. The cable is inside a spiral-wound metal sheath.

The male latches mounted to the firewall each have a pin that engages the female latches on the underside of the hood. The male latches in all 1968 and those 1969 cars assembled through approximately September 1969 use cone-shaped pins. All 1969 cars assembled thereafter use pyramid-shaped pins.

Another cable connects the two female latches mounted to the underside of the hood. In very early 1968, this cable is inside a wound metal sheath. This changes to a black nylon sheath for mid-production '68s and then to a white nylon sheath for later '68s and all '69s.

In 1968 this underhood crossover cable is fastened at its ends with small brass cylinders and silver-cadmium-plated hex-head set screws. In 1969 flat tabs of metal containing multiple holes are attached to the cable's ends. The flat tabs are secured to the hood latches with small clevis pins fitted with flat washers and cotter pins.

In 1968 and early 1969, two clips held by indented hex-head bolts fasten the cable to the underside of the hood. Beginning in approximately September 1969, the two clips are replaced with a single clip centered under the hood.

1968–1969 CHASSIS
Chassis

All 1968 and 1969 Corvette chassis are painted semi-gloss black. Chassis for automatic transmission–equipped cars have a removable, bolt-on center crossmember, while standard transmission–equipped cars have a welded-on center crossmember. Also, automatics do not have a clutch cross shaft tower welded on top of the chassis behind the left front wheel as standard transmission cars do.

A pair of one-inch-high chassis part number sequences is painted in white on the frame with a stencil. One sequence is the A. O. Smith part number (this company fabricated the chassis for GM), and the other sequence is the Chevrolet part number.

A manufacturing date code is stenciled on the rail as well. The date contains one or two numbers representing the month, one or two numbers indicating the day, and two numbers denoting the year.

The stencil numbers and date code usually appear on the outside of the right frame rail and are usually upside down.

All 1968 and 1969 Corvettes have serial numbers stamped into their chassis in two locations. They are typically found in the left-side rail slightly forward of the number-4 body mount bracket. They are also typically found on the left-side rear kickup above the wheel area, slightly forward of the number-3 body mount bracket.

Body mounts from 1968 and 1969 are not made from rubber as in 1967 and older Corvettes. Instead, they are thick aluminum discs that get sandwiched between the body and the chassis's body mount bracket.

Steel shims are frequently utilized at body mount points to make up for irregularities in fit. If present, shims are usually taped to the body mount bracket with 1½-inch masking tape.

The number of shims needed at each body mount bracket is typically written on the chassis adjacent to the bracket with a green or white grease crayon. Unlike earlier cars, this number is usually an actual number rather than slash marks.

Front Suspension

Upper and lower front control arms are painted semi-gloss to gloss black. Ball joints are installed after the arms are painted and are therefore not painted. Crushed steel rivets (not bolts) hold ball joints on and are also natural in finish.

Control arm cross shafts are painted semi-gloss black on some cars and unpainted on others. Cars with painted cross shafts typically have control arm bushing retention washers and bolts that are also painted semi-gloss black. Cars with unpainted cross shafts typically have retention washers that are gray phosphate plated and bolts that are black phosphate plated.

Front coil springs are natural in finish and sometimes have an irregular bluish cast from the manufacturing process. A green paper sticker contains two black letters indicating the spring's broadcast code (application), as well as a black GM part number.

Front and rear shock absorbers are manufactured by Delco and are oil hydraulic, not gas filled. They are painted semi-gloss gray and have "DELCO REMY DAYTON OHIO U.S.A. PLIACELL" and a date code stamped in around the bottom. The Julian date code contains three numbers indicating the day and two numbers denoting the year. In addition, there is a small paper sticker with a two-letter broadcast code on the side of the shock.

All 1968 and 1969 big-block Corvettes and all small-block-equipped cars with optional F41 suspension utilize a $^{15}/_{16}$-inch front sway bar. All small-blocks not equipped with F41 utilize a ¾-inch bar. Some cars have a sway bar painted semi-gloss black, while others have a natural, unpainted finish bar.

Bushings mounting the front sway bar to the chassis, as well as bushings in the end links, are unpainted black rubber. Stamped-steel brackets painted semi-gloss black hold the bar to the chassis.

End link bolts are zinc plated 5/16-24 SAE fine thread and have the manufacturer's logo, "WB," on their heads. End link spacers are zinc plated, have a split seam, and typically "K" or "C" stamped in.

Steering Box and Steering Linkage

All 1968 and 1969 Corvettes use a cast steering gear. It is usually natural in color, though some are painted semi-gloss black. The steering box cover is aluminum and does not have any symbols or writing in it. A daub of yellow paint is frequently seen on top of the box.

A forged pitman arm links the steering box to the relay rod. The pitman arm is natural in color and is often seen with a blue or green daub of paint. The steering relay rod and idler arm are typically natural in finish. Both parts are forged and tend to have a bluish gray tint. Original idler arms do not have grease fittings.

Tie rod ends are natural in finish and also typically have a bluish gray color cast. Daubs of yellow paint are often seen on tie rod ends. Tie rod end sleeves are painted semi-gloss black. Tie rod end clamps have two reinforcing ridges around their circumferences and are sometimes painted semi-gloss black and sometimes left unpainted.

Outer tie rod ends can install into either of two holes in the steering knuckles. Cars equipped with standard, nonpower steering have the outer tie rod ends installed into the rear holes, while cars equipped with power steering and cars equipped with an L88 or ZL1 engine have them in the forward holes. On those cars equipped with power steering, the unused steering knuckle hole is plugged with an aluminum plug inserted from the bottom.

On those cars so equipped, the power steering control valve and hydraulic cylinder are both painted semi-gloss black. The nut and washers retaining the hydraulic cylinder's ram to the frame bracket are zinc plated. The frame bracket may be painted semi-gloss black or unpainted. Original power steering hoses typically have longitudinal ridges around their entire circumferences, while later replacements don't.

Rear Suspension

All 1968 and 1969 Corvettes equipped with standard suspension utilize a nine-leaf rear spring. Cars equipped with optional F41 suspension utilize a seven-leaf spring. No band clamps are used on original springs. All springs are painted light gray and have black plastic liners between the leaves. Nine-leaf springs do not have a liner between leaf six and leaf seven (with the bottom leaf being number one).

The center rear spring-mount bracket is painted semi-gloss black. The four bolts retaining the spring to the differential typically have the manufacturer's logo, "WB," on their heads and are either black phosphate or zinc plated. The outer spring bolts and nuts are usually black phosphate plated, and the washers are typically silver cadmium plated or natural.

Rear trailing arms are painted semi-gloss to gloss black. Rear wheel bearing carriers (also called spindle supports) are natural and have a part number and date code cast in. The date code has a letter representing the month, with "A" for January, "B" for February, and so on, one or two numbers for the day, and one number for the final digit of the year. So the date code for a rear bearing carrier made on August 18, 1969, would read "H 18 9."

All 1968 and 1969 Corvettes equipped with F41 suspension or a big-block engine have a rear stabilizer bar. The bar is $^{9}/_{16}$-inch diameter and may be painted semi-gloss black or unpainted. It mounts to the chassis with stamped-steel brackets painted semi-gloss black. At each end, the bar has a link bracket painted semi-gloss black that attaches to brackets bolted to the trailing arms. The brackets on the trailing arms have plating that is sometimes called pickling. It results in a brownish olive color. These brackets attach to the trailing arm via bolts that thread into small, unpainted steel plates that slip into the rear of the arms.

Rear camber adjustment rods (also called strut rods) are usually natural and often have a bluish gray tint. Some rods are painted semi-gloss black or are partially painted during the undercarriage "blackout" process. Original rods have 1½-inch-diameter ends, while 1974 and newer rods have 1¾-inch-diameter ends.

The outboard ends of the camber adjustment rods are held to the rear wheel bearing carriers with forged L-shaped pins that also serve as the lower mounts for the rear shock absorbers. These pins, which are sometimes called rear shock brackets, contain a raised part number. Originally, there was a left and a right pin, with each having a slight bend to angle it upward when installed. Later GM replacements are not angled, so the left and right side interchange.

Special bolts attach the inboard ends of the camber adjustment rods to a bracket that's painted semi-gloss black. These bolts have integral off-center washers that, when rotated, move the rods in or out and thus allow for rear wheel camber adjustment. The camber adjustment bolts are usually silver cadmium plated, though they may be black phosphate plated instead.

Rear wheel toe adjustment is set with the use of shims placed on either side of the trailing arms where they mount to the chassis. The adjusting shims are unpainted rectangular pieces of steel in varying thicknesses. Correct shims have equally sized holes at each end, and when installed, one end protrudes from the chassis pocket where the end of the trailing arm resides. Later cars use a shim with a slot in one end that slips over the trailing arm mount bolt.

Rear axle shafts (often called half shafts) are made from forged ends welded to extruded steel tubes. The axle shafts are natural, with the tube shiny silver and the ends a dull gray. Original axle shaft tubes are approximately 2½ inches in diameter. Later tubes are considerably larger than this.

U-joints do not have grease fittings and do have raised part numbers on the body. They are natural and tend to have that faint bluish tint that is characteristic of forged parts.

The outboard axle shaft U-joints are pressed into a flange that is natural in color. The flange is held to the rear wheel bearing carrier by four bolts that are usually black phosphate plated. The bolts are prevented from turning out by two pairs of French locks, the tabs of which are bent over to contact the bolt heads. The French locks are zinc plated and typically have only one of the two tabs adjacent to each bolt bent over.

The inboard axle shaft U-joints are held to the differential output yokes by one of two methods. Forged caps retained by hex-head bolts are used on Corvettes equipped with big-block engines, and U-shaped strap clamps with nuts are used on cars equipped with small-block engines.

Front Wheel Assemblies

Front spindles and steering knuckles are natural and tend to have a bluish tint to their gray color. In addition, the lower portions of the spindles are frequently seen with orange or white paint, as though the bottoms of the spindles were dipped into it.

Original front brake backing plates are zinc plated and then chromate dipped. This results in varying finishes, ranging from gold with a faint rainbow of other colors throughout to a dull silver with only a trace of the yellowish chromate coloring. Well-preserved original backing plates typically appear dull silver, probably because the chromate dip deteriorates over time, leaving only the zinc plating behind.

Front brake caliper support brackets are plated silver cadmium or cadmium dichromate, which results in a translucent gold color with varying degrees of other colors present in a rainbowlike pattern.

Cars equipped with J56, the heavy-duty brake option, have a number of special components. These include front calipers that use two pins to hold the pads instead of the standard one, extra front caliper supports, semi-metallic brake pads, heat insulators on the face of all caliper pistons, and a proportioning valve mounted beneath the master cylinder.

The J56 proportioning valve was made by Kelsey-Hayes and has "K-H" cast into its side. The body is painted semi-gloss black, and the front adjusting nut and its shaft are silver cadmium plated. The stamped-steel bracket that mounts it below the master cylinder is painted semi-gloss black.

Front brake calipers are painted semi-gloss black and frequently have blue or white daubs of paint on the side. Painting is done before the caliper halves are machined, and therefore machined surfaces are unpainted. Bleeder screws are zinc plated and remain unpainted.

Caliper hoses are black rubber with gold-iridite-plated end hardware. Federally mandated DOT specifications are written on the hose in red ink. In addition, a red longitudinal stripe on the hoses makes it easier to see if they are twisted. Original hoses typically have raised longitudinal ridges around their entire circumferences, while later replacements are typically smooth.

Front brake rotors are natural in finish. The front wheel bearing carrier (also called a hub) is riveted to the rotor disc.

Rear Wheel Assemblies

As with the fronts, original rear brake backing plates are zinc plated and then chromate dipped. This results in varying finishes, ranging from gold with a faint rainbow of other colors throughout to a dull silver with only a trace of yellowish chromate coloring. Well-preserved original backing plates typically appear dull silver, probably because the chromate dip deteriorates over time.

Rear brake caliper support brackets are natural, and hence a dull gray, or on occasion painted flat to semi-flat black.

Rear brake calipers are painted semi-gloss black and frequently have blue or white daubs of paint on the side. Painting is done before the caliper halves are machined, and therefore machined surfaces are unpainted. Bleeder screws are zinc plated and remain unpainted.

Rear brake rotors are natural in finish. They are riveted to the rear spindle, which is pressed into the rear wheel bearing carrier. To service the park brake assembly or the rear wheel bearings, the rivets are often drilled out. The wheel lug nuts retain the rotor in the absence of the rivets.

Transmission

Automatic-equipped 1968 and 1969 Corvettes utilize a Turbo Hydra-Matic 400 transmission. The main case and the tail housing are both cast aluminum with a natural finish. The fluid pan is stamped steel and is also natural.

Automatic transmissions contain an identification plate on the right side. The plate has two alphanumeric sequences stamped in. The bottom sequence is the car's serial number, and the top sequence is referred to as a production code. The first two numbers of this code indicate the model year. Next comes a letter that denotes the car model (in our case Corvette) and the engine. This is followed by three numbers that represent the day the transmission was assembled.

The transmission assembly date is a modified version of the Julian calendar system. The three numbers represent the day of the year, but unlike most applications of the Julian calendar system in dating Corvette components, with transmissions, the count does not begin with the first day of the year. Instead, for 1968 Corvettes, it begins with January 1, 1967, and continues sequentially through calendar year 1968. Similarly, for 1969 models, it begins January 1, 1968, and continues through calendar year 1969.

This dating system sounds confusing, but it's easy once you get the hang of it. For example, in the production code 68K018, the "68" represents the 1968 model year, "K" represents the application code (1968 and 1969 small-block), and "018" represents the 18th day from when the count begins. Remember, the count begins on January 1 of the preceding year, so this transmission was assembled January 18, 1967. Had that same transmission been assembled on January 18, 1969, the code would read "69K384," with January 18, 1969, being 384 days after the count for the 1968 model year began (factoring in that 1968 was a leap year).

The application codes for 1968 and 1969 Corvettes include a "K" for all small-blocks, an "S" for hydraulic lifter big-blocks, and a "Y" for solid lifter big-blocks.

Four-speed manual transmissions have cast-aluminum main cases, side covers, and tail housings that are natural in color. A steel tag with a part number is affixed to the transmission with one of the side cover bolts.

Two alpha-numeric sequences are stamped into the main case on a vertical surface at the front of the right side. One of these sequences is a derivative of the car's serial number. The other is a production code and the date the transmission was originally assembled.

The production code begins with a letter to indicate the source for the transmission. All Corvette four-speeds were obtained from Muncie, which is represented by the letter "P." This is followed by a number representing the last digit of the model year. Next there is a letter indicating the month of production, followed by two numbers denoting the day of the month. Various letters are not used in denoting the month, so refer to this chart when determining assembly date:

A	January
B	February
C	March
D	April
E	May
H	June
K	July
M	August
P	September
R	October
S	November
T	December

The final character in the production code is a letter commonly called a suffix code. This letter indicates which of the three available four-speeds the unit is. "A" indicates a wide-ratio M-20 with a 2.52:1 first-gear ratio. "B" indicates a close-ratio M-21 with a 2.20:1 first-gear ratio. "C" denotes a close-ratio M-22 "heavy-duty" transmission, which also has a 2.20:1 first-gear ratio.

An example of a four-speed transmission code is P9M24A. This identifies an M-20 wide-ratio Muncie four-speed assembled on August 24, 1969.

Differential and Driveshaft

All 1968 and 1969 Corvettes are equipped with a non-limited-slip differential as standard. A Posi-Traction limited-slip differential is available both years as an extra cost option, and approximately 95 percent of the 1968 and 1969 Corvettes came with it. The differential case and cover are both natural-colored castings and thus are a dull silvery gray.

A plastic triangular tag is attached to Posi-Traction differentials by means of the square-head oil fill plug. The tag is red, with white lettering that says "USE LIMITED SLIP DIFF. LUBRICANT ONLY." The fill plug is natural and has a large "W" cast into the square. Even though the red tag described above is specific to Posi-Traction differentials, it is often seen on non-Posi-Traction units as well.

Front differential input yoke and side output yokes are forgings that are natural in color. Because they are forged, they have a somewhat smoother surface than the case and cover, and they tend to have a slight bluish tint to their dull gray color.

Differential cases and covers both have casting numbers and a casting date that includes a letter for the month (with "A" representing January, "B" representing February, and so on), one or two numbers indicating the day of the month, and one number indicating the last digit of the year.

In addition to the cast-in dates, all cases also have a stamped-in production code. The production code is on the bottom, rear edge of the case, adjacent to where it meets the cover. The code begins with a number that indicates the assembly shift that built the unit. This is followed by a two- or three-letter code indicating the gear ratio. Next comes a date code that includes one or two numbers for the month, one or two numbers for the day, and two numbers for the year. The final character in the production code is a letter that indicates the specific plant that built the differential. (Refer to Appendix E for differential gear ratio codes.)

The transmission and differential are connected by a driveshaft made from extruded steel tubing, welded at each end to a forged universal joint coupling. As with the axle shafts, the driveshaft is natural in color. The center tube portion is bright silver, with longitudinal extrusion lines sometimes visible, and the ends are a dull silvery gray with a slight bluish hue at times.

A part number stenciled on the driveshaft tube in yellow or white paint is sometimes seen. One or two green circumferential stripes on the tube and daubs of variously colored paint on the forged ends are sometimes seen as well.

Exhaust System

All 1968 and most 1969 Corvettes use an undercar, carbon-steel exhaust system manufactured by Walker for Chevrolet. Side-mount exhaust was available as an option in 1969 only.

All 1968 cars equipped with a big-block engine or the optional N11 off-road exhaust utilize 2½-inch exhaust pipes. All other cars utilize 2-inch pipes. All 1969 cars with undercar exhaust systems, including those equipped with big-blocks, utilize 2-inch pipes.

All cars except those equipped with an L88 or ZL1 engine use a heat riser valve at the base of the passenger-side exhaust manifold. The manifold studs are longer to accommodate the valve, and the exhaust pipe is correspondingly shorter. L88 and ZL1 engines use a spacer in place of the valve. The spacer resembles a valve without the butterfly or counterbalance weight.

Mufflers are galvanized on the exterior and have an embossed "W" to represent the manufacturer. At the rear of each muffler is one welded-on bracket to which the rear hangar bolts. Mufflers are welded to the intermediate exhaust pipe, not clamped. On those 1968 Corvettes so equipped, 2½-inch intermediate pipes are flattened somewhat where they pass underneath the rear camber adjustment rod bracket for additional ground clearance. Two-inch pipes are not flattened.

In 1968 and 1969, a round, chrome-plated steel exhaust tip is clamped to each muffler. The tips, which are the same in both years, measure 10⅝ inches long on top and 8 inches long on the bottom. The difference is due to the diagonal cut at the outboard end.

Fuel Lines, Brake Lines, and Miscellaneous Chassis and Underbody Components

All 1968 and 1969 fuel lines run along, and at times through, the right-side chassis rail. All cars except those equipped with an L88, L89, L71, or ZL1 engine have two fuel lines. In other words, only Holley-carburetor-equipped cars have a single fuel line, and all Quadrajet-equipped cars have two lines. One supplies fuel from the tank to the carburetor, and the other is a return line. The two lines run parallel to one another.

Fuel lines are galvanized carbon steel. Black rubber fuel hose connects the lines to the tank and the fuel pump. Galvanized tower clamps are used to secure the hose to its line in 1968. Zinc-chromate-plated spring clamps are usually used in 1969. Exceptions include the hoses on the fuel return line, which may use small, galvanized tower-style clamps in 1969.

Brake lines are galvanized carbon steel. Brake line end fittings are brass. Fittings at the master cylinder are often seen with red or blue dye, which was probably used to denote the two different sizes of fittings. In addition, daubs of yellow paint are sometimes seen on the fittings at junction blocks.

Various heat shields are affixed to the underside of the body to help insulate the passenger compartment from engine and exhaust system heat. All cars are fitted with transmission tunnel insulation. A semi-rigid foil-wrapped blanket in the shape of the tunnel is fastened above the transmission with clips riveted to the underbody.

Early 1968s have an aluminum-foil-backed fiberglass insulation pad at the base of the firewall. Later 1968s use a white plastic shield in this area instead. Early '68s also utilize a semi-gloss painted triangular steel shield on each side underneath the firewall area.

On late 1968s and all 1969s the previously used foil-backed insulation and triangular steel heat shield are replaced with a large rectangular steel shield. This shield, which is gray phosphate plated, is mounted on the lower vertical area of the firewall on both sides.

All cars, with the possible exception of some earlier 1968s, have a thick, black foam insulating pad attached to the underbody above the engine's bell housing. Also, a thick, white foam pad is fastened to the underbody on each side of the car just forward of the doors. Those 1969s equipped with side-mount exhaust do not have these pads.

A variety of steel plates are fastened to the underbody to mount components in the passenger compartment. These components include the battery, seats, and jack hold-down clips. All the plates are painted semi-gloss black and are retained by unpainted aluminum rivets.

Chapter 2
1970–1972

1970–1972 EXTERIOR
Body Fiberglass

In 1970 the Corvette's body was modified in subtle but easily recognizable ways. The front fender and the rear quarter panel area behind each wheel is flared out rather than tucked under as they had previously been. The flares are intended to catch stones and other road debris kicked up by the wheels. In fact they work quite well, preventing the chipped paint so prevalent on 1968 and 1969 models. The flares in the fenders and quarter panels continued unchanged for 1971 and 1972.

All 1970-72 body panels are made from press-molded fiberglass. The panels are smooth on both sides and are very dark gray.

Body Paint

All 1970–1972 cars were painted with acrylic lacquer. Factory paint is generally smooth and shiny, though some orange peel is evident throughout. Roughness and poor coverage is fairly typical along the very bottom edges of body panels. Clear coat was not used by the factory, even with metallic colors. Because clear coat was not used, metallic colors tend to be slightly mottled or blotchy.

Front Bumpers

Front bumpers are chrome plated and held to the car with steel brackets painted semi-gloss black. Cadmium-plated hex-head bolts are used to retain the bumper to the brackets, and cadmium and/or black oxide hex-head bolts hold the brackets to the chassis. The most commonly seen head markings on original bolts are "TR," "TRW," "RSC," "SCC," and "M." These head markings represent the respective bolt manufacturers.

Unpainted or silver-cadmium-plated shims are sometimes used between the front outer bumper mounts and the body.

Front Grille Area and Parking Lamps

The two front grille assemblies are made from silver gray cast metal with chrome trim. In 1970 they are retained by one chrome Phillips oval-head screw in the upper outside corner and three studs that are not readily seen when installed. In 1971–1972 they are retained by three screws. There is overlap, however, and late 1970s (assembled in June or July 1970) may have the later grilles, while early 1971s (assembled in December 1970 or earlier) may have the earlier units.

The front parking lamp housings are part of the front grilles. In 1970–1971 they get clear plastic lenses with

Integral fender flares behind all four wheels were introduced in 1970. The primary purpose of the flares was to protect body paint from debris thrown up by the wheels.

LT-1-powered 1970–1972 Corvettes are extremely popular with collectors. This beautifully preserved example from 1972 has traveled only 41,000 miles since it was new.

This 1972 is one of 2,763 Corvettes painted Classic White that year. The power dome on the hood, in conjunction with the double pinstripe outlining the dome, is unique to LT-1-powered cars.

A rear deck luggage rack was a popular accessory for early C3 Corvettes. Chevrolet never offered a rack as a regular production option, but they were sold through many Chevy dealers, along with various other comfort and convenience items.

The last year for a front chrome-plated bumper, removable rear coupe window, and the egg crate motif for front grilles and side fender trim was 1972.

amber-colored bulbs. In 1972 they get amber lenses with clear bulbs. Chrome Phillips-head screws hold in the lenses. All 1970s and 1971s assembled through the end of June '71 have a fiber optic cable inserted into the top of each parking light housing. Those 1971s built in July '71 and all 1972s have no fiber optics and no holes for cables in the parking light housings.

Rectangular side marker lamps are used at all four corners in 1970–1972. The lamp housings, which can be seen from behind the body panels, are made from die-cast aluminum. Later replacements have plastic bodies. Front side marker lamps have amber lenses while rears have red lenses.

Front License Plate Bracket

All 1970–1972 front license plate brackets are painted semi-gloss black and are held on by two cadmium-plated hex-head bolts. A small rubber bumper is inserted in a hole toward the

Front grille detail in an unrestored 1970. As shown here, in 1970 the L-shaped chrome trim used one screw in the upper corner adjacent to the park light housing and three studs that are visible only when the part is removed. Some late 1970s and all 1971–1972s used three screws to hold on the outer grille trim pieces.

Two different shades of blue were offered in 1970. This unrestored example is Mulsanne Blue.

Square mesh grilles and park lamp assemblies were new for 1970. Front parking lamps in 1970–1971 use clear lenses and amber bulbs, while 1972 lamps use amber lenses with clear bulbs.

The C3 Corvette design was based on Chevrolet's highly acclaimed 1965 Mako Shark show car. Beautiful proportions and sexy curves make these cars timeless styling classics.

bottom center, and two white plastic nuts insert into square holes in the upper corners. A small brown paper bag marked "license plate screws" came with the car. In it were four large, cadmium-plated, slotted pan-head screws for the front and rear license plates. All cars also came with two stainless-steel license plate frames sealed in plastic bags and placed in the luggage area. Original frames have stainless rivets, while service replacements have silver-cadmium-plated rivets.

Front Headlamps and Headlamp Bezels

All four headlamp bulbs in 1970–1972 were made by Guide and feature a Guide T-3 logo in the glass. All 1970–1971 bulbs have a centered triangle with "T-3" surrounded by vertical bars. Some late 1971s (assembled in May and June '71) and 1972s have the "T-3" enclosed in squares and rectangles centered at the bottom of the bulb's face.

Headlamp bezels are die-cast aluminum and painted body color. Paint on the bezels is usually not as shiny or smooth as it is on the body. All 1970s and early 1971s have two headlamp washer nozzles in the bezels. One nozzle is on the vertical surface, and the other is on the lower horizontal surface. Both nozzles are pointed at the low-beam (outer) bulb. Some very late 1970s and very early 1971s have both nozzles mounted on the vertical surface. Those 1971s assembled after December 1970 do not have the headlamp washer system, though cars assembled through at least March 1971 may have nozzles, bezels with nozzle holes but no nozzles, or nozzles on one bezel and just holes on the other.

A semi-gloss black plastic shield behind each front grille shields the headlamps from view when the light assemblies are in the down position. The shields are held to the body by three self-tapping, black phosphate Phillips pan-head screws with integral flat washers.

This 1971 is one of 4,891 Corvettes painted Ontario Orange that year. It has undergone an intensive and thorough restoration. That enabled it to earn a coveted NCRS Top Flight award.

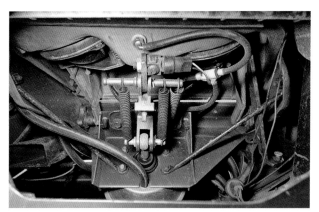

All 1970–1972 Corvettes came with vacuum-actuated pop-up headlamps. Hoses toward the top of this view of a headlamp housing's inner workings are for the headlamp washer system. All 1970 through mid-1971 cars had two wash fluid nozzles aimed at each low-beam bulb.

A cadmium-dichromate-plated vacuum actuator is mounted behind each headlamp assembly. Original actuators have a ¼-inch diameter hose connection tube that extends about ⁹⁄₁₆ inch out from the actuator body before its 90-degree bend. Replacement actuators have a ⁵⁄₁₆-inch diameter tube that extends about ⅜ inch from the body before turning 90 degrees. A translucent red ink marking is normally found on each actuator adjacent to the tube. A red-striped hose connects to the back of each actuator, and a green-striped hose connects to the front.

Front Fenders

Front fenders for 1970–1972 have a redesigned vent area, which features a cast-metal grille fastened into a recess in the fiberglass. Each grill is held in place by two recessed Phillips flathead screws at the top and a stud and nut on the bottom. Because the grilles were already mounted when the car was painted, the screw heads are body color and the underside of the rectangular boxes formed in the grille frequently show poor paint coverage. For 1970s and early 1971s (cars assembled up to approximately the first week of September 1970), fender grilles have chrome edges on horizontal surfaces only. Later 1971s and 1972s have chrome on vertical and horizontal surfaces.

Both fenders have an emblem reading "Stingray" above their grilles. The emblems are chrome, with the thin stepped edge surrounding each letter painted black. Emblems are held onto the body by a visible thick black adhesive strip. Each has four long studs used for positioning only, and therefore they do not get nuts. Original emblems feature an "i" without a dot, while later replacements have a small groove cut into the "i" to simulate the dot.

Hood

All 1970–1972 cars originally equipped with a small-block engine, except those with the optional LT1, have a low-profile hood with a single wind split down the middle. The hoods have no emblems, decals, or other markings. LT1- and 454-equipped cars have a raised area with twin simulated vents in the center of the hoods for added engine compartment clearance. The leading edge of each simulated vent has a cast-metal piece of trim. It is chrome except on the inside, which is painted semi-gloss black.

The 454-equipped cars have a "454" emblem on each side of the hood's bulge. The emblems are chrome with black-painted recesses. LT1-powered cars have special paint striping and LT1 decals on their hoods. There are two bands of striping, each consisting of two thin stripes. The stripes are either black or white, depending on what color the car is painted. In 1970 the individual thin stripes that comprise each of the two larger stripes differ in width in their front portions only. The front portion of the two inside thin stripes is ¼ inch wide, while the front portion of the two outside thin stripes is ⅛-inch wide. As the two ¼-inch thin stripes curve around the hood bulge and extend rearward, they taper down to ⅛ inch. The 1970 LT1s assembled through mid- to late July 1970 had these unequal stripes, while all four thin strips on very late 1970s through 1972s were ⅛ inch wide all the way around. The gaps between the two thin stripes in each band of striping are ⅛ inch for all 1970–1972 LT1s.

The 1970 hood stripes were originally applied with a four-piece mask, resulting in a sharp point where the stripes met in the middle of the hood. The mask was changed in 1971–1972 to three pieces, and the point was rounded instead of sharp. Whether created from the earlier four-piece or later three-piece mask, the stripes tend to be slightly misaligned

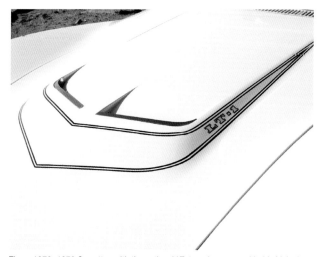

Those 1970–1972 Corvettes with the optional LT-1 engine came with this high-rise hood, adorned with LT-1 decals and spray-painted pinstriping. Those 1970s built through about July had stripes with two different widths—the inner about 1/4 inch thick, and the outer 1/8 inch thick. Cars built after late July 1970 had 1/8-inch inner and outer stripes. The pinstriping was done with multipiece masks, and slight misalignment between adjacent masks was quite common. This 1972 with original paint clearly shows misalignment forward of the LT-1 decals, where the stripes curve around the hood bulge contours.

where the mask sections meet. In addition, the edges of the stripes are normally not razor sharp along their entire length.

The LT1 decals are placed between the two stripes on each side of the hood bulge. Earlier 1970s assembled through mid-May 1970 have silver decals outlined in black, while later cars all had white decals outlined in black.

Windshield Vent Grille, Wiper Door, and Wipers

The windshield vent grille is painted body color and is retained by black oxide recessed Phillips flathead screws with fine threads. The windshield wiper door is also painted body color. A stainless-steel trim strip is on the windshield edge of the wiper door. The strip is painted body color except for an unpainted, polished bead that runs adjacent to the windshield. The strip is attached to the wiper door with small round-head rivets on either end in 1970 and part of 1971. Later 1971s and 1972s use small Phillips flathead screws.

Wiper arms and blade holders are dull black in color, and each holder says "TRICO" on one end. A length of washer tubing is soldered to a small tab at the end of each wiper arm and is further retained by one to four black plastic clips. (According to Chevrolet's *Assembly Instruction Manual*, three clips should hold the left tube and four should hold the right, but in reality the numbers vary from car to car.)

Wiper blade inserts say "TRICO" and have various patent numbers molded in. Two raised ribs are present below all the writing.

Windshield, Door Glass, and Back Glass

All 1970–1972 Corvette windshields were manufactured by Libby Owens Ford (LOF) utilizing Safety Plate glass. The LOF logo, "SAFETY PLATE," and a two-letter manufacturing date code are etched into the lower right side of the windshield. In the date code, one letter represents the month and the other denotes the year. There is no discernible pattern to the letter usage, so you must refer to the glass date codes in Appendix R.

The letters "ASI" are present in the upper right portion of the windshield. These letters are white and sandwiched between the laminates of glass, not etched into the surface like the logo and date code.

Both side windows are made from tinted LOF Safety Flo Lite glass. It has the manufacturer's logo and a two-letter date code etched in, just like the windshield. The words "Astro Ventilation" are silk-screened in white letters in the lower forward corner of each window.

Back windows in 1970–1972 coupes, like the windshields and side glass, have the LOF logo and the manufacturing date code etched in.

Door Mirror, Handles, and Locks

All 1970–1972 Corvettes have one outside rearview mirror mounted on the driver's door. A mounting base is held to the door by two screws. The mirror goes over the base and

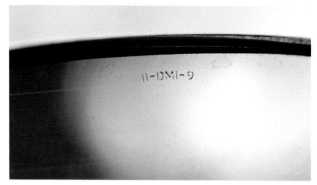

All 1970–1972 Corvettes came with a side mirror on the driver's door. The factory did not install a mirror on the passenger door. The mirror contains a manufacturing code and a date code on the edge of the glass. The first number indicates the month. The second number is the final digit of the year. In this example, the mirror was made in November 1969. "DMI" represents the manufacturer, Donnelly Mirror, Inc. Ajax Mirror Company was another supplier. Ajax mirrors typically have a letter for the month, with "A" representing January and so on, "AX" for the company's logo, and two numbers to represent the year.

is held on by a black oxide Allen-head screw. A thin gasket goes between the base and door and is visible when the mirror is installed.

The mirror's head is rectangular and measures 3⅞ inches high by 5⅜ inches wide. The glass is coded with the manufacturer's symbol and a date code. Mirrors supplied by Donnelly Mirror, Inc. have "DMI" in the code, and those supplied by Ajax Mirror have "AX." For example, the code in a Donnelly-supplied mirror manufactured in April 1971 would read, "4-DMI-1," while the code for an Ajax-supplied mirror manufactured in February 1970 would read, "2-AX-70."

All 1970–1972 door handles are a spring-loaded, press-flap design. On original handles, the spring action is provided by a coil spring on the hinge shaft. A butterfly spring covering a coil spring is incorrect. When the flap is depressed, the spring is visible. A thin black rubber gasket is visible between the handle and door.

The door locks, which are positioned below the door handles, feature a polished stainless-steel bezel. Original bezels are retained to the cylinders by a continuous crimp around the entire circumference. Incorrect replacement locks may have bezels retained by four tangs. A thin black rubber gasket is visible between the lock and door.

Side Rocker Moldings

Side rocker moldings for all 1970–1972s are brushed aluminum with a painted, ⅜-inch-wide flat black stripe along their length. In 1970–1971 they attach to the body with six black oxide Phillips oval-head screws. On 1972s the forward two and rearmost screws are often pan head instead of oval head.

In addition to the six screws that go through the face toward the top edge, original rocker moldings also have a single vertical fastener. It goes through a tab on the molding's lower lip near the front and into a J nut on the body. In 1970

A labor dispute in May 1969 led to 1969 Corvette production being extended, which in turn led to 1970 production being shortened. Some believe this played a role in the lack of changes to 1971 models, which were nearly identical to 1970s.

and part of 1971, a black oxide fillister-head screw is used here, while later 1971s and 1972s usually use a black oxide hex-head screw.

Radio Antenna

A radio was still an option for Corvettes in 1970–1972, and several hundred cars were built without one. Those cars have no radio antenna, but on all others an antenna was mounted on the driver-side rear deck. Most antennas utilize a fixed-height mast, though some originals have telescoping masts. Either way, the antenna ball is .300 inch in diameter, not .250 inch as seen on later replacements.

A black plastic gasket goes between the antenna base and the car's body. The base is also made of black plastic. It, along with the portion of the antenna assembly beneath the body, is retained by a chrome hex nut. A chrome cap with two flat areas for a wrench to grab holds the mast to the base.

Rear Deck Vent Grilles and Gas Fill Door

Two vent grilles are installed on the rear deck behind the back window (or behind the convertible top deck on convertibles). The vent grilles are painted body color and are each retained by four black oxide Phillips flathead screws. The lips in the body the grilles sit on and the vent channel below are sprayed with flat black paint in varying degrees of coverage.

Gas lid doors are painted body color and feature a chrome and painted crossed-flag emblem held on by cadmium- or chrome-plated acorn nuts, visible with the door open. In 1970 a latch that is part of the hinge assembly holds the door in the open position. A tab riveted to the underside of the door inserts into a receptacle in the body bezel formed from two pieces of white nylon to hold the door closed. In

1971–1972 an over-center spring integral to the hinge holds the door both open and closed.

For all years, gas lid door hinges are chrome plated, and the door is held to the hinge with chrome-plated Phillips fillister-head screws. The polished door bezel is held to the body with black oxide Phillips flathead screws. Doors from 1970 don't use any rubber bumpers, while 1971 and 1972 doors have two bumpers that insert into the bezel toward the rear of the car.

All 1970–1972s came with a twist-on gas cap, not a locking cap. The locking caps, which are usually flat and chrome plated, were dealer installed or aftermarket. The 1970 and early 1971 caps are cadmium plated, while later 1971 and 1972 caps are gold iridite plated. The 1970 caps have "SEALED" stamped into them, while 1971–1972s have "OPEN SLOWLY CAUTION" in addition to "SEALED." Some early 1971s have a separate red plate with "OPEN SLOWLY CAUTION" in white letters.

For all years, the cap has a handle for twisting it on and off. The handle is attached by two ears that are bent over and spot welded onto the cap. On original 1970 and early 1971 caps, the ears face down when the word "SEALED" is upright. With later 1971 and all 1972 caps, the ears face down when "SEALED" is upside down and "OPEN SLOWLY CAUTION" is upright.

A black rubber boot surrounds the gas filler neck on all 1970–1972s. The boot has a plastic nipple facing the rear of the car. A rubber drain hose attaches to it. The hose, which has a metal spring inside to prevent it from collapsing, runs down behind the gas tank and exits the body through a hole adjacent to one of the rear bumper braces. A black plastic tie wrap holds the hose to the bumper brace.

The first year that Chevrolet sold more Corvette coupes than convertibles was 1969. By 1971, when this stunning Ontario Orange example was made, coupes outnumbered convertibles by slightly more than two to one.

Rear Fascia, Taillamps, Bumpers, and Related Parts

The rear body panel has "CORVETTE" spelled out in eight individual letters centered between the taillamps. Each letter is chrome plated with silver paint in its recessed face.

An audio alarm was optional in 1970–1971 and standard equipment in 1972. All cars so equipped have a lock cylinder switch on the rear body panel between the taillamps and above the "Corvette." Those 1970s assembled until sometime in June 1970 use an open-style lock cylinder, while subsequent cars use cylinders with spring-loaded face plates and crimped-over bezels like those used in the door locks. As with the door locks, the bezel should be crimped around its full circumference. Incorrect replacement locks have bezels with four tabs that bend over.

The recessed area of the body where the rear license plate mounts is covered by a chrome-plated, die-cast surround trim. A lamp assembly mounts at the top of the recess behind the rear body panel and illuminates the rear license plate. For 1970–1971s, a fiber optic cable inserts into the license lamp housing. A black rubber bumper is inserted into the rear valance panel centered toward the lower edge of the license plate. Two white plastic push nuts insert into square cutouts in the rear body panel for the license plate retaining screws.

All 1970–1972s utilize four rear lamps. The two outer ones utilize red lenses that function as taillamps, stop lamps, and turn signals. The two inner ones utilize red lenses with clear plastic centers that function as backup lamps. All 1970s and early 1971s (through January 1971 production) use a conical backup lens with concentric grooves on the inside. Later 1971s and 1972s have a rounded lens with a checkerboard pattern on the inside. All lenses are retained with three black oxide Phillips pan-head screws.

Rear bumpers are chrome plated and are attached to the body with brackets painted semi-gloss black. As with the front bumpers, cadmium-plated hex-head bolts retain the bumpers to the brackets, and cadmium- and/or black-oxide-plated hex-head bolts hold the brackets to the chassis.

The rear valance panel is painted body color but often shows poor paint quality, including runs or sparse coverage along the bottom edge. It is retained to the body by four cadmium-plated indented hex-head bolts. The two outer ones utilize integral washers, while the two inners have separate flat washers.

All 1970–1972s originally came with undercar exhaust systems, not side pipes. The exhaust tips exit the rear of the car through rectangular cutouts in the body. The cutouts are trimmed with rectangular, chromed, die-cast bezels with open bottoms. The bezels are retained by chrome Phillips oval-head screws.

Convertible Tops

Convertible tops are made from vinyl with a woven pattern. The convertible top is available in either white or black, regardless of exterior body color. The front header roll and tack strip cover are also vinyl but have a grained rather than a woven pattern. Two small stainless-steel trim pieces cover the ends of the tack strip. The trim pieces are flared around their perimeter and attach with one small, bright Phillips flathead screw. The convertible-top window is clear vinyl and is heat sealed, not sewn, to the top.

The convertible-top back window contains a manufacturer's logo, a manufacturing date, "VINYLITE, TRADE MARK, AS-6," and "DO NOT RUB DRY WASH WITH WATER SOAKED CLOTH" heat stamped in the

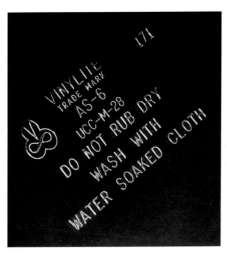

The convertible top vinyl rear window had the manufacturer's logo, specifications, cleaning instructions, and a manufacturing date heat stamped in the lower driver-side corner. In this example, the date code "171" translates to January 1971.

driver-side lower corner. The date code is normally three or four numbers, with the first one or two representing the month and the second two representing the year. For example, a convertible top manufactured in April 1971 would have a date code of 471.

A paper "caution" label is sewn into the top in the driver-side corner below the heat-stamped logo and date in the window. The label reads:

**WARNING
DEALER—DO NOT REMOVE
FOR CARE OF REAR WINDOW
AND TOP MATERIAL
SEE BOOKLET
"HOW TO OPERATE FOLDING TOP"**

The purchaser could choose either a soft top or a hardtop, or both as an extra cost option. The hardtop is painted body color unless it is vinyl covered. All vinyl-covered hardtops are black.

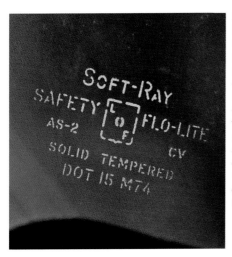

All body glass is imprinted with the manufacturer's logo, date of production, and other information. Libby Owens Ford glass was used throughout, and each piece should have a two-letter date code. In this example, "CV" reveals that the glass was made in November 1969.

The hardtop rear window contains the LOF manufacturing logo and is date coded with two letters like the remainder of the body glass. The first letter represents the month of production, and the second represents the year of production. (Refer to Appendix R for glass date codes.)

Tires, Wheels, and Wheel Covers

The majority of 1970–1972 Corvettes have either Goodyear or Firestone F70x15 bias-ply nylon cord tires. Raised-white-letter US Royal tires are believed correct for 1972 only.

The standard tire for all three years is a blackwall. Whitewalls and raised-white-letter tires are available as extra cost options. Whitewalls are either Firestone Super Sport Wide Ovals or Goodyear Speedway Wide Treads. The Firestones have a ⅜-inch white stripe that is 1⅛ inches from the bead edge. The Goodyears have a ⁵⁄₁₆-inch white stripe that is 1 inch from the bead edge.

Raised-white-letter Goodyears say "Goodyear Wide Tread F70-15" in block letters. Raised-white-letter Firestones say "Firestone Wide Oval" in block letters. Raised-white-letter US Royals say "Uniroyal Tiger Paw" in block letters.

All 1970–1972s are equipped with steel rally wheels. The color for all three years is called Argent Silver, but actually two different colors are used. The 1970 Argent Silver has a slight greenish hue, while 1971–1972 Argent Silver is noticeably brighter and more silvery. The back sides of the rally wheels are painted semi-flat black and always have silver overspray, since the front side was painted silver after the black was applied to the rear.

All wheels are stamped with a date code and size code on the front face. All 1970–1972 Corvette wheels are 15 by 8 inches and have the code "AZ" stamped in to indicate this. The "AZ" is adjacent to the valve stem hole.

Also adjacent to the valve stem hole is the manufacturer's logo and date code stamping. On one side of the hole it says "K," which is believed to represent the wheel manufacturer, Kelsey Hayes. This is followed by a dash and a "1," which likely represents Chevrolet, though it might represent a specific wheel plant. Next comes another dash and either a "0," "1," or "2" to denote the last digit of the year of manufacture. This is followed by a space and one or two numbers to indicate the month of manufacture. On the other side of the valve stem hole are one or two numbers that represent the day of manufacture.

Stainless-steel trim rings and chrome center caps are standard for all cars. Original trim rings are held to the wheel by four steel clips. Center caps should read "Chevrolet Motor Division" in black-painted letters.

A full wheel cover is available as an extra cost option for all 1970–1972 Corvettes. Called option PO2, this cover has a stainless-steel outer rim and closely spaced radial fins that converge outward toward a protruding ornamental disc in the center. The disc is chrome around its edge, black in the middle, and contains the Corvette crossed-flag emblem.

This full wheel cover was option P02 in 1970–1972. Similar covers were available on other Chevrolet cars, but the protruding center ornament with the recessed emblem distinguishes Corvette covers from those installed on Chevy passenger cars. The passenger car covers had a flat center ornament and emblem.

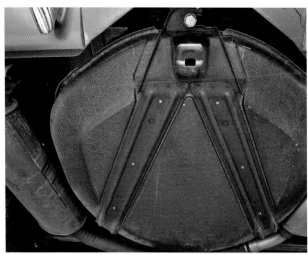

The spare tire carrier was made from molded black fiberglass. The fiberglass was not painted but may have some overspray from the chassis blackout process. The V-shaped carrier support bracket was painted semi-gloss black. Because the bracket was riveted onto the carrier after it was painted, the rivets should not be painted.

Other Chevrolet products use a similar wheel cover but have a flat center disc instead of the protruding disc utilized for Corvettes.

Wheels on cars equipped with standard trim rings and center caps utilize black rubber valve stems that measure approximately 1¼ inches long. These are fitted with caps that come to a point and have longitudinal ridges around entire perimeter and the manufacturer's name, Dill, molded into them.

Wheels on cars equipped with optional full wheel covers have extensions threaded onto the standard valve stems. The extensions have white inner shafts, which are visible because they are not fitted with caps. The name of the manufacturer, Schrader, is molded into the end.

To ease the balancing process, wheels are sometimes marked with a tiny weld drop or paint dot at their highest point. This mark is lined up with an orange dot on the tire. Balance weights are the type that clamp onto the edge of the rim and are placed on the inside of the wheel only. Original balance weights usually have "OEM" molded into their faces. There is usually a small dot of white or colored paint on the tire adjacent to each balance weight.

All cars have a full-size spare tire and wheel that are identical to the other four tires and wheels. The spare wheel is not fitted with a wheel covering like the other four.

The spare tire and wheel are housed in a carrier bolted to the rear underbody area. The carrier is fiberglass with steel supports. The fiberglass is unpainted, and the steel support is painted semi-gloss black. The tire tub portion of the carrier has a fair amount of flat to semi-gloss black paint on its outside surface, applied during the blackout process. A lock covered by a black rubber boot goes over the spare tire carrier access bolt.

1970–1972 INTERIOR
Trim Tag
Interior trim color and material, as well as exterior body color and body assembly date, are stamped into an unpainted stainless-steel plate attached to the driver's door hinge pillar by two aluminum pop rivets. This plate is commonly called a trim plate or trim tag.

All 1970–1972 Corvettes came with a stainless-steel trim tag riveted to the driver-side door hinge pillar. The trim code indicates the original interior color and material. The paint code reveals the original body color. The three-character code in the upper right is the date the body reached the point on the assembly line where the tag was riveted on. The letter represents the month, with "A" for the first month of production, "B" for the second month, and so on. Production began in January for model year 1970 and in August for model years 1971 and 1972. The two numbers represent the day. In this 1971 example, "H08" translates to March 8, 1971.

This is an original, unrestored, standard vinyl 1970 interior.

Trim color and material are indicated in the plate by a three-number code. For example, in 1970 trim code "424" indicates saddle color with leather seat covers. Exterior body paint is likewise indicated by a three-number code stamped in the trim plate. For example, in 1972 code "946" indicates Elkhart Green. (Refer to Appendix T for paint and interior trim codes.)

The body build date represents the date when the painted and partially assembled body reached that point on the assembly line where the trim plate was installed. The car's final assembly date is typically one to several days after the body build date. A letter indicating the month, followed by two numbers indicating the day, represents the body build date. The letter "A" was assigned to the first month of production, which was January in 1970 and August in 1971 and 1972. The second month of production was assigned the letter "B," and so on. A body assembled on the August 6, 1971, would have "A06" stamped into the trim plate, for example, and a body built on May 11, 1970, would have "E11" stamped into its plate. (Refer to Appendix S for body build date codes.)

Seats

Standard seat upholstery was a combination of very slightly grained flat vinyl with Chevrolet's "comfort-weave" vinyl inserts sewn into the seat bottoms and backs. Vinyl seats for 1970–1972 all had vertical insert panels. Leather was available as an extra cost option but only in black or saddle. Leather

The optional custom interior trim package included leather seat covers, but these were available in black or saddle only. All 1970 and most 1971 leather seats featured vertical panels, as seen here. Late 1971 and 1972 leather upholstery was sewn with horizontal panels.

seats from 1970 through late 1971 had vertical panels, while late 1971s and all 1972s had horizontal panels.

Each seat rests on two seat tracks, which allow for forward and rearward adjustment of the seat's position. The tracks are black phosphate, and each is held to the floor by one black phosphate indented hex-head bolt at either end for a total of four per seat. The front bolts are covered by a cutaway flap of carpet, while the rear bolts simply pass through the carpet. The seat adjust lever is black phosphate with a chrome ball screwed onto its end.

Seat back details in an unrestored 1970. Everything shown here is factory original. Shoulder belts were standard in all coupes and optional in convertibles.

Hamill manufactured all 1970–1972 Corvette seat belts. All belts had a label printed with manufacturing information. In 1970–1971 the label was made from a thin, silklike material. A thicker, paperlike material was used starting in 1972. The first two numbers represent the week of the year, and the last two numbers are the final digits of the year. In this example, "52 B 69" translates to a manufacture date of the 52nd week of 1969. The meaning of the letter "B" is not known.

The seat backs are made of molded plastic and match interior color. The seat back release button and its bezel are both chrome plated. Two bolts that allow for adjustment of seat back position are bright silver and get a rubber cushion over their heads. Those 1970s assembled prior to April 1970 do not have plastic washers under the seat back release bezel or adjustment bolts. Later 1970s and all 1971s and 1972s do have them in these places.

Lap and Shoulder Belts

All 1970–1972 coupes were equipped with lap and shoulder belts, while convertibles came with lap belts as standard and shoulder belts as an extra cost option. All belts were manufactured by a company called Hamill, and a tag bearing that name is sewn to them. Original tags used in 1970, 1971, and part of 1972 were made from a thin, silklike woven material. At some point during 1972, production tags made from a thicker, paperlike material began to be used. This tag indicates the date the belt was manufactured by an ink stamping, with a number representing the week of the year and another number representing the year. For example, a

stamping of "10 D 72" means that the belt was made the 10th week of 1972. The meaning of the letter between the numbers is not known with certainty, but it may denote the day of the week or the manufacturing plant where the belt was made.

In addition to the tag bearing the manufacturer's name and date code, another, smaller tag is sewn to the outboard lap belts close to the male latch. This tag reads "IMPORTANT wear lap belt at all times. Adjust snugly." A similar tag is sewn at the same position on each of the shoulder harness belts. This tag reads "IMPORTANT Attach shoulder harness securely to lap belts. Do not use if wearer is less than 4 feet 7 inches tall. Do not use without a lap belt."

All belts are made from a three-row webbing material and are the same color as the carpet. The material used for lap belts is slightly thicker than that used for shoulder belts.

In 1970 and 1971, a chrome clip attached to the front of each seat bottom holds the outboard lap belts when they are not in use. Also for these two years, a plastic collar around each outboard belt and its tail (the loose end or slack in the belt used for adjustment) keeps the tail from flapping around. The plastic collar is the same color as the belts.

In 1972 the outboard belts are on a spring-loaded retractable coil, so the retaining clips on the seat bottoms and plastic tail collars are eliminated. The retractor in 1972 also includes an integral switch that controls the seatbelt alarm buzzer. The retractors are beneath each seat under a plastic cover.

Inboard portions of the seatbelts are encased in a semi-rigid plastic that goes over part of the female buckles. The buckles are brushed silver in color. The black release buttons each have a rigid metallic sticker that says "GM" in silver letters on a blue background.

The factory attached inner window felt strips to door panels with staples. The use of pop rivets, screws, or any fasteners other than staples is not correct.

Door Panels and Door Hardware

All door panels are made from molded vinyl and match the interior color. With standard interiors (that is, interiors with vinyl seat covers), the door panels are plain and utilize no trim. Custom interiors include fancier door panels, in addition to either saddle or black leather seat covers. A piece of plush cut pile carpet is added along the bottom of the panels, and a strip of chrome trim covers the gap where the carpet meets the vinyl. In addition, custom door panels include a band of veneered walnut wood trim in the middle. With both standard and custom interiors, inside window felts are attached to the upper edge of the door panels with heavy staples, not pop rivets.

Door panels are attached to the doors by means of black phosphate clips along the front, bottom, and rear. The clips insert into a cutout in the back of the panel and get fastened to the door with black phosphate Phillips pan-head screws. In addition, a chrome Phillips oval-head screw goes through the face of each panel at the upper front and rear corners. In

1970 and part of 1971, these screws had a separate finishing washer. For part of 1971 and all of 1972, the screws utilized an integral finishing washer.

Inside door release handles are chrome with black paint in the knurled center area. A round black emblem features the crossed-flag logo. The inside lock knob is chrome with a black stripe painted in the center indent. The inside door pull is a grained vinyl handle that matches interior color. Cars equipped with standard manual windows have chrome window cranks with opaque plastic knobs. Unlike some later replacements, the knobs on original cranks are about one inch away from the door panel's surface.

Door Jambs and Door Perimeters

The jambs and perimeter of each door are painted body color, with the exception of the top front of each door, which is painted semi-gloss black. The door striker, which is the large pin threaded into the doorpost, and its corresponding receiver in the door are cadmium plated. The striker is a special indented hex-head bolt on 1970s built through January 1970. In early February 1970, they changed to an indented star-head design.

The courtesy light pin switches and "door ajar" warning light/alarm system pin switches are cadmium plated and should not have any paint overspray. All pin switches have "SX," the manufacturer's logo, stamped into the head of the plunger.

As with the pin switches, door strikers, and door striker receivers, door alignment blocks and door weather strips were added after the body was painted and should not have any body paint overspray. The main door weather stripping is two separate pieces and typically shows a gap in the center on the bottom of the door.

In 1970 and 1971, the water deflecting strips pop riveted to each doorpost near the "door ajar" warning light/alarm system pin switches are painted body color, as they were already installed when the body was painted. These

These original 1972 door panels came with the optional custom interior trim. They differ from the standard panels by virtue of the walnut veneer insert, plush carpet strip along the bottom, and related trim surrounding the veneer and carpet.

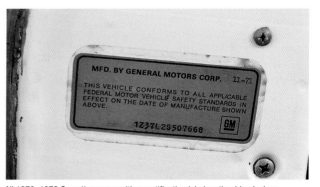

All 1970–1972 Corvettes came with a certification label on the driver's door jamb. The decal was blue with a clear vinyl coating that overlapped all around the perimeter. The date in the upper right is the date the car was produced. The number along the bottom is the car's VIN. The label shown here was used from 1970 through early 1972. Beginning in January 1972, axle loading and gross vehicle weight rating information was added to the decal.

strips were not used in 1972. Likewise, door hinges, bolts, and return springs (there should be one spring in each top hinge) are also painted body color.

The blue vehicle certification label glued toward the top of the rear portion of the driver's door is unpainted. It contains the VIN and the month and year the vehicle was produced. At the end of calendar year 1971 (during early 1972 production), axle loading and gross vehicle weight ratings were added to the labels.

Door sills are bright aluminum with black-painted ribs. Each sill is held on with four black phosphate Phillips oval-head screws.

Kick Panels, Quarter Trim Panels, Pedals, and Carpet

The kick panels beneath the dash just forward of the doors are molded plastic and are interior color. On air-conditioned cars, the passenger-side panel was cut by hand for increased clearance, and the cut is frequently rough. One chrome Phillips oval-head screw in the forward, upper corner of each panel holds it in place. The panels have a bevy of small holes for the speakers that mount behind them. Speakers were never mounted in the kick panels. Some replacement kick panels have a slot in the speaker grille area, and others have a solid rectangular area in the middle of the speaker grille holes. Neither style is original for 1970–1972.

The quarter trim panels just rearward of the doors are molded plastic to match the interior color. They are each held in place by a piece of metal trim retained by four chrome Phillips oval-head screws. The quarter trim panels on coupes also have one chrome Phillips oval-head screw, with a trim washer at the top.

In standard interiors, carpet is made from an 80/20 loop pile molded material. In custom interiors, it is made from plush cut pile material. In all cases it matches interior color. Three rubber plugs in the driver's foot well and three more in the passenger's foot well help hold the carpet in place. The plugs pass through the carpet near its upper front edge and have the GM part number 3868790 molded into the top surface.

Carpet covers the bulkhead behind the seats and has sewn-on binding on the lower edge where it overlaps the front floor carpet behind the seats. Rear storage compartment doors each have carpet under their frames. One piece of carpet covers the rear storage area floor and extends up the rear bulkhead. The edge at the top of the bulkhead is trimmed with sewn-on binding and is held by three rubber plugs. Separate pieces of untrimmed carpet cover the two wheelwells.

The carpet has a molded vinyl accelerator heel pad in the corner of the driver's footwell, adjacent to the accelerator pedal. Heel pads in 1970s and in 1971s assembled through approximately March 1971 have horizontal ribs that extend up to the top stitching holding the pad to the carpet. Pads for later 1971s and for 1972s have ribs that stop about ⅜ inch from the stitching. The earlier pads have "IMCo," the Interstate Manufacturing Company's logo, molded in.

An original carpet heel pad from 1970. This kind of pad, with the ribs running all the way to the top in the section beneath the accelerator pedal, was used in all 1970s and most 1971s. A heel pad with a smooth area in the section beneath the accelerator pedal was used intermittently beginning in mid-1971 and throughout 1972.

Some 1970s had a sewn-in, molded vinyl dimmer switch pad, but most did not. Early 1971s with the first heel pad design have a dimmer switch pad that also bears the IMCo logo.

For all 1970–1972s, accelerator, brake, and clutch pedals have black rubber pads with horizontal ribs. All 1970–1971 pedals have a polished metal surround, while 1972 pedals do not. In 1970–1971s, the accelerator pedal measures 5⅝ inches high by 2 inches wide. In 1972 the pedal is 4 inches high, 1⅞ inches wide at the top, and 1⅝ inches wide at the bottom.

Dash Pad and Dash Panels

Upper dash pads, as well as driver's and passenger's dash panels, are made of soft vinyl and match interior color. The two vertical panels are attached to the upper pad by means of six Phillips oval-head screws with conical washers. The screw heads are painted to match interior color, except in 1970 and early 1971s fitted with black interiors. In that case, the screws are finished in a black oxide plating. Later 1971s and 1972s with black interiors use black-painted screws. Dash pads have white stitching across their tops, regardless of interior color. An interior color hard plastic grille is located in the defroster opening of the upper pad.

A three-pocket storage area is inset into the passenger-side dash panel. The storage pocket assembly is made from vinyl and is the same color as the interior. The dash panel has stitching around the opening for the storage pockets. The

This is an original headlamp switch knob, and it is correct for 1972 only.

These are original override controls for the headlamps and wipers. The large round plastic knob on the wiper motor override switch should be all black. Later service replacements and reproductions of this knob have a stainless-steel center section.

two smaller, outboard pockets are retained to the larger one with a single chrome-plated snap. A spring-loaded retainer behind the dash holds the three-pocket assembly tight against the dash panel.

Interior Switches, Controls, and Related Parts

All 1970–1972s have a headlamp switch mounted in the upper left corner of the driver-side dash pad. The 1970–1971 headlight knobs are gloss black grained plastic with a chrome disc in the center. A black plastic bezel behind the knob reads "LIGHTS" in white letters. The 1972 headlight knobs are grained soft black vinyl, with an image of a headlamp with light rays coming out of it.

This is the correct headlamp knob and bezel for 1970–1971.

All 1970–1972 Corvettes have air vents on both sides of the dash toward the lower, outboard corner. The vent mechanisms are chrome spheres that rotate to change the direction of airflow. A push/pull knob next to each sphere controls the flow of air. In 1970–1971, the knob is chrome, and in 1972 it is black.

A small black T-handle pull mechanism beneath the driver's side dash on the left side releases the hood latch. The handle is black with the words "HOOD RELEASE" in painted white block letters across its face. The hood release cable is in a spiral wound metal sheathing.

A semi-gloss black bracket beneath the steering column mounts the wiper door override switch, wiper arm override switch, and headlamp door override switch. The trip odometer reset knob is mounted to the left of this and has a grooved black rubber cover. The wiper door override switch has a large, round, shiny black knob with grooved edges. The wiper door override switch and headlamp door override switch are both vacuum switches that mount to either side of the wiper arm switch. The two vacuum switches have dull black plastic push/pull knobs.

Steering Wheel and Steering Column

All 1970–1972 steering wheels are black regardless of interior color. All wheels have grained vinyl rims molded to a three-spoke stainless-steel hub. Each spoke has a brushed finish with a pattern of parallel lines extending from the center of the wheel to the outer rim.

The standard steering column and optional tilt-telescoping column in 1970–1972 is painted interior color in a semi-gloss finish. The tilt-telescoping column has a thick locking ring below the steering wheel to control the telescoping function. The ring is painted to match the rest of the column. Twisting the lever on the ring releases the locking mechanism and allows the column to telescope.

A lever similar to but shorter than the turn signal lever controls the tilt function of the optional steering column. The tilt lever is located between the turn signal lever and the dash.

All columns have a four-way flasher switch mounted on the right side. All 1970 and those 1971s built through approximately February 1971 and equipped with a standard steering column use a switch with a one-piece, chrome-plated knob with black-painted, debossed letters in the head reading, "FLASHER." Later 1971s with a standard steering column

The steering column was painted to match interior color. The hazard light switch shown here is correct for 1972 only.

The steering column was painted semi-gloss to match the interior color. The lock ring behind the horn button is for the optional tilt-telescopic steering column. The horn button was the same for 1970–1972, with the exception of the black-and-white pattern on the emblem's checkered flag. This example is from 1971 and was unique to that year. The black-and-white pattern was opposite in 1970 and 1972.

use a black metal knob on the flasher switch instead of a chrome one. As in earlier cars, "FLASHER" is debossed in the top of the knob, but in later 1971s, the letters are painted white instead of black.

All 1970s and 1971s built through about March 1971 and equipped with the optional tilt-telescoping steering column use a different chrome flasher knob than do cars with standard columns. The knob has a longer shaft, and "FLASHER" is pressed into the shaft rather than into the head. As with the standard column, the letters are painted black.

In 1972 the same flasher switch knob is used for both the standard steering column and the optional tilt-telescoping column. The knob is black with white lettering but is made of plastic rather than metal, as it previously was. And unlike earlier versions, the 1972 knob has a black Phillips-head screw through its center.

The 1970 and 1971 models used two different turn signal levers. Both have a chrome-plated shaft, but the molded-on plastic ends differ. Very early 1970s use a gloss black plastic end with molded-in grooves parallel to the chrome shaft. For the remainder of 1970 and for 1971s built through approximately September 1970, this first design continues to be used, but a second design is added as well. The second design is similar to the first but does not have grooves in the gloss black plastic end. Instead, the end is grained. Later 1971s, built from approximately September 1970 onward, use the lever with a grained end.

The 1972 (and possibly some late 1971) models use a third turn signal lever. This design has a dull black rubber end with a single concentric groove near the tip.

Cars equipped with standard steering columns and tilt-telescoping columns use the same turn signal levers, but the method of attachment differs slightly. On standard columns, the lever is attached with a screw, while on tilt-telescoping columns, the lever threads in.

All 1970–1972 models use a textured metal horn button painted to match the interior. A crossed-flag emblem is in the center of the button. In 1970 and 1972, the upper right square of the flag in the emblem is black, while in 1971 this same square is white.

Interior Windshield Moldings, Sun Visors, and Rearview Mirror

Three pieces of vinyl-covered molding matched to the interior color cover the inside of the windshield frame for all 1970–1972 Corvettes. The two side pieces are held on by plastic retainers attached to the reverse side. The plastic retainers are not visible when the moldings are installed. In addition, each side molding has one chrome Phillips-head screw retaining it at the top. The top piece of molding is retained by chrome recess-head Phillips screws.

Sun visors are covered with padded soft vinyl with the same "comfort-weave" pattern as the vinyl seat covers. Each sun visor is held to the windshield frame with chrome recess-head Phillips screws.

Beginning in approximately January 1972, a sticker describing the proper engine starting procedure is glued to the top of the driver-side sun visor. The sticker is white with black lettering and is made of nylon cloth.

All 1970–1972 Corvettes have an interior day/night rearview mirror mounted to the center of the upper windshield frame. The mirror is eight inches wide and is held to its mount with a slotted oval-head screw. A piece of trim covered with interior color vinyl is mounted over the base of the mirror mount at the windshield frame. All 1970–1971 and some early 1972 interior mirrors have a stainless-steel housing with gray rubber trim around the perimeter. A gray lever at the bottom center moves the mirror between its day and night positions. All 1972 interior mirrors, with the exception of some early cars, have black vinyl with a grain pattern covering their housing. The vinyl-backed mirrors have black rubber trim around the perimeter but still use a gray day/night lever like the earlier stainless housed mirrors.

Instruments and Radio

The center console instrument cluster housing is cast metal painted semi-gloss black. In 1970 and 1971, a solid bar separates the seat-belt warning light from the button below it. Later replacement housings don't have this bar. The 1972s have the seat-belt warning light and a buzzer but don't have a button below to turn them off. Early 1972s have a timer that shuts both the light and buzzer off after about 15 seconds. In later '72s, the light and buzzer go off only after the seat belt is extended or the parking brake is applied.

The windshield wiper/washer control switch is mounted above the center console instrument cluster housing. The switch knob is hard black plastic with "WASHER-PUSH" in painted white block letters on its face.

All gauges, including the speedometer and tachometer, have a flat black background and a straight red needle. Gauge numerals are slightly greenish in 1970 and 1971 and white in 1972. Tachometer redlines vary according to the engine. The high-beam indicator light is red in cars assembled during January 1970 and blue in all cars thereafter.

All 1970–1972 Corvettes came standard without a radio. For those cars not equipped with a radio, a block-off plate is fitted to the cutout where the radio would otherwise go. The block-off plate for all three years is painted semi-gloss black and has a flat face with a thin, raised chrome border around its perimeter near the edge.

As an extra cost option, one of two different Delco radios could be ordered. The first is an AM/FM pushbutton, and the second is an AM/FM pushbutton with stereo reception. Both radios have a small slide bar above the dial that changes reception between AM and FM, and both have "Delco" written in script lettering across the lens face.

All 1970–1972 stereo radios have indicator lights that come on when FM stereo is being received. In 1970 and 1971, "STEREO" appears in green, and in 1972 an orange circle lights up.

In 1970 and 1971, radio knobs are shiny black plastic with silver accents. In 1972 the knobs are dull black rubber with white pictorial inserts. The on/off/volume knob on the left has a musical note, while the tuning knob on the right has an antenna with a radiating signal.

Beneath the main radio knobs on all 1970–1972s is a secondary control, which is chrome plated. The one on the left controls tone. The one on the right, which is functional only on stereo-equipped cars, controls balance.

In 1970–1971 a bar separated the seat-belt warning lamp and the reset button. The bar was part of the center instrument housing's casting on original housings. Some reproduction housings have the bar glued in place. In 1972 there were just warning lamps, with no bar and no reset button in this position.

All 1972 instruments had white numerals and markings. The tachometer redline correlates to the engine. In this example from 1972, the 6,500-rpm redline was for LT-1 engines only.

This is an original AM/FM radio in a 1971. The light green numerals and the knobs are correct for 1970–1971. The 1972 radios used white numerals and different knobs.

AM/FM radio and AM/FM stereo were options in 1970–1972. The radio knobs shown here are correct for 1972 only. White radio numerals are also correct for 1972 only.

The 1970–1971 engine identification plate listed horsepower, torque, compression ratio, and displacement. The 1972 plate listed compression ratio, torque, and engine size but not horsepower. All 1970s and 1971s through approximately VIN 21,000 had the fiber optic system.

Center Console, Shifter, and Park Brake

All 1970–1972 center consoles are made from molded vinyl in the same color as the interior. Park brake lever consoles are made from rigid molded plastic and also match interior color.

The shifter surround insert on the top of the center console is painted semi-gloss black. Engine specifications are debossed into the rectangular area below the shifter. In 1970 and 1971, horsepower, torque, compression ratio, and engine displacement are indicated. In 1972 the horsepower designation was dropped, and only torque, compression ratio, and engine size are specified.

In manual transmission–equipped cars, the shift pattern is indicated next to the shifter. The shift pattern area is semi-gloss black, and the letters and numbers are chrome, as is a border around the pattern.

The shifter boot for all 1970–1972 manual transmission cars is made from black leather and has a sewn seam toward

the passenger side of the car. Manual shifters for all years have a chrome shaft and threaded-on black chrome ball. A T-handle integral to the shaft controls the reverse lockout.

On Corvettes equipped with an automatic transmission, the shift pattern is also next to the shifter. Chrome letters are used to indicate shifter position in 1970s built through approximately June 1970. Those 1970s built after approximately June 1970, as well as '71s and '72s, use a plastic

An original center console area in an unrestored 1970.

The custom interior trim option included a walnut veneer insert on top of the center console in most 1970 and all 1971–1972 Corvettes. Reproductions are made from plastic, not real walnut. A matching walnut veneer insert in each door panel, carpet along the bottom of the panels, and leather seat covers were also part of the interior option package.

Details of a 1970 center console.

An original 1970–1972 park brake lever.

lighted band with painted letters. The letters are painted to match the instrument faces: slightly greenish in 1970 and '71 and white in '72.

Rather than a boot, automatic transmission shifters are surrounded by a gloss black plastic seal that slides back and forth as the shifter is moved. Automatic shifters for all 1970–1972s are made from a chrome shaft topped by a black plastic ball. The ball has a chrome, spring-loaded button in the top to release the detent and to allow the shifter to be moved.

Two types of heater/air conditioning control assemblies are used in 1970 to 1972. The first, which is used in 1970 and 1971, has green letters and a separate fan switch plate inset into the larger assembly. In 1972 the letters are white, and the fan switch is mounted directly behind the larger assembly, not in a separate small rectangle. With both control assemblies, a chrome lever is used to set fan speed. All air-conditioned cars use a switch with four positions, in addition to "off." Switches in non-air-conditioned cars have only three positions, in addition to "off."

Whether the car is equipped with air conditioning or not, its control assembly employs two large black plastic rotary thumbwheels on either side. The left thumbwheel controls temperature, and the right thumbwheel controls the system setting.

All 1970–1972 non-air-conditioned cars have only two fresh air vent controls on the center console. The controls are sliding levers made from small black plastic balls with a flat area mounted to black oxide metal arms. In 1970–1971 the balls are smooth and shiny on their rounded portions and their flat faces. In 1972 the balls are still shiny black on the flat faces but change to dull black with a grained pattern on the rounded portions only. Balls from all three years say "CLOSE" in painted white letters and have a white arrow on the flat face.

All 1970–1972s have an ashtray inset into the center console insert next to the heater/air conditioning control assembly. The ashtray door is semi-gloss black and slides back and forth with slight resistance. The ashtray is chrome plated and can be removed for cleaning.

All cars are equipped with a cigarette lighter. All 1970–1971s and most '72s use a lighter with a shiny black plastic knob with a white circle and white concentric grooves in its face. Some '72s use a lighter with a chrome knob. The lighters with black knobs have "63 CASCO 12V" stamped in the element, while the lighters with chrome knobs have "72 CASCO 12V" stamped in.

On those 1970–1972 Corvettes equipped with the optional rear window defogger, a control switch is mounted on the left trim panel, forward of the center console. The switch uses a large, round, chrome-plated knob.

All 1970–1972 Corvettes have a park brake lever mounted between the seats. The lever's handle is made from hard, shiny black plastic, with a crosshatch pattern to enhance grip. Chrome trim separates the black plastic grips. A release button on the top of the lever is made from hard, shiny black plastic also. The slotted opening in the park brake lever console is covered by a rippled black plastic cover that slides along with the movement of the lever.

Rear Storage Compartments and Their Contents, Battery, Rear Window Storage Tray

All 1970–1972s feature three enclosed storage compartments behind the seats. The lids for these compartments are made from pressboard and are covered with carpet that matches the interior carpet. The underside of each lid is painted flat black. A white vehicle maintenance sticker is on the underside of the center compartment lid for 1971s manufactured starting in mid-March 1971 and all 1972s. Stickers for tire pressure, jacking instructions, and the limited-slip differential are on the underside of the passenger-side compartment lid.

Each lid is surrounded by a molded plastic border painted to match interior color. The entire assembly of all three lids is also surrounded by a color-matched molded plastic border. Each lid is hinged and latches with a spring-loaded mechanism. Each lid has a chrome button to release its latch and a vinyl hoop to pull it open. The vinyl hoop is the same color as the interior and is retained to the lid by a chrome Phillips-head screw.

In 1970–1971 the center compartment is fitted with a locking chrome release button. In 1972 the center compartment does not have a locking button, but the passenger side compartment does. For 1970s built through mid-June 1970, the same key operates the storage compartment lid lock and the spare tire compartment lock; however, a different key operates the antitheft alarm switch on those cars equipped with the optional antitheft burglar alarm. For 1970s built after mid-June 1970, as well as 1971s and 1972s, the key for the storage compartment lid lock is the same as the keys for the antitheft alarm and spare tire storage compartment.

Each molded plastic border is held to its lid by chrome flathead Phillips screws. Each lid is held to its hinge by black oxide round-head Phillips screws fitted with integral black oxide flat washers. Each hinge is held to the compartment surround by rivets. The whole assembly is held to the body by chrome flathead Phillips screws. The screws holding the rear of the assembly have chrome countersunk integral washers.

The compartment directly behind the driver's seat holds the vehicle's battery. It has a thin foam seal around the perimeter of the door opening to help keep battery fumes from entering the passenger compartment. This seal is not one continuous piece of foam but instead has a seam where the two ends of the strip meet.

All 1970–1972 Corvettes use a side terminal Delco battery. Those 1970s manufactured through approximately early June 1970 use two different model batteries. Big-block-equipped cars or those with the heavy-duty battery option (option T60) use Delco model R 79W. Delco model R 79S is standard for all small-block cars not equipped with the optional battery.

Those 1970s assembled after early June 1970, as well as 1971s and 1972s, use Delco battery model R 89S for small-blocks and model R 89W for big-blocks and cars equipped with the heavy-duty battery option.

All batteries used in 1970–1972 have six cells covered by two plastic caps, each covering three cells. Each cap has three Delco split circle logos molded into its top. The split circles are painted dark orange. A black rubber vent hose runs from each of the caps through a hole in the underbody.

All 1970–1972 battery cables are side terminal style and have red positive ends and black negative ends. For 1970s assembled through approximately the end of March 1970, battery cables have a raised Delco split circle logo on both cable terminals. Both terminals are fastened to the battery with a $\frac{7}{16}$-inch hex-head bolt.

For 1970s assembled from approximately April 1970 through early June 1970, the Delco split circle logo disappears from the battery cable terminals. Instead, the positive cable terminal has a plus sign and the negative terminal has a minus sign. The cables are still retained with $\frac{7}{16}$-inch hex-head bolts.

Those 1970s made from approximately mid-June onward may utilize $\frac{5}{16}$-inch hex-head retention bolts instead of the previously used $\frac{7}{16}$-inch bolts. It is possible that some 1970s made after mid-June use a $\frac{5}{16}$-inch hex-head bolt for one cable and a $\frac{7}{16}$-inch bolt for the other cable. The later a 1970 is, the more likely it is to use the smaller bolts. It is believed that all 1971s and 1972s use the $\frac{5}{16}$-inch hex-head bolts.

The battery cable itself changes in 1972. Each cable is thicker, and the insulation has "COPPER CLAD ALUMINUM" written in white block letters.

The passenger-side storage compartment contains a removable insert. The insert, which is like a squared off bucket, is made from grayish black fiberboard and measures $6\frac{1}{4}$ inches deep. For 1970–1972 convertibles only, the fiberboard insert contains a ½-inch open-ended wrench for installation and removal of the hardtop.

Also inside the fiberboard insert is an off-white cotton pouch with a yellow drawstring. The drawstring is held on by an encasement stitched with red thread. The pouch contains eight silver washers and four oblong, gray phosphate shims used to adjust seat backs to the preferred position.

In addition to the hardtop wrench and seat hardware pouch, the storage insert holds a number of other items. A small white paper envelope with the "GM mark of excellence" logo and instructions printed in black letters contains the car's keys and the key knockouts. A small brown paper envelope contains license plate screws. "LICENSE SCREWS" is written in black ink on the envelope. Another small brown paper envelope is included with Corvettes equipped with optional P02 deluxe wheel covers. This envelope contains four extensions for the valve stems.

The final item in the storage insert is the owner's packet. This packet included an owner's manual, warranty folder, Protect-O-Plate, consumer information booklet, trim ring installation instruction card, and radio instruction sheet. Those 1970s equipped with the optional stereo radio also have a stereo instruction sheet. Some 1971s and 1972s have the stereo sheet and some do not. Cars that did not come with a radio did not have the radio instruction sheet or the stereo instruction sheet. In 1972 only an emissions control systems booklet is included in the packet.

The above-described contents of the owner's packet are in a clear vinyl envelope. In 1970 and 1971, the same envelope, which carries the part number 3950779, is used. It has a yellow key with blue letters reading, "Don't invite car theft." Cars from 1972 have similar envelopes, but without the yellow key or blue writing.

The fiberboard insert in the passenger-side rear storage compartment lifts out to reveal an additional storage area beneath. A jack and jack handle are mounted to the bottom of the compartment (to the car's floor panel) with a black spring that latches onto a black hook riveted to the floor.

All jacks are painted semi-gloss black and have "A" stamped into the chassis contact pad. This is the logo for Auto Specialties Manufacturing, the company that made the jacks. In addition to the manufacturer's logo, all jacks contain a date code stamping. The stamping is on the jack's large side arm and contains a number for the year followed by a letter for the month, with "A" representing January, "B" representing February, and so on. For example, the date code stamping for a jack manufactured in June 1971 would be "1 F."

All jack handles are painted semi-gloss black and include a pivoting ¾-inch boxed hex wrench on the end for removing and installing lug nuts. A thick rubber ring is fitted around the hex wrench end to prevent rattling.

In addition to the jack and jack handle, electrical relays and a flasher unit are mounted underneath the fiberboard insert on those cars equipped with the audio antitheft alarm system.

All 1970–1972 coupes have two storage bags to hold the T-tops when they are removed. Some cars have bags dyed to match interior color, while others have black bags regardless of interior color. Earlier cars for each year are more likely to have a color-matched bag. Later cars are more likely to have black bags.

All bags have a date code stamped inside in ink. Typical date stampings contain a month and year designation. For example, bags manufactured in October 1970 read "10-70." In addition to the date stamping, bags may contain a logo stamping representing the manufacturer. The most common

In 1970–1971 coupe rear window storage trays were held up with this latch. Some later 1971s and all 1972s used a different latch. It featured a push-button release and had no words or markings.

logo is "TEX." All bags have a flap that closes over the opening and is retained by three chrome-plated snaps.

All 1970–1972 coupes have adjustable T-top hold-down straps. As with the T-top bags, early cars tend to have straps dyed to match interior color, and later cars tend to have black straps regardless of interior color. All 1970 coupes have two straps attached to chrome-plated anchors. The anchors are fastened to the floor of the rear luggage area. The 1971 and 1972 coupes use only a single strap harness, which is attached to the rear bulkhead in the luggage area and extends to a chrome-plated anchor attached to the front bulkhead between the seats.

All 1970–1972 coupes have molded vinyl trim mounted to the underside of the T-tops. The vinyl is the same color as the interior.

The convertible top storage area is typical of 1970–1972 production. The underside of the convertible top, the top frame, and the fiberglass header panel are all black, regardless of interior or exterior color.

All 1970–1972 coupes have a rear window storage tray mounted above the rear luggage area. Trays in 1970–1971s assembled through approximately mid-March 1971 have a thin steel latch marked "Rear Window Storage." This latch holds the hinged storage tray up. Releasing the latch allows the tray to drop down. Most '71s assembled from mid-March 1971 forward and all '72s utilize a push-button release instead of the spring steel latch to drop the storage tray down. The push-button release has no writing or markings on it.

Some 1970 and early '71 coupes have latches mounted on the inside of the window storage tray to hold the window in place while it is being stored. These inside hold-down latches are not used at all after early 1971 production.

Convertible Top Frames

For all 1970–1972 convertibles, top frames are painted semi-gloss black. A black fiberglass header panel is secured to the front underside of the top frame. Three chrome-plated latches secure the front top header to the windshield frame. Black rubber coats the latch levers, and each latch is accompanied by an adjustable rubber-tipped tensioning bolt.

The convertible top frame's rear bow is secured to the body deck lid with two chrome-plated pins that insert into chrome-plated receptacles affixed to the body. Chrome Phillips oval-head screws hold the pins to the rear bow.

The underside of the convertible top, including the top material itself and the pads, is always black, regardless of interior color. The optional removable hardtop on those convertibles so equipped has a padded vinyl headliner color matched to the interior. Front latches for the hardtop are chrome plated, but unlike the soft top, the levers on these latches are not rubber coated.

The underside of the convertible deck lid is painted body color. Deck lid release levers, release cables, and lock mechanisms were all mounted prior to painting and should therefore also be painted body color.

The latch receptacles for the pins in the rear bow of the convertible top, as well as the rods that control the receptacles, are black. Deck lid rubber bumpers are black, as are their brackets.

Those 1970 convertibles assembled through approximately July 1970 have two round rubber bumpers mounted to the underside of the deck lid. When the soft top is down in its storage compartment and the lid is closed, these rubber bumpers contact the black fiberglass header panel mounted to the front underside of the top frame. Most very late 1970s, as well as most '71s and early to mid-'72s, have only one such bumper. Most late '72s again have two bumpers.

1970–1972 MECHANICAL
Engine Blocks

Engine block casting numbers for all 1970–1972 engines are located on the top, rear, driver side of the block, on the flange that mates to the transmission bell housing. All 1970–1971 and most '72 small-block cars use number-3970010 blocks. Some '72s assembled beginning in March 1972 use a number-3970014 block. All 1970–1971 big-block cars use number-3963512 blocks. All '72 big-blocks use number-3999289 blocks.

Engine block casting dates for all 1970–1972 small- and big-block Corvettes, with the exception of small-blocks utilizing number-3970014 blocks, are located on the top rear passenger side of the block, on the flange that mates to the transmission bell housing. The casting date for the number-3970014 block is on the top rear driver side flange, adjacent to the casting number.

The engine block casting date for number-3970010 small-blocks and all big-blocks consists of a letter for the month, one or two numbers for the day, and one number for the year. For example, a number-3970010 block cast on June 17, 1972, would have a casting date of "F 17 2."

Number-3970014 small-blocks found in some late 1972s use a similar date code system, except the year is designated by two numbers rather than one. For example, a number-3970014 block cast on June 17, 1972, would have a casting date of "F 17 72."

All 1970–1972 engines contain two distinct stampings on a machined pad on top of the passenger side between the cylinder head and the water pump. One stamping is commonly referred to as the assembly stamping, and the other is commonly called the VIN derivative stamping.

The assembly stamping begins with a prefix letter to indicate the engine assembly plant. "V" indicates the Flint plant, where all small-blocks were assembled, and "T" designates the Tonawanda plant, where all big-blocks were assembled. Following the prefix letter are four numbers

With the exception of 1970s made during the first few days of production, all 1970–1972 Corvette engines had a VIN derivative, assembly date, and suffix code stamped into a pad on the front passenger side of the block, immediately adjacent to where the water pump mounts. In very early 1970s, the VIN derivative was stamped on the side of the block, just above the oil filter. This 1971 stamping is from car number 194371S111560. The "V" tells us that the engine was produced in the Flint V-8 engine plant. The date code "0220" indicates that it was assembled on February 20, 1971. The suffix code "CGZ" tells us that it was an LT-1 coupled to a manual transmission.

This is an extremely original, unrestored 1970 engine compartment. Note the many subtle variations in surface finishes and textures.

indicating the month and day of assembly. After the numbers indicating the assembly date are three suffix letters denoting the particular engine. This suffix code is often referred to as the engine broadcast code, or simply the engine code. (Refer to Appendix C for engine suffix codes.)

To illustrate what a typical engine assembly stamping looks like, consider the following 1971 combination: a base 350/270-horsepower engine built on April 5 and coupled to a four-speed transmission. The assembly stamping for such an engine would be "V0405CJL."

Always remember that the engine assembly date must come after the engine block casting date (you can't assemble an engine before the block is cast), and both the casting date and assembly date must precede the final assembly date of the car (you can't final assemble a car before the engine has been cast and assembled). The great majority of engines were cast and assembled less than a few weeks prior to the car's assembly date. Some engines, however, were cast and/or assembled months prior to installation in a car. Six months is generally accepted as the outer limit between an engine assembly or casting date and the final assembly date of the car.

The VIN derivative stamping, as the name implies, is a stamping containing a portion or a derivative of the car's vehicle identification number. For 1970 Corvettes, this stamping begins with "70" for model year 1970. This is followed by "S" for St. Louis, where all 1970–1972 Corvettes were built. The "S" is followed by the final six digits of the car's VIN. For example, the VIN derivative stamping for the very first 1970 assembled would be "70S400001." The second car would be "70S400002," and so on.

VIN derivative stampings in early 1971s built in August and very early September 1970 follow the same pattern as the stampings used in all of 1970. The very first 1971, for example, would have a VIN derivative stamping of "71S100001." After early September 1970, however, the beginning of the stamping is changed, with "C11" replacing the two-number designation for the year. So the 4,000th 1971 built would have a VIN derivative stamping of "C11S104000." The "C" represents Chevrolet, the first "1" designates the Chevrolet car line, and the second "1" designates the 1971 model year.

For model year 1972, the VIN derivative stamping was again changed. The "C" was dropped, but the "1" immediately following it was retained to designate the Chevrolet car line. So the VIN derivative stamping in the 4,000th 1972 built would be "12S504000."

On big-block engines, the assembly stamping is normally on the left and toward the rear of the pad when viewing it to read the stamping. The VIN derivative stamping is to the right and toward the front of the pad. On small-block engines, this positioning is reversed.

A notable exception occurred in the first few days of 1970 production. Very early '70 engines have been observed with the VIN derivative stamping on the bottom driver side of the block above the oil filter.

All 1970–1972 engine blocks are cast iron, and all are painted Chevrolet Engine Orange. Blocks were originally painted before exhaust manifolds were installed. Therefore coverage on the sides of blocks behind the manifolds is good. The engine stamp pad was normally covered up when the engine was painted. Therefore it normally appears unpainted.

Cylinder Heads

As with engine blocks, all 1970–1972 cylinder heads have both a casting number and a casting date. As with blocks and other cast parts, the cylinder head casting date typically has a letter to indicate month, one or two numbers to indicate the day of the month, and one number to indicate the year. (Refer to Appendix G for cylinder head casting numbers.)

All 1970–1972 engines utilize cast-iron cylinder heads, with the exception of the optional 1971 LS6 engine, which has aluminum cylinder heads.

All cylinder heads and head bolts, with the exception of the aluminum heads installed on 1971 LS6 engines, are painted Chevrolet Engine Orange.

Intake Manifolds

All 1970–1972 intake manifolds are cast iron except for those on optional LT1 small-blocks and LS6 big-blocks, which are cast aluminum.

As with engine blocks and cylinder heads, intake manifolds contain casting numbers and casting dates. As with other cast engine parts, the casting date consists of a letter designating the month, one or two numbers designating the day of the month, and a number denoting the year.

Casting numbers for all manifolds are on the top surface, as are casting dates for cast-iron manifolds. For aluminum manifolds, casting dates are on the underside and are therefore not visible when the manifold is installed on an engine. (Refer to Appendix H for intake manifold casting numbers.)

During the first few days of 1970 production, the VIN derivative was stamped on the side of the engine block above the oil filter, rather than on the passenger-side pad adjacent to the water pump, where it is normally found. In this example, from the 28th Corvette built in 1970, the VIN derivative was stamped twice, likely because the first stamping was done at an angle that made the top half deep and the bottom half extremely weak.

No original 1970–1972 Corvette intakes have a machined opening at the forward edge for an oil fill tube, as is seen on earlier intakes and some later replacements.

All 1970–1972 Corvette engines utilize an aluminum thermostat housing that does not have a hole for a temperature sending unit. Housings used on certain other Chevrolets and some replacement housings have a tapped hole. Aluminum thermostat housings are painted orange when mounted to cast-iron intakes and left unpainted when mounted to aluminum intakes.

With original 1970–1972 intake manifold side gaskets, but not with later GM replacements, semicircular tabs stick up between the runners for cylinders three and six and from the exhaust heat crossover passage. Also, original front and rear intake gaskets do not have side tabs for locating the gaskets on the block's rail, as do later replacements.

All intake manifolds are held on by 3⁄16-inch hex-head bolts. The bolts do not get any type of washer when used for cast-iron intakes and 1970–1971 aluminum intakes. For aluminum intakes in 1972, however, those intake bolts not also used to hold a bracket in place received flat washers.

Engine lifting brackets are attached to most 1970–1972 Corvettes. In 1970 all small-blocks have one bracket attached to the second intake manifold bolt from the front on the driver side. All 1971–1972 small-blocks and all 1970–1972 big-blocks have a front bracket that attaches to the first and second intake manifold bolts from the front on the driver side. A second bracket attaches to the upper bell-housing-to-block bolt on the passenger side for all 1970–1972 small-blocks except those mated to an automatic transmission. Small-blocks mated to automatics did not get a rear lift bracket at all. A second bracket attaches to the rear of the passenger-side cylinder head for all 1970–1972 big-blocks.

The front bracket is painted orange on those 1970–1972 engines equipped with cast-iron intake manifolds

and painted silver on 1970 LT1s. Brackets on 1971–1972 LT1s are typically unpainted toward the bottom and painted orange toward the top. The rear bracket is painted orange for all 1970–1972 engines except LS6s. LS6 rear brackets are unpainted, as are LS6 front brackets.

All cast-iron intake manifolds are painted Chevrolet Engine Orange. Some small-block aluminum intakes are painted with dull aluminum paint, while others are unpainted. LS6 aluminum intakes are unpainted

All intake manifolds, including aluminum examples, were installed before engines were painted. Therefore, on those engines with cast-iron intakes, hold-down bolts, as well as any exposed portions of gaskets, are painted Chevrolet Engine Orange.

Aluminum intakes were crudely masked off prior to the engine being painted. Therefore engines with aluminum intakes may have orange paint overspray on edges, bolts, and gaskets. If orange overspray was excessive, the factory sometimes sprayed the area along the edges of the manifold silver, resulting in silver overspray on bolts, gaskets, and sometimes even cylinder heads.

Distributor and Ignition Coil

All 1970–1972 Corvettes use a mechanical tach drive Delco Remy distributor. All distributors have a thin aluminum identification band secured around the housing in a recess just above where the distributor hold-down clamp rests.

The identification band is natural on one side and dyed pinkish red on the other. While the majority of cars have the dye on the outside of the band, some have it on the inside, making it difficult to see when the band is installed on the distributor.

The identification band has "DELCO REMY" stamped into it. This is followed by a seven-character part number and a date code. (Refer to Appendix K for distributor part numbers.)

The date code, which represents the day the distributor was assembled, consists of a number representing the year, a letter representing the month, and one or two numbers representing the day of the month. For 1970–1972 distributor date codes, the letter "A" represents January, "B" represents February, and so on. As is typical of stamped-in date codes, the letter "I" is skipped, so September is represented by "J." So the date code on a distributor assembled on March 17, 1972, would read "2 C 17," and one assembled November 21, 1970, would read "0 L 21."

While most distributors were made several weeks before the engine was assembled, several months can separate the two. As with most other components, six months is the generally accepted maximum.

Those 1970 Corvettes assembled through approximately the middle of the model year utilize a distributor housing without a small hole opposite the tachometer drive gear. Mid-1970 and 1971–1972 housings do have this small hole.

Distributor housings are painted semi-gloss black and have a daub of colored paint just below the distributor cap on the passenger side toward the front of the car.

All distributors are fitted with a vacuum advance unit. Vacuum advances have part numbers stamped into the bracket that mounts the vacuum canister to the distributor.

All 1970–1972 Corvettes use a black Delco Remy distributor cap with "Delco Remy Pat. Pend. R." molded into the top between the towers.

All 1970–1972s use a Delco Remy ignition coil. All coils are held by a silver-cadmium-plated, stamped-steel bracket. The coil is clamped into the bracket with a slotted round-head machine screw, and the bracket is held to the intake manifold by two hex-head bolts. If the car is equipped with a radio, a capacitor is held to the coil bracket with a clamp retained by a single screw.

Coils are painted gloss black and have the last three numbers of their Chevrolet part number embossed in the housing from the inside out, so they are raised up. (Refer to Appendix L for coil numbers and applications.)

In addition to the final three numbers of the part number, some ignition coils also have "B-R" embossed in their cases. Coils utilized with the optional transistor ignition system have a red, black, and silver foil sticker that reads "Delco Remy Ignition Coil for Transistor Ignition."

Transistor ignition was a distinct option in 1970, was available only with LT1 and LS6 in 1971 as part of those options, and was not available at all in 1972. Transistor ignition includes a different distributor, a special wire harness, a different ignition coil, and a pulse amplification box. The amplification box is mounted to the front of the driver-side front inner wheelwell. It is visible if you look between the driver-side front inner wheelwell and the driver-side front corner of the body with the hood in the raised position.

The correct 1970–1971 pulse amplification box is part number 1115343. It has a three-wire pigtail that terminates in a plug connector. The plug connector is mated with a corresponding plug connector in the transistor ignition harness. Earlier versions of the amplification box have a female plug directly on the box rather than a short pigtail of wire with a plug on the end.

Ignition Shielding

All 1970–1972 Corvettes equipped with a radio are outfitted with ignition shielding. All pieces of shielding are plated with flash chrome. The quality and appearance of the chrome are not very good.

All 1970 small-block cars assembled through approximately early July 1970 have a two-section main ignition shield. It consists of a surround that completely encapsulates the distributor and coil and a lid for the surround.

The surround for 1970s assembled through approximately the end of February 1970 is actually two pieces held together by two small Phillips-head screws. The two halves in cars assembled after approximately the end of February 1970 are spot welded together rather than screwed.

A translucent plastic shield is held to the underside of the top lid by four plastic rivets. Three chrome-plated wing bolts retain the lid to the surround.

The main shield, or top shield as it is sometimes called, attaches to support brackets with two chrome wing bolts on each side. The support brackets are painted Chevrolet Engine Orange and attach to the intake manifold bolts.

Those 1970 small-blocks assembled after approximately early July 1970, and all 1971–1972 small-blocks, utilize a one-piece top ignition shield. The one-piece shield is held to the support brackets by one chrome-plated wing bolt on each side.

All 1970–1972 small-blocks have four cadmium-plated spark plug heat shields, each covering two plugs. Each heat shield is retained to the engine block by a single silver-cadmium-plated indented hex-head bolt.

Small-block-equipped 1970s assembled through approximately June 1970 (the cars with two-section top shields) have four chrome-plated spark plug shields, each covering two plugs. The spark plug shields are retained to cadmium-plated brackets with chrome-plated wing bolts. The brackets have "FPM" stamped in to represent the manufacturer. Later, incorrect GM replacement brackets have "CNI" stamped in.

After approximately June 1970, more or less concurrent with the change to a one-piece top shield, use of the two forward spark plug shields was discontinued. The rearward two shields remained, covering the plugs in cylinders five, seven, six, and eight.

All 1970–1972 small-blocks use a pair of boomerang or V-shaped sections of chrome-plated shielding to encapsulate the spark plug wires. The boomerang shielding runs from the bottom of the vertical shields to the area beneath the spark plugs.

Small-block cars not originally equipped with a radio still have the two main shield support brackets on the back of the intake manifold and the cadmium-plated spark plug heat shields. They do not have any of the chrome shielding, however.

Those 1970 big-blocks assembled through approximately early July 1970 have a two-section main ignition shield just like small-block-equipped cars. Very late 1970 and all 1971–1972 big-blocks have the second kind of shielding. This is the one-piece shield held to the support brackets by one chrome-plated wing bolt on each side.

Rather than spark plug wire and spark plug shields like small-blocks, big-blocks have special spark plug wires covered with braided stainless-steel wire. The braid toward the end of each wire ends in a hoop that fastens to the valve cover bolts to provide a ground. In 1970–1971 the hoops on the right side attach in pairs to the forward-most

Though LT-1 engines lacked the brute power of 454 engines, many preferred the more balanced performance they delivered.

bolt and the third bolt back. On the left side of the engine, they attach to the second and fourth bolts back. In 1972 the left side is also attached in pairs to the second and fourth bolts back, but the right side has a single wire on the first and second bolts and a pair of wires on the third bolt back.

Beginning sometime in the 1971 model year, big-block engines were fitted with spark plug heat shields. Each heat shield is a cadmium-plated steel tube with a welded-on tab. The tab allows each shield to be mounted to an exhaust manifold bolt.

Big-block cars not originally equipped with a radio do not have the main shield support brackets or braided steel spark plug wires but do have the heat shields.

In addition to the external ignition shielding fitted to all 1970–1972 Corvettes equipped with a radio, some cars had an additional shield covering the ignition points beneath the distributor cap. Called a radio frequency interference (RFI) shield, it was used on standard ignition distributors (that is, nontransistor ignition distributors) in 1971–1972 and in 1970s assembled after approximately August 1970. Its use in 1970 appears to correlate to the use of the 1971-style external shielding, which was also installed on 1970 models assembled from approximately August 1970 onward.

Spark Plug Wires

All 1970–1972 Corvettes use black spark plug wires manufactured by Packard Electric. All wires are ink stamped every few inches with the words "Packard T V R Suppression" and a date code. The date code indicates the quarter and the year of manufacture. For example, wires labeled "2Q-71" were made in the second quarter of 1971.

Wires for small-block engines have black boots with 90-degree bends at the spark plug end and straight black boots at the distributor end. The 1970–1971 big-block wires have gray boots with 135-degree bends at the spark plug end and 90-degree bends at the distributor end. The 1972 big-block wires are the same, except the boots at the spark plug ends are straight.

Carburetors and Choke

All 1970–1972 Corvettes are carbureted. Original carburetors come from either Rochester, Holley, or Carter. Carter was at times contracted to manufacture Rochester Quadrajet carburetors for General Motors, so the Carter-built Quadrajets are almost identical to the Rochester-built ones. Carter-built Quadrajets are identified as being manufactured by Carter and use Carter's system of date coding rather than Rochester's system. (Refer to Appendix J for carburetor numbers.)

Rochester-built Quadrajets contain an alphanumeric sequence stamped into a flat, vertical area of the main body on the rear of the driver side. Either the full seven-digit GM part number or the final five digits of the part number are stamped in. Several letters, which identify the specific plant where the carburetor was made, may be stamped here as well. Finally, four numbers denoting the date of manufacture are also stamped into this area.

Rochester utilized the Julian calendar for date coding its carburetors. With this system of dating, the first three numbers represent the day of the year, and the final number is the last digit of the specific year. For example, the Julian date code for a carburetor made on January 1, 1972, would be "0012." The first three digits, "001," represent the first day of the year. The final digit, "2," represents 1972.

The Julian date code for a carburetor made on December 31, 1971, would be 3651. The first three digits, "365," represent the 365th day of the year, which in 1971 was December 31. The final digit, "1," represents 1971.

The letter in the date code for Carter-built Quadrajets represents the month, while the number that follows is the last digit for the year of manufacture. For example, a date code of "C1" indicates that the carburetor was made in March 1971.

Holley carburetors have three distinct stampings on the front driver side of the air horn. The top stamping is the seven-digit GM part number, which may be followed by one or two letters.

Below the GM part number is the Holley list number. The list number corresponds to Holley's part number. This

Holley carburetors were stamped on the front of the air horn with a GM part number, Holley list number, and manufacturing date code. This is an original carburetor for a 1971 LT-1. The first digit of the date code is the last digit of the year. The second digit is the month, and the final digit is the week. In this example, the date code "122" means the carburetor was manufactured during the second week of February 1971.

stamping says "LIST," followed by four numbers and then an additional number, a letter, or a combination of numbers and letters.

Below the Holley list number is the date code. Holley date codes in 1970–1972 utilize three numbers. The first is the last digit of the year, the second is the month of production, and the third is the week of production. For the month of production, the numbers one through nine denote January through September, "O" denotes October, "A" denotes November, and "B" denotes December. A Holley carburetor manufactured on March 3, 1970, would have a date code of "031," with "0" representing 1970, "3" representing March, and "1" representing the first week of March.

All 1970–1972 carburetors are plated gold dichromate. Rochester carburetors tend to be darker and more uniform in color than Holleys.

All carburetors have an insulator separating them from the intake manifold. Those 1970 Corvettes equipped with a Rochester carburetor and sold new in all states except California utilize a ⅛-inch-thick insulator. The 1970 Rochester-equipped cars delivered new in California have a ³⁄₁₆-inch-thick insulator.

All 1970–1972 Holley-equipped Corvettes, as well as all 1971–1972 Rochester-equipped ones, have ¼-inch-thick insulators.

Those 1970 Corvettes sold new in California were required to have option NA9, called an evaporative emissions system. NA9 includes a thin, brushed-aluminum heat shield that goes beneath the carburetor. In addition to the aluminum shield, NA9 also includes heat-insulating inserts that go over the carburetor mounting bolts to discourage heat transfer through the bolts into the carburetor.

All 1970–1972 carburetors use a single accelerator return spring. It is black phosphate plated and mounts from the primary shaft bell crank to the accelerator cable mount.

All 1970–1972 Corvettes utilize a mechanical carburetor choke controlled by a thermostatic coil. The coil is mounted

All Quadrajet carburetors installed in 1970–1972 Corvettes had identifying information stamped into the main body on the driver side. Rochester and Carter were both suppliers of Quadrajets to GM. Part number "7040203" indicates that this carburetor is for a 1970 base engine car. "M9" is the date code, which tells us that this is a Carter Quadrajet made in December 1969. The © symbol is a Carter logo, and "DB" is believed to represent the specific assembly plant where this carburetor was manufactured.

Driver-side carburetor details from an unrestored 1970.

in a recess on the passenger side of the intake manifold and is covered by a cadmium-plated steel housing. A rod links the coil to the choke linkage on the carburetor. In 1970 the rod is secured to the linkage with a clip that locks back on the choke rod. In 1971–1972 it is secured with a clip that locks over a groove in the end of the rod.

Air Cleaner

The majority of 1970 Corvettes use an open element air cleaner assembly. Those 1970s assembled after approximately mid-June 1970, except for LT1-equipped cars, use the 1971–1972 closed element air cleaner. LT1s continue to use an open element design.

All 1971–1972s use a closed element design except for LT1s and LS6s, which continue to use the open element air cleaner. The closed element design uses a housing that is enclosed except for two forward-facing snorkels that allow air to enter. The housing is painted gloss black.

All air cleaners, including both open and closed element designs, have chrome-plated lids. All 1970–1971 lids have a decal identifying engine displacement and horsepower rating. The 1972 lids do not have a decal.

All open element air cleaner lids have service instructions and the replacement filter part number silk-screened on the underside.

Closed element air cleaner assemblies do not have anything on the underside of the lid. Instead, the replacement filter number and other information are on a sticker affixed to the outside of the air cleaner housing. The sticker is white with "CR" and the number "6485887" on it.

Original 1970–1972 air filter elements for both open and closed element air cleaner assemblies are AC Delco number A 212 CW. Original elements, unlike later replacements, have a fine wire screen around the outside in a vertical (not diagonal) pattern. The horizontal and vertical wire forms rectangles, with the longer measurement running vertical when the element is installed.

Valve Covers

All 1970–1972 base engines are fitted with stamped-steel valve covers painted Chevrolet Engine Orange. These are held on with hex-head bolts and metal tabs that are also painted orange. Original valve covers have more rounded corners than later replacements. Also, original covers do not have spark plug wire brackets welded to them. Stamped-steel valve covers do have small tabs welded to the side to hold electrical wires, however. In 1970 small-blocks have one tab welded on the passenger side, while big-blocks have two welded on the passenger side. In 1971 and 1972, all engines with steel valve covers have two tabs welded on the driver side.

A PCV valve inserts into a rubber grommet in the driver-side valve cover. A hose connects the PCV valve to the carburetor. A crankcase vent intake hose connects from a nipple in the passenger-side valve cover to a nipple on the air cleaner base.

All 1970 base engines use a steel twist-on oil fill cap in the driver-side valve cover. The oil cap has a square rivet in its center and is painted orange. The 1971 and most '72 base engines use a push-in black rubber plug with "OIL" molded into the top. Some late 1972 base engines use a steel twist-on oil cap. It's the same as the 1970 style, but it has "ENGINE OIL FILL AC-FC2" stamped in a circle around the center rivet.

The 1970 L46 (350/350 horsepower) and 1970–1972 LT1s have cast-aluminum valve covers with longitudinal ribs. As with the painted steel covers, a vent hose connects the passenger-side valve cover to the air cleaner base, and a PCV valve is in the driver-side valve cover. Aluminum valve covers are retained by silver-cadmium-plated indented hex-head bolts.

All 1970 aluminum valve covers have chrome-plated twist-in oil fill caps on the driver side. A large "S" for Stant, the manufacturer of the caps, is stamped into the center rivet. All 1971 and most 1972s use a rubber push-in-style oil fill plug with "OIL" molded into the top.

Both passenger- and driver-side aluminum valve covers are made from the same mold. The only difference is that the driver-side cover has a hole for the oil fill cap. The passenger-side cover does not have. On the passenger side, where the hole would go, there is a rigid disc with the crossed-flag emblem glued on.

All 1970 big-block valve covers are plated with low-quality chrome. They have internal drippers spot welded on, and the spot welds show as irregular indents on the outside of the cover. The passenger- and driver-side covers each have two welded-on brackets to hold plastic spark plug wire looms. The rear of the driver-side cover has a large depression to clear the power brake booster. This cover is used on cars with both power and nonpower brakes. A foil decal reading "Tonawanda #1 Team" is on the top of the passenger-side cover toward the front. A twist-on chrome-plated oil fill cap is located on the passenger side.

All 1970–1972 Corvettes came with a Delco Remy starter motor. A part number and manufacturing date code were stamped into each motor's case. This 1970 motor is part number "1108338." Its assembly date of "9M12" indicates that it was made on December 12, 1969.

The 1971 big-block valve covers are the same as those used in 1970, except they are painted Chevrolet Engine Orange instead of chrome plated. Also, only very early '71s have the "Tonawanda #1 Team" decal on the valve cover. As with '71 small-block covers, a rubber push-in plug with "OIL" molded into the top is used for the oil fill. It is located on the passenger side.

The 1972 big-block valve covers are the same as those used in 1971, except for the spark plug wire brackets. Instead of the two brackets seen in 1970–1971, the '72 covers each have one bracket welded toward the middle rear. It holds a four-wire plastic loom. In addition, only 1972 covers have four single-wire retainers welded along the bottom edge. A rubber push-in plug with "OIL" molded into the top is located on the passenger side for oil fill.

Exhaust Manifolds

All 1970–1972 exhaust manifolds are cast iron. They contain a casting number that is normally on the side facing away from the engine and a casting date that is normally on the side facing the engine. (Refer to Appendix I for exhaust manifold casting numbers.)

Small-block exhaust manifold casting dates normally include a letter denoting the month and one or two numbers denoting the day of the month. Big-block exhaust manifolds normally include a letter denoting the month, one or two numbers denoting the day of the month, and two numbers denoting the year.

Small-block exhaust manifolds were not yet installed when engines were originally painted, so they show no signs of overspray. Big-block manifolds may or may not have Chevrolet Engine Orange paint overspray.

No 1970–1972 exhaust manifolds use a gasket where they mount to the cylinder head.

Small-block manifolds use ⅜-inch hex-head bolts with two concentric rings on their heads. The front two bolts and rear two bolts on both sides of the engine get French locks, with one of the two tabs bent over to prevent the bolts from loosening. In addition, the same front and rear bolts on each side get thick, flat washers that sit between the French lock and manifold. But if the exhaust manifold bolt also retains a bracket (such as an air-conditioning bracket), the flat washer is not used.

Bolts holding big-block manifolds have been observed with three different kinds of heads. The most prevalent has two concentric rings like small-block manifold bolts. A second design has an integral washer, a recessed hex head, and "A" (the manufacturer's logo) in the center of the head. A third variety is a simple hex head with no markings.

The 1970 big-block exhaust manifolds do not have French locks or any type of washers used with the bolts. Some 1971 big-blocks have French locks, and all '72 big-blocks have them.

Starter Motor

All 1970–1972 Corvettes have a Delco Remy starter motor. Automatic-transmission-equipped cars utilize starters with aluminum noses, while starters for manual-transmission-equipped cars have cast-iron noses.

Motor housings and cast-iron noses are painted semi-gloss black. Aluminum noses are unpainted.

The starter's part number and assembly date are stamped into the side of the motor housing. The date code contains a number representing the last digit of the year and a letter denoting the month, with "A" representing January, "B" representing February, and so on. As is typical of stamped-in date codes, the letter "I" is skipped, so September is represented by "J." One or two numbers indicating the day follow the letter denoting the month. For example, a date code of "2B14" indicates that the starter was made on February 14, 1972. (Refer to Appendix N for starter motor part numbers.)

Starter solenoids have a black Bakelite cover for the electrical connections. Solenoid housings may be painted semi-gloss black or be silver cadmium plated.

All starters use a stamped-steel brace to support the forward end (the end facing the front of the car when the starter is installed). The brace mounts to a stud on the starter's end plate and to a threaded boss in the engine block. The brace is painted semi-gloss black.

Every starter has a heat shield to protect it from exhaust system heat. Small-block engines are fitted with rectangular shields, while big-blocks get larger, irregularly shaped shields. Small-block shields are painted semi-gloss black, and big-block shields are plated with poor-quality flash chrome. Heat shields attach to the solenoid screws with barrel nuts.

Oil Filter

All 1970–1972 engines, including both small and big-blocks, utilize an AC Delco spin-on oil filter. Original filters are

All 1970–1972 Corvettes came with a Delco Remy alternator mounted on the driver side of the engine. A part number, amp rating, and date code are stamped into the alternator housing. This information faces up and is easily read on all applications, except cars equipped with a 454 engine and power steering, in which case the stamped information is on the underside of the alternator. In this example, the part number is "1100950," and the "1A16" date code translates to January 16, 1971. The "RF" ink stamping is a broadcast code. It indicates that this alternator is correct for the standard 350 and optional LT-1.

white with a red AC logo, blue circumferential stripes, and blue lettering reading "FULL FLOW" and "TYPE PF-25." It is likely but not certain that at least some original filters had "BEST WAY TO PROTECT YOUR ENGINE—REPLACE WITH AC TYPE PF25" embossed on the bottom. Later service replacement GM filters are painted dark blue, with a sticker bearing the AC and GM logos.

Alternator

All engines are fitted with a Delco Remy alternator mounted on the driver side. Alternator housings are made from cast aluminum and are not painted or coated with anything.

The front half of the housing has the unit's part number, amperage rating, and assembly date code stamped in. The date code contains a number for the year and a letter for the month, with "A" representing January, "B" representing February, and so on. As is typical of stamped-in date codes, the letter "I" is skipped, so September is represented by "J." The letter denoting the month is followed by one or two numbers for the day. For example, an alternator stamped "2D17" was assembled on April 17, 1972.

The alternator pulley on all LT1s without air conditioning and all LS6s was machined from solid material and is silver cadmium plated. While this high-performance pulley is randomly seen on other engines, most other applications used a zinc-plated, stamped-steel pulley.

The lower alternator bracket on 1970 and '71 small-blocks is stamped steel painted Chevrolet Engine Orange. The 1972 small-blocks use a cast lower bracket painted semi-gloss black.

The lower alternator bracket on all 1970–1972 big-blocks without power steering is cast and painted semi-gloss black. The bracket for big-block cars equipped with

power steering is stamped steel painted semi-gloss black. All 1970–1972 Corvettes utilize a stamped-steel upper alternator bracket. This bracket is painted semi-gloss black.

Power Steering Pump and Fuel Pump

Small-block 1970–1972 cars equipped with power steering use a power steering pump painted semi-gloss black, with a neck that is the same diameter from top to bottom. The necks on big-block pumps, in contrast, widen toward the bottom. Small-block pumps have a semi-gloss black, stamped-steel belt guard bolted to the body.

Small-block cars equipped with air conditioning usually use a semi-gloss black, stamped-steel pulley for the power steering pump. Non-air-conditioned small-blocks usually use a cast pulley with open spokes. All big-block-equipped cars use a double groove, open spoke, cast pulley for the power steering pump.

All 1970–1972 power steering pumps, regardless of engine, use a semi-gloss painted, stamped-steel support bracket.

All 1970–1972 Corvettes use an AC brand fuel pump that's a natural dull silver color. The pumps have "AC" cast into the top or side of the upper housing and a five-character part number stamped into the underside of the mounting flange. Base engines and L46s used pump 40769. LT1s used pump 40709 in 1970–1971 and pump 40956 in '72. LS5s and LS6s used number 40770.

Water Pump, Engine Fan, and Fan Clutch

All 1970 small-blocks use casting number 3782608 water pumps. Their front bearings are smaller in diameter than 1971 and newer pumps, so the snout of the housing is smaller. Also, the snout does not have reinforcing ribs, and the top of the pump housing does not have a boss for a bypass hose fitting.

All 1971 and those '72 small-blocks assembled through approximately the end of May 1972 use casting number 3991399 water pumps. These have reinforcing ribs on the snout and their front bearings are larger in diameter than 1970 pumps. As in 1970, these do not have a boss for a bypass hose fitting on top.

Those 1972 small-blocks assembled after approximately the end of May 1972 use casting number 330813 water pumps. These pumps have front bearings with a large diameter and reinforcing ribs on the snout. They also have flat bosses on the top for bypass hose fittings, though the bosses are not drilled and tapped.

Those 1970 big-blocks assembled through at least January 1970 use casting number 3992077 water pumps. Later '70s and those '71 big-blocks assembled through approximately the end of August 1970 use casting number 3856284 water pumps. Most 1971s and '72s use casting number 386100 water pumps. All big-block pumps utilize a bypass hose connected to a screwed-in fitting on top of the housing.

All 1970–1972 Corvettes came with a viscous drive fan clutch. As shown here, the clutch was mounted to the water pump with studs, nuts, and split-ring lock washers, not bolts. The shaft and mounting flange were typically painted silver. An inspection mark, which is most often yellow, is sometimes seen on the mount flange. A green mark is often seen on the clutch's fins. A date code and manufacturer's logo were stamped into the edge of the mounting flange. This example was made on August 1, 1969. "SC" represents the manufacturer, Schwitzer Corporation.

All solid lifter engines utilize a deep groove water pump pulley, while pulleys on hydraulic lifter engines have a shallower groove. Most water pump pulleys are painted semi-gloss black, though some originals have a black phosphate finish.

All 1970–1972 Corvettes use a thermostatically controlled, viscous coupled fan clutch. Original clutches usually have a date code stamped in the edge of the flange that goes against the water pump pulley. Clutches (as well as water pump pulleys) are retained by studs and nuts that thread into the pump's front hub.

All 1970–1972s use a cooling fan painted gloss black and mounted to the fan clutch. Cars equipped with air conditioning use a seven-blade fan with a part number and

date code stamped into the edge of one or more blades. The date code contains a letter for the month, with "A" designating January, "B" designating February, and so on. As is typical of stamped-in date codes, the letter "I" is skipped, so September is represented by "J." Following the letter indicating the month are two numbers to denote the year.

Small-block air-conditioned cars use a seven-blade fan that is essentially flat along the outer edge of each blade. In contrast, the ends of blades on big-block air-conditioned cars are irregularly shaped and come to an off-center point. Cars not equipped with air conditioning use a five-blade fan. Five-blade fans do not have part numbers or date codes stamped in.

A minority of air-conditioned cars have five-blade fans instead of the more commonly seen seven-blade unit. The five-blade fan differs from the one seen in non-air-conditioned cars in that its blades are pitched at a more severe angle.

Radiator, Hoses, and Related Parts

All 1970–1972 Corvettes use either a copper or an aluminum radiator, depending on the engine and transmission choice and on whether the car is equipped with air conditioning.

Aluminum radiators have a part number and date code stamped into the top left side. The date code consists of two numbers to denote the year and a letter to indicate the month, with "A" representing January, "B" representing February, and so on. To the right of the stamping is a rectangular foil sticker printed "HARRISON," the name of the manufacturer. Aluminum radiators are painted semi-gloss to gloss black.

Those 1970–1972 Corvettes equipped with option ZR1 or the combination of an LT1 and M22 transmission, and 1971s with option ZR2, utilize a unique aluminum radiator. It resembles the aluminum radiator used in other Corvettes but is slightly larger. Also, its top neck is long and curved instead of short and straight.

Copper radiators were also manufactured by Harrison and have that name debossed in the passenger-side radiator tank. In addition, a stamped-steel tag with a two-letter broadcast code and a part number is attached to the passenger side of copper radiators. As with the aluminum, the copper radiators are painted semi-gloss to gloss black.

All cars except 1971s with option ZR2 and 1972s with option ZR1 use a fan shroud. Most cars with copper radi-ators use an unpainted black or very dark gray plastic shroud, though some 1970 big-block cars have light gray plastic shrouds.

All cars fitted with aluminum radiators use a semi-gloss painted, stamped-steel shroud.

Some 1970–1972 Corvettes are fitted with an aluminum expansion tank. Some are fitted with a brass tank, and some don't have a tank at all. Generally, cars with aluminum radiators got aluminum expansion tanks, and cars with copper radiators did not get tanks. The exception to the latter is LS5-equipped cars, which had copper radiators and brass tanks.

This is the correct fan for 1970–1972 Corvettes fitted with both a 454-cid engine and air conditioning. This fan has seven blades and is distinguished by the pointed tips on each blade.

Those 1970–1972 Corvettes with an aluminum radiator were fitted with a steel fan shroud painted semi-gloss black. A small number of 1970 LS5 cars had a light gray fiberglass shroud. All other cars had the black fiberglass shroud seen here. Note the one-piece triangular black foam strip used to seal the radiator support to the hood in this original 1972. Starting in 1971 after about VIN 8,000, this type of seal was used on all cars with the LT-1/big-block "power bulge" hood.

Aluminum tanks are unpainted and have the Harrison logo debossed in the side. Embossed in the same side is a part number, "FILL 1/2 WHEN COLD," and a manufacturing date code. The date code contains two numbers to denote the year and a letter to indicate the month, with "A" representing January, "B" representing February, and so on. Unlike earlier aluminum tanks that have only one outlet in the bottom, the tanks used in 1970–1972 have two outlets.

Brass expansion tanks are longer and thinner than their aluminum counterparts. They measure approximately 3 inches in diameter by 20 inches in length. A thin brass tag with "Harrison," a part number, and a date code stamped in is soldered to the side of the tank. The whole tank is painted semi-gloss to gloss black.

Cars that don't have an expansion tank use an RC-15 radiator cap rated at 15 psi and installed directly on the radiator. Cars with a brass expansion tank use the same cap installed on the tank. Cars with an aluminum expansion tank use an RC-26 cap, also rated at 15 psi, installed on the tank.

Cars equipped with a copper radiator or brass expansion tank used a 15-psi RC-15 radiator cap. As this original example illustrates, the cap is cadmium plated, while the center rivet is unplated brass. Original caps have a flat or slightly depressed rivet, while some reproductions have a rounded rivet.

All radiator and heater hoses are molded black rubber. Stamped-on radiator hoses in white ink are a part number, the GM logo, and several letters that are believed to be manufacturer's codes. In addition, a colored line usually runs the length of the hose. On air-conditioned big-block cars, the lower radiator hose is two pieces joined by a steel tube in the middle.

Heater hoses usually contain a GM logo in white ink. They sometimes have "DL" or "U" stamped on also. Most original hoses have three or four thin ridges running lengthwise.

All cars use SURE-TITE brand stainless-steel worm drive clamps for the radiator hoses. All applications use size-28 clamps except air-conditioned big-blocks, which use size 32 on the lower hose only. Original clamps have "SURE-TITE" in italics stamped into the band along the circumference. In addition, "WITTEK MFG. CO. CHI. U.S.A." is stamped into the worm screw's housing.

All cars use tower-style clamps for the heater hoses. The ⅝-inch heater hoses use 1¹⁄₁₆-inch clamps. This clamp has a galvanized finish and contains the size, "WITTEK MFG. CO. CHICAGO U.S.A.," and a date code stamped into the band. The first number of the date code denotes the quarter, and the following two numbers indicate the year.

The ¾-inch heater hose uses 1¼-inch clamps. These clamps have a cadmium dichromate finish that results in a translucent goldish tint, as opposed to the smaller clamps' dull silver color. The larger 1¼-inch clamps contain the manufacturer's logo and size designation but no date code. Instead, they have "DCM" stamped into the band.

Brake Master Cylinder and Related Components

All master cylinders are manufactured by Delco Moraine, are painted semi-gloss black, and contain a casting number and the Delco split circle logo on the inboard side. Non-power-assist master cylinders are casting number 5455509, and power-assist masters are casting number 5480346.

In addition to the casting number, each master contains a stamped-in two-letter application code. For 1970–1972 cars assembled through approximately mid-June 1970, this code was stamped into a flat, machined boss on the top front of the unit. Later 1972s were stamped on a flat surface by the front brake line fitting. Most masters also have a date code stamped in this area.

Most cars with power-assist brakes have "PG" stamped into the master cylinder, and most without power assist have "DC" stamped in. Some 1972s use "MK" for power-assist masters and HC or ZC for non-power assist. Very late '72s with the stamping by the front brake line fitting use the code "TG."

All masters contain two bleeder screws above the brake line ports, and two steel bail wires that hold the cover on. A small vinyl sticker with two letters is folded around one of the bail wires. This sticker is white with red letters, reading "TG"

The master cylinder used in 1970s, 1971s, and most 1972s produced during calendar year 1971 had a two-letter code stamped into the flat spot at the front top of the casting. "DC" was for manual brake master cylinders, and "PG" was for power brake masters.

for power brake cars, "YA" for 1970 through early '72 manual brake cars, and "HC" for later '72 manual brake cars.

All master cylinders use a stamped-steel, cadmium-dichromate-plated cover and rubber gasket. The cover has two domes that are not connected by a small ridge like later units. "SERVICE WITH DELCO PARTS" is stamped into one dome, while "USE DELCO SAE J 1703 BRAKE FLUID" or "SERVICE WITH SAE J 1703 BRAKE FLUID" is stamped into the other dome.

Power brake boosters, on cars so equipped, are painted gloss black and frequently have a spot of yellow or white paint somewhere. The paint is thought to be an inspection mark or an application code.

Some boosters have a Julian date code stamped in on top opposite the vacuum valve. The code contains a number corresponding to the final number of the year and three numbers denoting the day of the year. For example, a booster stamped "1134" was manufactured on the 134th day of 1971.

Air Conditioning and Heating System Components

All 1970–1972 Corvettes equipped with air conditioning utilize a model A-6 Frigidaire compressor. Compressors are painted semi-gloss black and have a green, black, and silver

foil sticker on top of the housing. The sticker contains, among other things, the compressor's model number. For 1970 and '71 454s, the model number is 5910740, and for 1972 454s it's 5910797. For 1970 and early 1971 350s, the model number is 5910741. For later 1971s, it's 5910778, and for 1972s, it's 1131002.

The air-conditioning system for all cars includes a POA valve assembly that is natural aluminum in color. The thermostatic expansion valve, the tubing crimped onto the ends of the hoses, and the manifold block that connects the hoses to the back of the compressor are also unpainted.

An unpainted, dark gray fiberglass housing covers the evaporator. There is a Harrison foil sticker on the housing, as well as a fan relay. In 1970 and '71, the relay has a cover painted gloss black with "DELCO REMY" stamped in from the inside. In 1972 the cover is zinc or cadmium plated and does not have any words stamped in.

Those 1970–1971 Corvettes with air conditioning have a vacuum-actuated valve spliced into the heater hose. When the air conditioning is on, this valve shuts off the flow of engine coolant to the heater core. The valve was not used in 1972.

The blower motors for both air-conditioned and non-air-conditioned cars are painted gloss black. Motors on air-conditioned cars have a rubber tube that extends from the motor housing to the evaporator housing. Motors on non-air-conditioned cars do not have this tube. Motors have a part number and date code stamped into their mounting flanges. The date code contains one or two numbers to denote the month and two numbers to indicate the year.

Windshield Wiper Door Mechanism, Wiper Motor, and Related Components

All 1970–1972 Corvettes have a vacuum-actuated wiper door. The door is moved up and down by a vacuum motor mounted on the upper right side of the firewall. In 1970 the vacuum connection nipple protruding from the front of

Engine compartment details from a low-mileage, unrestored 1970. Note the correct master cylinder cap and emissions decal and the correct component finishes.

Passenger-side firewall details from an unrestored 1970. All components and component finishes shown are correct.

Note the many different surface finishes, hose markings, and wire routing in this correctly restored 1971 engine compartment. Sloppy use of sealant and roughness of fiberglass is very typical of factory appearance.

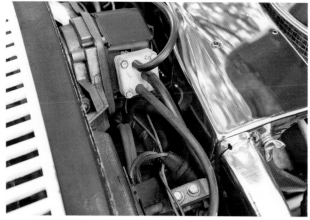

Cars from 1970 through mid-1971 were fitted with a five-port windshield washer pump. Later 1971 through 1972 cars got the three-port pump shown here. Original pumps do not have a part number stamped on the lower passenger side, while service replacement pumps do.

the motor is straight, while in 1971–1972 it has a 90-degree bend. All vacuum motors are cadmium dichromate plated.

The vacuum motor is controlled by a vacuum valve mounted to the upper left side of the firewall for all 1970 and some '71 cars. For some 1971 and all '72 cars, this valve is mounted on the right side inner wheelwell. As with the vacuum motor, the valve is plated cadmium dichromate.

The wiper motor and windshield washer pump are an integral assembly for all 1970–1972 Corvettes. The motors are natural die-cast silver, and the washer pump is white

plastic. A black plastic cover goes over the wiper motor. (Refer to Appendix P for wiper motor part numbers.)

The washer pump utilized for 1970 and '71 models assembled through approximately mid-March 1971 has five ports. Cars assembled after mid-March 1971 use pumps with three ports. The two additional ports found on the earlier pumps are for the headlight washer nozzles. Those 1971s assembled after December 1970 do not have the headlamp washer system, so from approximately December 1970 to mid-March 1971 there are two unused ports on the washer

The only year buyers could have an LT-1 engine and air conditioning was 1972. When the two were combined, the base engine's tachometer face had a 5,600-rpm redline, instead of the normal 6,500-rpm tach used with LT-1s. It was thought that the lower redline would discourage drivers from hitting engine speeds that could detach the air-conditioner compressor's belt.

1970–1972

pumps. The two ports are connected to each other with a short length of hose.

For 1970 Corvettes without air conditioning, the windshield washer fluid reservoir is mounted on the rear, engine compartment side of the right inner wheelwell. The reservoir is rigid white plastic and does not have any writing. All 1971 and '72 cars have a similar reservoir mounted in the same location, but these include a long fill neck that extends slightly below the fender lip. All air-conditioned cars use an off-white flexible plastic bag to hold washer fluid. This bag is mounted on the lower left side firewall.

Air Injection Reactor System and other Emissions Components

An air injection reactor (AIR) emission control system is used in most 1970–1972 Corvettes. Engines fitted with AIR include all LT1s, LS6s, 1972 bases, and LS5s. In addition, all Corvettes delivered new in California got an AIR system. The AIR system includes black-cadmium-plated tubes that thread into each of the four runners on both exhaust manifolds. Therefore all AIR-equipped cars have four holes drilled and tapped into each manifold.

Corvettes not originally equipped with AIR systems have exhaust manifolds that are not drilled and tapped. Possible exceptions are 1970 LS5s made in approximately the last three weeks of March 1970. Exhaust manifolds on LS5s made during this time may have drilled and tapped holes closed off with steel pipe-thread plugs with recessed squares for a driving tool.

The AIR pump body is die-cast aluminum and natural in color. A rough-textured, sand-cast plate painted semi-gloss black covers the back of the pump. Original covers have "7801149" cast in.

All pumps contain a centrifugal filter behind the pulley. A white plastic filter was used for 1970 through early '72 cars, and a black plastic filter was utilized thereafter.

Small-block engines use a steel spacer between the front pump pulley and the centrifugal filter. Big-blocks do not use a spacer. The spacer is zinc or silver cadmium plated and the

An original AIR injection pump. The finned centrifugal filter behind the pump pulley was opaque white in 1970 through early 1972. Later 1972s had a black centrifugal filter, as shown here.

pulley is gray phosphate plated or painted semi-gloss black. Pulleys used on small-blocks have the part number 3917234 stamped in, while those used on big-blocks have part number 3925522 stamped in.

Most pumps are date coded, though the date can be difficult to see with the pump installed. It is stamped into a boss on the rear underside of the body. The sequence may begin with a letter to indicate the assembly plant or specific line. Then one or three numbers indicate the day of the year on the Julian calendar. Earlier dates (prior to the 100th day) may start with two zeros or may not. For example, a pump assembled on the fifth day of the year may be stamped "005" or simply "5." A fourth (or second) number follows to denote the last digit of the year. This is followed by a number indicating the shift and a letter indicating the model of the pump.

The lower pump bracket is painted Chevrolet Engine Orange, and the upper bracket is painted semi-gloss black. For small-blocks, the lower bracket is cast and contains the number "3923214." For big-blocks, the lower bracket is stamped steel.

The diverter valve body is natural in color, while the diaphragm cover and check valves are cadmium dichromate. The diaphragm cover has a round sticker with a two-letter broadcast code printed on it. The diverter valve muffler is plated gray phosphate. The diverter valve part number is stamped into the valve below the muffler. Check valves have a part number stamped into their center ridges.

Hoses connecting the various parts of the AIR system are molded black, and hose clamps are tower style. Clamps have a galvanized finish and contain the size, "WITTEK MFG. CO. CHICAGO U.S.A.," and a date code stamped into the band. The first number of the date code denotes the quarter. The following two numbers indicate the year.

The following 1970–1972 Corvettes were originally equipped with an AIR system: all LS6s, all LT1s, all 1972

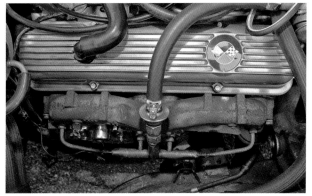

Passenger-side AIR plumbing details in a 1972 LT-1.

LS5s, and all 1972 ZQ3 base engine cars fitted with option NB2 (exhaust emission control), which was required on all cars delivered new in California. All other 1970–1972 Corvettes do not have an AIR system.

Those 1970 Corvettes equipped with option NA9 (California emissions equipment) and all 1971–1972 Corvettes are fitted with an evaporative control system. This system includes a black carbon-filled canister mounted to the lower left inner wheelwell. One hose runs from the canister to a fitting on the positive crankcase ventilation (PCV) valve, and another goes to a steel line attached to the chassis.

All 1970–1972 Corvettes have a PCV valve located in the left valve cover. The valve has a part number stamped into it. For those engines equipped with a Holley carburetor, the PCV valve is part number CV746C, and for those equipped with a Rochester carburetor, it is number CV736C.

All 1970–1972 Corvettes have a transmission controlled spark (TCS) solenoid. On 1970 and 1972 small-block engines, it is attached to an intake manifold stud toward the passenger-side rear of the carburetor. On 1970 big-blocks, it is on a stud toward the passenger-side front of the carburetor, and on 1972 big-blocks, it is mounted to the right coil bracket bolt.

All 1971s have the TCS integrated into a throttle position solenoid, and the two together are called a combined emissions control (CEC). The CEC is mounted with a bracket to the forward driver side of the carburetor base.

All 1972s have an antidiesel solenoid mounted to the carburetor base with a bracket. The bracket is cadmium dichromate plated, and the solenoid housing is silver cadmium plated.

All 1970–1972 Corvettes have an emissions label glued to the upper left area of the firewall. The labels are either white or yellow. They contain engine tune-up specifications as well as information about the car's emission control systems.

The radiator and fan shroud in an unrestored, original 1970. Early 1970s, including this example, were fitted with three pieces of sealing foam on top of the shroud. Later 1970 through 1972 cars with the standard small-block hood used a single piece of foam on top. Those 1970 through mid-1971 cars with the LT-1 and big-block hood used a three-piece seal, while later 1971s and all 1972s with the "power bulge" hood used a taller, triangular, one-piece seal.

Engine Compartment Brackets, Latches, Wiring, and Related Components

The firewall, underside of the hood, and engine compartment side of the inner wheelwells are painted semi-gloss black. The wheel side of the front and rear inner wheelwells are also painted semi-gloss black, though coverage is usually sparse. In addition, the rear areas of the wheel sides normally have some undercoating.

All 1970s and some '71s have engine compartment wiring harnesses and vacuum hoses bundled together in a circle. Some '71s and all '72s have the harnesses and adjacent hoses bundled together in a row, so rather than forming a circle, they are flat. The harnesses and hoses are held to each other with black plastic tie wraps.

All vacuum hose is color coded with an ink stripe that runs the length of the hose. Larger hoses have a green, red, or yellow striping, while smaller hoses usually have a white stripe.

All 1970–1972 Corvettes equipped with a big-block have a small oil pressure line bracket on the left side of the engine block. A steel tube goes from the brass block fitting to a junction at this bracket. A black plastic tube continues up to the oil pressure gauge.

All 1970–1972 small-block-equipped cars utilize black plastic tubing that goes directly from the engine block fitting to the oil pressure gauge. The plastic line has tiny white lettering and is fastened at both ends with brass fittings.

All cars have a horn relay mounted to the inner wheelwell. The 1970 relays have a zinc-plated cover with "DELCO REMY, MADE IN THE USA," and four letters stamped in from the inside. The cover sits on a black plastic base with a silver-cadmium-plated metal bracket attached for mounting.

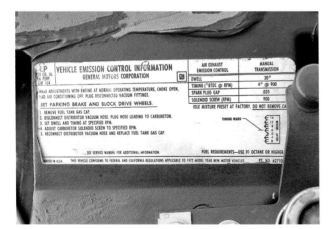

All 1970–1972 Corvettes came with one or two emission control information decals on the driver-side firewall adjacent to the male hood latch. The specific label used depended on a number of different factors, including the engine and transmission combination the car came with.

This beautifully restored 1971 LS5 engine compartment illustrates the complexity and richness of component finishes. Note the subtle differences in the level of gloss of painted surfaces and the paint color. The windshield washer pump should be white, not black.

This 1972 LT-1 engine compartment is unrestored and entirely original.

The 1971 horn relays are the same as '70 units, except the mounting bracket is black plastic and is part of the base rather than a separate metal piece.

The 1972 horn relay has a short, squared-off silver cadmium cover with nothing stamped in. The plain cover sits on a black plastic base and for mounting relies on a black plastic tab that forms part of the black plastic base.

All 1970 Corvettes have two horns, a high and a low note. The high note is part number 9000246, and it mounts on the driver side. The low note is part number 9000245, and it mounts on the passenger side. In 1971 and '72, only one horn is installed. It is part number 9000245 in 1971 and part number 9000032 in 1972.

Horns have the last three digits of the part number and a manufacturing date code stamped into flat areas near the sound opening. The date code contains a number denoting the year, a letter denoting the month (with "A" representing January, "B" representing February, and so on), and another number indicating the week. For example, a horn stamped "1D2" was made the second week of April 1971. Each horn is attached to a mounting bracket, and the whole assembly is painted semi-gloss black. (Refer to Appendix O for horn relay and horn numbers.)

Hood hinges are silver cadmium plated and usually have both body color and underhood black overspray on them. Hinges are usually fastened by black-phosphate-plated indented hex-head bolts.

The hood support is silver cadmium plated. The 1970 and '71 supports have two sections that telescope together as the hood is lowered. The 1972 supports have two hinged sections that fold as the hood is lowered.

The hood latches are black phosphate plated and mount with black-phosphate-plated hardware. The driver-side male latch has the hood release cable attached with a brass barrel cable stop that utilizes a hex bolt to lock the stop to the cable. The cable is inside a spiral-wound metal sheath.

The female hood latches were plated with black phosphate and installed after the underside of the hood was painted.

Another cable connects the two female latches mounted to the underside of the hood. This cable is inside a black nylon sheath, and its ends are secured to the latches with small clevis pins fitted with flat washers and cotter pins.

1970–1972 CHASSIS
Chassis

The 1970–1971 Corvette chassis are painted semi-gloss black. Chassis for automatic-transmission-equipped cars have a removable, bolt-on center crossmember, while standard-transmission-equipped cars have a welded-on center crossmember. Also, cars with automatics do not have a clutch cross shaft tower welded on top of the chassis behind the left front wheel as standard transmission cars do.

A pair of one-inch-high chassis part number sequences is painted in white on the frame with a stencil. One sequence is the part number from A. O. Smith (the company that fabricated the chassis for GM). The other sequence is the Chevrolet part number.

A manufacturing date code is stenciled on the rail as well. The date contains one or two numbers representing the month, one or two numbers indicating the day, and two numbers denoting the year.

The stencil numbers and date code usually appear on the outside of the right frame rail and are usually upside down.

All 1970–1972 Corvettes have a serial number stamped into the chassis in two locations. It is typically found in the left rail slightly forward of the number-four body mount bracket. It is also typically found on the left rear kickup above the wheel area, slightly forward of the number-three body mount bracket.

Steel shims are frequently utilized at body mount points to make up for irregularities in fit. If present, shims are usually taped to the body mount bracket with 1½-inch masking tape. The number of shims needed at each body mount bracket is typically written on the chassis adjacent to the bracket with a green or white grease crayon. Unlike earlier cars, this number is usually an actual number rather than slash marks.

Body mounts are not made from rubber as in 1967 and older Corvettes. Instead, they are thick aluminum discs that get sandwiched between the body and the chassis's body mount bracket.

Front Suspension

Upper and lower front control arms are painted semi-gloss to gloss black. Ball joints are installed after the arms are painted and are not painted. Crushed steel rivets (not bolts) hold ball joints on and are also natural in finish.

Control arm cross shafts are painted semi-gloss black on some cars and unpainted on others. Cars with painted cross shafts typically have control arm bushing retention washers and bolts that are also painted semi-gloss black. Cars with unpainted cross shafts typically have gray-phosphate-plated retention washers and black-phosphate-plated bolts.

All 1970–1972 front coil springs were unpainted. They came with a green paper tag containing a two-letter broadcast code and a GM part number wrapped around one of the coils. This is an original tag in a 1970.

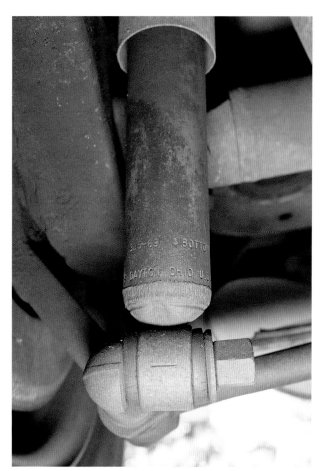

Original shocks have various things stamped into the lower tube along the bottom, including the words "DELCO REMY PLIACELL, DAYTON OHIO U.S.A.," and a date code. The date code consists of three numbers representing the day of the year and two numbers denoting the year. In this example, the date code of "335-69" indicates that the shock absorber was made on the 335th day of 1969.

Front coil springs are natural in finish and sometimes have an irregular bluish cast from the manufacturing process. A green paper sticker contains two black letters indicating the spring's broadcast code (application), as well as a black GM part number.

Front and rear shock absorbers are manufactured by Delco and are oil hydraulic, not gas filled. They are painted semi-gloss gray and have "DELCO REMY PLIACELL" and a date code stamped in around the bottom. The Julian date code contains three numbers indicating the day and two numbers denoting the year. In addition, there is a small paper sticker with a two-letter broadcast code on the side of the shock.

The front upper shock mount rubber bushings are unpainted black rubber. The top upper bushing is larger in diameter than the bottom upper bushing, and the upper shock washer is gray phosphate plated. The front lower shock mount rubber bushings and both rear shock mount bushings are integral and are therefore painted along with the shock.

All 1970–1972 big-block Corvettes and all small-block-equipped cars with optional F-41 suspension utilize a $^{15}\!/_{16}$-inch front sway bar. All small-blocks not equipped with F-41 utilize a ¾-inch bar. Some cars have a semi-gloss black sway bar, while others have a natural, unpainted finish bar.

Bushings mounting the front sway bar to the chassis, as well as bushings in the end links, are unpainted black rubber. Stamped-steel brackets painted semi-gloss black hold the bar to the chassis.

End link bolts are zinc plated 5/16-24 SAE fine thread and have the manufacturer's logo "WB" on their heads. End link spacers are zinc plated, have a split seam, and typically have "K" or "C" stamped in.

Steering Box and Steering Linkage

All 1970–1972 Corvettes use a cast steering gear that is usually natural in color, though some are painted semi-gloss black. The box cover is cast aluminum and is retained by three black-oxide-plated hex-head bolts. A daub of yellow or blue paint is frequently seen on top of the box.

A forged pitman arm links the steering box to the relay rod. The pitman arm is natural in color and is often seen with a blue or green daub of paint. The steering relay rod and idler arm are typically natural finish. Both parts are forged and tend to have a bluish gray tint. Original idler arms do not have grease fittings.

Tie rod ends are natural finish and also typically have a bluish gray color cast. Daubs of yellow paint are often seen on tie rod ends. Tie rod end sleeves are painted semi-gloss black. Tie rod end clamps have two reinforcing ridges around their circumference and are sometimes painted semi-gloss black and sometimes left unpainted.

Outer tie rod ends can install into either of two holes in the steering knuckles. Cars equipped with standard, nonpower steering have the outer tie rod ends installed into the rear holes, while cars equipped with power steering have

The steering box was usually unpainted in earlier cars and painted semi-gloss black in later cars. Two inspection marks made with yellow paint are commonly seen. The 1972 boxes are sometimes seen with "CM" stamped in yellow.

The date code for a rear bearing carrier made on April 18, 1971, for example, would read "D 18 1."

All 1970–1972 big-blocks have a rear stabilizer bar. The bar is 9/16-inch diameter and may be painted semi-gloss black or unpainted. It mounts to the chassis with semi-gloss black stamped-steel brackets. At each end, the bar has a semi-gloss black link bracket that attaches to brackets bolted to the trailing arms. The brackets on the trailing arms have plating that is sometimes called pickling. It results in a brownish olive color. These brackets attach to the trailing arm via bolts that thread into small, unpainted steel plates that slip into the rear of the arms.

Rear camber adjustment rods (also called strut rods) are usually natural and often have a bluish gray tint. Some rods are painted semi-gloss black or are partially painted during the undercarriage "blackout" process. Original rods have 1½-inch-diameter ends, while 1974 and newer rods have 1¾-inch-diameter ends.

The outboard ends of the camber adjustment rods are held to the rear wheel bearing carriers with forged L-shaped pins that also serve as lower mounts for the rear shock absorbers. These pins, which are sometimes called rear shock brackets, contain a raised part number.

The inboard ends of the camber adjustment rods attach to a semi-gloss black bracket with special bolts. These bolts have integral off-center washers that, when rotated, move the rods in or out and thus allow for rear wheel camber adjustment. The camber adjustment bolts are usually silver cadmium plated, though they may be black phosphate plated instead.

Rear wheel toe adjustment is set with the use of shims placed on either side of the trailing arms where they mount to the chassis. The adjusting shims are unpainted, rectangular pieces of steel that vary in thickness. In 1970 the shims have equally sized holes at each end, and when installed, one end protrudes from the chassis pocket where the end of the trailing arm resides. The last few hundred 1970s produced and all 1971–1972 cars use a different shim. This second design has a slot in one end that slips over the trailing arm mount bolt. Rather than protruding from the chassis pocket, the other ends of shims are rotated upward, so their holes align with corresponding holes in the chassis. A long cotter pin passes through the stacks of shims on both sides of the trailing arm and through the hole in the chassis.

Rear axle shafts (often called half shafts) are made from forged ends welded to extruded steel tubes. The axle shafts are natural, with the tube being shiny silver and the ends being dull gray. In 1972 shafts sometimes have a faint "alligator" pattern in the tube. Slashes, or green, blue, or white paint, are sometimes seen on axle shaft tubes.

U-joints do not have grease fittings and do have raised part numbers on the body. They are natural and tend to have that faint bluish tint that is characteristic of forged parts.

The outboard axle shaft U-joints are pressed into a flange that is natural in color. The flange is held to the rear wheel

them in the forward holes. On those cars equipped with power steering, the unused steering knuckle hole is plugged with an aluminum plug inserted from the bottom.

On those cars so equipped, the power steering control valve and hydraulic cylinder are painted semi-gloss black. The nut and washers retaining the hydraulic cylinder's ram to the frame bracket are zinc plated. The frame bracket may be painted semi-gloss black or unpainted. Original power steering hoses typically have longitudinal ridges around their entire circumference, while later replacements don't.

Rear Suspension

All 1970–1972 Corvettes equipped with standard suspension utilize a nine-leaf rear spring. Cars equipped with optional F-41 suspension utilize a seven-leaf spring. All springs are painted light gray and have black plastic liners between the leaves. Nine-leaf springs do not have a liner between leaf six and leaf seven (with the bottom leaf being number one).

The center rear spring mount bracket is painted semi-gloss black. The four bolts retaining the spring to the differential typically have the manufacturer's logo "WB" on their heads and are either black phosphate or zinc plated. The outer spring bolts and nuts are usually black phosphate plated, and the washers are typically natural.

Rear trailing arms are painted semi-gloss to gloss black. Rear wheel bearing carriers (also called spindle supports) are natural and have a part number and date code cast in. The date code has a letter representing the month, with "A" for January, "B" for February, and so on, one or two numbers for the day, and one number for the final digit of the year.

bearing carrier by four bolts that are usually black phosphate plated. The bolts are prevented from turning out by two pairs of French locks, the tabs of which are bent over to contact the bolt heads. The French locks are zinc plated and typically have only one of the two tabs adjacent to each bolt bent over.

The inboard axle shaft U-joints are held to the differential output yokes by one of two methods. Forged caps and bolts are used on Corvettes equipped with a 454 engine, and U-shaped strap clamps with nuts are used on cars equipped with a 350 engine.

Front Wheel Assemblies

Front spindles and steering knuckles are natural and tend to have a bluish tint to their gray color. In addition, the lower portions of the spindles are frequently seen with orange or white paint, as though the bottoms of the spindles were dipped into it.

Original front brake backing plates are zinc plated and then chromate dipped. This results in varying finishes, ranging from gold with a faint rainbow of other colors throughout to a dull silver with only a trace of yellowish chromate coloring. Well-preserved original backing plates typically appear dull silver, probably because the chromate dip deteriorates over time.

Front brake caliper support brackets are plated silver cadmium or cadmium dichromate, which results in a translucent gold color with varying degrees of other colors present in a rainbowlike pattern.

Cars equipped with option ZR1 or ZR2 have a heavy-duty brake package. This package includes front calipers that use two pins to hold the pads instead of the standard one, extra front caliper supports, semi-metallic brake pads, heat insulators on the face of all caliper pistons, and a proportioning valve mounted beneath the master cylinder.

Front brake calipers are painted semi-gloss black and frequently have blue or white daubs of paint on the side. Painting is done before the caliper halves are machined. Therefore machined surfaces are unpainted. Bleeder screws are zinc plated and remain unpainted.

Caliper hoses are black rubber with gold-iridite-plated end hardware. Federally mandated DOT specifications are written on the hose in red ink. In addition, a red longitudinal stripe on the hose makes it easier to see if it is twisted. Original hoses typically have raised longitudinal ridges around the entire circumference, while later replacements are typically smooth.

Front brake rotors are natural in finish. The front wheel bearing carrier (also called a hub) is riveted to the rotor disc.

Rear Wheel Assemblies

As with the fronts, original rear brake backing plates are zinc plated and then chromate dipped. This results in varying finishes, ranging from gold with a faint rainbow of other

colors throughout to a dull silver with only a trace or yellowish chromate coloring. Well-preserved original backing plates typically appear dull silver, probably because the chromate dip deteriorates over time.

Rear brake caliper support brackets are natural and hence a dull gray. On occasion they are painted flat to semi-flat black.

Rear brake calipers are painted semi-gloss black and frequently have blue or white daubs of paint on the side. Painting is done before the caliper halves are machined, and therefore machined surfaces are unpainted. Bleeder screws are zinc plated and remain unpainted.

Rear brake rotors are natural in finish. They are riveted to the rear spindle, which is pressed into the rear wheel bearing carrier. For servicing the park brake assembly or the rear wheel bearings, the rivets are often drilled out. The wheel lug nuts retain the rotor in the absence of the rivets.

Transmission

Automatic-equipped 1970–1972 Corvettes utilize a Turbo Hydra-matic 400 transmission. The main case and the tail housing are both cast aluminum with a natural finish. The fluid pan is stamped steel and is also natural.

Automatic transmissions contain an identification plate on the right side. The plate has two alphanumeric sequences stamped in. The bottom sequence is the car's serial number, and the top sequence is called a production code. The first two numbers of the code indicate the model year. Next comes a letter that denotes the car model (in our case, Corvette) and the engine. This is followed by three numbers that represent the day the transmission was assembled.

The transmission assembly date is a modified version of the Julian calendar system. The three numbers represent the day of the year, but unlike most applications of the Julian calendar system in dating Corvette components, with transmissions the count does not begin with the first day of the year. Instead, for 1970 Corvettes, it begins with January 1, 1969, and continues sequentially through calendar year 1970. Similarly, for 1971 models, it begins on January 1, 1970, and continues through calendar year 1971. And for 1972 models, it begins on January 1, 1971, and continues through calendar year 1972.

This dating system sounds confusing, but it's easy once you get the hang of it. For example, in the production code 71Y018, "71" represents the 1971 model year, "Y" represents the application code (1971 Corvette with a 454 engine), and "018" represents the eighteenth day from when the count begins. Remember, the count begins on January 1 of the preceding year, so this transmission was assembled on January 18, 1970. Had that same transmission been assembled on January 18, 1971, the code would read, "71Y383," with January 18, 1971, being 383 days after the count for the '71 model year began.

The application codes for 1970–1972 Corvettes include "K" for all small-blocks, "S" for 1972s with 454 engines, and the aforementioned "Y" for 1970–1971s with 454 engines.

Four-speed manual transmissions have cast-aluminum main cases, side covers, and tail housings that are natural in color. A steel tag with a part number is affixed to the transmission with one of the side cover bolts.

Two alphanumeric sequences are stamped into the main case on a vertical surface at the front of the right side. One of these sequences is a derivative of the car's serial number. The other is a production code and the date the transmission was originally assembled.

The production code begins with a letter to indicate the source for the transmission. All Corvette four-speeds were obtained from Muncie, which is represented by the letter "P." This is followed by a number representing the last digit of the model year. Next is a letter indicating the month of production, followed by two numbers denoting the day of the month. Various letters are not used in denoting the month, so refer to this chart when determining assembly date:

A   January
B   February
C   March
D   April
E   May
H   June
K   July
M   August
P   September
R   October
S   November
T   December

The final character in the production code is a letter commonly called a suffix code. This letter indicates which of the three available four-speeds the unit is. The suffix code "A" indicates a wide-ratio M-20 with a 2.52:1 first-gear ratio. "B" indicates a close-ratio M-21 with a 2.20:1 first-gear ratio. "C" denotes a close-ratio M-22 "heavy-duty" transmission, which also has a 2.20:1 first-gear ratio.

An example of a four-speed transmission code is "P1D18A." This identifies an M-20 wide-ratio Muncie four-speed assembled on April 18, 1971.

Differential and Driveshaft

All 1970–1972 Corvettes are equipped with a Posi-Traction limited-slip differential. The differential case and cover were made from cast iron and not painted or coated with anything, so both are natural colored and appear dull silvery gray.

A plastic triangular tag is attached to the differential by means of the square-head oil fill plug. The tag is red with "USE LIMITED SLIP DIFF. LUBRICANT ONLY" in

white lettering. The fill plug is natural and has a large "W" cast into the square.

The front input yoke and side output yokes are forgings that are natural in color. Because they are forged, they have a somewhat smoother surface than the case and cover and tend to have a slight bluish tint to their dull gray color.

Differential cases and covers both have casting numbers and a casting date that includes a letter for the month (with "A" representing January, "B" representing February, and so on), one or two numbers indicating the day of the month, and one number indicating the last digit of the year.

In addition to the cast-in dates, all cases have a stamped-in production code. The production code is on the bottom rear edge of the case, adjacent to where it meets the cover. In 1970 the code begins with a number that indicates the assembly shift that built the unit. This is followed by a three-letter code indicating the gear ratio. Next comes a modified Julian date code that includes one or two numbers for the month, one or two numbers for the day, and two numbers for the year. The final character in the 1970 production code is a letter that indicates the specific plant that built the differential.

For 1971 and 1972, the differential production code begins with two letters to indicate the gear ratio. This is followed by a single letter denoting the assembly plant. Then come one, two, or three numbers representing the day the unit was assembled. After this comes a single letter indicating the source for the Posi-Traction unit (which was not necessarily the company that assembled the differential). The final number in the sequence represents the assembly shift that built the unit. (Refer to Appendix E for differential gear ratio codes.)

The transmission and differential are connected by a driveshaft made from extruded steel tubing welded at each

All differential housings were stamped with a production code and a date of assembly on the bottom edge, where the housing meets the rear cover. In this example, the stamping "1 CAV 12 11 69 W" translates as follows: "1" tells us that this differential was built during the first shift of the day. "CAV" indicates a 1970 Posi-Traction differential with a 3.08:1 gear ratio. The numbers "12 11 69" indicate that this unit was assembled on December 11, 1969. "W" reveals that the Warren Motive plant built it.

end to a forged universal joint coupling. As with the axle shafts, the driveshaft is natural in color. The center tube portion is bright silver, with longitudinal extrusion lines sometimes visible, and the ends are dull silvery gray with a slight bluish hue at times.

A part number stenciled on the driveshaft tube in yellow or white paint is sometimes seen. One or two green circumferential stripes on the tube and daubs of paint in various colors on the forged ends are sometimes seen as well.

Exhaust System

All 1970–1972 Corvettes use an undercar, carbon steel exhaust system manufactured by Walker for Chevrolet. All cars equipped with a big-block engine or an LT1 engine utilize 2½-inch exhaust pipes. All other cars utilize 2-inch pipes.

Even though LT1 engines get 2½-inch pipes, they still use the same 2-inch outlet exhaust manifolds as other small-blocks. This is accomplished by swaging the 2½-inch front engine pipes down to 2 inches at their ends.

Mufflers are galvanized on the exterior and have an embossed "W" to represent the manufacturer. At the rear of each muffler is one welded-on bracket to which the rear hangar bolts. Mufflers are welded to the intermediate exhaust pipe, not clamped. 2½-inch intermediate pipes are flattened somewhat where they pass underneath the rear camber adjustment rod bracket for additional ground clearance. Two-inch pipes are not flattened.

A rectangular, chrome-plated carbon steel exhaust tip is clamped to each muffler. Two different tips are used in 1970–1972. Tips used on 1970s assembled through approximately mid-July 1970 have a weld bead where the rectangular portion is fastened to the flat back portion. The underside of the rectangular portion does not have a weld bead or anything stamped in. It is smooth and flat.

After mid-July 1970, a second tip began to be used. The second design is the same as the first, except it has a weld seam on the underside of the rectangular section. Either the first or second design, or one of each, is seen on very late 1970s (cars made after mid-July 1970) and those '71s assembled through approximately early May 1971. Those 1971s assembled after approximately early May 1971 and all 1972s have the second exhaust tip design.

Fuel Lines, Brake Lines, and Miscellaneous Chassis and Underbody Components

All 1970–1972 fuel lines run along, and at times through, the right chassis rail. All cars except those equipped with an LT1 engine have two fuel lines. One supplies fuel from the tank to the carburetor, and the other is a return line.

In addition to the one or two fuel lines on the right side of the chassis, all 1971s, all '72s, and those '70s equipped with NA9 (evaporative emission control, which was required

The driveshaft was made from an extruded steel tube that was not painted. A stenciled part number was applied and is still visible on this extremely original 1970.

for all cars delivered new in California) have a vapor return line on the left side of the chassis.

Fuel lines are galvanized carbon steel. Black rubber fuel hose connects the lines to the tank and the fuel pump. Zinc-chromate-plated spring clamps are usually used to secure the hose to its line. Exceptions include hoses on the fuel return line in 1970 and most of 1971. These use small galvanized tower-style clamps.

Brake lines are galvanized carbon steel. Brake line end fittings are brass. Fittings at the master cylinder are often seen with red or blue dye, which was probably used to denote the two different sizes of fittings. In addition, daubs of yellow paint are sometimes seen on the fittings at junction blocks.

Various heat shields are affixed to the underside of the body to help insulate the passenger compartment from engine and exhaust system heat. A sheet steel shield, which is gray phosphate plated, is mounted on the lower vertical area of the firewall on both sides. In addition, 1970s assembled through approximately February or March 1970 and equipped with a big-block engine have two similar shields underneath the floor, below the seat area.

All cars are fitted with transmission tunnel insulation. A semi-rigid foil-wrapped blanket in the shape of the tunnel is fastened above the transmission with clips riveted to the underbody.

All cars have a thick black foam insulating pad attached to the underbody above the engine's bell housing. A thick white foam pad is fastened to the underbody on each side of the car, just forward of the doors.

A variety of steel plates are fastened to the underbody to mount components in the passenger compartment. These components include the battery, seats, and jack hold-down clips. The plates are painted semi-gloss black and are retained by unpainted aluminum rivets.

Chapter 3
1973-1977

1973-1977 EXTERIOR
Body Fiberglass and Body Paint

All 1973–1977 Corvette body panels are made from press-molded fiberglass, with the exception of 1973–1977 front bumper covers and 1974–1977 rear bumper covers, which are urethane. The fiberglass panels are smooth on both sides and are very dark gray.

All 1973–1977 cars were painted with acrylic lacquer. Factory paint is generally smooth and shiny, though some orange peel is evident throughout. Roughness and poor coverage is fairly typical along the very bottom edges of body panels. Overall paint quality was relatively poor, and as consumers became more demanding, the factory made a greater effort to eliminate flaws before the cars were shipped. As a result, many mid-1970s Corvettes left the St. Louis factory with considerable paint touchups.

Clear coat was not used by the factory, even with metallic colors. Because clear coat was not used, metallics tend to be slightly mottled or blotchy.

Roof structure details in an unrestored 1975 coupe. Note the rough finish of the fiberglass and body paint in this area, which is typical of normal factory production.

Only 1,664 Corvettes were painted Bright Green in 1975, the only year this color was offered.

This Corvette Orange 1974 is one of 32,028 coupes made that year.

The first year Corvettes did not come with chrome-plated front bumpers was 1973. Federally mandated standards led to the use of a urethane-covered, energy-absorbing bumper assembly that could withstand impacts of five miles per hour without significant damage.

An original 1973–1974 cloisonné nose emblem. A similar emblem with a chrome ring around the outside and "CORVETTE" on the red sunburst was used in 1975–1976.

Front Bumpers

All 1973–1977 Corvettes are fitted with impact-absorbing front bumper assemblies. The cover is made from urethane painted body color. A flex additive is mixed with the paint used on the bumper cover to discourage the paint from cracking. The flex additive often causes the paint on the bumper to be a slightly different shade than the paint on the rest of the car.

The remainder of the bumper assembly, which is covered by the urethane piece, is comprised of several steel components painted semi-gloss black. Black-phosphate- or silver-cadmium-plated hex-head bolts are used to retain the underlying bumper structure to the chassis.

The 1975–1977 Corvette front bumpers were redesigned to include two black rubber-tipped protrusions on either side of the license plate area. The underlying energy-absorbing bumper assembly was modified in 1975. It went from an extruded bolt system to a collapsing cone design, which was in use on other GM vehicles.

Front Grille Area, Parking Lamps, and Front License Plate Area

Corvettes delivered new in states that required a front license plate have two front grille sections, while cars delivered in states that didn't require a front plate have three grille sections. In states requiring only rear license plates, the center grille was placed inside the car for dealer installation. This center grille matches the two outer grilles. Cars delivered new in states requiring two license plates got a front license plate mounting assembly instead of the center grille.

In 1973 the front grille assemblies are made from die-cast pot metal. They are painted semi-gloss black, with the leading edges of the horizontal bars chrome plated. In 1974 they are made from die-cast aluminum instead of pot metal and are painted entirely semi-flat black with no chrome accents.

For all 1973–1977 Corvettes, the front parking lamp housings are mounted in the front grilles. In 1973 the park

This remarkably well-preserved 1977 has traveled a little more than 31,000 miles and is still in the hands of its original purchaser.

The final year for the third-generation Corvette's notchback styling was 1977.

All 1973–1977 front-side marker lamp lenses were amber, with "SAE AP2 3 Y" and a manufacturing logo molded in.

lamp lenses are made from clear plastic with silver painted horizontal lines. In 1974–1977 they have black-painted horizontal lines. All years have amber bulbs.

Rectangular side marker lamps are used at all four corners in 1973–1977. The lamp housings, which can be seen only from behind the body panels, are made from die-cast aluminum in 1973s and some early '74s. Later '74s and subsequent years have plastic-bodied side marker lamps. All front side marker lamps have amber lenses, while rears have red lenses.

On those 1973–1975 cars so equipped, front license plate brackets are painted semi-gloss black and are held on by four black oxide Phillips oval-head screws with integral washers. During 1976 the design of the front license plate bracket changed. It is held by six screws instead of four. For all years, a small rubber bumper is inserted in a hole toward the bottom center of the bracket, and two white plastic nuts insert into square holes in the upper corners.

A stainless-steel license plate frame (two frames in cars delivered to states requiring two plates) was in the luggage compartment when the car was new. In addition, a small brown paper bag marked "UNIT NUMBER 3875313" across the top, "LICENSE ATTACHING" on one side, and "REAR PLATE PARTS" on the other, came in the car originally. In it were four large cadmium-plated, slotted pan-head screws for the front and rear license plates.

Corvettes in 1977 got a lot of interior changes, but the exterior is nearly identical to the year prior.

1973–1977

All 1973–1977 Corvettes came with Guide "power beam" headlamp bulbs.

All 1973–1976 Corvettes came with this fender vent and Stingray emblem. The emblem is held in place by adhesive and four long studs that pass through holes in the fender. These studs are for correctly positioning the emblem and did not get nuts. A later GM service replacement has shorter studs than the original Stingray emblem and a groove cut into the base below the dot in the letter "i."

Front Headlamps and Headlamp Bezels

All four headlamp bulbs in 1973–1977 were made by Guide and feature a Guide "power beam" logo in the glass. This logo is a circle with the word "POWER" above it and the word "BEAM" below it.

Very early 1973s, assembled through approximately December 1972, may have headlamp bezels made from die-cast aluminum. Later '73s and all 1974–1977 cars have bezels made from fiberglass. All bezels are painted body color. Paint on the bezels is usually not as shiny or smooth as it is on the body.

A cadmium-dichromate-plated vacuum actuator is mounted behind each headlamp assembly. Original actuators have a ¼-inch diameter hose connection tube that extends about ⁹⁄₁₆ inch from the actuator body before its 90-degree bend. Replacement actuators have a ⁵⁄₁₆-inch diameter tube

that extends about ⅜ inch from the body before turning 90 degrees. A translucent red ink marking is normally found on each actuator, adjacent to the tube. A red-striped hose connects to the back of each actuator, and a green-striped hose connects to the front. The vacuum hoses normally don't have any clamps, but some cars may have left the factory with spring clamps.

Front Fenders

Front fenders in 1973–1977 got a redesigned vent area, which features a molded-in recess in the fiberglass. In 1973–1976 both fenders have an emblem reading "Stingray" above the fender vents. The emblems are chrome, with the thin stepped

Headlamp actuators and related hoses. White, red, yellow, and green lines on hoses help identify their routing and function. Black vinyl tape and plastic cable ties were used to secure hoses. Body color overspray on the nose supports is normal. Vacuum actuators are plated zinc dichromate, and a black stamped number is often visible on them.

A new sales record was set in 1977 with 49,213 Corvettes built. This original paint example is Corvette Light Blue, the third most popular color in 1977 behind Classic White and Classic Black.

edge surrounding each letter painted black. Emblems are held onto the body by a visible thick black adhesive strip. Each emblem has four long studs used for positioning only, so they do not get nuts.

Early 1977s do not have the "Stingray" or any other emblem on the front fender. Later '77s have a crossed-flag emblem on each fender. The emblem is held on by an adhesive backing.

All 1973–1977 Corvettes are equipped with an anti-theft alarm system. In '73 the key switch for the alarm is in the taillamp panel, as before. In 1974 through mid-1977, it is in the driver-side front fender, above the forward edge of the fender vent. In mid-1977 the switch was deleted from the fender and incorporated into the driver-side door lock cylinder.

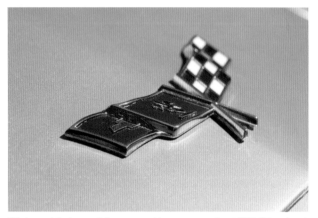

This is an original crossed-flags nose emblem on an unrestored 1977. This replaced the cloisonné nose emblem used from 1973–76 and was itself replaced in 1978, when all Corvettes got a special 25th anniversary nose emblem.

All 1973–1977 Corvettes came with a Stingray emblem on each front fender. The emblem is held in place by adhesive and four short studs that pass through holes in the fender. These studs are for correctly positioning the emblem and did not get nuts. Compared with this original Stingray emblem, a later GM service replacement has a groove cut into the base below the dot in the letter "i." The lock switch to the left of the emblem is for the audio alarm system that was standard in all 1973–1977 Corvettes. The switch was located here from 1974 through approximately VIN 23736 in 1977, after which it was integrated into the driver-side door lock. In 1973 the switch was in the taillamp panel.

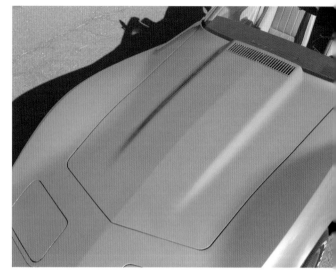

Corvettes in 1973–1975 used a functional cowl induction hood. The 1976 hoods had the air intake vent at the rear, but the cowl induction feature was not functional. The 1977 hood did not have the vent.

For the fender-mounted alarm key switches, the bezel should be crimped over around its full circumference just like the door locks. Incorrect replacement key switches have bezels with four tabs that bend over.

Hood

All 1973–1975 cars have a functional cowl induction hood. Outside air ingested at the base of the windshield is routed through the raised area down the middle of the hood and into the carburetor. An electrically actuated solenoid under the hood vent opens a valve when the throttle is sufficiently advanced, allowing additional cold air to flow to the carburetor.

The hood vent centered at the rear of the hood's power bulge is metal painted body color. Six black phosphate plated acorn nuts on the underside of the hood retain the vent.

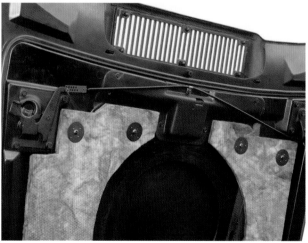

Underhood details from an original 1973 LS4.

All 1973–1974 Corvettes equipped with an optional LS4 454-cid engine came with "454" emblems on the hood. Each number is held by studs and nuts beneath the insulation on the underside of the hood. It is believed that some late 1974 cars with LS4 did not get the hood emblem.

The functional cowl induction system is eliminated in 1976, but the hood vent remains throughout the year. In 1977 the nonfunctional hood vent is eliminated.

There are no emblems, decals, or other markings on the hood for cars with base engines. Those 1973 and '74 Corvettes fitted with a 454 engine have a "454" emblem on each side of the hood's bulge. The emblems are chrome, with painted black recesses. The numbers that form each emblem are joined by a base, unlike earlier hood emblems that have individual numbers.

Those 1975–1977 Corvettes equipped with the optional L82 engine have an "L-82" emblem on either side of the hood. Some early 1975 L82s do not have the emblem.

Windshield Wipers and Windshield Washers
Wiper arms and blade holders are dull black in color, and each holder says "TRICO" on one of its ends in 1973. In 1974–1977 Anco brand blade holders were also used. On those 1973s assembled through approximately mid-October

1972, a length of metal washer tubing is soldered to a small tab at the end of each wiper arm and is further retained by one to four black plastic clips. On those '73s assembled thereafter and on all 1974–1977 cars, the metal tube is replaced with rubber hose.

Wiper blade inserts say "TRICO" or "ANCO" and have various patent numbers molded in. Two raised ribs are typically present below the writing.

In 1973 and 1974, the wiper blades rest against a square metal bracket when they are parked. In 1975–1977 the blades rest against a V-shaped metal bracket.

Windshield Trim
The top and sides of the windshield are surrounded by stainless-steel trim. In 1973–1976 this trim is unpainted and highly polished. In 1977 the windshield trim is painted satin black. In 1973–1975 the upper trim is comprised of two sections, and normally silver sealant is visible where they meet. In 1976–1977 the upper trim is a single piece.

Windshield, Door Glass, and Back Glass
All 1973–1977 Corvette windshields were manufactured by Libby Owens Ford (LOF) utilizing Safety Flo-Lite glass. The LOF logo, "SHADED SOFT RAY," "SAFETY FLO-LITE," "LAMINATED DOT 15 M24," and a two-letter manufacturing date code are etched into the lower right side of the windshield. In the date code, one letter represents the month and the other denotes the year. There is no discernible pattern to the letter usage, so you must refer to the glass date codes in Appendix R.

The letters "ASI" are present in the upper right portion of the windshield. The letters are white and are sandwiched between the laminates of glass, not etched into the surface like the logo and date code.

Both side windows are made from tinted LOF Safety Flo-Lite glass, with the manufacturer's logo and a two-letter

Those 1975–1977 Corvettes equipped with the optional L82 engine got this emblem on either side of the hood's "power bulge." Some very early 1975s with L82s may not have gotten the emblems.

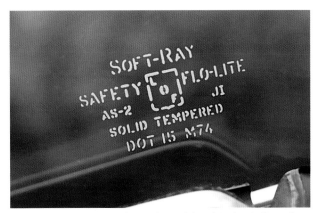
All body glass is imprinted with the manufacturer's logo, date of production, and other information. Libby Owens Ford SAFETY FLO-LITE tinted glass was used throughout, and each piece should have a two-letter date code. In this example, "JI" reveals that the glass was made in May 1975.

date code etched in, just like the windshield. The words "Astro Ventilation" are silk-screened in white letters in the lower forward corner of each window in 1973s and most '74s. The designation was eliminated toward the end of the 1974 model run but is occasionally seen in very early 1975 coupes and convertibles and in very late '75 convertibles.

Back windows in 1973–1977 coupes, like the windshields and side glass, have the LOF logo and manufacturing date code etched in. Starting in 1973, back windows are not removable as they had been previously.

Door Mirror, Handles, and Locks
All 1973–1976 and most '77 Corvettes have an outside rearview mirror mounted on the driver's door. A mounting base is held to the door by two screws. The mirror goes over the base and is held on by a black oxide Allen-head screw. A thin gasket goes between the base and door and is visible when the mirror is installed.

Option D35, first available in 1977, substituted dual sport mirrors for the single chrome one. Each door got a sport mirror, which are painted exterior color. A passenger door mirror was not available as a factory option in 1973–1976 but was offered as a dealer-installed accessory.

In 1973 and 1974, the mirror's rectangular head measures 3⅞ inches high by 5⅜ inches wide. In 1975 a larger mirror measuring 3¾ inches high by 6¼ inches wide was introduced, but some early '75s have the smaller mirror. All 1976–1977s have the larger one. For all years, the glass is coded with the manufacturer's symbol and a date code. The majority of 1973–1977 mirrors were supplied by Donnelly Mirror, Inc. These have "DMI" in the date code, while mirrors supplied by Ajax Mirror have "AX." So the code in a Donnelly-supplied mirror manufactured in April 1975 would read, "4-DMI-5," while the code for an Ajax-supplied mirror manufactured in February 1973 would read "2-AX-73."

All 1973–1977 door handles are a spring-loaded, press-flap design. On original handles, a coil spring on the hinge shaft provides the spring action. A butterfly spring covering a coil spring is incorrect. When the flap is depressed, the spring is visible. A thin black rubber gasket is visible between the handle and door.

The door locks, which are positioned below the door handles, feature a polished stainless-steel bezel. Original bezels are retained to the cylinders by means of a continuous crimp around the entire circumference. Incorrect replacement locks may have bezels retained by four tangs. A thin black rubber gasket is visible between the lock and door.

Side Rocker Molding
Side rocker moldings for all 1973–1977 cars are brushed aluminum with a painted ⅜-inch-wide flat black stripe along their length. They attach to the body with six black oxide Phillips oval-head screws. The forward and rearmost screws are sometimes pan head instead of oval head. Through

approximately November 1974, rocker moldings also have a single vertical fastener. It goes through a tab on the molding's lower lip near the front and into a J nut on the body. A black oxide fillister-head screw or a black oxide hex-head screw is used at this mounting point.

Radio Antenna
A radio was still an option for Corvettes in 1973–1977, and several thousand cars were built without one. Those cars have no radio antenna, but on all others, an antenna was mounted on the driver-side rear deck.

A black plastic gasket goes between the antenna base and the car's body. The base is also made of black plastic and is retained by a chrome hex nut. A chrome cap with two flat areas for a wrench to grab holds the mast to the base.

Original antenna bases have a continuous taper, while some later service replacements and reproductions have a two-step taper. The total height of the antenna should be approximately 32 inches, and the ball on top of the mast should be .30 inches in diameter. Some replacement masts have a .25-inch ball.

Rear Deck Vent Grilles and Gas Fill Door
In all 1973–1975 cars, two vent grilles are installed on the rear deck behind the back window (or behind the convertible top deck on convertibles). The vent grilles are painted body color and are each retained by four black oxide Phillips flathead screws. The lips in the body the grilles sit on and the vent channel below are sprayed with flat black paint in varying degrees of coverage.

The deck vent grilles remain open in all 1973s and in those 1974s and '75s not equipped with air conditioning. The vents exhaust passenger-compartment air in non-air-conditioned cars. In 1974 and '75 coupes equipped with air conditioning, the vents are present but get blocked with plates painted flat black. In 1974 and '75 convertibles with air conditioning, the vents are not blocked.

The underside of a rear deck shows unpainted fiberglass panels and a bonding strip with handwritten numbers and letters. Though writing on the underside of body panels is commonly seen, the meaning of most of it is unknown.

In 1975 33,836 coupes and only 4,629 convertibles were made. Buyers' clear preference for coupes led Chevrolet to stop offering C3 convertibles after 1975.

Most 1973 Corvettes have this crossed-flag emblem on the body color gas lid door. Late 1973 and all 1974 cars do not have an emblem on the gas lid door.

This crossed-flag emblem is correct for 1977. It was held in place with black-oxide-plated acorn nuts on earlier cars and by adhesive on later cars. The "UNLEADED FUEL ONLY" decal used white letters with darker color cars and black letters with lighter colors.

All 1975–1976 Corvettes used a cloisonné emblem on the gas filler door. The letters on the clear Mylar fuel warning decal were either black or white, depending upon body color.

Gas lid doors are painted body color for all 1973–1977s. The doors in most '73s feature a chrome and painted crossed-flag emblem held on by cadmium acorn nuts visible with the door open.

Late 1973s and all '74s don't have any emblem on the gas lid door. All 1975 and '76 cars have a round cloisonné emblem in the door. This emblem has a red sunburst pattern with crossed flags in the center. The 1977s use a simple crossed-flag emblem in the gas lid door. Black oxide acorn nuts hold the emblems in 1975–1977.

Beginning in 1975, a decal reading "UNLEADED FUEL ONLY" was affixed to the rear edge of the gas lid door. The decal is clear Mylar with white letters when body paint is dark and with black letters when body paint is light.

This is an original gas cap in a 1975 Corvette. Though difficult to see because of deterioration of the original zinc dichromate plating, "UNLEADED GASOLINE ONLY" is stamped into the top of the cap.

An over-center spring integral to the hinge holds the gas lid door open. A C-shaped spring clipped to the lid holds the door closed. The door hinge is chrome plated, and the door is held to the hinge with chrome-plated Phillips fillister-head screws fitted with external star lock washers. The polished door bezel is held to the body with black oxide Phillips flathead screws. Two rubber bumpers insert into the bezel toward the rear of the car to cushion the door.

All 1973–1977s come with a gold-iridite-plated, twist-on gas cap, not a locking cap. The locking caps, which are usually flat and chrome plated, were dealer installed or aftermarket.

The 1973 and 1974 caps resemble 1963–1972 units in their general appearance. Each has a handle for twisting on and off. The handle is attached by two ears that are bent over and spot welded onto the cap. The words "OPEN SLOWLY," "CAUTION," and "SEALED" are stamped into the top

side of the cap. The manufacturer's logo, a stylized "SM," is stamped into a circle on the cap's underside.

The 1975–1977 gas caps are a different design than earlier units. The twist handle is stamped into the cap from underneath rather than being a separate, welded-on piece. In addition, the outer perimeter has serrations formed in the metal. Wording stamped into the top reads "UNLEADED GASOLINE ONLY." A part number is also stamped into the top.

A black rubber boot surrounds the gas filler neck on all 1973–1977s. The boot has a plastic nipple facing the rear of the car. A rubber drain hose attaches to it. The hose, which has a metal spring inside to prevent it from collapsing, runs behind the gas tank.

Rear Fascia, Taillamps, Bumpers, and Related Parts

In 1973 the rear body panel has "CORVETTE" spelled out in eight individual letters centered between the taillamps. Each letter is chrome plated, with silver paint in its recessed face. Rear bumpers are chrome plated and are attached to the body with brackets painted semi-gloss black. Cadmium-plated hex-head bolts retain the bumpers to the brackets and cadmium- and/or black-oxide-plated hex-head bolts hold the brackets to the chassis.

Only 1973s still have a distinct lower rear valance panel. It is painted body color but often shows poor paint quality, including runs or sparse coverage along the bottom edge. It is retained to the body by four cadmium-plated indented hex-head bolts. The two outer ones utilize integral washers, while the two inners have separate flat washers.

In 1974–1977 the rear body panel, chrome bumpers, and lower valence are all replaced with an impact-absorbing bumper assembly. As in the front, this assembly consists of a

The last year Corvettes came with chrome-plated rear bumpers was 1973. The following year they were replaced with a urethane-covered energy-absorbing bumper assembly.

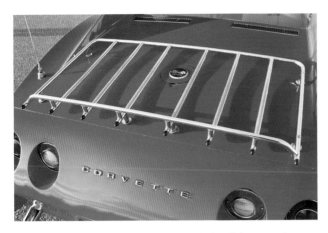

A deck-mounted luggage rack was offered as a dealer-installed accessory in 1973–1976 and as a regular production option in 1977. As shown here, the rack offered by Chevrolet dealers in 1973–1975 had six mounting points. The rack sold in 1976–1977 had two additional mounting points.

The 1973 taillamp lenses have concentric grooves and stainless-steel trim rings. Each lens is held in place by three black oxide Phillips-head screws.

body-colored urethane cover fitted over a multipiece metal understructure. In 1974 only, the urethane cover is two pieces, with a vertical seam at the centerline of the car. In 1975–1977 the cover is one piece, so the seam is eliminated.

All 1974 and 1975 cars have "CORVETTE" spelled out in eight individual letters centered between the taillamps. The 1976 and 1977 cars have "CORVETTE" spelled out in a single nameplate rather than individual letters. Earlier '76s use a six-inch-wide emblem and have a recess molded into the bumper for the emblem. Later '76s and all '77s use an eight-inch-wide emblem and do not have a recess.

Recesses for taillamps and a license plate are molded into 1974–1977 rear bumper covers. All 1975–1977 cars also have two black-rubber-tipped protrusions toward the lower, outboard corners of the rear bumper cover.

In 1973 the recessed area of the body where the rear license plate mounts is covered by a chrome-plated die-cast surround trim. A lamp assembly mounts at the top of the recess, behind the rear body panel, and illuminates the rear license plate. The lens for the lamp has "Guide 35 SAE L66" cast into its face. A black rubber bumper is inserted into the rear valance panel, centered toward the lower edge of the license plate. Two white plastic push nuts insert into square cutouts in the rear body panel for the license plate retaining screws.

In 1974–1977 the license plate recess is molded into the rear bumper cover. It uses no bezel or other trim. Instead of a single light above the license plate, 1974s utilize two smaller lights, with one on either side of the plate. Each lens has "SAE L 74 Guide 1A" cast into its face. All 1975–1977 cars use a single lamp above the rear license plate. The clear lens on this lamp has "SAE L 75 Guide 4Y" cast into its face.

All 1973–1977s utilize four rear lamps. The two outer ones utilize red lenses that function as taillamps, stop lamps, and turn signals. The two inner ones utilize red lenses with

clear plastic centers that function as backup lamps. Each lamp has a very small moisture wick protruding from the bottom of the lens. The wick material resembles a cigarette filter.

In 1973 only, taillamp lenses are separate from their housings. The lenses are slightly convex, with a checkerboard pattern on the inside. They are retained with three black oxide Phillips pan-head screws. The clear plastic centers in the inboard lenses are glued in place. The glue was often sloppily applied.

Starting in 1974, the taillamp lenses are integral to the housings, eliminating the need for screws to hold the lens on. The inner 1974 lenses have "SAE AR 74 Guide 1Y" cast in, and the outer '74 lenses have "SAE 15T 74 Guide 1Y" cast in. In 1975–1977 the inner lenses have "SAE AR 75 Guide 1Y," and the outers have "SAE 1ST 75 Guide 1Y."

All 1973–1977s originally came with undercar exhaust systems, not side pipes. For 1973 only, the exhaust tips exit

All 1974–1977 taillamp lenses were retained by chrome-plated Phillips-head screws.

Taillamp, park lamp, and side marker lamp lenses all contain manufacturing information and the date of production. The "74" in this taillamp lens represents 1974.

the rear of the car through rectangular cutouts in the body. The cutouts are trimmed with rectangular, chromed die-cast bezels with open bottoms. The bezels are retained by chrome Phillips oval-head screws. The tailpipes in 1974–1977 cars exit below the rear bumper assembly. There are no cutouts as in 1973.

Convertible Tops

The final year for the convertible body style, until it was revived in 1986, was 1975. All 1973–1975 convertible tops are made from vinyl with a woven pattern. The convertible top is available in either white or black, regardless of exterior body color. The front header roll and tack strip cover are also vinyl, but have a grained pattern rather than a woven pattern. Two small stainless-steel trim pieces cover the ends of the tack strip. The trim pieces are flared around the perimeter and attach with one small, bright Phillips flathead screw. The convertible top window is clear vinyl and is heat sealed, not sewn, to the top.

The convertible top back window contains a manufacturer's logo, manufacturing date, and the words "VINYLITE, TRADE MARK, AS-6," and "DO NOT RUB DRY WASH WITH WATER SOAKED CLOTH" heat stamped in the driver-side lower corner.

A paper "caution" label is sewn into the top in the driver-side corner below the heat-stamped logo and date in the window. The label reads:

**WARNING
DEALER—DO NOT REMOVE
FOR CARE OF REAR WINDOW
AND TOP MATERIAL
SEE BOOKLET
"HOW TO OPERATE FOLDING TOP"**

As an extra cost option, a removable hardtop was available in addition to the standard soft top for convertibles. The hardtop is painted body color unless vinyl covered. All vinyl-covered hardtops are black. The hardtop rear window contains the LOF manufacturing logo and is date coded with two letters like the remainder of the body glass. The first letter represents the month of production, and the second represents the year of production. (Refer to Appendix R for glass date codes.)

Tires, Wheels, and Wheel Covers

The first year Corvettes came with radial tires was 1973. All 1973–1977s are equipped with size GR-70 radials. The standard tire for all years is a blackwall. Whitewalls and raised-white-letter tires are available as extra cost options in 1973–1976, while only raised-white-letter tires were available as an option in 1977. It's likely that all factory-installed tires are either Firestone Steel Radial 500s or Goodyear Steelgards, but it's possible that B. F. Goodrich and/or Uniroyal tires were factory installed.

Raised-white-letter Goodyears say "Goodyear Steelgard" in block letters. Raised-white-letter Firestones say "Firestone Steel Radial 500" in block letters. In addition, Firestone raised-white-letter tires on those 1973s assembled through approximately June 1973 also have a raised, white-outlined triangle with a raised-white "F" in the middle.

Every 1973–1977 tire has a ten- or eleven-digit "tire identification number" stamped into the sidewall. The first letter of the code indicates the manufacturer, with Goodyear represented by "M" and Firestone by "V." The second character denotes the location of the plant that manufactured the tire. For example, "K" represents Goodyear's plant in Union City, Tennessee, and "N" represents Firestone's plant in Joliette, Quebec, Canada. The third and fourth digits are "U5," to indicate the tire's size, GR70-15. The following three

All 1973–1977 Corvettes came with GR70-15 Goodyear Steelgard or Firestone Steel Radial 500 tires. Blackwall tires were standard, and whitewall or raised-white-letter tires were optional until 1976. In 1977, only raised-white-letter tires were optional. Firestone Steel Radial 500 tires were susceptible to tread separation. As a result, in November 1978, Firestone initiated what would become the most extensive tire recall ever. The original owner of this 1977 did not participate in the recall. She still has the original tires delivered with her Corvette.

or four letters denote the type of tire construction. The next two numbers indicate the week of the year the tire was made, with "01" designating the first week of the year and "52" being the last. The final number is the last digit of the year of manufacture. Thus a tire stamped "MKU5 FMH394" is a GR70-15 Goodyear Steelgard Radial manufactured in the Union City plant during the 39th week of 1974.

After problems with tread and inner belt separation came to light, Firestone announced, on November 29, 1978, the recall of 14.5 million Steel Radial 500 tires. On July 16, 1980, the company announced the recall of an additional 5 million such tires. These recalls covered virtually every Steel Radial 500 manufactured, including those installed on new 1973–1977 Corvettes.

All 1973–1977 Corvettes are equipped with steel rally wheels as standard equipment. They are a color called Argent Silver on the front side. The back sides are painted semi-flat black and always have silver overspray, since the front side was painted silver after the black was applied to the rear.

All wheels are stamped with a date code and size code on the front face. All 1970–1972 Corvette wheels are 15 by 8 inches and have the code "AZ" stamped in to indicate this. The "AZ" is adjacent to the valve stem hole.

Also adjacent to the valve stem hole is the manufacturer's logo and date code stamping. On one side of the hole it says "K," which is believed to represent the wheel manufacturer, Kelsey-Hayes. This is followed by a dash and a "1" that likely represents Chevrolet, though it may represent a specific wheel plant. Next comes another dash and either a "0," "1," or "2" to denote the last digit of the year of manufacture. This is followed by a space and one or two numbers to indicate the month of manufacture. On the other side of the valve stem hole are one or two more numbers that represent the day of manufacture.

Stainless-steel trim rings and chrome center caps are standard for all cars. Original trim rings are held to the wheel by four steel clips. Center caps should read "Chevrolet Motor Division" in black paint.

A full wheel cover is available as an extra cost option in 1973 only. Called option PO2, this cover has a stainless-steel outer rim and closely spaced radial fins converging outward toward a protruding ornamental disc in the center. The disc is chrome around its edge and black in the middle, and it contains the Corvette crossed-flag emblem. Other Chevrolet products use a similar wheel cover, but those have a flat center disc instead of the protruding disc utilized for Corvettes.

Aluminum wheels were first offered as an option in 1973, but according to Chevrolet records, only four cars were actually delivered with them that year. The wheels posed quality-control problems, and they were not offered again until the 1976 model year. Aluminum wheels are polished and coated with a clear paint finish. "Kelsey-Hayes," the manufacturer, and "Made in Mexico," are stamped into the backs of the wheels.

Wheels on cars equipped with standard trim rings and center caps utilize black rubber valve stems that measure approximately 1¼ inches long. These are fitted with caps that come to a point and have longitudinal ridges around the entire perimeter.

Wheels on 1973s equipped with optional full wheel covers have extensions threaded onto the standard valve stems. The extensions have white inner shafts that are visible because they are not fitted with caps.

To ease the balancing process, steel wheels are sometimes marked with a tiny weld drop or paint dot at their highest point. This mark is lined up with an orange dot on the tire. Balance weights are the type that clamp onto the edge of the rim and are placed on the inside of the wheel only. Original balance weights usually have the letters "OEM" molded into their faces. There is usually a small dot of white or colored paint on the tire adjacent to each balance weight.

All cars have a full-size spare tire and wheel. In 1973 only, those cars equipped with the optional aluminum wheel had a matching aluminum wheel for the spare. Later cars fitted with aluminum wheels, and all cars equipped with standard steel wheels, had a steel wheel for the spare. Those 1973 cars equipped with optional P02 full wheel covers do not have a fifth cover for the spare wheel.

The spare tire and wheel are housed in a carrier bolted to the rear underbody area. The carrier is fiberglass with steel supports. The fiberglass is unpainted, and the steel support is painted semi-gloss black. The tire tub portion of the carrier has a fair amount of flat to semi-gloss black paint on its outside surface, applied during the blackout process. A lock covered by a black rubber boot goes over the spare tire carrier access bolt.

1973–1977 INTERIOR
Trim Tag
Interior trim color and material, as well as exterior body color and body assembly date, are stamped into an unpainted stainless-steel plate attached to the driver's door hinge pillar by two aluminum pop rivets. This plate is commonly called a trim plate or trim tag.

Trim color and material are indicated in the plate by a three-digit code. For example, in 1974 trim code 413 indicates dark blue color with vinyl seat covers.

Exterior body paint color is indicated in the trim plate by a three-number code in 1973 and 1974 and by a two-letter code in 1975–1977. The two-letter code is followed by an "L" to indicate lacquer paint. For example, code 33L in 1976 indicates dark green. (Refer to Appendix T for paint and interior trim codes.)

The body build date is the date when the painted and partially assembled body reached that point on the assembly line where the trim plate was installed. The car's final assembly date is typically one to several days after the body build date. A letter indicating the month followed by two

The blue interior in this 1977 is extremely original and unrestored.

A driver-side view of an unrestored 1977 interior.

All 1973–1977 Corvettes were fitted with a trim tag in the driver-side door hinge pillar. The tag was attached with pop rivets, while the body was on the paint line, between the application of the second and third color coats, so the tag is normally painted body color. A three-character code for the date the tag was affixed to the body is stamped in the upper right corner. A letter represents the month, with "A" representing the first month of production, "B" the second, and so on. The two numbers following the letter represent the day. The example shown is from 1977. "G11" indicates a date of February 11, 1977.

numbers indicating the day represents the body build date. The letter "A" was assigned to the first month of production, which was August 1972 for '73 models, August 1973 for '74 models, October 1974 for '75 models, August 1975 for '76 models, and August 1976 for '77 models. The second month of production was assigned "B," and so on. A body assembled on August 6, 1975, would have "A06" stamped into the trim plate, for example, and a body built on January 11, 1975, would have "D11" stamped into its plate. (Refer to Appendix S for body build date codes.)

Seats

Standard seat upholstery in 1973–1976 is a combination of very slightly grained flat vinyl with Chevrolet's "comfort-weave" vinyl inserts sewn into the seat bottoms and backs. Vinyl seats for 1973–1976 all have vertical insert panels. Leather seat upholstery was standard beginning in 1977.

All 1973–1975 seats have a chrome-bordered black trim insert at the top of the seat back, while 1976 and 1977 seats do not. The 1975 vinyl seats are distinguished from 1973 and 1974 by the position of the horizontal stitch seam in the lower cushion. In 1975 this seam was moved forward, toward the center of the cushion.

A custom interior trim option package was offered in 1973–1976. This package includes leather seat covers and a strip of carpet on the bottom of the door panels. All 1973–1977 leather seats have horizontal panels. In 1973 and 1974, leather seats have eight stitched seams in the lower cushion, while 1975–1977 seats have six seams in

Original "medium saddle" vinyl interior in an unrestored 1975.

Original vinyl seat in an unrestored 1975. Leather upholstery was optional in 1973–1976 and standard in 1977.

Details of a 1973–1977 seat back panel and its hardware.

This is an original, unrestored 1973 interior with the custom interior trim option. This option package included leather seat covers, walnut veneer inserts on the center console and door panels, lower carpet trim on door panels, and plush cut pile carpet on the floor in place of standard carpet.

Vinyl seat upholstery was standard in 1973–1976. Leather upholstery was optional only as part of the custom interior trim option package. The side "skirt" portion of the leather seat covers was actually vinyl, not leather. The custom interior trim option was available only in black, silver, or saddle.

The original carpet in an unrestored 1975 illustrates how the factory normally cut and glued down a flap to cover the front seat mounting bolts. Note the absence of a clear plastic backing on the carpet flap. Some reproduction carpet has a clear plastic backing, which was not present on factory-installed carpeting.

this cushion. Only the faces of leather-covered seats are real leather. The sides of the covers are vinyl.

In 1977 leather seat covers became standard. Combination leather and cloth upholstery was offered in 1977 as a no additional cost option. The center sections of the seats are cloth with horizontal stitching.

Each seat rests on two seat tracks, which allow for forward and rearward adjustment of the seat's position. The tracks are black phosphate, and each is held to the floor by one black phosphate, indented hex-head bolt at either end, for a total of four per seat. The front bolts are covered by a cutaway flap of carpet, while the rear bolts simply pass through the carpet. The seat adjust lever is black phosphate, with a chrome ball screwed onto its end.

The seat backs are made of molded plastic and match interior color. The seat back release button, its bezel, and the brackets that attach the seat back to the bottom are all chrome plated. Two bolts that allow for adjustment of seat back position are bright silver and get rubber cushions over their heads. Black plastic trim washers are under the seat back release bezel and adjustment bolts.

Lap and Shoulder Belts

All 1973–1977 coupes were equipped with lap and shoulder belts, while 1973–1975 convertibles came with lap belts as standard and shoulder belts as an extra cost option. All 1973 and 1974 belts were manufactured by a company called Hamill. A tag bearing that name is sewn to them. Firestone bought Hamill in 1975, and tags sewn to 1975–1977 seat belts may say "Hamill" or "Firestone." Some cars have tags from both manufacturers.

The tag with the manufacturer's name also indicates the date the belt was manufactured by an ink stamping, with a number representing the week of the year and another number representing the year. For example, a stamping of "01 D 73" indicates that the belt was made during the first week of January 1973. The meaning of the letter between the numbers is not known with certainty, but it may denote the day of the week or the manufacturing plant where the belt was made.

In addition to the tag bearing the manufacturer's name and date code, another, smaller tag is sewn to both lap and shoulder belts. This second tag contains safety instructions.

All belts are made from a three-row webbing material and are the same color as the carpet. The material used for lap belts is slightly thicker than that used for shoulder belts.

Outboard belts are on a spring-loaded retractable coil for all 1973–1977 cars. The retractors are beneath each seat, under a plastic cover.

Inboard portions of the seat belts are encased in a semi-rigid plastic that goes over part of the female buckles. The buckles are brushed silver in color, and the black release buttons each have a rigid metallic sticker that says "GM" in silver letters on a blue background.

All 1973–1977 lap and shoulder belts are made from three-bar webbing that's color matched to the carpet. Lap belts are made from slightly thicker material than shoulder belts. Reproduction shoulder belts are usually made from the thicker lap belt webbing. Original belts have warning and information tags sewn on. The information tag includes the GM part number, model number, manufacturer, and manufacturing date. In this example, the date code "22 E 75" indicates that the belt was made in the 22nd week of 1975. The meaning of the letter "E" is not clear. Some believe it represents the day of the week, with "A" denoting Monday, "B" Tuesday, and so on. But this is unlikely, since the vast majority of original belts have an "E," which would mean the vast majority were made on Friday.

This "caution" message was printed in white letters on a clear plastic clip that went over the shoulder harness webbing. This example is in an unrestored 1975 coupe.

This is an original door panel for a 1975 standard interior. Panels were virtually identical in 1973–1976. The 1977 panel is similar but has a strip of carpet along the bottom and a textured, semi-gloss black panel insert above the armrest.

An original 1973 door panel in a car with the custom interior trim option. The option adds a walnut veneer insert and accompanying trim, as well as a lower plush cut pile carpet insert and accompanying trim.

Door Panels and Door Hardware

All door panels are made from molded vinyl and match the interior color, unless that color is white, in which case the door panel, carpet, and certain other interior trim are keyed to exterior color. With standard interiors (that is, interiors with vinyl seat covers), the door panels are plain and utilize no trim. Custom interiors include fancier door panels. A piece of plush cut pile carpet is added along the bottom of the panels, and a strip of chrome trim covers the gap where the carpet meets the vinyl. In addition, custom door panels include a band of simulated walnut wood trim in the middle in 1973–1976. In 1977 a satin black insert replaces the simulated wood insert. With both standard and custom interiors, inside window felts are attached to the upper edge of the door panels with heavy staples, not pop rivets.

Door panels are attached to the doors by means of interlocking plastic clips fastened to the back of the panel and the door frame. Black phosphate clips at the bottom

This is an original 1977 door panel. It is the only door panel used in 1977 because the custom interior trim option available in 1973–1976 was discontinued when leather seats became standard in 1977.

of the front and rear of the panel also hold it on. The clips insert into a cutout in the back of the panel and get fastened to the door with black phosphate Phillips pan-head screws. Finally, a chrome Phillips oval-head screw with integral washer goes through the face of each panel at the upper front and rear corners.

Inside door release handles are chrome with black paint in the knurled center area. A round black emblem features the crossed-flag logo. The inside lock knob is chrome with a black stripe painted in the center indent. The inside door pull is a grained vinyl handle that matches interior color. Cars equipped with standard manual windows have chrome window cranks with black plastic knobs.

Door Jambs and Door Perimeters

The door jambs and perimeter of each door are painted body color, with the exception of the top front of each door, which is painted semi-gloss black in 1973 through early 1975, and in 1977. Later 1975s and '76s were painted body color in the top front area of the door jamb. The door striker, which is the large pin threaded into the doorpost, and its corresponding receiver in the door are both cadmium plated. The striker is a special indented star-head design.

All 1973–1975 convertibles have an additional striker in the door jambs. A cone-shaped male insert is mounted to the door, and a hollow cone-shaped female receiver is mounted to the body jamb. The male piece is chrome plated, while the female piece is black with a brass insert.

The 1973–1976 courtesy light pin switches and "door ajar" warning light/alarm system pin switches are cadmium plated and should not have any paint overspray. These pin switches have "SX," the manufacturer's logo, stamped into the head of the metal plunger. In 1977 a pin switch with a nylon plunger was introduced. The nylon head of the plunger may have "M" or "B" molded in.

As with the pin switches, door strikers, and door striker receivers, the door alignment blocks and the door weather strip were added after the body was painted and should not have any body paint overspray.

In 1973 the main door weather stripping is two separate pieces and typically shows a gap in the center on the bottom of the door. Starting in 1974, it is one piece and therefore does not have a gap. The 1975 convertibles have an additional piece of weather strip at the top rear of the door jamb.

The vehicle certification label glued toward the top of the rear portion of the driver's door is unpainted. It's blue in 1973 through mid-1975 and white thereafter. It contains the car's VIN, the month and year the vehicle was produced, axle loading and gross vehicle weight ratings, and a statement that reads "THIS VEHICLE CONFORMS TO ALL

An original interior door release handle and lock knob in a 1973. All 1974–1977s used the same components. A thin white plastic insert was installed between the lock knob and the door panel.

All 1973–1976 and some 1977 Corvettes used a metal "door ajar," alarm, and courtesy light plunger switch. "B" or "SX" was stamped into the head to denote the manufacturer. During 1977 production, a switch with a nylon head on the plunger was introduced. The switch was installed after the body was painted and should have not overspray.

Door striker bolts were silver cadmium plated. The number of black-phosphate-plated spacers behind the striker varied.

A 1973–1977 doorsill plate with correct black oxide Phillips oval-head retaining screws.

All 1973–1977 Corvettes came with a vehicle certification decal and a tire pressure decal on the driver's door jamb. The 1973 through early 1975 certification decals had a blue background. Later 1975s and 1976–1977s had a white background. The blue decal on the left is from a March 1975 car. The white one on the right is from a July 1975 car.

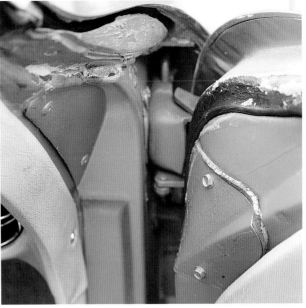

Passenger-side forward door jamb and hinge pillar details in an unrestored 1975. Note the sloppy application of the yellow weather strip adhesive and the very rough appearance of the area between the front fender and the hinge pillar. Both are characteristic of typical factory production.

APPLICABLE MOTOR VEHICLE SAFETY STANDARDS IN EFFECT ON THE DATE OF MANUFACTURE SHOWN ABOVE."

Beginning in 1973, a tire pressure sticker appears below the vehicle certification label. This sticker specifies tire pressure, tire size, and recommended vehicle capacity.

Door sills are bright aluminum with black-painted ribs. Each sill is held on with four black phosphate Phillips oval-head screws.

Kick Panels, Quarter Trim Panels, Pedals, and Carpet

The kick panels beneath the dash, just forward of the doors, are molded plastic and are interior color. On air-conditioned cars, the passenger-side panel was cut by hand for increased clearance, and the cut is frequently rough. One chrome Phillips oval-head screw in the forward, upper corner of each panel holds it in place. The panels have a bevy of small holes

for the speakers that mount behind them. There is no ridge at the rear edge of the panel in 1973–1977. A ridge does appear in 1978.

The quarter trim panels just rearward of the doors are molded plastic to match the interior color. They are each held in place by a piece of metal trim retained by four chrome Phillips oval-head screws. The quarter trim panels on coupes also have one chrome Phillips oval-head screw with a trim washer at the top.

In standard 1973–1976 interiors, carpet is made from an 80/20 loop pile molded material. In custom interiors and all 1977s, it is made from plush cut pile material. Carpet matches interior color unless the interior is white, in which case carpet color is determined by exterior color.

The original center console in an unrestored 1975. This console, and related parts, was used in 1973–1976. The original console featured real stitching along the top edges, while some reproductions have simulated stitching molded in.

Original heel pad and driver-side carpet in an unrestored 1975 Corvette.

All 1973–1977 Corvettes came with a three-pocket map compartment on the passenger-side dash. Pockets are mounted with spring tension retainers that hold the pockets nearly closed and close to the dash. A single snap holds the two smaller pockets to the larger one. This original example shows stitching along the edges and around the perimeter of the pockets. Some reproductions do not have the correct stitching.

A black rubber flap on the firewall insulation retains the upper edge of the front carpeting on both sides.

Carpet covers the bulkhead behind the seats and has sewn-on binding on the lower edge where it overlaps the front floor carpet behind the seats. Rear storage compartment doors each have carpet under their frames. One piece of carpet covers the rear storage area floor and extends up the rear bulkhead. The edge at the top of the bulkhead is trimmed with sewn-on binding. Convertibles have a two-step tab, and coupes have a one-step tab. Separate pieces of untrimmed carpet cover the two wheelwells.

Carpet has a molded vinyl accelerator heel pad in the corner of the driver's footwell adjacent to the accelerator pedal. The main section of the pad is rectangular and has horizontal bars molded in. Extensions come off the main section and extend up the transmission tunnel and under the accelerator pedal.

In 1973–1976 a sewn-in, molded vinyl dimmer switch pad is on the carpet above the dimmer switch. As with the accelerator heel pad, the dimmer switch pad is color matched to the interior. In 1977 the dimmer switch is incorporated into the turn signal stalk, eliminating the need for a dimmer switch pad in the carpet.

Dash Pad and Dash Panels

The upper dash pad, as well as driver's and passenger's dash panels, are made of soft vinyl and match interior color. With light color interiors, the upper pad is usually a darker shade. For example, tan interiors typically have brown upper pads.

The two vertical panels are attached to the upper pad by means of six Phillips oval-head screws with conical washers. The screw heads are painted to match interior color. In 1977 the dash screws may be unpainted or black and may be Pozidriv instead of Phillips head.

In 1973–1975 dash pads have color-matched stitching across the top. In 1976 the stitching may be color matched or white. In 1977 the stitching was replaced by a molded indentation. An interior-color hard plastic grille is located in the defroster opening of the upper pad.

A three-pocket storage area is inset into the passenger-side dash panel. The storage pocket assembly is made from vinyl and is the same color as the interior. The dash panel has stitching around the opening for the storage pockets. The two smaller, outboard pockets are retained to the larger one with a single chrome-plated snap. A spring-loaded retainer behind the dash holds the three-pocket assembly tight against the dash panel.

Interior Switches, Controls, and Related Parts

All 1973–1977 Corvettes have a headlamp switch mounted in the upper left corner of the driver-side dash pad. All 1973–1976 and some 1977 headlight switch knobs are soft black grained vinyl with an image of a headlamp with light rays coming out of the center. Other 1977 knobs are hard black plastic with a white or chrome circle in the middle.

All 1973–1977 Corvettes have air vents on both sides of the dash, toward the lower, outboard corner. The vent mechanisms are chrome spheres that rotate to change the direction of airflow. A black push/pull knob next to each sphere controls the flow of air.

A small black T-handle pull mechanism beneath the driver-side dash on the left side releases the hood latch. The handle is black with the words "HOOD RELEASE" in white-painted block letters across its face. The hood release cable is in a spiral wound metal sheathing.

The headlamp door override switch is mounted in a semi-gloss black bracket beneath the steering column. It is a vacuum switch with a dull black plastic push/pull knob. A

A 1973–1976 headlamp knob and bezel. The 1977 knobs vary, with some identical to this and some made from hard, glossy black plastic with a white or chrome circle in the middle.

trip odometer reset knob is mounted beneath the dash to the left of the headlamp door override switch. The reset knob has a grooved black rubber cover.

Steering Wheel and Steering Column

All 1973–1975 steering wheels are black regardless of interior color. The wheels have grained vinyl rims molded to a three-spoke stainless-steel hub. Each of the spokes has a brushed finish with a pattern of parallel lines extending from the center of the wheel to the outer rim.

All 1976 and those '77 Corvettes with standard steering columns utilize a four-spoke steering wheel. The entire wheel, including the spokes, is covered with padded vinyl that matches interior color. Those 1977s equipped with the optional tilt and telescoping steering column utilize a three-spoke steering wheel. The spokes for this wheel are brushed stainless steel, and the rim is covered with leather.

The standard steering column and optional tilt-telescoping column in 1973–1977 are painted whatever the interior color is, in a semi-gloss finish. The 1977 columns are

This 1975 steering wheel is 15 inches in diameter, with a black textured vinyl rim and stainless-steel spokes. This was the only wheel available in 1973–1975. A different wheel, featuring four vinyl-wrapped spokes and a vinyl-wrapped rim, was used in 1976. The vinyl-wrapped wheel was also used in 1977, but only with the standard steering column. The tilt-telescopic column got a three-spoke wheel with a leather-wrapped rim.

Those 1977 Corvettes fitted with the standard steering column got a vinyl-covered four-spoke steering wheel. Cars equipped with the optional tilt-telescopic steering column option came with this leather-covered three-spoke steering wheel.

1973–1977

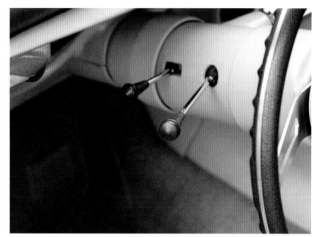

A 1973–1976 turn signal lever and tilt-telescopic steering column tilt adjustment lever.

Original steering column ignition lock and hazard lamp switch details in an unrestored 1975.

Beginning in 1977, a stalk with turn signal, headlight dimmer, and windshield wiper/washer controls is mounted into the steering column.

All 1973–1976s and those 1977s with standard columns use a textured metal horn button painted to match the interior. The button on 1973–1976 standard columns is slightly smaller, with sharper edges compared with the button on tilt-telescopic columns. Those 1977s with the optional tilt-telescopic steering column built through approximately early January 1977 have an unpainted, brushed-aluminum horn button. After approximately January 1977, the horn button on tilt-telescopic columns is smooth aluminum, painted interior color. The unpainted aluminum buttons were recalled by Chevrolet because strong reflections from the surface could interfere with the driver's ability to see, so at least some 1977s that came with them don't have them now.

A crossed-flag emblem is in the center of all 1973–1977 horn buttons. In 1973–1975, the emblem is relatively large, with a silver circle that cuts through the flags. In 1976 and 1977, the silver circle is eliminated and the emblem is smaller.

Interior Windshield Moldings, Sun Visors, and Rearview Mirror

Three pieces of vinyl-covered molding matched to the interior color cover the inside of the windshield frame for all 1973–1977 Corvettes. The two side pieces are held on by plastic retainers attached to the reverse side. The plastic retainers are not visible when the moldings are installed. In addition, each side molding has one chrome Phillips-head screw retaining it at the top. The top piece of molding is retained by black oxide, recess-head Phillips screws.

Sun visors are covered with padded soft vinyl. In cars with standard interior trim, they have the same "comfort-weave" pattern as the vinyl seat covers. In cars with the custom interior trim, they have a Madrid pattern in the vinyl. In 1974, when the interior rearview mirror was made larger, sun visors became smaller and differently shaped.

Each sun visor is held to the windshield frame with chrome recess-head Phillips screws. In 1977 sun visor mounts are changed to allow the visors to swivel.

A label describing engine starting procedures is affixed to the driver-side sun visor in 1973–1975. This label is made from a woven material in 1973 and from paper in 1974–1975. All 1975 Corvettes also have a push start procedure label on the driver-side sun visor. In 1976 this label is on the passenger-side visor, and a catalytic converter label is on the driver side. In 1977 a label pertaining to the optional sport mirrors is affixed to the passenger-side visor on those cars so equipped, and a label for the sunshade sleeve is on the driver-side visor.

All 1973–1976 Corvettes have an interior day/night rearview mirror mounted to the center of the upper wind-

about two inches shorter than earlier columns, resulting in the steering wheel being closer to the dash.

The tilt-telescoping column has a thick locking ring below the steering wheel to control the telescoping function. The ring is painted to match the rest of the column in most 1973–1977 Corvettes. Those 1977s made from approximately mid-October 1976 through mid-January 1977 came with an unpainted, brushed aluminum locking ring on tilt-telescopic columns.

A lever similar to, but shorter than, the turn signal lever controls the tilt function of the optional steering column. The tilt lever is located between the turn signal lever and the dash.

All columns have a four-way flasher switch mounted on the right side. The knob for this switch is black with white lettering spelling the word "FLASHER."

All 1973–1976 Corvettes use a turn signal lever with a chrome-plated shaft and a dull black rubber end. The end is grained and has a single concentric groove near the tip.

This is option UF1, a map light mounted on the underside of the interior rearview mirror. It was offered from 1973 through 1976.

Instruments and Radio

The center console instrument cluster housing is cast-metal painted semi-gloss black in 1973–1976. In 1977 it's black plastic. In 1973–1976 the windshield wiper/washer control switch is mounted above the center console instrument cluster housing. The wiper/washer switch moves to the steering column in 1977.

The original windshield wiper and washer control assembly in an unrestored 1975. The assembly is the same in 1973–1976, with the possible exception of the lettering along the top. In 1973–1975, the "OFF," "HIGH," and "PUSH" letters are chrome. In 1976 they are white.

shield frame. Beginning in 1977 (or possibly late 1976), the mirror is mounted onto the upper windshield itself, instead of the frame.

In 1973 only, the mirror is eight inches wide and is held to its mount with a slotted oval-head screw. It is backed with black-grained vinyl and has black rubber trim. The day/night lever is black as well, with the possible exception of some very early cars, which may utilize a gray lever. Vinyl trim dyed interior color covers the mirror's mount at the windshield header.

Beginning in 1974, the interior rearview mirror is 10 inches wide. In 1973–1976 a mirror-mounted map light was offered as option UF1. This light is on the bottom of the passenger side of the mirror. It has a clear plastic lens and a black sliding switch. A clear or black sticker with silver letters provides instructions on how to change the bulb.

In 1973–1976 a slotted oval-head screw adjusts the tension between the mirror and its mount. In 1977 an Allen screw adjusts tension. All mirrors say "Made in the USA" on the bottom, adjacent to the day/night lever, and "Guide Glare Proof" on top of the mirror between the two rivets.

Center stack instrument faces were redesigned for 1977.

All gauges, including the speedometer and tachometer, have a flat black background and a straight red needle. Tachometer redlines vary according to the engine. Beginning in 1975, speedometers include kilometers per hour markings in addition to miles per hour markings.

Beginning in 1975, fuel gauges have "UNLEADED FUEL ONLY" written below the needle. In 1973 the oil pressure gauge reads to 70 psi, and the water temperature gauge is marked at 100, 210, and 250 degrees. Beginning in 1974, the oil pressure gauge reads to 80 psi, and the temperature gauge is marked at 100, 200, and 280 degrees.

An original speedometer in an unrestored 1975.

An original speedometer in a 1973. The same speedometer was used in 1974.

An original 1977 speedometer and tachometer. The tachometer redline varied according to which engine the car came with.

A 1973–1977 tachometer. The redline varied, depending on which engine the car was equipped with.

The correct center stack instruments and AM/FM stereo radio in an unrestored 1973. In 1974–1977 the oil pressure gauge reads "0," "40," and "80" rather than "0," "35," and "70," as in 1973. In 1974–1977 the water temperature gauge reads "100," "200," and "280" instead of "100," "210," and "250," as in 1973.

In 1977 the faces of all the small gauges were redesigned. In addition, the ammeter gauge utilized previously was replaced with a voltmeter gauge.

All 1973–1977 Corvettes came standard without a radio. For those cars not equipped with a radio, a block-off plate is fitted to the cutout where the radio would otherwise go. The block-off plate is painted semi-gloss black and has a flat face with a thin, raised-chrome border around its perimeter near the edge.

As an extra cost option, one of two different Delco radios could be ordered in 1973–1976. The first is an AM/FM pushbutton, and the second is an AM/FM pushbutton with stereo reception. Both radios have a small slide bar above the dial that changes reception between AM and FM. A third optional radio was offered in 1977. Dubbed option UM2, it is an AM/FM stereo with an eight-track player.

All 1973–1976 radio knobs are dull black rubber with white pictorial inserts. The on/off/volume knob on the left has a musical note, while the tuning knob on the right has an antenna with a radiating signal. Beneath the main radio knobs is a secondary control, which is chrome plated around the edge and black in the middle. The one on the left controls tone, and the one on the right, which is functional only on stereo-equipped cars, controls balance.

An original 1975 center gauge cluster and AM/FM radio. The 1973 cluster and gauges are nearly identical, but oil pressure reads to 70 psi, and the temperature gauge is marked at 100, 210, and 250 degrees. The 1974 and 1976 gauges are identical. In 1977 the clock and fuel gauge face designs differed, and the ammeter was replaced with a voltmeter. In 1977 the word "Delco" on the radio face was in block lettering, not script as seen here. Also, the positioning of the fuel and water temperature gauges was reversed in 1977.

All 1973–1977 Corvettes came standard without a radio. An AM/FM radio and AM/FM stereo were optional all years. In 1977 a third choice, AM/FM stereo with an eight-track tape player, was also offered. This is an original U58 AM/FM stereo in an unrestored 1973. The small light in the upper right corner of the radio's dial was used on stereos only. It glowed orange when stereo FM was received.

The original center console in an unrestored 1975. This console, and related parts, was used in 1973–1976. The original console featured real stitching along the top edges, while some reproductions have simulated stitching molded in.

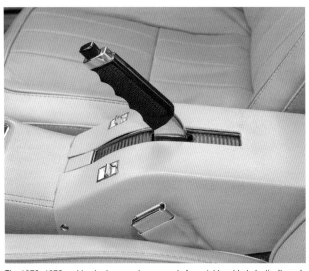

The 1973–1976 parking brake console was made from rigid molded plastic. It used the ribbed black plastic park brake handle sliding surround shown here.

The 1977 radio knobs have serrated silver edges and a black center with a silver circle in the middle. Secondary controls behind the main knobs are gloss black plastic.

Center Console, Shifter, and Park Brake

All 1973–1977 center consoles are made from molded vinyl in the same color as the interior. All 1973–1976 park brake lever consoles are made from rigid molded plastic and also match interior color. The 1977 park brake consoles are made from a flexible molded vinyl material in the same color as the interior.

The insert in the top of the center console is painted semi-gloss black and is the same design in 1973–1976. In 1977 the entire top of the center console is redesigned, and it is also semi-gloss black. Those 1973–1976 cars equipped with the custom interior trim option have a simulated wood insert in the top of the center console.

In 1973–1976 cars, engine specifications are debossed into an insert below the shifter. These specifications include the compression ratio and engine size.

In cars with manual transmission, the shift pattern is indicated next to the shifter. The shift pattern area is semi-gloss black, and the letters and numbers are chrome. All 1973–1976 cars, but not '77s, also have a chrome border around the pattern.

This is the correct automatic transmission shifter for 1973–1977.

The walnut veneer insert in the center console was part of the custom interior trim option. Original center consoles have real stitching. Some reproductions have simulated stitching molded into the vinyl.

The console-mounted engine data plate used in 1973–1974 includes engine displacement, torque rating, and compression ratio.

The console-mounted engine data plate used in 1975–1976 includes engine displacement and compression ratio information.

The shifter boot for manual transmission cars is made from black leather and has a sewn seam toward the passenger side of the car. Manual shifters have a chrome shaft and a threaded-on black chrome ball. A T-handle integral to the shaft controls the reverse lockout.

On those Corvettes equipped with an automatic transmission, the shift pattern is also next to the shifter. A plastic lighted band with painted letters is used to indicate shifter position. In 1973–1976 automatic transmission shifters are surrounded by a gloss black plastic seal that slides back and forth as the shifter is moved. In 1977 the shifter is surrounded by a leather boot.

Automatic shifters are made from a chrome shaft topped by a black plastic ball. The ball has a chrome spring-loaded button in the top to release the detent and allow the shifter to be moved.

The heater/air-conditioning control assembly utilized in 1973–1976 has white letters and a fan control switch mounted directly behind the larger assembly, not in a separate small rectangle. A chrome lever is used to set fan speed. All air-conditioned cars use a switch with four positions, in addition to "off." Switches in non-air-conditioned cars have only three positions in addition to "off."

Whether the car is equipped with air conditioning or not, in 1973–1976 its control assembly employs two large black plastic rotary thumbwheels on either side. The left side thumbwheel controls temperature, and the right side thumbwheel controls the system setting.

Non-air-conditioned 1973–1976s have two fresh-air vent controls on the center console. The controls are sliding levers made from small black plastic balls with a flat area mounted to black oxide metal arms. The balls are shiny black on the flat face but change to dull black with a grained pattern on the rounded portion only. The word "CLOSE" in white paint and a white arrow appear on the balls' flat faces.

The 1977 Corvettes use an entirely different type of heater/air-conditioning control assembly. Instead of the previous thumbwheel switch assembly, the new unit relies

1973–1977

A 1973–1976 heater and air-conditioning control assembly. The surrounding wood veneer indicates that this car came with the custom interior trim option.

A switch for the optional C50 rear window defroster was on the driver side of the center console. All 1973s and those 1974s made through approximately February 1974 used a round, chrome-plated knob with a black center and knurled edge on the switch. Later cars used the three-position black rocker switch shown here.

This is an original 1973 heater and air-conditioning control panel. The same basic design was used through 1976.

This is a correct 1973–1976 park brake handle. Switches for optional power windows are chrome plated. The 1977 handle was made from lightly textured rubber, rather than hard plastic with a more pronounced texture, as shown here.

on horizontal sliding levers to control function and temperature. A separate fan speed switch is located to the left of the control unit.

All 1973–1976s have an ashtray inset into the center console insert next to the heater/air-conditioning control assembly. All 1977s have a wider ashtray inset into the console below the heater/air-conditioning control unit. The ashtray door is semi-gloss black and slides back and forth with slight resistance. All cars are equipped with a cigarette lighter.

On those 1973–1977 Corvettes equipped with the optional rear window defogger, a control switch is mounted on the left side trim panel, forward of the center console. In 1973 the switch is one speed and uses a large round chrome-plated knob. Thereafter it has three speeds and uses a toggle switch lever.

All 1973–1977 Corvettes have a park brake lever mounted between the seats. The lever's handle is made from hard, shiny black plastic, with a crosshatch pattern to enhance grip. Chrome trim separates the black plastic grips in 1973 and 1974. In 1975–1977 the chrome trim is eliminated. A release button on the top of the lever is also made from hard, shiny black plastic. A chrome band separates the button from the remainder of the handle for all years.

In 1973–1976 the slotted opening in the park brake lever console is covered by a rippled black plastic cover that slides along with the movement of the lever. In 1977 the rubber park brake console has a slit that the lever passes through.

Rear Storage Compartments and Their Contents, Battery, and Rear Window Storage Tray

All 1973–1977s feature three enclosed storage compartments behind the seats. The lids for these compartments are made from molded fiberglass, with the exception of those found in some early '73s, which are made from pressboard. All lids are covered with carpet that matches the interior carpet. The underside of each lid is painted flat black. A white vehicle maintenance sticker is on the underside of the center compartment lid. A sticker for jacking instructions is on the underside of the passenger-side compartment lid. In 1973 and 1974, a sticker for the limited-slip differential is also on the underside of the passenger compartment lid.

Each lid is surrounded by a molded plastic border painted to match interior color. The entire assembly of all three lids is also surrounded by a color-matched molded plastic border.

Each lid is hinged and latches with a spring-loaded mechanism. Each lid has a chrome button for releasing the latch and a hoop for pulling it open. The hoop, which is leather in cars with leather seats and vinyl in cars with vinyl seats, is the same color as the interior and is retained to the lid by a chrome Phillips-head screw.

One of the rear compartments is fitted with a locking chrome release button. The lock is usually in the passenger-side compartment door but is sometimes found on one of the other doors instead. The key for the storage compartment lid lock is the same as the keys for the antitheft alarm and spare tire storage compartment.

The compartment directly behind the driver's seat holds the vehicle's battery. It has a thin foam seal around the perimeter of the door opening to help keep battery fumes from entering the passenger compartment.

All 1973–1977 Corvettes use a side-terminal Delco battery. For each year, two different model batteries were used. In 1973–1975 the battery is called Delco Energizer, and in 1976–1977 it's called Delco Freedom.

In 1973 cars equipped with the standard engine or optional L82 engine use Delco model R 88ST. Those cars equipped with either a big-block engine or the heavy-duty battery option (option T60) use Delco model R 88WT.

In 1974 cars equipped with the standard engine or optional L82 engine use Delco model R 89ST. Those cars equipped with either a big-block engine or the heavy-duty battery option (option UA1) use Delco model R 89WT.

In 1975 cars equipped with the standard engine or optional L82 engine use Delco model R 89ST. Those cars equipped with the heavy-duty battery option (option UA1) use Delco model R 89WPT.

In 1976 cars equipped with the standard engine or optional L82 engine use Delco model R 87-5. Those cars equipped with the heavy-duty battery option (option UA1) use Delco model R 89WP.

In 1977 cars equipped with the standard engine or optional L82 engine use Delco model R 87-5. Those cars equipped with the heavy-duty battery option (option UA1) use Delco model R 89-5.

All batteries used in 1973–1975 have six cells covered by two plastic caps, each of which covers three cells. In those '73s assembled through approximately January 1973, each cap has three Delco "split circle" logos molded into its top. The split circles are painted dark orange. The caps in '73s assembled after approximately January 1973, as well 1974 and 1975 cars, have flat tops with no markings. In all 1973–1975 cars, a black rubber vent hose runs from each of the caps through a hole in the underbody.

The 1973–1975 Delco Energizer batteries say "Delco Energizer" in raised letters on top of the case. A black and silver label is also on top of the case. This label reads "REPLACE WITH ENERGIZER R-88 ST" (or whatever model the particular battery is).

Delco Freedom batteries used in 1976 and 1977 do not have cell caps. Instead they have two large raised squares in the top of the battery. One of the squares contains the "Delco Eye," a small circle of glass utilized to indicate battery condition.

The top of the Delco Freedom battery is blue, and the sides are white. A "caution" label is affixed to the top. Also, the words "Delco Freedom Battery" are written across the top.

All 1973–1977 battery cables are side-terminal style and have a red positive end and a black negative end. The positive cable terminal has a plus sign molded in, and the negative terminal has a minus sign molded in.

The cables themselves are covered with black insulation with the words "COPPER CLAD ALUMINUM" in white block letters. The cables are retained with $\frac{5}{16}$-inch hex-head bolts.

The passenger-side storage compartment contains a removable insert. The insert, which is like a squared-off bucket, is made from grayish black fiberboard and measures about 6¼ inches deep. The inside has a material called flock. It consists of small strands of black fiber and resembles velvet.

The fiberboard insert contains an off-white cotton pouch with a yellow drawstring. The drawstring is held on by an encasement stitched with red thread. The pouch contains eight silver washers and four oblong, gray phosphate shims for adjusting seat backs to the preferred position.

In addition to the seat hardware pouch, the storage insert holds a number of other items. A small white paper envelope with the "GM mark of excellence" logo and instructions printed in black letters contains the car's keys and the key knockouts.

A small brown paper envelope contains license plate screws. This bag is marked "UNIT NUMBER 3875313" across the top, "LICENSE ATTACHING" on one side, and "REAR PLATE PARTS" on the other side.

Another small brown paper envelope is included with those Corvettes equipped with the optional P02 deluxe wheel covers. This envelope contains four extensions for the valve stems.

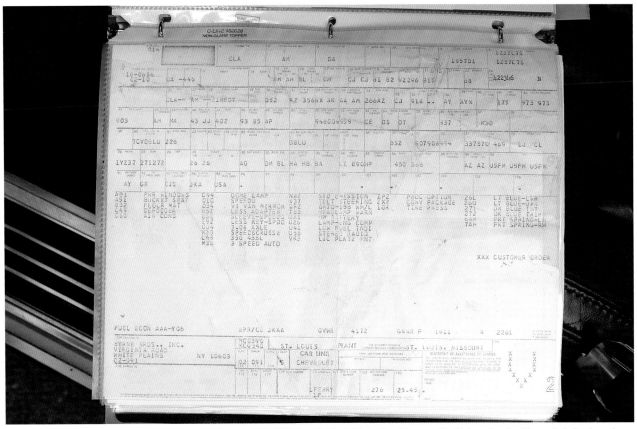

A document commonly called a build sheet was generated for each 1973–1977 Corvette. The build sheet contains a wealth of information about the car, including the options it came with and identifying information for some of the parts it was built with. A copy of the build sheet is often found somewhere in the car, with likely locations being under the carpet, inside a seat, behind the dash, or on top of the fuel tank. This example is from a 1977.

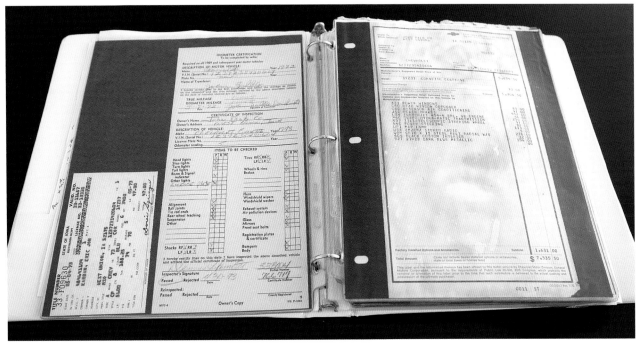

Original sales documents and other original paperwork are highly desirable to collectors. Sometimes paperwork has remained with the car through the years. Sometimes you can procure it by tracking down the car's previous owners.

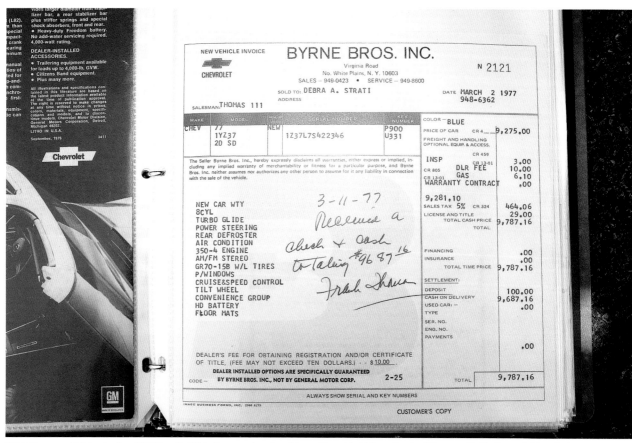

This is the new vehicle invoice for a 1977 Corvette. Original paperwork such as this provides a lot of information about the car and is highly coveted by collectors.

The final item in the storage insert is the owner's packet. This packet includes an owner's manual, warranty folder, Protect-O-Plate, consumer information booklet, trim ring installation instruction card, tire warranty booklet, and radio instruction sheet (if the car has a radio). For 1974 the packet also has a seat-belt instruction addendum. All these items are in a clear vinyl envelope.

The fiberboard insert in the passenger-side rear storage compartment lifts out to reveal additional storage area beneath. A jack and jack handle are mounted to the bottom of the compartment (to the car's floor panel) with a black spring that latches onto a black hook riveted to the floor.

All jacks are painted gloss or semi-gloss black and have the letter "A" stamped in the chassis contact pad. This letter is the logo for Auto Specialties Manufacturing, the company that made the jacks.

In addition to the manufacturer's logo, all jacks contain a date code stamping. The stamping is on the jack's large side arm and contains a number for the year followed by a letter for the month, with "A" representing January, "B" representing February, and so on. So the date code stamping for a jack manufactured in June 1975 would say "5 F."

All jack handles are painted gloss or semi-gloss black and include a pivoting ¾-inch boxed hex wrench on the end for removing and installing lug nuts. A thick rubber ring is fitted around the hex wrench end to prevent rattling.

In addition to the jack and jack handle, electrical relays and a flasher unit are mounted in the area underneath the fiberboard insert. These components are part of the antitheft alarm system.

All 1973–1977 coupes have two storage bags to hold the T-tops when they are removed. Some cars have bags dyed to match interior color, while others have black bags regardless of interior color. Earlier cars for each year are more likely to have color-matched bags, and later cars are more likely to have black bags.

All bags have a date code stamped inside in ink. Typical date stampings contain a month and year designation. For example, bags manufactured in October 1974 read "10-74." In addition to the date stamping, bags might also contain a logo stamping representing the manufacturer. The most common logo seen is "TEX."

All bags have a flap that closes over the opening and is retained by three chrome-plated snaps.

All 1973–1977 coupes have adjustable T-top hold-down straps. Tops are held by a single harness that attaches to the rear bulkhead in the luggage area and extends to a chrome-plated anchor attached to the front bulkhead between the

Original 1975 T-top guide pin and hold-down latch details. Note the sloppy application of yellow weather strip adhesive, which is typical of factory production.

An original T-top from an unrestored 1975.

seats. As with the T-top bags, early cars tend to have straps dyed to match interior color, and later cars tend to have black straps regardless of interior color.

All 1973–1977 coupes have molded vinyl trim mounted to the underside of the T-tops. The vinyl is the same color as the interior. Beginning in late 1976, a dome light is found in the center of the interior roof trim.

Convertible Top Frames

For all 1973–1975 convertibles, top frames are painted semigloss black. A black fiberglass header panel is secured to the front underside of the top frame. Three chrome-plated latches secure the front top header to the windshield frame. Black

rubber coats the latch levers, and each latch is accompanied by an adjustable, rubber-tipped tensioning bolt.

The convertible top frame's rear bow is secured to the body deck lid with two chrome-plated pins that insert into chrome-plated receptacles affixed to the body. Chrome Phillips oval-head screws hold the pins to the rear bow.

The underside of the convertible top, including the top material itself and the pads, is always black regardless of interior color.

The optional removable hardtop on those convertibles so equipped has a padded vinyl headliner color matched to the interior. Metal trim pieces on the underside of the hardtop are also painted to match interior color. Front latches for the hardtop are chrome plated, but unlike the soft top, the levers on these latches are not rubber coated.

The underside of the convertible deck lid is painted body color. Deck lid release levers, release cables, and lock mechanisms were all mounted prior to painting and should therefore also be painted body color.

The latch receptacles for the pins in the rear bow of the convertible top, as well as the rods that control the receptacles, are black. Deck lid rubber bumpers are black, as are their brackets.

1973–1977 MECHANICAL
Engine Blocks

The engine block casting number for all 1973–1977 engines is located on the top rear driver side of the block, on the flange that mates to the transmission bell housing.

Some very early 1973 small-block-equipped Corvettes utilize a block with the casting number 3970014. All other '73s and all 1974–1977 small-block cars use a number-3970010

Every Corvette engine block has a casting number on the top driver-side rear of the block, immediately adjacent to where the bell housing mounts to the engine. Casting number "3999289" indicates that this is a 1973 or 1974 454-cid block.

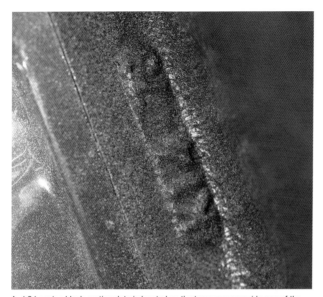
An LS4 engine block casting date is located on the top passenger-side rear of the block, immediately adjacent to where the bell housing mounts to the engine. The casting date consists of a letter representing the month, two numbers denoting the day, and two more numbers indicating the year. In this example, "K14 73" tells us that this block was cast on November 14, 1973.

block. All 1973 and 1974 big-block cars use number-3999289 blocks.

Engine block casting dates for all 1973–1977 small- and big-block Corvettes, with the exception of small-blocks utilizing number-3970014 blocks, are located on the top rear passenger side of the block, on the flange that mates to the transmission bell housing. The casting date for the number-3970014 cast block is on the top rear driver side flange adjacent to the casting number.

The engine block casting date for number-3970010 small-blocks and all big-blocks consists of a letter for the month, one or two numbers for the day, and one number for the year. For example, a number-3970010 block cast on June 12, 1975, would have a casting date of "F 12 5."

Number-3970014 small-blocks found in some very early 1973s use a similar date code system, except the year is designated by two numbers rather than one. For example, a number-3970014 block cast on August 21, 1972, would have a casting date of "H 21 72."

All 1973–1977 engines contain two distinct stampings on a machined pad on the top of the passenger side between the cylinder head and water pump. One stamping is commonly

The passenger-side L48 engine compartment in an unrestored 1977. The GM parts label wrapped around the air-conditioning hose indicates that the hose was likely replaced at some point.

referred to as the assembly stamping; the other is commonly called the VIN derivative stamping.

The assembly stamping begins with a prefix letter to indicate the engine assembly plant. "V" indicates the Flint plant, where all small-blocks were assembled, and "T" designates the Tonawanda plant, where all big-blocks were assembled. Following the prefix letter are four numbers indicating the month and day of assembly. After the numbers indicating the assembly date are three suffix letters denoting the particular engine. This suffix code is often referred to as the engine broadcast code or simply the engine code. (Refer to Appendix C for engine suffix codes.)

To illustrate what a typical engine assembly stamping looks like, consider the following 1977 combination: a base 350/180-horsepower engine built on April 5 and coupled to a four-speed transmission. The assembly stamping for such an engine would read "V0405CKZ."

Always remember that the engine assembly date must come after the engine block casting date (you can't assemble an engine before the block is cast), and both the casting date and assembly date must precede the final assembly date of the car (you can't final assemble a car before the engine has been cast and assembled). The great majority of engines were cast and assembled a few weeks prior to the car's assembly date. Some engines were cast and/or assembled months prior to installation, however. Six months is generally accepted as the outer limit between an engine assembly or casting date and the final assembly date of the car.

The VIN derivative stamping, as the name implies, is a stamping containing a portion or a derivative of the car's vehicle identification number. For 1973–1977 Corvettes, the VIN derivative stamping begins with a "1" to designate the Chevrolet car line. This is followed by the final eight characters of the car's VIN. So the VIN derivative stamping in the engine for the 8,612th 1976 built would read "16S408612."

On big-block engines the assembly stamping is normally on the left and toward the rear of the pad when viewing it to read the stamping. The VIN derivative stamping is to the right and toward the front of the pad. On small-block engines, this positioning is reversed.

All 1973–1977 engine blocks are cast iron. In 1973–1976 the blocks are painted Chevrolet Engine Orange. In 1977 they are painted blue.

A driver-side L48 engine compartment in an unrestored 1977. Note how crooked the "Keep your GM car all GM" decal on the air cleaner base is. This shows that Corvettes were largely hand assembled, mass-produced cars that were less than perfect in many areas.

All 1973–1977 Corvettes were fitted with a black metal plate containing the car's vehicle identification number. The VIN plate was attached to the driver-side windshield pillar with a rosette-head rivet on either end. The heads of the rivets are beneath the pillar's interior trim.

A 1974 LS4 bell housing with casting number "3899621." The bell housing was on the engine when it was painted Chevrolet Engine Orange.

All 1973–1977 Corvette engines came with two alphanumeric stampings in the flat pad on top of the block at the forward passenger side, immediately adjacent to the water pump. On big-block engines, the assembly code was outboard and the VIN derivative was inboard. On small-blocks it was opposite. In this 1974 example, "T" represents the Tonawanda engine plant, "1120" denotes November 20, and "CWM" represents a 454-cid, 270-horsepower V-8 coupled to a manual transmission. In the VIN derivative stamping, "1" stands for Chevrolet Division, "4" represents model year 1974, "S" is for the St. Louis Assembly Plant, "4" denotes the Corvette model, and "10617" tells us that this engine went into the 10,617th 1974 Corvette built.

Small-blocks were originally painted before exhaust manifolds were installed. Therefore coverage on the sides of the block behind the manifolds is good. It is believed that all or most big-blocks were painted with exhaust manifolds installed. The engine stamp pad and timing tab on the timing chain cover were normally covered up when the engine was painted. Therefore they normally appear unpainted.

Cylinder Heads

As with engine blocks, all 1973–1977 cylinder heads have both a casting number and a casting date. As with blocks and other cast parts, the cylinder head casting date typically has a letter to indicate month, one or two numbers to indicate the day of the month, and one number to indicate the year. (Refer to Appendix G for cylinder head casting numbers.)

All 1973–1977 engines utilize cast-iron cylinder heads. All cylinder heads and head bolts are painted engine color.

Intake Manifolds

All 1973–1977 intake manifolds are cast iron and painted engine color. As with engine blocks and cylinder heads, intake manifolds contain casting numbers and casting dates. As with other cast engine parts, the casting date consists of a letter designating the month, one or two numbers designating the day of the month, and a number denoting the year.

Casting numbers and casting dates for all manifolds are on the top surface. (Refer to Appendix H for intake manifold casting numbers.)

All 1973–1977 Corvette engines utilize an aluminum thermostat housing painted engine color. With the exception of some late 1977s, the housing does not have a hole for a temperature sending unit.

Unlike those used on earlier cars, original 1973–1977 intake manifold side gaskets do not have semicircular tabs visible between the runners for cylinders three and six and for the exhaust heat crossover passage.

All intake manifolds are held on by 9/16-inch hex-head bolts. The bolts do not get any type of washer. Engine lifting brackets are attached to the engines in all 1973–1977 Corvettes. The brackets are painted engine color.

All 1973–1974 intake manifolds are made from cast iron and contain both a casting number and casting date on top. The casting number in this example, "336789," is correct for a 1974 LS4. The casting date of "K14 73" indicates that the manifold was cast on November 14, 1973.

All small-blocks have one bracket attached to the first and second intake manifold bolt from the front on the driver's side. On four-speed cars, a second bracket is attached to the rear of the engine, with one of the bolts holding the bell housing to the block. Some cars with automatic transmission do not have a rear bracket, and some have one attached to the rear of the intake manifold on the passenger side.

All big-blocks have a front bracket that attaches to the first and second intake manifold bolts from the front on the driver's side. A rear bracket is fastened to the rear of the cylinder head on the passenger side.

All 1973–1977 Corvette ignition distributors had an identification band wrapped around the housing. This band, which was removed for the photograph, shows part number "1112114" and manufacture date code "3 K 2." The part number indicates that it is correct for a 1973 or 1974 LS4 engine's distributor. The first number of the code is the final digit of the year, the letter represents the month, and the final number indicates the day, so this example was made on October 2, 1973.

Distributor and Ignition Coil

All 1973 and 1974 Corvettes use a mechanical tach drive Delco Remy point distributor. All 1975–1977 cars use a Delco HEI distributor and an electronic tachometer.

All 1973 and 1974 point distributors have a thin aluminum identification band secured around the housing in a recess just above where the distributor hold-down clamp rests. The identification band is natural on one side and dyed pinkish red on the other. While the majority of cars have the dye on the outside of the band, some have it on the inside, making it difficult to see when the band is installed on the distributor. The identification band has the words "DELCO REMY" stamped into it. This is followed by a seven-character part number and a date code.

All 1975–1977 HEI distributors have part numbers and date codes stamped directly into their aluminum housings. These stampings are on the driver side. (Refer to Appendix K for distributor part numbers.)

The date code, which represents the day the distributor was assembled, consists of a number representing the year, a letter representing the month, and one or two numbers representing the day of the month. For distributor date codes, the letter "A" represents January, "B" represents February, and so on. As is typical of stamped-in date codes, the letter "I" is skipped, so September is represented by "J." The date code on a distributor assembled on January 17, 1973, for example, would read "3 A 17."

While most distributors were made several weeks before the engine was assembled, it is entirely possible that several months can separate the two. As with most other components, six months is the generally accepted maximum.

All 1973 and 1974 distributor housings are painted semi-gloss black and have a daub of one of several colors of paint just below the distributor cap on the passenger side toward the front of the car. The 1975–1977 distributor housings are unpainted.

All distributors are fitted with a vacuum advance unit. Vacuum advances have part numbers stamped into them in the bracket that mounts the vacuum canister to the distributor.

All 1973–1977 Corvettes use a black Delco Remy distributor cap. The 1973 and 1974 caps have the words "Delco Remy" and a patent number molded into the top between the towers.

All 1973 and 1974 Corvettes use a separate Delco Remy ignition coil. A silver-cadmium-plated, stamped-steel bracket holds the coil. The coil is clamped into the bracket with a slotted round-head machine screw, and the bracket is held to the intake manifold by two hex-head bolts. If the car is equipped with a radio, a clamp retained by a single screw holds a capacitor to the coil bracket.

Coils are painted gloss black and have the last three numbers of their Chevrolet part number embossed in the housing from the inside out, so they are raised up. In addition to the final three numbers of the part number, ignition coils have "B-R" embossed in their cases.

The ignition coil for 1975–1977 cars is integral to the distributor cap. It is manufactured by Delco and is black. It says "DELCO REMY" and "MADE IN THE USA" on top. The word "LATCH" appears on the top twice.

This is a correct coil for 1973–1974 Corvettes with the optional LS4 engine. The correct coil for small-block cars has the same configuration, with the final three digits of the GM part number and "B-R" embossed on. Small-block coils are part number 1115270, so they have "270" embossed near the top of the canister.

Ignition Shielding

All 1973–1977 Corvettes equipped with a radio are outfitted with ignition shielding. All pieces of shielding are plated with flash chrome. The quality and appearance of the chrome are not very good.

All small-blocks utilize a one-piece top ignition shield. A translucent plastic shield is held to the underside of the top ignition shield by four plastic rivets.

The ignition shield is held to its two support brackets by one chrome-plated wing bolt on each side. The support brackets are painted engine color and attach to the intake manifold bolts.

Small-block-equipped cars have two chrome-plated spark plug shields, each covering two plugs at the rear of the engine. The spark plug shields are retained to cadmium-plated brackets with chrome-plated wing bolts. The brackets are cadmium plated and have "FPM" stamped in to represent the manufacturer. Later, incorrect GM replacement brackets have the letters "CNI" stamped in.

Small-blocks have four cadmium-plated spark plug heat shields, each covering two plugs. Each heat shield is retained to the engine block by means of a single silver-cadmium-plated indented hex-head bolt.

All small-block-equipped cars also use a pair of boomerang or V-shaped sections of chrome-plated shielding to encapsulate the spark plug wires. The boomerang shielding runs from the bottom of the vertical shields to the area beneath the spark plugs.

Those 1973–1977 Corvettes equipped with a radio were fitted with chrome ignition shielding to shield the radio from interference generated by the ignition system. All 1973–1976s and some 1977s used two chrome-plated wing bolts to hold the top shield on. Some 1977s used black-phosphate-plated hex-head bolts to hold the top shield on.

Driver-side details of 1974 Rochester Quadrajet.

Small-block cars not originally equipped with a radio still have the two main shield support brackets on the back of the intake manifold and the cadmium-plated spark plug heat shields. They do not have any of the chrome shielding, however.

Like small-blocks, 1973 and 1974 big-blocks each have a one-piece top ignition shield held to two support brackets by one chrome-plated wing bolt on each side.

However, rather than vertical spark plug wire shields and spark plug shields like small-blocks, big-blocks have special spark plug wires covered with braided stainless-steel wire. The braid toward the end of each wire ends in a hoop that fastens to the valve cover bolts to provide a ground. The four driver-side hoops are attached in two pairs to the second and fourth bolts back. The passenger side has a single hoop on the first and second bolt and a pair of hoops on the third bolt back. The valve cover bolts holding the hoops are unpainted. All other valve cover bolts are painted engine color.

All big-block engines are fitted with spark plug heat shields. Each heat shield is a cadmium-plated steel tube with a welded-on tab. The tab allows each shield to be mounted to an exhaust manifold bolt. Big-block cars not originally equipped with a radio do not have the main shield support brackets or braided steel spark plug wires, but they do have the heat shields.

In addition to the external ignition shielding fitted to all 1973–1977 Corvettes equipped with a radio, 1973 and 1974 cars had an additional shield covering the ignition points beneath the distributor cap. This additional shield is called a radio frequency interference (RFI) shield.

Spark Plug Wires

All 1973–1977 Corvettes use spark plug wires manufactured by Packard Electric. All wires are ink stamped every few inches with the words "Packard T V R Suppression" and a date code. The date code indicates the quarter and the year of manufacture. For example, wires labeled "2Q-76" were made in the second quarter of 1976.

Wires are black in 1973 and most of 1974 and gray in 1975–1977. Small-block engines have boots with 90-degree bends at the spark plug end and no bends at the distributor end. The 1973 and 1974 big-block wires have straight boots at the spark plug ends and boots with 90-degree bends at the distributor ends. Both black and gray boots were used, with no clear pattern for which color was used when.

Carburetors

All 1973–1977 Corvettes have a Rochester Quadrajet carburetor. Carter was at times contracted to manufacture Rochester Quadrajet carburetors for General Motors, and the Carter-built Quadrajets are almost identical to the Rochester-built ones. Carter-built Quadrajets are identified as being manufactured by Carter and use Carter's system of date coding rather than Rochester's system. (Refer to Appendix J for carburetor numbers.)

Rochester-built Quadrajets contain an alphanumeric sequence stamped into a flat, vertical area of the main body on the rear of the driver side. Either the full seven-digit GM part number or the final five digits of the part number are stamped in. Several letters, which identify the specific plant where the carburetor was made, may be stamped here as well. Finally, four numbers denoting the date of manufacture are also stamped into this area.

Rochester utilized the Julian calendar for date coding its carburetors. With this system of dating, the first three numbers represent the day of the year, and the final number is the last digit of the specific year. For example, the Julian date code for a carburetor made on January 1, 1974, would read "0014." The first three digits, "001," represent the first day of the year. The final digit, "4," represents 1974.

Carter-built Quadrajets don't use a Julian calendar date coding system. Instead, they use a single letter and a single number. The letter denotes the month, with "A" indicating January, "B" indicating February, and so on. The letter "I" is not used, so September is represented by "J." The number in the date code for Carter-built Quadrajets is the last digit for the year of manufacture. For example, a date code of "C5" indicates that the carburetor was made in March 1975.

All carburetors are plated gold dichromate. Plating tends to be rather dark and uniform in color. All carburetors have an insulator separating them from the intake manifold.

All 1973 carburetors use a single accelerator return spring. It is natural or silver cadmium plated and mounts from the primary shaft bell crank to the accelerator cable mount. The 1974–1977 carburetors use two accelerator return springs, a silver one inside a blue one.

Carburetors utilize a mechanical choke controlled by a thermostatic coil. The coil is mounted in a recess on

All 1973–1977 Corvettes came with a Quadrajet carburetor. All Quadrajets had identifying information stamped into the main body on the driver side. Part number "7045222" indicates that this carburetor is for a 1975 L48. "R6" is believed to denote the specific plant where the carburetor was manufactured, and "1275" indicates that this carburetor was made on the 127th day of 1975.

the passenger side of the intake manifold and is covered by a cadmium-plated steel housing. A rod links the coil to the choke linkage on the carburetor. The rod is secured to the linkage with a round clip that locks over a groove in the end of the rod.

Air Cleaner

All 1973–1975 Corvettes use an air cleaner design that works in conjunction with the fresh-air induction hood. This design uses a housing with two forward-facing snorkels that allow air to enter.

The housing is painted gloss black, as is the lid. There are no decals on the lid. A decal on the side of the housing reads "KEEP YOUR GM CAR ALL GM." This sticker is white with red and blue lettering.

In addition to the two forward-facing snorkels, 1973–1975 air cleaners also receive air from the hood cowling at times. A stepped rubber gasket and steel flange on the edge of the air cleaner base seal against the duct in the underside of the hood.

All 1976 and 1977 Corvettes use a different air cleaner assembly. The assembly is entirely closed and does not mate to the hood. For cars with base engines, the housing has a single snorkel pointing toward the front of the car, with a slight offset to the driver side. The air cleaner housing in cars equipped with an L-82 engine has two forward-facing snorkels.

On base engines the snorkel is connected to a black molded plastic plenum on top of the fan shroud by means of a duct. The duct is made from black paper over coiled

The unrestored underside of a 1975 hood. As shown, 11 large, round, black-phosphate-coated push-on retainers hold the insulation in place. In 1976–1977, only eight retainers were used.

wire and has an accordion shape. It is retained at each end by means of a built-in clamp that snaps into position.

The snorkel has a vacuum motor that opens to permit the flow of warmed air from a metallic tube connected to the driver-side exhaust manifold. The vacuum motor is painted semi-gloss black and has the words "AUTO THERMAC" embossed on the top side.

On L82 engines, both snorkels are connected to a molded plenum. It is similar to the plenum on cars with base engines, except it has two connection points.

Air cleaner assemblies have the replacement filter number and other information on a white sticker affixed to the outside of the air cleaner housing.

Original 1973–1977 air filter elements, unlike later replacements, have a fine wire screen around the outside in a vertical (not diagonal) pattern. The horizontal and vertical wire forms rectangles, with the longer measurement running vertical when the element is installed.

This is an extremely correct L48 engine compartment in a low-mileage, unrestored 1975. The alarm pin switch, radiator cap, and AIR pump belt are not correct.

Valve Covers

All 1973–1977 base engines are fitted with stamped-steel valve covers painted engine color. These are held on with hex-head bolts and metal tabs that are also painted engine color.

Two metal wire retention clips are spot welded to the passenger-side cover. This cover also has a crankcase vent intake hole. The hole gets a black rubber grommet. A tube inserts into the grommet and connects to the air cleaner base.

On cars with base engines, two metal wire retention clips are spot welded to the driver-side cover. This cover also has a PCV valve inserted into a hole fitted with a rubber grommet. A hose connects the PCV valve to the carburetor. The driver-side cover has a provision for the oil filler cap.

Optional L82 small-blocks utilize cast-aluminum valve covers with longitudinal ribs. As with the painted steel covers, a vent hose connects the passenger-side valve cover to the air cleaner base, and a PCV valve is in the driver-side valve cover.

A yellow decal containing the engine suffix code and measuring 1⅛ by 2¼ inches was normally placed on the rear of the passenger-side valve cover. It is likely that the decal was sometimes placed on the front of the passenger-side valve cover. This example, from an unrestored 1973, indicates that the engine is an LS4 coupled to an automatic transmission.

Passenger-side engine compartment details in an original 1973. The rubber oil fill cap in the valve cover is normally painted, but it is believed that some LS4-equipped cars were delivered new with unpainted caps.

Aluminum valve covers are retained by silver-cadmium-plated, indented hex-head bolts.

Passenger- and driver-side aluminum valve covers are both made from the same mold. The only difference is that the driver-side cover has a hole for the oil fill cap, and the passenger side does not. On the passenger side, where the hole would go, is a rigid disc with the crossed-flag emblem glued on. All 1973 and 1974 big-block valve covers are made from stamped steel painted engine color. Unlike earlier covers, they do not have internal drippers that are spot welded on.

The passenger-side cover has a hole fitted with a black rubber grommet. A long black-phosphate-plated steel tube inserts into the grommet and connects to the rear of the air cleaner housing.

The passenger-side big-block cover has a welded-on bracket at the rear to hold a plastic spark plug wire loom. Two metal brackets are spot welded on toward the top edge of the cover. These brackets retain wires and hose. Four individual brackets along the bottom edge of the cover hold each of the passenger-side spark plug wires. Another wire retention bracket is welded on the bottom toward the rear.

The driver-side big-block cover has the PCV valve and a welded-on bracket at the rear to hold a plastic spark plug wire loom. The bracket has a hole to receive a clip that holds wire to the carburetor solenoid. A metal bracket is spot welded on toward the top edge of the cover. This bracket also retains the wire to the carburetor solenoid. Four individual brackets along the bottom edge of the cover hold each of the driver-side spark plug wires. A bracket is also welded on the bottom edge toward the middle.

The curve of the inner front corner of the driver-side big-block cover is interrupted by a small flat indentation. The curve of the outer rear corner is recessed to provide clearance for the power brake booster.

Aluminum valve covers used on L82 engines have chrome-plated twist-in oil fill caps on the driver side. A large "S" for Stant, the manufacturer of the caps, is stamped into the center rivet. Base engines use a steel twist-on oil fill cap in the driver's side valve cover. As with the L82 cap, a large "S" for Stant is normally stamped into the center rivet. An "X" instead of an "S" is sometimes in the rivet on original caps. Some 1975–1976 caps have "Engine Oil Fill" and

"AC FC2" stamped in. Base-engine oil fill caps are painted engine color.

All 1973 and 1974 big-block engines use a rubber push-in-style oil fill plug with the word "OIL" molded into the top. Since the plug was installed before the engine was painted, it too is painted Chevrolet Engine Orange.

Exhaust Manifolds

All 1973–1977 exhaust manifolds are cast iron. The casting number is normally on the side facing away from the engine, and the casting date is normally on the side facing toward the engine. (Refer to Appendix I for exhaust manifold casting numbers.)

Small-block exhaust manifold casting dates normally include a letter denoting the month and one or two numbers denoting the day of the month. Big-block exhaust manifolds normally include a letter denoting the month, one or two numbers denoting the day of the month, and two numbers denoting the year.

Small-block exhaust manifolds were not yet installed when engines were originally painted, so they show no signs of overspray. Big-block manifolds were installed before engines were painted and therefore have Chevrolet Engine Orange paint overspray.

No 1973–1977 exhaust manifolds use a gasket where they mount to the cylinder head.

Small-block manifolds use ⁷⁄₁₆-inch hex-head bolts with two concentric rings on the heads. The front two bolts and rear two bolts on both sides of the engine get French locks, with one of the two tabs bent over to prevent the bolts from loosening. In addition, the same front and rear bolts on each side get thick flat washers that sit between the French lock and manifold. But if the exhaust manifold bolt also retains a bracket (such as an air-conditioning bracket), the flat washer is not used.

Bolts holding big-block manifolds have three different kinds of heads. The most prevalent has two concentric rings like small-block manifold bolts. A second design has an integral washer, a recessed hex head, and the letter "A" (the manufacturer's logo) in the center of the head. A third variety is a simple hex head with no markings.

The 1973 and 1974 big-block exhaust manifolds do not have French locks or any type of washers used with the bolts.

Starter Motor

All 1973–1977 Corvettes use a Delco Remy starter motor. Automatic-transmission-equipped cars utilize starters with aluminum noses, while starters for manual-transmission-equipped cars have cast-iron noses. Motor housings and cast-iron noses are usually painted semi-gloss black, but it is believed that some left the factory unpainted. Aluminum noses are unpainted.

The starter's part number and assembly date are stamped into the side of the motor housing. The date code contains a number representing the last digit of the year and a letter denoting the month, with "A" representing January, "B" representing February, and so on. As is typical of stamped-in date codes, the letter "I" is skipped, so September is represented by "J." One or two numbers indicating the day follow the letter denoting the month. For example, a date code of "7B14" indicates that the starter was made on February 14, 1977. (Refer to Appendix N for starter motor part numbers.)

Starter solenoids have a black Bakelite cover for the electrical connections. Solenoid housings may be painted semi-gloss black or be silver cadmium plated.

All starters use a stamped-steel brace to support the forward end (the end facing the front of the car when the starter is installed). The brace mounts to a stud on the starter's end plate and to a threaded boss in the engine block. The brace is painted semi-gloss black.

Every starter has a heat shield to protect it from exhaust system heat. Small-block engines are fitted with a rectangular shield, while big-blocks get a larger, irregularly shaped shield. Small-block shields are painted semi-gloss black, and big-block shields are plated with poor-quality flash chrome. Heat shields attach to the solenoid screws with barrel nuts.

Oil Filter

All 1973–1975 and some 1976 engines, including both small and big-blocks, utilize an AC Delco spin-on oil filter. It's painted white, with a red AC logo, blue circumferential stripes, and blue lettering reading "FULL FLOW" and "TYPE PF-25." It is likely but not certain that at least some original filters had "BEST WAY TO PROTECT YOUR ENGINE —REPLACE WITH AC TYPE PF25" embossed on the bottom. Beginning in 1976, Corvettes had AC Delco PF-25 spin-on oil filters painted dark blue. These filters have a dark blue sticker bearing the AC and GM logos. The sticker has a

Both small- and big-block exhaust manifolds have a casting number on the outer surface. The casting number "3880828" is correct for a right-side big-block manifold. This same casting was used from 1966 to 1974, so to determine whether a given manifold is correct for a specific car, you need to also check the casting date, which is on the reverse side.

An original Delco Remy alternator in an unrestored 1973. Because this car came with a 454 engine and power steering, the alternator is mounted upside down from its usual position. As a result, the part number and date code stampings are on the underside. The two-letter broadcast code was stamped on the side facing up, however. The "RH" indicates that this is a number-1100544, 61-amp alternator.

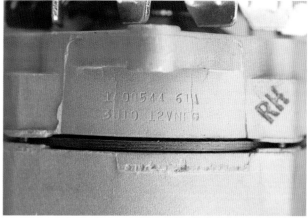

All 1973–1977 Corvettes came with a Delco Remy alternator, which was mounted on the driver side of the engine. A part number, amp rating, and date code were stamped into the alternator housing. In this example, the part number is "1100544," which is the correct alternator in 1973 through early 1975 air-conditioned cars. The "3J10" date code translates to September 10, 1973.

white border and white lettering and contains the part number 6438261. Original stickers do not say "DURAGUARD," as do stickers on later AC Delco PF-25 filters.

Alternator

All engines are fitted with a Delco Remy alternator mounted on the driver side. Alternator housings are made from cast aluminum and are not painted or coated with anything.

The front half of the housing has the unit's part number, amperage rating, and assembly date code stamped in. The date code contains a number for the year and a letter for the month, with "A" representing January, "B" representing February, and so on. As is typical of stamped-in date codes, the letter "I" is skipped, so September is represented by "J." The letter denoting the month is followed by one or two numbers for the day. For example, an alternator stamped "4B11" was assembled February 11, 1974. (Refer to Appendix M for alternator part numbers.)

The alternator pulley for most small-blocks is made from zinc-plated stamped steel. Some L82 engines have alternator pulleys machined from solid material. Alternators on air-conditioned cars have a 2.65-inch diameter pulley with "6" stamped in the face. On cars without air conditioning, the alternator pulley is 2.83 inches in diameter and has a "7" stamped in the face.

All 1973 and 1974 big-blocks utilize an alternator pulley with a deeper groove than that found in small-block pulleys. The center hub is machined from solid material, and the pulley is silver cadmium plated.

The lower alternator bracket on all small-block-equipped 1973–1977 cars is cast metal painted semi-gloss black. The upper bracket is stamped steel painted semi-gloss black.

The lower alternator bracket on all 1973 and 1974 big-blocks without power steering is cast and painted semi-gloss black. The bracket for big-block cars equipped with power steering is stamped steel painted semi-gloss black. A third bracket attaches to the lower bracket and to the water pump mount bolt underneath the brace for the air injection reactor (AIR) pump. This third bracket is painted semi-gloss black.

Power Steering Pump and Fuel Pump

Small-block 1973–1977 cars equipped with power steering use a power steering pump painted semi-gloss black, with a neck that is the same diameter from top to bottom. The necks on 1973 and 1974 big-block pumps, in contrast, widen toward the bottom. Small-block pumps have a semi-gloss black, stamped-steel belt guard bolted to the body.

Power steering pump pulleys on base-engine-equipped cars are cast with open spokes. Pulleys on L82-equipped cars are stamped steel painted semi-gloss black. All big-block-equipped cars use a double groove, open spoke, cast pulley for the power steering pump.

All 1973–1977 power steering pumps, regardless of engine, use two stamped-steel support brackets painted semi-gloss black.

All 1973–1977 Corvettes use an AC brand fuel pump. The pumps usually have "AC" cast into the top or side of the upper housing and a part number stamped into the underside of the mounting flange. All 1973–1977 small-blocks use pump number 6470308, and big-blocks use pump number 6470309. All pumps have natural, dull silver, cast-aluminum bodies with gold-iridite-plated lower covers.

Water Pump, Engine Fan, and Fan Clutch

Early 1973 small-block cars use a water pump with an undrilled bypass hose boss. Later 1973 pumps have the boss drilled and tapped. The tapped hole is closed with a

The water pump housing has a casting date on the driver-side front. The small-block pump date has a letter representing the month, two numbers representing the day, and a single number denoting the year. Big-block pumps, such as the one shown here, have two numbers representing the year. This example, dated "J 22 73," was cast on September 22, 1973.

This is an original seven-blade fan as was used on most 1973–1977 Corvettes with air conditioning. The original water pump is painted engine color and has a square plug in the top hole, as shown from late 1973 through 1977. Early 1973 pumps had an undrilled boss on top.

square-head plug. Unlike earlier water pumps, the snout on 1973–1977 pumps has reinforcing ribs. Small-block pumps usually have casting number "330818" in the housing.

Very early 1973 big-block water pumps utilize number-3992077 housings. Later 1973 and 1974 big-blocks use number-386100 water pumps. All big-block pumps utilize a bypass hose connected to a screwed-in fitting on top of the housing.

All water pump housings have a cast-in date code. The first character of the code is a letter denoting the month, with "A" representing January, "B" representing February, and so on. The second character is one or two numbers denoting the day. For small-block pumps, this is followed by a single number denoting the year. For big-blocks it is followed by two numbers denoting the year.

Most water pump pulleys are painted semi-gloss black, though some originals have been observed with a black phosphate finish.

All 1973–1977 Corvettes use a thermostatically controlled, viscous coupled fan clutch. Those 1973 Corvettes assembled through approximately July 1973 use one clutch, and all cars assembled thereafter use a second clutch. The first design uses a flat, rectangular, bimetallic strip on its front face as a thermostat. The second design uses a metallic coil instead.

Original clutches usually have a date code stamped in the flange that goes against the water pump pulley. Clutches (as well as water pump pulleys) are retained by studs and nuts that thread into the pump's front hub.

All 1973–1977 Corvettes use a cooling fan painted gloss black and mounted to the fan clutch. Cars equipped with air conditioning use a seven-blade fan with a part number and date code stamped into the edge of one or more of the blades. The date code contains a letter for the month,

with "A" designating January, "B" designating February, and so on. As is typical of stamped-in date codes, the letter "I" is skipped, so September is represented by "J." Following the letter indicating the month are two numbers to denote the year.

Small-block air-conditioned cars use a seven-blade fan that is essentially flat along the outer edge of each blade. In contrast, the ends of the blades on big-block air-conditioned cars are irregularly shaped and come to an off-center point.

Cars not equipped with air conditioning use a five-blade fan. Five-blade fans do not have a part number or date code stamped in.

Radiator, Hoses, and Related Parts

All 1973–1977 Corvettes use a copper radiator. Radiators were manufactured by Harrison and have that name debossed in the passenger-side radiator tank. In addition, radiators have a stamped-steel tag with a two-letter broadcast code and a part number attached to the passenger side. All radiators are painted semi-gloss to gloss black.

All cars use a black or dark gray plastic fan shroud. In 1973 both small- and big- block engines have the same shroud but use a different lower extension. The small-block extension is part number 331870, and the big-block extension is part number 336152.

The 1974 Corvettes use a different fan shroud than 1973s, but, again, both small- and big-block engines have the same shroud and use a different lower extension. The lower extensions are the same as in 1973.

All 1973–1977 cars use a white plastic coolant recovery tank. The tank for 1973 is part number 334762. It has a pointed edge adjacent to the inner wheelwell. Starting in 1974, the number-339185 tank is used. This tank has a noticeably rounder edge where it meets the inner wheelwell.

Fan shroud and upper radiators details in an unrestored 1975. Note the foam seals between the radiator and support and between the support and the hood.

This engine cooling system warning decal was placed on the top of the fan shroud in 1973 through part of 1975.

Radiator and fan shroud details in an original 1973 with an LS4 engine option. Note the correct upper radiator hose, the worm-style stainless-steel hose clamp, and the foam seals between the radiator and radiator support and between the support and the hood.

Some very early 1973s may have used an RC-29 radiator cap, but all other 1973–1977 Corvettes used this AC RC-33 cap. The center brass rivet should be unplated and flat, as seen here, or indented with a V shape, not rounded.

With the possible exception of 1973s assembled through approximately early October 1973, all cars use an RC-33 radiator cap rated at 15 psi and installed directly on the radiator. Some very early '73s may use an RC-29 cap.

RC-33 caps contain the AC logo in a circle. They also contain the words "DO NOT OPEN, CHECK LEVEL IN BOTTLE, CLOSED SYSTEM, ALIGN ARROW & VENT TUBE."

RC-29 caps have a thin round disc attached to the top. The disc is silver with a blue stripe and reads "CLOSED SYSTEM." Above the blue stripe in red letters it reads "DO NOT OPEN." Below the stripe in blue letters it reads "ALIGN STRIPE WITH OVERFLOW TUBE." Also below the stripe, but in red letters, it reads "15lbs. RC29."

All radiator and heater hoses are molded black rubber. Stamped on radiator hoses in white ink are a part number, the GM logo, and several letters that are believed to be manufacturer's codes. In addition, a colored line usually runs the length of the hose.

In 1973 only, on air-conditioned big-block cars, the lower radiator hose is two pieces joined by a steel tube in the middle. The steel tube is painted semi-gloss black and has a small depression to provide added clearance for the engine cooling fan. The 1974 big-blocks use a one-piece lower hose.

Heater hoses usually contain a GM logo in white ink. They sometimes also have the letters "DL" or "U" stamped on. Most original hoses have three or four thin ridges running lengthwise.

All cars use SURE-TITE brand stainless-steel worm drive clamps for the radiator hoses. All applications use size-28 clamps, except 1973 air-conditioned big-blocks, which use size 32 on the lower hose only. Original clamps have "SURE-TITE" stamped into the band along the circumference. In addition, "WITTEK MFG. CO. CHI. U.S.A." is stamped into the worm screw's housing.

With the possible exception of very late 1977s, all cars use tower-style clamps for the heater hoses. The ⅝-inch heater hoses use 1¹⁄₁₆-inch clamps. This clamp has a galvanized

An original upper radiator hose in an unrestored 1977 with an L48 engine.

finish and contains the size, the words "WITTEK MFG. CO. CHICAGO U.S.A." and a date code stamped into the band. The first number of the date code denotes the quarter, and the following two numbers indicate the year.

The ¾-inch heater hose uses 1¼-inch clamps. These clamps have a cadmium dichromate finish that results in a translucent goldish tint, as opposed to the smaller clamps' dull silver color. The larger 1¼-inch clamps contain the manufacturer's logo and size designation but do not have a date code. Instead, they have the letters "DCM" stamped into the band.

Brake Master Cylinder and Related Components

All master cylinders are manufactured by Delco and contain a casting number and the Delco split circle logo on the inboard side. Non-power-assist master cylinders are casting number 5455509, and power-assist masters are casting number 5480346.

In addition to the casting number, each master also contains a two-letter application code stamped on a flat surface by the front brake line fitting. A Julian date code is also stamped in this location. The date code typically contains a number indicating the year, followed by three numbers denoting the day of the year. For example, a stamping of "3219" represents the 219th day of 1973.

Most cars with power-assist brakes have "TG" stamped into the master cylinder, and most without power assist have "HC" or "YA" stamped in. The entire master cylinder is semigloss black, except for machined areas, which are natural.

All 1973 and some very early 1974 masters contain two bleeder screws above the brake line ports. Later 1974s and 1975–1977 masters do not have bleeder screws. The bleeders are zinc-plated steel.

For all master cylinders, two steel wire bails hold the cover on. A small vinyl sticker with two letters is folded around one of the bail wires. This sticker is white with red letters, which are usually "TG" for cars with power brake and "YA" or "HC" for cars with manual brakes.

All master cylinders use a stamped-steel, cadmium-dichromate-plated cover and a rubber gasket. The cover has two domes connected by a pressure relief tunnel, which forms a visible ridge between them in 1973. In 1974–1977 the cover's domes are not connected by a small ridge. In 1973–1975 covers, "SERVICE WITH DELCO PARTS" is stamped into one dome, and "USE DELCO SAE J 1703 BRAKE FLUID" or "SERVICE WITH SAE J 1703 BRAKE FLUID" is stamped into the other dome. In 1976–1977 covers, "WARNING CLEAN FILLER CAP BEFORE REMOVING" is stamped into one dome, and "USE ONLY DOT 3 FLUID FROM A SEALED CONTAINER" is stamped into the other dome.

Power brake boosters, on cars so equipped, are painted gloss black in 1973–1976. The 1977s use a gold-iridite-plated booster, but boosters on some very early 1977s were painted black. The booster frequently has a spot of yellow or white paint somewhere. The paint is thought to be an inspection mark or an application code.

Some boosters have a Julian date code stamped on top. The code contains a number corresponding to the final number of the year and three numbers denoting the day of the year. For example, a booster stamped "3168" was manufactured on the 168th day of 1973.

A correct master cylinder and brake booster in a 1973. A tag with the "TG" broadcast code was normally wrapped around forward bail wire but may have been placed on rearward wire at times. Zinc-plated bleeder screws in the master are correct for 1973, but 1974 masters did not have bleeder screws. The master cylinder cap shown is correct for 1973 only. The cap in 1974 had a pressure relief tunnel between the two domes. Though difficult to read because the stamping is light along the top edge, a part number and date code were stamped into the top of the power booster.

This original, unrestored master cylinder and power brake booster are in a 1977. Though not visible here, a two-letter broadcast code and date code are stamped into the flat area of the master cylinder above the forward brake line. The power booster in 1973–1976 was painted gloss black. In 1977 it was plated gold iridite. Some very early 1977s have had a black-painted booster.

All 1973–1976 and some very early 1977 power brake boosters were from Bendix and got painted gloss black. Most 1977 boosters were supplied by Delco Moraine and were gold iridite plated. Bendix boosters have a date code and part number stamped in the top of the forward half of the housing. The first number is the last digit of the year, and the next three numbers are the day of the year. The fifth character is typically an "A" or "B," which probably represents first or second shift. The final five numbers are the last five numbers of the part number. In this example, "5" represents 1975, "170" represents the 170th day of 1975, "A" probably denotes the first shift, and "10842" represents the full part number, "2510842."

All 1975 and most 1976 Corvettes equipped with air conditioning came with a model A-6 Frigidaire axial-style compressor. "CODE NO." is a manufacturing date code, with the first two numbers representing the month, the next two numbers indicating the day, the fifth number denoting the year, and the final number indicating the shift. In this example, "060552" translates to June 5, 1975, second shift.

Air-Conditioning and Heating System Components

All 1973–1975 and most '76 Corvettes equipped with air conditioning utilize a model A-6 axial-type Frigidaire compressor. Starting in late 1976 and continuing in '77, Corvettes use a radial-type Frigidaire compressor.

Both types of compressors are painted semi-gloss black. A-6 axial compressors have a green, black, and silver foil decal on the top of the housing. The sticker contains, among other things, the compressor's model number and a date code. The

date code contains two numbers for the month, two numbers for the day, one number for the year, and one number for the shift. For example, a date code of "031952" translates to March 19, 1975, second shift. Radial-type compressors have a yellow, silver, and black decal with a variety of information, including the unit's model number and date code.

Unlike earlier systems that utilize a separate POA valve assembly, thermostatic expansion valve, and receiver-dehydrator, 1973–1977 systems have all of these components

Delco Air radial-style R-4 air-conditioning compressors were installed in Corvettes beginning late in model year 1976. The six-number manufacturing date code printed next to "CODE NO." on the foil label contains two numbers for the month, two for the day, one for the final digit of the year, and one for the shift. In this example from 1977, "090461" indicates a compressor made on September 4, 1976, during the first shift.

An original 1974 windshield wiper motor and wash pump assembly.

A 1973 A-6 air-conditioning compressor with the original foil label. "CODE NO." is a manufacturing date code, with the first two numbers representing the month, the next two numbers indicating the day, the fifth number denoting the year, and the final number indicating the shift. In this example, "030631" translates to March 6, 1973, first shift.

combined into one unit mounted beneath the heater/air-conditioning fan housing.

An unpainted, dark gray, fiberglass housing covers the evaporator. The housing has a blue and silver Harrison foil sticker, as well as a fan relay. The relay cover is zinc or cadmium plated and does not have any words stamped in it.

Most Corvettes with air conditioning have a vacuum-actuated valve spliced into the heater hose. When the air conditioning is on, this valve shuts off the flow of engine coolant to the heater core.

The blower motors for both air-conditioned and non-air-conditioned cars are painted semi-gloss to gloss black. Motors on air-conditioned cars have a rubber tube that extends from the motor housing to the evaporator housing. Motors on non-air-conditioned cars do not have this tube. Motors have a part number and date code stamped into the mounting flange. The date code contains one or two numbers to denote the month and two numbers to indicate the year.

Windshield Wiper Motor and Related Components

The wiper motor for all 1973–1977 Corvettes uses an unpainted cast-aluminum housing and transmission case. A black plastic cover goes over the wiper motor transmission assembly. A silver-colored foil sticker containing the motor's part number and date of manufacture is on the motor housing.

In 1973 the wiper motor is part number 5044784. In 1974 it is part number 5044811. In 1975, 1976, and part of 1977, it is part number 5044814. Other 1977s use motor number 5044314. (Refer to Appendix P for wiper motor part numbers.)

Date codes for wiper motors use the Julian calendar. One, two, or three numbers indicate the day of the year. This is followed by a single number denoting the year.

The windshield washer pump utilized in 1973–1977 has three ports. The center one is an intake port that connects to the fluid reservoir, and the other two feed fluid to the nozzles.

In 1973 and 1974, the washer fluid pump is integral to the wiper motor assembly. In 1975–1977 it is a separate unit mounted at the base of the fluid reservoir.

The windshield washer fluid reservoir is mounted on the engine compartment side of the left inner wheelwell. The reservoir is rigid white plastic and does not have any writing or fluid level marks. A long fill neck inserts in the reservoir and extends up slightly below the fender lip.

Air Injection Reactor System and other Emissions Components

All 1973–1977 Corvettes, except 1974–1977s with L48 engines and M40 automatic transmission, are equipped with an AIR system. In 1973 and 1974, the AIR system includes black-cadmium-plated tubes that thread into each of the four runners on both exhaust manifolds. In 1975 and 1976, the AIR system is connected by a single tube to the passenger-side

An original AIR pump on an unrestored 1975 L48 engine. All 1973–1977 Corvettes, except 1974–1977s with an L48 engine and M40 automatic transmission, came equipped with an air injection reactor system.

exhaust pipe below the heat riser valve. In 1977 the system is connected to the driver-side manifold with four tubes and to the passenger-side manifold with two tubes.

The AIR pump body is die-cast aluminum and natural in color. A rough-textured, sand-cast iron plate painted semi-gloss black covers the back of the pump. In 1973–1975 the iron plate contains casting number 7801149, and in 1976–1977 it contains casting number 7817872. All pumps contain

a centrifugal filter behind the pulley. This filter, which looks more like a fan, is made from black plastic with rounded fins.

Small-block engines use a steel spacer between the front pump pulley and the centrifugal filter. Big-blocks do not use a spacer. The spacer is zinc or silver cadmium plated, and the pulley is gray phosphate plated or painted semi-gloss black. Pulleys used on small-blocks have part number 3917234 stamped in, while those used on big-blocks have part number 330552 stamped in.

Most pumps are date coded, though the date can be difficult to see with the pump installed. It is stamped into a boss on the rear underside of the body. The sequence may begin with a letter to indicate the assembly plant or specific line. Then one or three numbers indicate the day of the year on the Julian calendar. Earlier dates (prior to the 100th day) may start with two zeros or may not. For example, a pump assembled on the fifth day of the year may be stamped "005" or simply "5." A fourth (or second) number follows to denote the last digit of the year. This is followed by a number indicating the shift and a letter indicating the model of the pump.

The lower pump bracket is painted engine color, and the upper bracket is semi-gloss black. For earlier small-blocks, the lower bracket is cast and contains the number 3923214. Later service replacement small-block lower brackets have casting number 14007354. For big-blocks, the lower bracket is stamped steel.

The last year without a catalytic converter was 1974. It was also the last year for C3s with true dual exhaust. It was the first year with urethane-covered, impact-absorbing bumpers on the front and rear.

The diverter valve body is natural in color, while the diaphragm cover and check valves are cadmium dichromate. The diaphragm cover has a round sticker printed with a two-letter broadcast code. The diverter valve muffler is plated gray phosphate. The diverter valve part number is stamped into the valve below the muffler. Check valves have a part number stamped into the center ridge.

Hoses connecting the various parts of the AIR system are molded black, and hose clamps are tower style. Clamps have a galvanized finish and contain the size, the words "WITTEK MFG. CO. CHICAGO U.S.A.," and a date code stamped into the band. The first number of the date code denotes the quarter, and the following two numbers indicate the year.

All 1973 Corvettes were originally equipped with an AIR system. All 1974s with manual transmission and all 1974s equipped with the California emissions package (option NB2) got AIR systems. In 1975–1977 all cars equipped with option L82, NB2, or NA6 (the high-altitude emissions package) also have an AIR system.

All 1973–1977 Corvettes are fitted with an evaporative control system. This system includes a black carbon-filled canister mounted to the lower left side inner wheelwell.

All 1973–1977 Corvettes have a PCV valve located in the left side valve cover. The valve has a part number stamped into it. In 1973 the valve is number CV736C. Thereafter it is number CV774C for the base engine and number CV775C for the L82 engine.

Most 1973–1977 Corvettes have a transmission controlled spark (TCS) system. This system includes a solenoid, timer, temperature switch, transmission switch, and vacuum advance solenoid.

The timer is usually mounted on the firewall, and the temperature switch is in the passenger-side cylinder head. On small-block engines the solenoid is attached to an intake manifold stud toward the front, passenger-side of the carburetor. On 1973 and 1974 big-blocks, it is mounted on the intake manifold to the right side of the coil bracket.

All 1975–1977 Corvettes are equipped with an early fuel evaporation (EFE) system. With this system, a vacuum-actuated valve is mounted to the passenger-side exhaust manifold. The valve is controlled by a thermal vacuum switch mounted adjacent to the thermostat housing. This switch is later placed in the housing.

All cars have an antidiesel solenoid mounted with a bracket to the carburetor base. The bracket is cadmium dichromate plated, and the solenoid housing is silver cadmium plated.

All 1973–1977 Corvettes have an emission system information decal. In most cars it is on the driver-side upper firewall adjacent to the hood latch. In 1976, from approximately February through the end of production, the decal was placed on top of the power brake booster if the car had power brakes. This label is either white or yellow. It contains engine tune-up specifications as well as information about the emission control systems installed in the car.

All 1973–1977 Corvettes came with one or two vehicle emission system information decals. From approximately February 1976 through the end of 1976 production, the decal was placed on top of the power brake booster in power-brake-equipped cars. In all other cars, the decal was affixed on the driver-side firewall adjacent to the hood latch. The specific label used varied in accord with several factors, including the model year, whether the car was to be delivered in California, and engine choice. The decals varied depending upon which engine was in the car and the specifics of the emission control system it was equipped with. This example is in an unrestored 1973.

Engine Compartment, Wiring, Horns, and Related Components

The firewall, underside of the hood, and engine compartment side of the inner wheelwells are painted semi-gloss black. The wheel side of the front and rear inner wheelwells are also painted semi-gloss black, though coverage is usually sparse. In addition, the rear areas of the wheelwells normally have some undercoating.

In all cars, wire harnesses and adjacent hoses are bundled together in a row, so rather than forming a circle, they are flat. The harnesses and hoses are held to each other with black plastic tie wraps.

All vacuum hose is color coded, with an ink stripe that runs the length of the hose. Larger hoses have a green, red, or yellow stripe, while smaller hoses usually have a white stripe.

All 1973 and 1974 Corvettes equipped with a big-block have a small oil pressure line bracket on the left side of the engine block. A steel tube goes from the brass block fitting to a junction at this bracket. A black plastic tube continues up to the oil pressure gauge.

All 1973 small-block-equipped cars utilize black plastic tubing that goes directly from the engine block fitting to the oil pressure gauge. The plastic line has tiny white lettering and is fastened at both ends with brass fittings.

All 1974–1977 Corvettes are fitted with electric oil pressure gauges. A gold-iridite-plated metal sending unit is threaded into the engine block above the oil filter.

In 1973 a horn relay is mounted to the driver-side inner wheelwell. It has a short, squared-off silver cadmium cover that has nothing stamped in. The plain cover sits on a black plastic base. Starting in 1974, the horn relay is mounted under the dash adjacent to the fuse block.

This unrestored 1973 LS4 engine compartment is exceptionally well preserved.

Note the many variations in surface finishes on 1973 driver-side engine compartment components. Pop rivets holding vacuum hose and wiring clips were installed before the body was painted and are therefore blue. The male hood latch bracket is black phosphate plated, while the pin is silver cadmium.

In 1973 one horn is installed on the driver side near the headlight vacuum canister. In 1974 and 1975, a single horn is standard equipment, but a second horn is available as option U05. The second horn is a lower note than the standard one. In 1976 and 1977, dual horns are standard.

Horns have the last three digits of the part number and a manufacturing date code stamped into flat areas near the sound opening. The date code contains a number denoting the year, a letter denoting the month (with "A" representing

January, "B" representing February, and so on), and another number indicating the week. For example, a horn stamped "3F2" was made the second week of June 1973. Each horn is attached to a mounting bracket, and the whole assembly is painted semi-gloss black. (Refer to Appendix O for horn relay and horn numbers.)

Hood hinges are silver cadmium plated and usually have both body color and underhood black overspray on them. Hinges are usually fastened by black-phosphate-plated, indented hex-head bolts.

The hood support is silver cadmium plated. It has two hinged sections, which fold as the hood is lowered.

The hood latches are black phosphate plated and mount with black-phosphate-plated hardware. The driver-side male latch is attached to the hood release cable with a brass barrel cable stop. A hex bolt locks the stop to the cable. The cable is inside a spiral wound metal sheath.

Another cable connects the two female latches mounted to the underside of the hood. This cable is inside a black nylon sheath. Is ends are secured to the latches with small clevis pins fitted with flat washers and cotter pins.

In 1977 a different hood latch system is employed. Hook-shaped latches replace the older pin-style latches on the firewall. A hood lift spring topped with a black rubber bumper is on either side of the firewall.

An original 1973 LS4 engine compartment. Every component and surface finish seen here is correct.

Between the last week of August and the first week of September 1976, GM's Flint V-8 Engine Plant started painting Corvette engines Corporate Blue instead of Chevrolet Orange. This is a driver-side view of an unrestored 1977 L48.

This is an extremely correct L48 engine compartment in a low-mileage, unrestored 1975. The master cylinder, upper radiator hose, and AIR pump belt are not correct.

The underside of 1973 LS4 hood. The hood hinges were the only underhood components installed before the body was painted and the engine compartment was sprayed black. Therefore they are the only components that may correctly show body color or blackout overspray.

The hood was mounted to the body when it when through the paint process, so hood hinges normally show body color overspray, as well as black from the engine compartment blackout spray.

Passenger-side hood pin details in an unrestored 1975. Note the rough texture of the firewall and the crude transition from body color to blackout paint on the hood ledge.

Hood latches and the bolts that hold them were plated with black phosphate, not painted. This same plating was used for the insulation retainers as well.

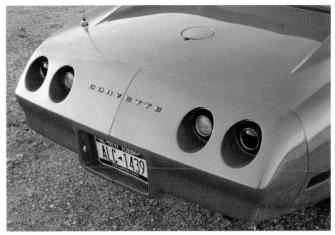

An impact-absorbing rear bumper was first used on Corvettes in 1974. The impact-absorbing assembly was covered with a two-piece urethane bumper cover with a vertical seam in the middle. After 1974 the rear bumper cover was one piece. Compared with originals, replacement 1974 rear bumper covers are thicker and more rigid.

Driver-side hood latch details in an unrestored 1975. Note the sloppy application of yellow weather strip adhesive along the edge of the hood and subtle variations in surface finishes among the latch components.

Each Corvette normally has the final nine characters of its VIN stamped into its frame on top of the driver-side main rail beneath the door area and on top of the driver-side rear kickup slightly forward of the rear body mount bracket. Not all frames have the VIN derivative stamping in these two spots. This example from 1974 reads "14S410617" and is located on the kickup above the driver-side rear wheel, just forward of the body mount bracket.

1973–1977 CHASSIS
Chassis

All 1973–1977 Corvette chassis are painted semi-gloss black. Chassis for automatic-transmission-equipped cars have a removable bolt-on center crossmember, while standard-transmission-equipped cars have a welded-on center crossmember. Automatics do not have a clutch cross shaft tower welded on top of the chassis behind the left front wheel as cars with standard transmission do.

In 1974 the chassis was modified in the rear with the addition of a bracket and extension to accommodate the rear-impact-absorbing bumper assembly. In 1975 the chassis was again modified in the rear. The rear crossmember was made about two inches wider.

A pair of one-inch high chassis part number sequences is painted in white or yellow on the chassis with a stencil. One sequence is the part number from A. O. Smith (the company that fabricated the chassis for GM). The other sequence is the Chevrolet part number. These part numbers are usually found on the passenger side of the chassis, behind the front wheel.

A manufacturing date code is stenciled on the rail as well. The date contains one or two numbers representing the month, one or two numbers indicating the day, and two numbers denoting the year.

Most 1973–1977 Corvettes have the serial number stamped into their chassis in two locations. It is typically found in the left-side rail, slightly forward of the number-four body mount bracket. It is also typically found on the left-side rear kickup above the wheel area, slightly forward of the number-three body mount bracket.

Steel shims are frequently utilized at body mount points to make up for irregularities in fit. If present, shims are usually taped to the body mount bracket with 1½-inch-wide masking tape. The number of shims needed at each body mount bracket is typically written on the chassis, adjacent to the bracket, with a green or white grease crayon. Unlike earlier cars, this number is usually an actual number rather than slash marks. The 1973–1977 body mount cushions are made from rubber.

Front Suspension

Upper and lower front control arms are painted semi-gloss to gloss black. Ball joints are installed after the arms are painted and are therefore not painted. Crushed steel rivets (not bolts) hold ball joints on and are also natural in finish.

Control arm cross shafts are painted semi-gloss black on some cars and unpainted on others. Cars with painted cross shafts typically have control arm bushing retention washers and bolts that are also painted semi-gloss black. Cars with unpainted cross shafts typically have retention washers that are gray phosphate plated and bolts that are black phosphate plated.

Front coil springs are natural in finish and sometimes have an irregular bluish cast from the manufacturing process. A green paper sticker contains two black letters indicating the spring's broadcast code (the application), as well as a black GM part number.

Front and rear shock absorbers are manufactured by Delco and are oil hydraulic, not gas filled. They are painted semi-gloss gray in 1973–1976 and semi-flat black in 1977. Shocks have the words "DELCO REMY DAYTON OHIO U.S.A. PLIACELL" and a date code stamped around the bottom. The Julian date code contains three numbers indicating the day and two numbers denoting the year. In addition, there is a small paper sticker with a two-letter broadcast code on the side of the shock.

The front upper shock mount rubber bushings are unpainted black rubber. The top upper bushing is larger in diameter than the bottom upper bushing, and the upper shock washer is gray phosphate plated. The front lower shock mount rubber bushings and both rear shock mount bushings are integral and are therefore painted along with the shock.

All 1973 and 1974 big-block Corvettes and all 1973–1977 small-block-equipped cars with optional FE7 or Z07 suspension utilize a $^{15}/_{16}$-inch front sway bar. Those 1973–1974s with a small-block engine and standard suspension utilize a $^{3}/_{4}$-inch bar, while 1975–1977s with standard suspension utilize a $^{7}/_{8}$-inch bar. Some cars have a sway bar painted semi-gloss black, while others have a natural, unpainted bar.

Bushings mounting the front sway bar to the chassis, as well as bushings in the end links, are unpainted black rubber. Stamped steel brackets painted semi-gloss black hold the bar to the chassis.

End link bolts are zinc plated 5/16-24 SAE fine thread and usually have the manufacturer's logo "UB" or "WB" on their heads. End link spacers are zinc plated, have a split seam, and typically have a "K" or a "C" stamped in.

A 1974 steering box. It is common to see one bolt with different head markings from the others.

Steering Box and Steering Linkage

All 1973–1977 Corvettes use a cast steering gear that is either natural in color or painted semi-gloss black. The box cover is cast aluminum. It is retained by three black-oxide-plated hex-head bolts. A daub of yellow or blue paint is frequently seen on top of the box. Two ink-stamped letters such as "CM" or "WZ" are sometimes seen on the steering box as well.

A forged pitman arm links the steering box to the relay rod. The pitman arm is natural in color and is often seen with a daub of blue or green paint.

The steering relay rod and idler arm are typically natural finish. Both parts are forged and tend to have a bluish gray tint. Original idler arms do not have grease fittings.

Tie rod ends are natural finish and also typically have a bluish gray color cast. Daubs of yellow paint are often seen on tie rod ends.

Tie rod end sleeves are painted semi-gloss black. Tie rod end clamps have two reinforcing ridges around the circumference and are sometimes painted semi-gloss black and sometimes left unpainted.

Outer tie rod ends can install into either of two holes in the steering knuckles. Cars equipped with standard, nonpower steering have the outer tie rod ends installed into the rear holes, while cars equipped with power steering have them in the forward holes. On those cars equipped with power steering, an aluminum plug inserted from the bottom plugs the unused steering knuckle hole.

On those cars so equipped, the power steering control valve and hydraulic cylinder are painted semi-gloss black. The nut and washers retaining the hydraulic cylinder's ram to the frame bracket are zinc plated. The frame bracket may be painted semi-gloss black or unpainted. Original power steering hoses typically have longitudinal ridges around their entire circumference, while later replacements don't.

Rear Suspension

All 1973–1974 Corvettes equipped with standard suspension utilize a 9-leaf rear spring. All 1975–1977s with standard suspension use a 10-leaf rear spring. Cars equipped with optional FE7 or Z07 suspension utilize a 7-leaf spring. All springs are painted light gray and have black plastic liners between the leaves. Nine-leaf springs may not have a liner between leaf six and leaf seven (with the bottom leaf being number one).

The center rear spring mount bracket is painted semi-gloss black. The four bolts retaining the spring to the differential typically have the manufacturer's logo, "WB," on their heads and are either black phosphate or zinc plated. The outer spring bolts and nuts are usually black phosphate plated, and the washers are typically natural.

Rear trailing arms are painted semi-gloss to gloss black. Rear wheel bearing carriers (also called spindle supports) are natural and have a part number and date code cast in. The date code has a letter representing the month, with "A" for January, "B" for February, and so on; one or two numbers for the day; and one number for the final digit of the year. The date code for a rear bearing carrier made on April 18, 1975, for example, would read, "D 18 5."

All 1973 and 1974 big-blocks, as well as all cars equipped with FE7 or Z07 suspension, have a rear stabilizer bar. The bar is ⁹⁄₁₆ inch in diameter and may be painted semi-gloss black or unpainted. It mounts to the chassis with stamped-steel brackets painted semi-gloss black. At each end, the bar has a link bracket painted semi-gloss black that attaches to brackets bolted to the trailing arms. The brackets on the trailing arms have plating that is sometimes called pickling. It results in a brownish olive color. These brackets attach to the trailing arm via bolts that thread into small unpainted steel plates that slip into the rear of the arms.

Rear camber adjustment rods (also called strut rods) are usually natural and often have a bluish gray tint. Some rods are painted semi-gloss black or are partially painted during the undercarriage "blackout" process. In 1973 and early 1974, the rods have 1½-inch diameter ends. Later '74s and all 1975–1977 cars have rods with 1¾-inch diameter ends.

The outboard ends of the camber adjustment rods are held to the rear wheel bearing carriers with forged L-shaped pins that also serve as lower mounts for the rear shock absorbers. These pins, which are sometimes called rear shock brackets, contain a raised part number.

The inboard ends of the camber adjustment rods attach to a bracket that's painted semi-gloss black. It has special bolts with integral off-center washers. When rotated, they move the rods in or out and thus allow for rear wheel camber adjustment. The camber adjustment bolts are usually silver cadmium plated, though they may be black phosphate plated instead.

Rear wheel toe adjustment is set with the use of shims placed on either side of the trailing arms where they mount to the chassis. The adjusting shims are rectangular pieces of unpainted steel in varying thicknesses. The shims have a slot in one end that slips over the trailing arm mount bolt. The other ends of all shims are rotated upward, so their holes each align with a corresponding hole in the chassis. A long cotter pin passes through the stacks of shims on both sides of the trailing arm and through the hole in the chassis.

Rear axle shafts (often called half shafts) are made from forged ends welded to extruded steel tubes. The axle shafts are natural, with the tube being shiny silver and the ends being a dull gray.

U-joints do not have grease fittings and do have raised part numbers on the body. They are natural and tend to have that faint bluish tint that is characteristic of forged parts.

The outboard axle shaft U-joints are pressed into a flange that is natural in color. The flange is held to the rear wheel bearing carrier by four bolts that are usually black phosphate plated. The bolts are prevented from turning out by two pairs of French locks, the tabs of which are bent over to contact the bolt heads. The French locks are zinc plated and typically have only one of the two tabs adjacent to each bolt bent over.

The inboard axle shaft U-joints are held to the differential output yokes by one of two methods. Forged caps and bolts are used on Corvettes equipped with 454 engines, and U-shaped strap clamps with nuts are used on cars equipped with 350 engines.

Front Wheel Assemblies

Front spindles and steering knuckles are natural and tend to have a bluish tint to their gray color. In addition, the lower portions of the spindles are frequently seen with orange or white paint, as though the bottoms of the spindles were dipped into it.

Original front brake backing plates are zinc plated and then chromate dipped. This results in varying finishes, ranging from gold with a faint rainbow of other colors throughout to a dull silver with only a trace of yellowish chromate coloring. Well-preserved original backing plates typically appear dull silver, probably because the chromate dip deteriorates over time.

Front brake caliper support brackets are plated silver cadmium or cadmium dichromate, which results in a translucent gold color with varying degrees of other colors present in a rainbowlike pattern.

Cars equipped with option Z07 have a heavy-duty brake package. This package includes front calipers that use two pins to hold the pads instead of the standard one, extra front caliper supports, semi-metallic brake pads, heat insulators on the face of all caliper pistons, and a proportioning valve mounted beneath the master cylinder.

Front brake calipers are painted semi-gloss black and frequently have daubs of blue or white paint on the side. Painting is done before the caliper halves are machined, and therefore machined surfaces are unpainted. Bleeder screws are zinc plated and remain unpainted.

Caliper hoses are black rubber with gold-iridite-plated end hardware. Federally mandated DOT specifications are written on the hose in red ink. In addition, a red longitudinal stripe on the hoses makes it easier to see if they are twisted. Original hoses typically have raised longitudinal ridges around the entire circumference, while later replacements are typically smooth.

Front brake rotors are natural in finish. The front wheel bearing carrier (also called a hub) is riveted to the rotor disc.

Rear Wheel Assemblies

As with the fronts, original rear brake backing plates are zinc plated and then chromate dipped. This results in varying finishes, ranging from gold with a faint rainbow of other colors throughout to a dull silver with only a trace of the yellowish chromate coloring. Well-preserved original backing plates typically appear dull silver, probably because the chromate dip deteriorates over time.

Rear brake caliper support brackets are natural and hence a dull gray. On occasion they are painted flat to semi-flat black.

Rear brake calipers are painted semi-gloss black and frequently have daubs of blue or white paint on the side. Painting is done before the caliper halves are machined. Therefore machined surfaces are unpainted. Bleeder screws are zinc plated and remain unpainted.

Rear brake rotors are natural in finish. They are riveted to the rear spindle, which is pressed into the rear wheel bearing carrier. The rivets are often drilled out to allow for servicing of the park brake assembly or the rear wheel bearings. The wheel lug nuts retain the rotor in the absence of the rivets.

Transmission

Automatic-equipped 1973–1977 Corvettes utilize either a Turbo Hydra-Matic 400 or a Turbo Hydra-Matic 350. All 1973–1975 cars, as well as all 1976–1977 cars equipped with an L82 engine, use the Turbo 400. All 1976 and 1977 cars with a base engine use a Turbo 350.

For both transmissions, the main case and the tail housing are cast aluminum with a natural finish. The fluid pan is stamped steel and is also natural.

Turbo 400 transmissions contain an identification plate riveted to the passenger side. The plate has two alphanumeric sequences stamped in. The bottom sequence is the transmission's serial number, and the top sequence is a production code. The first two numbers of this code indicate the model year. Next comes a letter that denotes the car model (in our case, Corvette) and the engine. This is followed by three numbers that represent the day the transmission was assembled.

The transmission assembly date is a modified version of the Julian calendar system. The three numbers represent the day of the year. But unlike most applications of the Julian calendar system in dating Corvette components, with transmissions the count does not begin with the first day of the year. Instead, for 1973 model Corvettes, it begins with January 1, 1972, and continues sequentially through calendar year 1973. Similarly, for 1974 models, it begins January 1, 1973, and continues through calendar year 1974. And for 1975 models, it begins January 1, 1974, and continues through calendar year 1975.

This dating system sounds confusing, but it's easy once you get the hang of it. For example, in the production code "74K018," the "74" represents the 1974 model year, "K" represents the application code (a 1974 Corvette with a base engine), and "018" represents the eighteenth day from the beginning of the count. Remember, the count begins on January 1 of the preceding year, so this transmission was assembled on January 18, 1973. Had that same transmission been assembled on January 18, 1974, the code would read, "74K383," with January 18, 1974 being 383 days after the count for the 1974 model year began.

The application codes for 1973–1977 Corvettes include a "K" for all base engines, an "S" for big-block engines, a "Y" for optional L82 engines in 1973, and a "Z" for optional L82 engines thereafter.

Each Turbo 400 transmission also contains the final eight characters of the serial number of the car it was originally installed into. This sequence is stamped into the case on the driver-side flange adjacent to the oil pan.

The identification numbers for Turbo 350 transmissions are different than the numbers for Turbo 400s. With Turbo 350s, the identification code is on the passenger side. This code has six characters. The first is a letter that denotes the manufacturing plant. The second is a number representing the year. The third is a letter denoting the month. The fourth and fifth are numbers representing the day of the month. The final letter is either a "D" for day shift or an "N" for night shift.

The letters designating the month of manufacture are as follows: "A" is January, "B" is February, "C" is March, "D" is April, "E" is May, "H" is June, "K" is July, "M" is August, "P" is September, "R" is October, "S" is November, and "T" is December.

In addition to the above-described production code, each Turbo 350 transmission contains the final eight digits of the serial number of the car it originally was installed into. This sequence is stamped into the case on the driver-side flange adjacent to the oil pan.

Four-speed manual transmissions manufactured by Muncie are used in 1973 and early 1974 Corvettes. Beginning in mid-1974, Borg Warner Super T-10 four-speeds are used. Those 1976 and 1977 Corvettes delivered new in California could not be equipped with a four-speed.

Four-speed Muncie transmissions have a cast-aluminum main case, side cover, and tail housing that are natural in color. A steel tag with a part number is affixed to the transmission with one of the side cover bolts.

Two alphanumeric sequences are stamped into the main case on a vertical surface at the front of the right side. One of these sequences is a derivative of the car's serial number. The other is a production code and the date the transmission was originally assembled.

The production code begins with a letter to indicate the source for the transmission. All Corvette four-speeds obtained

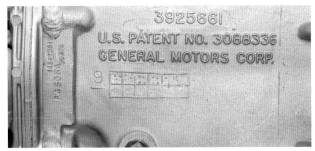

This is a 1974 Muncie four-speed transmission. The main case casting number "3925661" is correct for Corvette. The VIN derivative stamping "14S410617" indicates that this transmission was originally installed into the 10,617th 1974 Corvette. The production code stamping "P4S06A" translates as follows: "P" represents the supplier, Muncie; "4" represents model year 1974; "S" represents the month of November; "06" represents the sixth day of the month; and "A" indicates that this is a wide-ratio M20 with a 2.52:1 first gear.

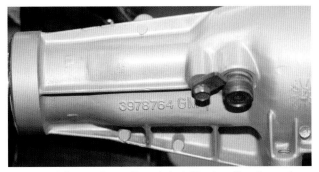

A 1974 Muncie four-speed manual transmission tail housing with casting number "3978764."

from Muncie are represented by the letter "P." This is followed by a number representing the last digit of the model year. Next is a letter indicating the month of production, followed by two numbers denoting the day of the month. Various letters are not used in denoting the month, so refer to this chart when determining assembly date:

A	January
B	February
C	March
D	April
E	May
H	June
K	July
M	August
P	September
R	October
S	November
T	December

The final character in the production code is a letter commonly called a suffix code. This letter indicates which of the three available four-speeds the unit is. The suffix code "A" indicates a wide-ratio M-20 with a 2.52:1 first-gear ratio. "B" indicates a close-ratio M-21 with a 2.20:1 first-gear ratio. "C" denotes a close-ratio M-22 "heavy-duty" transmission, which also has a 2.20:1 first-gear ratio.

An example of a four-speed transmission code is "P3M18A." This identifies an M-20 wide-ratio Muncie four-speed assembled on August 18, 1973.

With Borg Warner four-speeds, the car's serial number derivative, as well as the production code and assembly date, is stamped into the main case on the driver-side flange adjacent to where the tail housing attaches.

In the production code, the first letter is "W" to indicate Borg Warner. The next letter indicates the month of production, with "A" representing January, "B" representing February, and so on to "L," which represents December. The month code is followed by one or two numbers denoting the day. Next comes a single number to indicate the year. The last number indicates whether the transmission is a close- or wide-ratio unit. For example, a code of "WG2761" translates to a Borg Warner four-speed, built on July 27, 1976. The final "1" indicates that it is a wide-ratio unit.

Differential and Driveshaft

All 1973–1977 Corvettes are equipped with a Posi-Traction limited-slip differential. The differential case and cover are both natural-colored castings and as such are a dull silvery gray.

A plastic triangular tag is attached to the differential by means of the square-head oil fill plug. The tag is red, with white lettering that says "USE LIMITED SLIP DIFF. LUBRICANT ONLY." The fill plug is natural and often has a large "W" cast into the square.

Front input yoke and side output yokes are forgings that are natural in color. Because they are forged, they have a somewhat smoother surface than the case and cover, and they tend to have a slight bluish tint to their dull gray color.

Differential cases and covers both have casting numbers and a casting date that includes a letter for the month (with "A" representing January, "B" representing February, and so on), one or two numbers indicating the day of the month, and one number indicating the last digit of the year.

In addition to the casting date, all cases have a stamped-in production code. The production code is on the bottom rear edge of the case, adjacent to where it meets the cover. The differential production code begins with two letters to indicate the gear ratio. This is followed by a single letter denoting the assembly plant. Then come one, two, or three numbers representing the day the unit was assembled. After this is a single letter indicating the source for the Posi-Traction unit (not necessarily the same company that assembled the differential). The final number in the sequence represents the assembly shift that built the unit. (Refer to Appendix E for differential gear ratio codes.)

The transmission and differential are connected by a driveshaft made from extruded steel tubing, welded at each

All 1973–1977 Corvette differential housings are made from cast iron and have a casting date on the driver-side bottom. This example says "H233," which translates to a casting date of August 23, 1973.

end to a forged universal joint coupling. As with the axle shafts, the driveshaft is natural in color. The center tube portion is bright silver, with longitudinal extrusion lines sometimes visible, and the ends are a dull silvery gray with a slight bluish hue at times.

A part number stenciled on the driveshaft tube in yellow or white paint is sometimes seen. One or two green circumferential stripes on the tube and daubs of variously colored paint on the forged ends are sometimes seen as well.

Exhaust System

All 1973–1977 Corvettes use an undercar, carbon steel exhaust system manufactured by Walker for Chevrolet. All cars equipped with a big-block engine or an L82 engine utilize 2½-inch exhaust pipes. All other cars utilize 2-inch pipes.

Even though L82 engines get 2½-inch pipes, they still use the same 2-inch outlet exhaust manifolds as other small-blocks. This is accomplished by swaging the 2½-inch front engine pipes down to 2 inches at their ends.

Mufflers are galvanized on the exterior and may have an embossed "W" to represent the manufacturer. In addition, an embossed part number is sometimes found on each muffler. At the rear of each muffler is one welded-on bracket, to which the rear hangar bolts. Mufflers are welded to the intermediate exhaust pipe, not clamped. 2½-inch intermediate pipes are flattened somewhat where they pass underneath the rear camber adjustment rod bracket for additional ground clearance. Two-inch pipes are not flattened.

Beginning in 1974, small resonators are in each exhaust pipe beneath the seat area. Beginning in 1975, all Corvettes are equipped with a catalytic converter. The exhaust pipes connecting the converter to the engine are stainless steel.

A rectangular chrome-plated carbon steel exhaust tip is clamped to each muffler in 1973. Unlike some earlier tips, those used in 1973 each have a weld seam on the underside of the rectangular section. Mufflers from 1974–1977 do not have separate tips.

Fuel Lines, Brake Lines, and Miscellaneous Chassis and Underbody Components

All 1973–1977 fuel lines run along, and at times through, the right-side chassis rail. Most cars have two fuel lines. One supplies fuel from the tank to the carburetor. The other is a return line.

In addition to the one or two fuel lines on the right side of the chassis, all cars have a vapor return line on the left side of the chassis. This line is part of the evaporative emission control system.

Fuel lines are galvanized carbon steel. Black rubber fuel hose connects the lines to the tank and the fuel pump. Zinc-chromate-plated spring clamps are usually used to secure the hose to its line.

Brake lines are galvanized carbon steel. Brake line end fittings are brass. Fittings at the master cylinder are often seen with red or blue dye, which was probably used to denote the two different sizes of fittings. In addition, daubs of yellow paint are sometimes seen on the fittings at junction blocks.

Various heat shields are affixed to the underside of the body to help insulate the passenger compartment from engine and exhaust system heat. A sheet steel shield, which is gray phosphate plated, is mounted on the lower vertical area of the firewall on both sides.

All cars are fitted with transmission tunnel insulation. A semi-rigid foil-wrapped blanket in the shape of the tunnel is fastened above the transmission, with clips riveted to the underbody.

All cars have a thick, black foam insulating pad attached to the underbody, above the engine's bell housing. A thick, white foam pad is fastened to the underbody on each side of the car just forward of the doors.

A variety of steel plates are fastened to the underbody to mount components in the passenger compartment. These components include the battery, seats, jack hold-down clips, and so on. All these plates are painted semi-gloss black and are retained by unpainted aluminum rivets.

The underside of a 1974 shows unpainted fiberglass floor panels, steel brackets painted semi-gloss black with unpainted aluminum attachment rivets, and a foil-backed, fiber-based insulation panel held to the underside of the floor with pointed steel clips.

Chapter 4
1978–1982

1978–1982 EXTERIOR
Body Fiberglass and Body Paint

All 1978–1982 Corvette body panels are made from press-molded fiberglass. The panels are smooth on both sides and are very dark gray. Body panel alignment and fit is considerably better than it was in previous years, but it's still far from perfect.

The quality of the fit of all ancillary body components, such as doors, hoods, and headlamp doors, also varies and is at times poor. Factory assembly manuals call for the gap between most adjacent panels to be between ⅛ inch and ³⁄₁₆ inch wide. The manuals also specify that any differential in height be no more than ⅛ inch. The hood gap should be equal side to side within ¹⁄₁₆ inch, and the headlamp door gap should be equal side to side within ¹⁄₃₂ inch. Hood height is regulated in part by the use of small rectangular rubber blocks placed in the inner fender drip rails. The number and location of these blocks varies. Some cars don't have them at all.

All 1978–1980 cars were painted with acrylic lacquer. All 1981s assembled in the Corvette factory in St. Louis, Missouri, were also painted with acrylic lacquer. During 1981 production, Corvette assembly was moved to a new factory in Bowling Green, Kentucky. All 1981s assembled in

Bowling Green, as well as all 1982s, were painted with an acrylic enamel base coat/clear coat system.

On Corvettes assembled in St. Louis, factory paint is generally smooth and shiny, though some orange peel is evident throughout. Roughness and poor coverage is fairly typical along the very bottom edges of body panels. Clear coat was not used by the St. Louis factory, even with metallic colors. Because clear coat was not used, metallic paint tends to be slightly mottled or blotchy.

The new base coat/clear coat paint used on 1981s assembled in Bowling Green and on all 1982s generally resulted in a better quality finish than the old lacquer paint system. As the name implies, clear coat was applied over the base or color coat. As a result, metallic colors do not typically exhibit the mottling sometimes seen on cars painted with lacquer.

Front Bumpers

All 1978–1982 Corvettes are fitted with impact-absorbing front bumper assemblies. The cover is made from urethane that is painted body color. A flex additive is mixed with the paint used on the bumper cover to discourage the paint from cracking. The flex additive often causes the paint on the bumper to be a slightly different shade than the paint on the rest of the car.

By 1982 the Corvette body design dated to 1968. Its chassis went all the way back to 1963. Everyone expected an all-new Corvette for 1983, so Chevrolet forecast that 1982 sales would be rather poor. To help bolster sales and to celebrate the final year for a highly successful model, Chevy offered a Corvette Collector Edition Hatchback.

The black-over-silver paint scheme was unique to 1978 Limited Edition Corvette Pace Cars. Red striping and upgraded silver interior trim were also unique to pace car replicas.

Only 2,446 1979s were painted Corvette Dark Green, making it the second-least-popular color that year behind Corvette Yellow. The original owner of this stunning and remarkably original Corvette Dark Green 1979, who still owns it, says she loves green and didn't even consider other available colors.

Only 613 Corvettes were painted Charcoal Metallic in 1981, making them rather rare today. This pristine low-mileage example is all original except for the pinstriping along the tops of the fenders.

The 1982 Corvette Collector Edition Hatchback included special paint, body graphics, emblems, wheels, interior trim, and bronze-tinted T-tops.

Below: The 1982 Corvette Collector Edition Hatchback was the first Corvette to feature a functional rear glass hatch that lifted to provide access to the rear storage area.

Black was the second most popular color in 1980, behind only white. This example features original paint and is one of the nicest unrestored 1980 Corvettes in existence.

The first year for front and rear bumper covers with integral spoilers was 1980. Besides looking great, the new bumper covers reduced the car's coefficient of drag from .503 to .443 and increased the flow of cooling air to the radiator by 50 percent.

The St. Louis Corvette Assembly Plant was running at maximum capacity in 1979, when a record 53,807 Corvettes were built.

The front and rear spoilers introduced in 1978 on the limited edition Corvette pace car were offered as an option in 1979. This is one of 6,853 1979s that came with the $265 option.

The remainder of the bumper assembly, which is covered by the urethane piece, is comprised of several steel components painted semi-gloss black. Black-phosphate- or silver-cadmium-plated hex-head bolts are used to retain the underlying bumper structure to the chassis.

In 1978 and 1979, the front bumper fascias are the same as on previous Corvettes. In 1980–1982 the bumper fascias are a different design. They feature a noticeably revised shape that includes an integral spoiler. The new bumper design reduces drag coefficient from .503 to .443 while increasing airflow to the radiator by as much as 50 percent for improved cooling

In 1978–1979 a black plastic air deflector is bolted underneath the front bumper fascia toward the rear. Black oxide hex-head bolts with integral flat washers hold it on. On those cars equipped with option V01, a heavy-duty radiator, or the optional L82 engine, an additional air deflector is attached to the front of the first air deflector. The additional deflector is made from black rubber and is attached with eight aluminum pop rivets. A two-piece reinforcement, made from steel strips painted gloss black, is placed behind the second deflector.

All 1980–1982 cars use a two-piece air deflector extension bolted to reinforcements in the front bumper fascia underneath and toward the rear. These extensions are made from unpainted black rubber.

The impact-absorbing front bumper assembly is held to the car's chassis by steel brackets painted semi-gloss black. In addition to the steel brackets, the front bumper is held in place with fiberglass braces along each side. The braces are usually a raw, dark gray, though some are painted semi-gloss black. Because of production variances, shims were frequently used to adjust the fit of the bumpers to the car. These shims, which are typically found between the bumper brackets and the chassis, are plated silver cadmium.

The tubular crossmember included in the front bumper assembly also serves as the vacuum reservoir for the front headlamp system. Bolts retaining the front bumper brackets to the chassis are typically black oxide or gray phosphate in finish.

All 1978–1982 Corvettes came with black. injection-molded plastic front grilles and amber park lamps.

Front Grille Area, Parking Lamps, and Front License Plate Area

In 1978–1982 the left and right front grilles are made from black plastic. They are each one piece and are held to the car with black oxide Phillips screws in 1978 and 1979 and with black oxide hex-head bolts in 1980–1982.

All 1978 and 1979 cars have a front license plate mount bracket painted semi-gloss black. A single black rubber bumper is pressed into a hole toward the bottom center of the bracket. Two white plastic push nuts in the upper corners receive the license plate screws.

All 1980–1982 cars have a recess for the front license plate molded into the front bumper cover. Square holes are cut near the bottom corners of the recess. A black-phosphate-plated J nut is installed into each cutout to receive the license plate mount screws.

License plate mount screws are large slotted-head units with coarse threads. In 1978–1981 they are silver cadmium plated, and in 1982 they are dark cadmium plated. The screws came in a small brown paper bag marked "UNIT NUMBER 3875313" across the top, "LICENSE ATTACHING" on one side, and "REAR PLATE PARTS" on the other. The bag was placed inside the car in a storage compartment behind the seats.

In 1978 the front nose emblem and gas filler door emblem feature a design that commemorates the 25th anniversary of

Front grille details in unrestored 1979. All components shown, including the black-oxide-coated Phillips truss-head screws holding the grille, are factory correct.

The 1978 nose panel and gas filler door emblems celebrated Corvette's 25th anniversary. Emblems with black and silver paint, with red accents separating the two colors, were unique to 1978 Limited Edition Corvette Pace Cars.

the Corvette. This special emblem features the traditional crossed flags in a circle, with "CORVETTE" around the top edge and "1953 ANNIVERSARY 1978" around the bottom. Also, a "25" is above the crossed flags.

In 1979 the crossed flags alone are utilized for the front nose emblem and gas filler door emblem. In 1980 the crossed-flag emblem was redesigned. In 1980 and 1981, this new design is on the nose. In 1980 the staffs of the crossed flags are chrome plated, and in 1981 they are black.

In 1982 the crossed-flag nose emblem was again redesigned. The flags were shortened and widened, and the fleur-de-lis symbol found in the left flag for decades was replaced with the Chevrolet bowtie. "Collector edition" Corvettes from 1982 use special cloisonné emblems. In this design, the crossed flags are surrounded by a black ring, with the words "CORVETTE COLLECTOR EDITION" in gold letters.

In 1978 and 1979, the front park lamp lenses are made from clear plastic with black-painted horizontal lines that correlate to the lines in the front grille. The lenses attach with black oxide Phillips-head screws. In 1980–1982 the lenses are made from amber plastic and also have black-painted horizontal lines. They attach with black oxide Torx-head screws. All years have amber bulbs in the park lamps.

Rectangular side marker lamps are used at all four corners in 1978 and 1979. Lamp housings are made from plastic and are bordered with chrome stripes around the outer perimeter. All front side marker lamps have amber lenses, while rears have red lenses.

In addition to side marker lamps, 1980–1982 cars also have front cornering lamps that activate when the turn signal is turned on. Cornering lamp lenses are clear. Front side marker/cornering lamp assemblies are bordered by black plastic trim painted body color. As in 1978 and 1979, the rear side marker lamps used in 1980–1982 are bordered by chrome trim.

Front Headlamp Doors, Headlamps, and Headlamp Bezels

Headlamp housings are made from cast metal. The assemblies are painted body color. They typically show a dull or slightly rough paint finish except for the top of the housing, which should be consistent with the remainder of the exterior.

Low-beam headlamp bulbs in 1978–1982 were made by Guide and feature a Guide "power beam" logo in the glass. This logo is a circle with the word "POWER" above it and the word "BEAM" below it. It is believed that some cars got low-beam bulbs manufactured by GE or Wagner, though this is not the norm. High-beam bulbs in 1978 and those '79s assembled through approximately November 1979 are also Guide power beams. High-beam bulbs in those '79s assembled after approximately November 1979 and in all 1980–1982 cars are General Electric halogen sealed beams. They say "HALOGEN" in a rectangle in the center of the

All 1978–1982 Corvettes came with Guide "power beam" low-beam lamps. All 1978s and those 1979s made through approximately November 1978 also used power beam high-beam lamps. From approximately November 1978 through the end of 1982 production, all cars got General Electric halogen high-beam lamps. It is possible that a small number of cars came with low-beam lamps made by Wagner instead of Guide.

lens and "SEALED BEAM" near the bottom. "GENERAL ELECTRIC" also appears near the bottom.

All 1978–1982 cars have headlamp bezels made from fiberglass. All bezels are painted body color. On St. Louis–built cars especially, paint on the bezels is usually not as shiny or smooth as it is on the body. Bezels are retained by four chrome-plated Phillips oval-head screws. The two on the sides are fitted with integral countersunk washers, and the two on the front are not.

A cadmium dichromate vacuum actuator is mounted behind each headlamp assembly. A red-striped hose connects to the back of each actuator, and a green-striped hose connects to the front. The hoses are secured with yellow spring clamps.

Front Fenders

All 1978 and 1979 front fenders feature a molded-in recess as in previous years. In 1980–1982, front fenders got a redesigned vent area, which features an insert in the molded-in recess. The insert is black plastic, and the area behind it is painted semi-gloss black. The insert is held in place by black-oxide-plated Torx screws.

In 1978 and 1979 both fenders have a crossed-flag emblem above the vent area. The emblems used for early 1978 cars have a white square in the upper right corner of the checkered flag. Later 1978 and most 1979 cars have a black square in the upper right corner.

The 1978 Indy pace car replicas have a unique decal on each front fender, below the crossed-flag emblem. This decal is clear, with white lettering that reads "LIMITED EDITION."

All 1978 Limited Edition Corvette Pace Cars came with special decals for dealer installation if desired by the buyer. This extremely original example still wears its original paint. Its door decals remain in their original packaging.

No crossed-flag emblem is used on the front fenders of 1980–1982 Corvettes. Those 1980 cars equipped with an L82 engine have an emblem that says "L-82" above the fender vents. This emblem utilizes chrome-plated characters on a black base. In 1982 an emblem reading "CROSS-FIRE INJECTION" is above the fender vents. This emblem also has chrome-plated letters on a black base.

Hood

All 1978 and 1979 cars have the same hood design seen in preceding years. Corvettes in 1980–1982 have a revised hood design. The new design has a relatively subdued wind split in the middle, rather than the "power bulge" seen in previous years. Those 1978 and 1979 Corvettes equipped with the optional L82 engine have an "L-82" emblem on either side of the hood. This emblem feature red paint between the chrome-plated characters. No hood emblems are used on 1980–1982 Corvettes.

Windshield Wipers and Windshield Washers

Wiper arms and blade holders are dull black in color. Both arms and blades typically say "TRICO" on one of the ends. Some cars are equipped with blade holders manufactured by Anco instead of Trico. Anco blade holders are more prevalent in 1978–1980 than in 1981–1982. A length of rubber hose serves to convey washer fluid along the arms up to the windshield washer nozzles. When the wipers are parked, the passenger-side blade is above the driver-side blade.

Windshield, Door Glass, and Back Glass

All 1978–1982 Corvette windshields were manufactured by Libby Owens Ford (LOF) utilizing Safety Flo-Lite glass. The LOF logo, "SHADED SOFT RAY," "SAFETY FLO-LITE," "LAMINATED DOT 15 M24," and a two-letter manufacturing date code are etched into the lower right side of the windshield. In the date code, one letter represents the month and the other denotes the year. There is no discernible

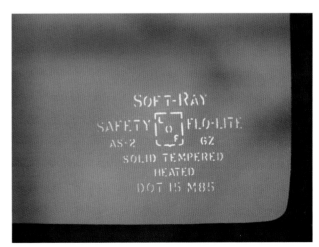

All body glass is imprinted with the manufacturer's logo, date of production, and other information. Libby Owens Ford "SAFETY FLO-LITE" tinted glass was used throughout, and each piece should have a two-letter date code. In this example, "GZ" reveals that the glass was made in April 1980.

pattern to the letter usage, so you must refer to the glass date codes in Appendix R.

The letters "ASI" are in the upper right portion of the windshield. These letters are white and sandwiched between the laminates of glass, not etched into the surface like the logo and date code.

All windshields are painted on the interior along the bottom edge and along the side edges with black paint. For all 1978–1982 cars, the exterior top and sides of the windshield are surrounded by stainless-steel trim. This trim is painted satin black.

In 1978–1982 both side windows are made from tinted LOF Safety Flo-Lite, Soft-Ray tinted glass. It has the manufacturer's logo and a two-letter date code etched in, just like the windshield.

All 1978–1982 Corvettes use a dramatically restyled back window area. Instead of the notch back design used in 1968–1977, the newer cars use a fastback design. Like the other glass in the cars, all back windows are tinted Safety Flo-Lite and have the LOF logo and manufacturing date code etched in.

The 1982 collector edition Corvettes utilize a back window that opens up. No other 1978–1982 Corvettes have this feature. The hardware and hinges for the functional hatch on the 1982 collector edition are semi-gloss black.

Rear window surround molding is stainless steel in all 1978–1982 Corvettes. The moldings utilized on those 1978 cars assembled through approximately mid-October 1977 are typically unpainted and polished along the outer edge, and painted satin black along the inner edge. The moldings on cars assembled from approximately mid-October 1977 through approximately the end of November 1977 are sometimes the same as in earlier cars and sometimes entirely unpainted and

A rear window defogger was an extra cost option in 1978–1982, and most of those Corvettes had it. The defogger relied on thin strips of a conductive material glued to the inside of the rear glass. When viewed from outside, the strips look reddish brown.

polished. Those 1978s assembled after approximately the end of November 1977 are typically seen with unpainted outer edges and black satin inner edges, as with earlier cars. All 1978 pace cars, as well as all 1979–1982 Corvettes, use rear window molding that is completely painted satin black.

Door Mirror, Handles, and Locks

One chrome-plated, outside rearview mirror mounted on the driver's door is standard in 1978 and most of 1979. In 1978 through late 1979, option D35 substituted dual sport mirrors for the single chrome one. Each door got a sport mirror, which was painted exterior color. The 1978 pace cars and silver anniversary models, late 1979s, and all 1980–1982s have dual sport mirrors as standard equipment.

For all years, the mirror glass is shaded and is coded with the manufacturer's symbol and a date code. The majority of

The 1978 Limited Edition Corvette Pace Car replica created a frenzy when it was announced to the public. Chevrolet ultimately built 6,502 examples.

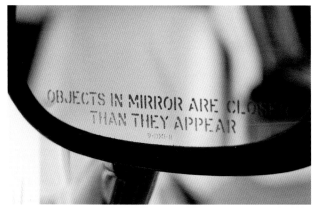

The door mirrors contain a manufacturer code and date code on the bottom of the glass. The first number indicates the month. The second number is the final digit of the year. In this example, the mirror was made in August 1979. "DMI" represents the manufacturer, Donnelly Mirror, Inc. Ajax Mirror Company was another supplier. Ajax mirrors typically have a letter for the month (with "A" representing January and so on), AX for the company's logo, and two numbers to represent the year.

1978–1982 mirrors were supplied by Donnelly Mirror, Inc. These have "DMI" in the date code, while mirrors supplied by Ajax Mirror have "AX" in the code. For example, the code in a Donnelly-supplied mirror manufactured in April 1979 would read, "4-DMI-9," while the code for an Ajax-supplied mirror manufactured in February 1980 would read "2-AX-80."

All 1978–1982 door handles are a spring-loaded, press-flap design. On original handles, the spring action is provided by a coil spring on the hinge shaft. A butterfly spring covering a coil spring is incorrect. When the flap is depressed, the spring is visible. No gasket is utilized between the handle and door.

The door locks, which are positioned below the door handles, feature a polished stainless-steel bezel. Original bezels have a thin black gasket and are retained to the cylinders by means of a continuous crimp around the entire circumference. Incorrect replacement locks may have bezels retained by four tangs.

Side Rocker Molding

Side rocker moldings for all 1978–1982 cars are brushed aluminum. All 1978–1980 models except '78 pace cars have moldings painted semi-flat black, with a thin strip of unpainted aluminum along the top. The rocker moldings for 1978 pace cars are unpainted, except for a painted ⅜-inch-wide semi-flat black stripe along their length. The moldings for 1981 and 1982 cars are completely painted semi-flat black.

Rocker moldings attach to the body with six black-oxide-plated Phillips oval head screws. The forward two and rearmost screws use a hex nut with an integral washer. The middle three screws go into nut plates in the body. The forward two and rearmost screws are sometimes pan-head instead of oval head. Original 1978–1982 rocker moldings do not have a tab on the lower lip near the front, as earlier moldings do.

Radio Antenna

On those 1978–1982 cars assembled without a radio, no radio antenna was installed. On all others, an antenna was mounted on the driver-side rear deck. A fixed-mast antenna was standard equipment on all 1978–1982 Corvettes fitted with a radio. A power antenna was available as an extra cost option for all years.

For fixed-mast antennas, a black plastic gasket goes between the antenna base and the car's body. The base is also made of black plastic. A chrome cap with two flat areas for a wrench to grab holds the mast to the base. The ball at the tip of the antenna is .300 inches in diameter in the vast majority of cars. Later GM service replacement masts have a .250-inch-diameter ball. Some original antennas might have the smaller ball.

The optional power antenna utilizes a black plastic bezel on very early 1978 models. Later '78s and early '79s use a chrome-plated bezel. Later '79s and 1980–1982 cars do not use a bezel. The antenna mounting nut for all cars is chrome plated and has four flat areas for a wrench.

Those 1978–1982 cars equipped with the optional CB radio have a unique antenna. It has a "loading coil" as part of the antenna mast. The loading coil is cylindrical and has a diameter that is slightly larger than the mast.

The antenna mounting area of the rear deck on all 1978 cars and those '79s assembled through approximately late February 1979 is flat and even with the remainder of the deck. The mounting area on '79 Corvettes assembled after approximately late February 1979 and on all 1980–1982 cars has a recess molded in. This recess allows the antenna to mount horizontally rather than on a slight angle.

Gas Lid Door and Gas Cap

Gas lid doors are painted body color for all 1978–1982 cars. The doors for all years are fitted with a crossed-flag emblem. It is held on by chrome or black oxide plated acorn nuts that are visible with the door open.

In 1978 the gas filler door was adorned with the 25th-anniversary emblem. This "UNLEADED FUEL ONLY" decal is original.

The underside of an unrestored gas lid door from 1979. Acorn nuts retaining the crossed-flag emblem are either black or chrome, as seen here. The letters "MDC" represent the manufacturer of the lid. The number sequences are GM and manufacturer part numbers.

The gas lid door bezel used on '78s assembled through approximately July 1978 is chrome plated. Thereafter, all gas lid door bezels are painted semi-gloss black. Both the chrome-plated and painted bezels are retained by four black-oxide-plated Phillips-head screws in 1978 and 1979. In 1980–1982 the bezel is retained by four black-oxide-plated Posidriv screws.

The gas lid door hinge is chrome plated, and the door is held to its bezel with chrome-plated Phillips fillister-head screws fitted with external star lock washers. Two black rubber bumpers with the letters "ABC" molded in support the gas lid door when it is closed.

A straight decal reading "UNLEADED FUEL ONLY," with silver letters outlined in black, was used from 1978 through early 1981. On pace cars and those '79 cars equipped with optional spoilers (option D80), the decal was affixed to the spoiler near the notch for the gas lid door. On all other 1978 and 1979 cars, it was affixed to the deck surface immediately behind the door.

Later 1981 and all 1982 Corvettes do not have an "UNLEADED FUEL ONLY" decal. Instead, their bezels are stamped with the words "UNLEADED FUEL ONLY" on the right side and "ESSENCE SANS PLOMB SEULEMENT" on the left side.

All 1978 and '79 Corvettes use a gold-iridite-plated, twist-on metal gas cap. The letters "NDH" and the numbers "559346" are stamped in around a recess in the center of the cap.

This gold-iridite-plated steel gas cap was used in 1980 only. The part number "22503147" and the manufacturer's logo are stamped into the center area. The caps were made by Stant.

This original 1978–1979 gas cap is gold iridite plated. It has the manufacturer's logo "NDH" and part number "559346" stamped in its top. Two small black rubber bumpers cushion the gas lid door when it's closed. Original bumpers have "ABC" in raised letters molded into their surface.

All 1981–1982 Corvettes were fitted with an ivory-colored plastic fuel cap. Most caps were manufactured by Stant and have an "S" or the Stant logo in the middle. It is believed that some original caps have the letters "CSM" in a circle.

All 1980 Corvettes also use gold-iridite-plated, twist-on metal gas caps. The caps were manufactured by Stant, and the company's logo, as well as "22503147," are stamped in.

In 1981 and 1982, Corvettes use an off-white plastic gas cap instead of the previous metal design. These caps were also manufactured by Stant and have a Stant logo molded in.

A black rubber boot surrounds the gas filler neck on all 1978–1982 cars. The boot has a plastic nipple facing the rear of the car. A rubber drain hose attaches to the nipple. The hose, which has a metal spring inside to prevent it from collapsing, runs down and exits behind the license plate area.

Rear Fascia, Taillamps, Bumpers, and Related Parts

All 1978–1982 Corvettes utilize an impact-absorbing rear bumper assembly. As in the front, this assembly consists of a body-colored urethane cover fitted over a multipiece metal understructure.

All 1978–1982 cars have "CORVETTE" spelled out in a single nameplate affixed to the rear bumper cover. The stylized lowercase letters are chrome plated and rest on a semi-gloss black base.

Recesses for taillamps are molded into the rear bumper cover. All 1978–1982 cars utilize four rear lamps. The two outer ones have red lenses that function as taillamps, stop lamps, and turn signals. The two inner ones have red lenses with clear plastic centers that function as backup lamps.

In 1978 and 1979, taillamps each have a stainless-steel ring around the outer perimeter and another stainless-steel ring around the center portion of the lens.

In 1980–1982 taillamp lenses each have a concentric groove molded in. Unlike earlier years, they do not have stainless-steel rings around the perimeter or the center of each lens.

Each lamp has a very small moisture wick that protrudes from the bottom of the lens. The wick material resembles a cigarette filter.

The rear bumper cover has a molded-in recess for a license plate in all years. A lamp with a plastic cover is mounted in a cutout above the license plate. The lamp assembly is held by chrome-plated Phillips-head screws.

Silver-cadmium-plated steel brackets for mounting the rear license plate are held to the bumper cover by pop rivets. Two white plastic push nuts insert into the brackets and receive the license plate retaining screws. As with the front, 1978–1981 license plate screws are plated silver cadmium. The 1982 screws are plated dark gray cadmium.

T-tops

All 1978–1982 Corvettes except 1978 pace cars and 1982 collector editions come standard with fiberglass T-tops painted body color. In 1978 tops are fitted with unpainted stainless-steel trim. In 1979–1982 the stainless trim is painted semi-gloss black.

Glass T-tops are standard on '78 pace cars and '82 collector editions and are optional on all other 1978–1982 Corvettes. Instead of stainless steel, glass tops are trimmed with black plastic.

All glass T-tops were manufactured by Libby Owens Ford and have the "LOF" manufacturer's logo etched in. As with the other glass in the car, glass T-tops have a two-letter date code indicating when they were made. (Refer to the glass date codes in Appendix R.)

Glass tops on all 1978–1980 Corvettes, and on those '81s assembled in St. Louis, are laminated. Glass tops on 1981s assembled in Bowling Green and on all '82s are solid tempered. Laminated tops have a bluish tint, while solid tempered tops have a grayish tint. Collector edition tops have a bronze tint.

Tires, Wheels, and Wheel Covers

All 1978–1982 Corvettes were equipped with Goodyear Polysteel P225/70R15 blackwall radials as standard

Front and rear spoilers were installed on all 1978 Limited Edition Corvette Pace Car replicas. No other 1978 Corvettes were delivered to retail customers with factory-installed spoilers. Spoilers were available in 1979 as option D80.

All 1978–1982 Corvettes came with a P225/70R15 radial blackwall tire as standard. These raised-white-letter Goodyear Polysteel Radials were an extra cost option. The semi-gloss finish of this aluminum wheel is factory correct.

Chevrolet produced 6,502 1978 Limited Edition Pace Car replicas. In addition to the Indianapolis Motor Speedway winged-tire logo decal on the rear quarter panel, pace car replicas came with large "OFFICIAL PACE CAR" decals for each door. The decals were shipped with the car for dealer installation if the original buyer wanted it.

equipment. These same tires with raised white letters were available as an extra cost option. The optional version says "GOODYEAR" and "POLYSTEEL RADIAL" in raised white block letters on the sidewall.

Available as an extra cost option was a larger Goodyear radial tire. This tire, sized at P255/60R15, was available only in raised-white-letter configuration. The raised white letters say "GOODYEAR" and "GT RADIAL" in 1978 through very early 1980. The optional larger tires in later 1980s and subsequent cars say "GOODYEAR" and "EAGLE GT." In 1978 and 1979, these larger tires necessitated trimming the front and rear lower edges of the front fenders for clearance.

Every 1978–1982 tire has a 10- or 11-digit "tire identification number" stamped into the sidewall. The first letter of the code indicates the manufacturer. The second character denotes the location of the plant that manufactured the tire. The third and fourth digits indicate the tire's size. The following three or four letters denote the type of tire construction. The next two numbers indicate the week of the year the tire was made, with "01" being the first week of the year and "52" being the last. The final number is the last digit of the year of manufacture.

All 1978–1982 Corvettes are equipped with steel rally wheels as standard equipment. They are a color called Argent Silver on the front side. The back sides are painted semi-flat black and always have silver overspray, since the front side was painted silver after the black was applied to the rear.

All wheels are stamped with a date code, manufacturer's logo, and size code on the front face. All 1978–1982 Corvette wheels are 15 by 8 inches and have the code "AZ" stamped in to indicate this. The "AZ" is adjacent to the valve stem hole.

Also adjacent to the valve stem hole is the manufacturer's logo and date code stamping. On one side of the hole it says "K" for the wheel manufacturer, Kelsey Hayes. This is followed by a dash and a "1" that represents Chevrolet. Next come another dash and a number to denote the last digit of the year of manufacture. This is followed by a space and one or two numbers to indicate the month of manufacture. On the other side of the valve stem hole are one or two more numbers that represent the day of manufacture.

Stainless-steel trim rings and chrome center caps are standard for all cars. Original trim rings are held to the wheel by four steel clips. Center caps should read "CHEVROLET MOTOR DIVISION" in black-painted letters.

Aluminum wheels were offered as an option in 1978–1982. In 1978 and 1979, the aluminum wheels on all Corvettes except pace cars have center sections painted semi-gloss black and small chrome-plated hubcaps with centers painted semi-gloss black. Also, the 1978 and 1979 aluminum wheels are unpainted inside the edges of the rectangular slots and are not clear coated.

The aluminum wheels used on pace cars are more highly polished overall. They do not have black-painted center areas or black-painted hub caps but are painted black in the inside edges of the rectangular slots. In addition, pace car wheels each have a red stripe painted around the outer edge.

Aluminum wheels used in 1980–1982, except on '82 collector edition cars, are essentially the same as those fitted to '78 pace cars, with the exception of the red stripe. The 1980–1982 wheels are highly polished overall, do not have black-painted center areas or caps, and are painted black in the inside edges of the rectangular slots. Unlike earlier versions, 1980–1982 aluminum wheels are clear coated. All 1978–1982 aluminum wheels are retained by chrome-plated lug nuts.

The 1982 collector edition wheels are made from aluminum but differ in design from the regular production

All 1982 collector edition Corvettes came with special aluminum wheels and P255/60R15 Goodyear Eagle GT tires. The same tires were available as an extra cost option on other 1978–1982 Corvettes.

All 1978–1982 Corvettes came with a Goodyear Polyspare space-saver spare tire. It is believed that a very small number of cars came with a full-size spare wheel and tire. All tires, including the spare, have manufacturing information molded into the sidewall. In this example, "MD" indicates the Goodyear manufacturing plant, "UH" relates to the size, "FBO" denotes the type and construction of the tire, and the final three numbers reveal the date of manufacture, the 21st week of 1982.

option aluminum wheels. These wheels utilize a center hub to cover the chrome-plated lug nuts. The center of the hub is fitted with a silver disc containing the 1982 crossed-flag logo.

All 1978–1982 wheels, including both standard steel rally wheels and optional aluminum wheels, utilize black rubber valve stems that measure approximately 1¼ inches long. These are fitted with caps that come to a point and have longitudinal ridges around their entire perimeter.

To ease the balancing process, steel wheels are sometimes marked with a tiny weld drop or paint dot at their highest point. This mark is lined up with an orange dot on the tire. Balance weights are the type that clamp onto the edge of the rim and are placed on the inside of the wheel only. Original balance weights usually have the letters "OEM" molded into their faces. There is usually a small dot of white or colored paint on the tire adjacent to each balance weight. All aluminum wheels are fitted with balance weights attached to the inside of the rim only.

Though it is probable that a very small number of 1978–1982 Corvettes left the factory with a full-size spare that matched the other four wheels and tires, the vast majority were equipped with a space-saver spare tire manufactured by Goodyear. This tire was called Polyspare by Goodyear and is sized at P195/80D15. The words "GOODYEAR," "TEMPORARY USE ONLY," and "MAX. SPEED 50 M.P.H." appear on the black sidewall. Regardless of what type of wheels the car is fitted with, the space-saver spare tire is mounted to 15-by-5-inch stamped-steel rim painted semi-gloss black. Some very early 1978 Corvettes have a spare tire rim painted very bright yellow instead of black.

Spare tire wheels are all stamped "YA," which is the size designation. They are also stamped with the manufacturer's logo, a code for the manufacturing plant, and a number to

The spare tire in 1978–1982 Corvettes was mounted on a 15-by-5-inch steel wheel. The "K" stamping represents the manufacturer, Kelsey Hayes, "3" identifies the specific plant where the wheel was made, and "2" indicates that it was made in 1982. The "6" to the left of the valve stem and the "1" to the right of it tells us the wheel was made on June 1, 1982.

indicate the year of production. A typical stamping reads "K39," with "K" indicating the manufacturer, Kelsey-Hayes, "3" indicating the plant where the wheel was made, and "9" indicating that the wheel was made in 1979.

The spare tire and wheel are housed in a carrier bolted to the rear underbody area. The carrier is fiberglass with steel supports. The fiberglass is unpainted, and the steel support is painted semi-gloss black. The tire tub portion of the carrier has a fair amount of flat to semi-gloss black paint on its outside surface, applied during the blackout process. A lock covered by a black rubber boot goes over the spare tire carrier access bolt.

All 1978–1982 Corvettes were fitted with a trim tag in the driver-side door hinge pillar. With St. Louis–built cars, the tag was attached with pop rivets while the body was on the paint line, between the application of the second and third color coats. So the tag is normally painted body color. A three-character code for the date the tag was affixed to the body is stamped in the upper right corner. A letter represents the month, with "A" representing the first month of production, "B" the second, and so on. Refer to Appendix S for body build date codes. The two numbers following the letter represent the day. The example shown is from 1979. "M11" indicates a date of August 11, 1979.

All 1978–1982 Corvettes were fitted with a trim tag in the driver-side door hinge pillar. Tags installed at the Bowling Green plant were unpainted. The first four characters indicated the body build date, with "B" representing model year 1981 and "C" denoting 1982. The next two numbers correlate to the month, and the letter indicates the week. In this example, the body was built the third week of August 1981. The "741" indicates that the car came with red cloth interior, and "39L 39U" tells us that it was painted Charcoal Metallic. Optional two-tone paint schemes were indicated by different upper and lower paint codes.

1978–1982 INTERIOR
Trim Tag

Interior trim color and material, as well as exterior body color and body assembly date, are stamped into a stainless-steel plate attached to the driver's door hinge pillar by two aluminum pop rivets. This plate is commonly called a trim plate or trim tag.

The trim tag for 1978–1980 and those '81 Corvettes assembled in St. Louis was installed before the body painting process was completed and was painted over. Tags on 1981 Corvettes assembled in Bowling Green and on all '82s were installed after the painting process was completed and therefore are unpainted.

The 1978 Limited Edition Corvette Pace Car replica featured a unique silver interior with high-back bucket seats. The blue hazard warning light operation instruction card shown was hung from the turn signal lever in each car when new.

1978–1982

Silver beige interior trim was unique to the Collector Edition. AM/FM stereo with an integral CB radio was optional in 1978–1982.

Trim color and material are indicated in the plate by a three-digit code. For example, in 1978, trim code 12C indicates Oyster White with cloth and leather seat covers.

Exterior body paint color is indicated in the trim plate by a three-character code or two three-character codes in cars with optional two-tone paint. For example, in 1980, code 52L indicates yellow. (Refer to Appendix T for paint and interior trim codes.)

The body build date represents the date when the painted and partially assembled body reached that point on the assembly line where the trim plate was installed. The car's final assembly date is typically one to several days after the body build date.

For 1978–1980 and those 1981 Corvettes assembled in St. Louis, a letter indicating the month followed by two numbers indicating the day represents the body build date. The letter "A" was assigned to the first month of production, which was September 1977 for '78 models, August 1978 for '79 models, October 1979 for '80 models, and August 1980 for '81 models. The second month of production was assigned "B," and so on. So a body assembled on August 6, 1978, would have "A06" stamped into the trim plate, and a body built on January 11, 1980, would have "D11" stamped into its plate.

The body build date code for those 1981 Corvettes assembled in Bowling Green and all '82 cars is different. It begins with a letter to designate the year, with "B" denoting 1981 and "C" denoting 1982. The letter is followed by two numbers that indicate the month, with "01" representing January, "02" representing February, and so on. The final character is a letter denoting the week of the month, with "A" representing the first week, "B" representing the second week,

Deep-bucket high-back seats, first introduced in 1978 limited edition pace car replicas, were standard in all 1979–1982 Corvettes. These are original leather seats, so the center sections are leather while the side bolsters are vinyl. Chevrolet used this design because side bolsters were subjected to more intense wear from people scraping across them while entering and exiting, and the vinyl material was more durable.

and so on. As an example, a body build code for a Bowling Green–assembled Corvette that reads "C 05 B" translates to a 1982 assembled in the second week of May.

Seats

All 1978 Corvettes except pace car replicas utilize the same high-back seats used in previous years. Pace cars and all 1979–1982 Corvettes use a completely revised seat design featuring deeper recesses and additional protrusions for side bolster support. The new seat backs tilt forward at a higher point than their predecessors. This permits the back to move

In 1981–1982 a power-adjustable driver seat was optional. Controls were located at the front of the outboard side of the seat base, housed in a molded plastic cover that was color matched to the interior trim.

Cloth seat upholstery was offered in 1978–1980 as a no additional cost option. The center sections of the seats are cloth with horizontal stitching, and the sides are vinyl. The no-cost cloth seat option in 1981–1982 utilized seat upholstery made entirely from cloth.

Each seat rests on two seat tracks, which allow for forward and rearward adjustment of the seat's position. The tracks are black phosphate, and each is held to the floor by one black phosphate indented hex-head bolt at either end, for a total of four per seat. The front bolts are covered by a cutaway flap of carpet. The carpet is usually trimmed away where the rear bolts pass through the floor, though in some cars the rear bolts simply pass through the carpet. The flaps of carpet are usually glued over the front seat bolts. The seat adjust lever is black phosphate with a plastic knob on its end. The knob has a grained texture and is the same color as the interior.

For all 1978s other than pace cars, the seat backs are made of molded plastic and match interior color. The seat back release button, its bezel, and the brackets that attach the seat back to the bottom are all chrome plated. Two bolts that allow for adjustment of seat back position are bright silver and get a rubber cushion over their heads. Black plastic trim washers are under the seat back release bezel and adjustment bolts.

Seats introduced with the '78 pace cars use a molded plastic shell for both the top and bottom sections of the seat.

much farther forward and thus gives improved access to the rear storage area.

Standard seat upholstery is leather for all 1978–1982 Corvettes. All 1978–1982 leather seats have horizontal panels, though the pattern is noticeably different in the new seat design fitted to '78 pace cars and all 1979–1982s. In all cars except the 1982 collector edition, only the faces of leather-upholstered seats are real leather. The sides of the covers are vinyl. The seat covers in the '82 collector edition are all leather.

The 1982 collector edition got unique seat upholstery and interior trim color.

Buyers could choose either cloth or leather seat upholstery in 1978–1982. The 1978–1980 cloth seats had cloth inserts with vinyl bolsters, while 1981–1982 seats were completely covered with cloth, as shown in this 1981 example.

High-back bucket seats used in 1978 limited edition pace car replicas and all 1979–1982 Corvettes had a carpet insert behind the upper section.

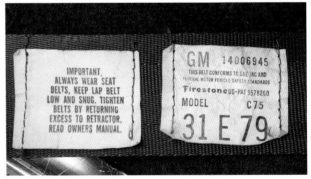

Firestone is believed to be the exclusive supplier of seat belts for 1978–1982 Corvettes. The 1978–1979 webbing has a pattern of four rows. The 1980–1982 webbing is comprised of four or five rows. All webbing is dyed to match interior color. The belt assembly's date of manufacture was ink stamped in the label to the right. In this case, "31 E 79" indicates that this belt was made during the 31st week of 1979. The meaning of the letter "E" is unknown.

The shells are color matched to the interior, and the back of the top shell has a carpet insert that is also color keyed to the interior. The 1978 pace cars and some very early '79 Corvettes have a vinyl border around the seat back carpet insert. Subsequent cars do not have this border.

These seats do not have any release hardware to tilt the seat back forward. Instead, the backs simply move forward. An inertial mechanism locks them in place in the event of a sudden stop. The seats have no means to adjust seat back angle.

Beginning in 1981, a six-way power driver side seat became optional. Externally, this seat appears essentially identical to the standard seat, with the exception of three switches mounted in the front left side of the seat bottom.

Lap and Shoulder Belts

All 1978–1982 Corvettes are equipped with combination lap and shoulder belts. All belts were manufactured by Firestone, and large tags sewn to the belts say "Firestone." In addition to the manufacturer's name, the tags indicate the model number and bear the date that particular belt was made. The model number for all 1978–1982 Corvette belts is C 75.

The lap and shoulder belt date is indicated by an ink stamping, with a number representing the week of the year, a letter whose meaning is not yet understood, and another number representing the year. For example, a stamping of "01 E 81" indicates that the belt was made in January 1981. The majority of 1978–1980 belts have the letter "E" in the date code, while the majority of 1981–1982 belts have the letter "L."

In addition to the tag bearing the manufacturer's name and date code, another, smaller tag is sewn to both lap and shoulder belts. This tag contains safety instructions.

In 1978–1979, belts are made from four-row webbing material, and 1980–1982 belts are made from four- or five-row material. In either case, the webbing is the same color as the carpet. The outboard portion of each belt is on a spring-loaded retractable coil.

Inboard portions of the seat belts are encased in a semi-rigid plastic that goes over part of the female buckles. The plastic is color matched to the interior. The buckles have a chrome-plated housing with a brushed-silver cover. The release buttons each have the GM logo.

Door Panels and Door Hardware

Most 1978–1982 door panels are made from molded vinyl with carpet along the bottom. Those 1978–1980 cars equipped with cloth seats have a cloth insert above the armrest. The 1982 collector edition has leather material on the door panels in place of vinyl. For all door panels, inside window felts are attached to the upper edge of the panels with heavy staples, not pop rivets.

The forward lower section of all door panels has a storage pocket covered with a section of carpet. The carpet is bound with vinyl trim and held shut with two Velcro-type fasteners.

This original 1981 door panel is typical of 1978–1982, with the exception of the 1982 collector edition and cars with cloth seats. The collector edition got unique leather-covered panels. Cars with cloth seats got matching cloth inserts above the armrests.

An original 1979 passenger-side door panel. Door panels in cars fitted with cloth seats had a matching cloth insert in the area above the armrest.

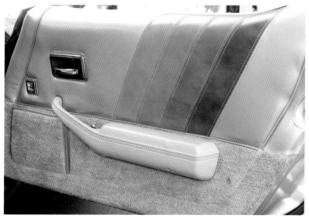

The upper portion of the 1982 Collector Edition door panel was covered in leather and featured four sewn-on strips of decorative leather. All other 1980–1982 door panels were covered with vinyl on the top half.

Door panel details from an unrestored 1979. Both the power lock switch and the mirror adjustment knob are chrome plated. The door handle trim plate is color keyed to the interior but often differs by a shade or two.

Door panels are attached to doors by means of interlocking plastic clips fastened to the back of the panel and the door frame. Black phosphate clips at the bottom of the front and rear of the panel also hold it on. The clips insert into a cutout in the back of the panel and get fastened to the door with black phosphate Phillips pan-head screws. Finally, three chrome Phillips-head screws with integral washers help retain the door panel. One, with a pan head, goes through the face of each panel at the upper rear. The two others, with oval heads, go through the carpeted area at the bottom.

Inside door release handles are chrome. They protrude from a rectangular, molded plastic escutcheon in the same color as the interior. The inside door pull is integral to the armrest. The armrest is molded vinyl and is held to the door with three black-oxide-plated Phillips-head screws.

Power windows were an option in 1978 and most of 1979 and became standard in May 1979. Cars equipped with standard manual windows have chrome window cranks with black plastic knobs. A thin plastic protective spacer is between the crank and the door panel.

Door Jambs and Door Perimeters

The jambs and perimeter of each door are painted body color, with the exception of the top front of each door, which is painted semi-gloss black. The door striker, which is the large pin threaded into the doorpost, and its corresponding receiver in the door are both cadmium plated. The striker is a special indented star-head design. Attached to the rear door jamb, toward the bottom, is a strip of aluminum and black rubber. This assembly is supposed to channel water outward.

The main door weather strip is one piece and therefore does not have a gap. It is held on with yellowish adhesive that is often sloppily applied. In addition to the adhesive, three Phillips pan-head screws also retain the weather strip, one at the forward end and two at the rearward end. In 1978 and early 1979, these screws are usually silver cadmium plated on

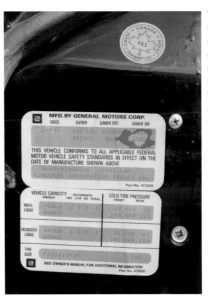

The original round and blue "Canada Transport" decal at the top of the door jamb was applied only to Corvettes exported to Canada. Note the somewhat sloppy application of yellow weather strip adhesive on the left and the equally sloppy application of black paint in the upper right. Both are quite typical of factory production.

the driver's door and black oxide plated on the passenger's door. Later cars tend to have black-oxide-plated screws on both doors.

The vehicle certification label glued toward the top of the rear portion of the driver's door is unpainted. It contains the car's VIN, the month and year the vehicle was produced, axle loading and gross vehicle weight ratings, and a statement that the vehicle conforms to all applicable motor vehicle safety standards in effect on the date of manufacture. In addition to the vehicle certification label, a tire information sticker appears on the rear of the driver's door. This sticker specifies tire pressure, tire size, and recommended vehicle capacity.

Most C3 Corvettes, including 1978–1982 examples, were extremely rough in the upper area of the front door jambs. The original, unrestored, one-owner 1979 shown here was delivered exactly as it appears.

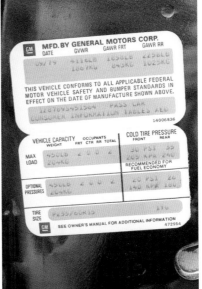

Two tamper-resistant decals were placed on the rear of the driver's door in most 1978 and all 1979–1982 Corvettes. Some early 1978s, in the vicinity of serial number 3,000 and earlier, have the decals on the driver-side door jamb, just below the striker. The top decal is a vehicle certification label, and the bottom contains tire pressure information. Both labels were covered with a clear film. The certification decal contains the car's VIN and date of manufacture.

In 1979–1982 the sill is unpainted aluminum, and it's much narrower than the sill used previously. The sill is held on with four chrome-plated Phillips oval-head screws.

Kick Panels, Quarter Trim Panels, Pedals, and Carpet

The kick panels beneath the dash just forward of the doors are molded plastic and are interior color. Panels are secured by an interference fit with the vertical door frame and by one chrome Phillips oval-head screw in the forward upper corner. Unlike 1977 and earlier kick panels, a ridge at the rear edge of 1978–1982 panels helps secure them to the body. Also unlike earlier panels, there is a carpet insert stapled to the kick panels. This insert matches the car's floor carpeting.

In all 1978–1982 Corvettes, carpet is made from plush cut pile material. In all cases it matches interior color. A black rubber flap on the firewall insulation retains the upper edge of the front carpeting on both sides. Carpet covers the bulkhead

behind the seats and has sewn-on binding on the lower edge where it overlaps the front floor carpet behind the seats. Rear storage compartment doors each have carpet under their frames. One piece of carpet covers the rear storage area floor and extends up the rear bulkhead. The edge at the top of the bulkhead is trimmed with a sewn-on binding, while the edges at the tops of the wheelwells are not trimmed. The only exception is carpet in 1978 pace cars, which is trimmed with vinyl on the edge above each wheelwell.

The carpet has a molded vinyl accelerator heel pad in the corner of the driver's footwell adjacent to the accelerator pedal. The main section of the pad is rectangular and has horizontal bars molded in. Extensions come off the main section and extend up the transmission tunnel and under the accelerator pedal. The heel pad is sewn to the carpet with a single filament thread that resembles fishing line. Some reproduction heel pads are sewn on with multifilament thread.

Dash Pad and Glove Box

The upper dash pad is made of soft vinyl and matches interior color along the edge closest to the passengers. The forward portion of the upper pad, which extends to the windshield, is flat black. Speaker grilles and the defroster outlet in the upper dash are also flat black.

A glove box door is inset into the passenger-side dash panel where a three-pocket storage area was placed in previous years. The door matches the dash panel in both texture and color. The door is released by means of a chrome-plated latch knob, which incorporates a key lock. The latch mechanism is made from unpainted pot metal components.

Two hinges are spot welded to the inside of the door. The hinges, as well as the back side of the door, are painted flat black. A small lamp is mounted on the right side of the glove box. It is activated by a plunger-type switch that utilizes a black plastic button surrounded by a chrome-plated bezel.

Lumpy fit of the rear carpet is typical. The Y-shaped adjustable strap was for securing T-tops when they were removed from the roof. T-top straps, trim around rear storage compartment doors, and speaker covers were color matched to interior.

An original carpet heel pad in a 1979. Original pads were sewn to the carpet with monofilament thread, which is similar to fishing line. The heel pads in some reproduction carpets were sewn with multifilament thread. Original heel pads have a flatter border than do reproductions.

Original paperwork enhances the collectability and value of vintage Corvettes. This array shows some of the papers that typically came with a 1979 Corvette.

Original documents delivered with new 1982 Corvettes are highly desirable to collectors. Some of the paperwork, such as the consumer information pamphlet and tire warranty brochure, were not keyed to each car individually and can be bought from literature dealers and others without much difficulty. Other items, including warranty papers, bills of sale, window stickers, build sheets, and order forms, are unique for each car and can't be replaced.

The glove box is formed from a black plastic liner retained by six black-oxide-plated Phillips pan-head screws. One of the liner screws also secures a metal shield for the glove box lamp. On those cars equipped with a cassette or eight-track player, a tape rack is installed in the glove box. This rack is made from black plastic.

The glove box contains a clear plastic envelope with no writing. Inside this envelope are the owner's manual, tire guide and warranty folder, maintenance folder, consumer information booklet, battery information card, vehicle and emissions warranty folder, CB radio manual (if the car is so equipped), and ETR radio manual (if the car is so equipped.)

Interior Switches, Controls, and Related Parts

All 1978–1982 Corvettes have a headlamp switch mounted in the upper left corner of the driver-side dash pad. In

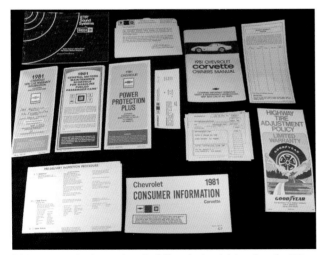

Original paperwork enhances the collectibility and value of vintage Corvettes. This array shows the papers that typically came with a 1981 Corvette.

The correct headlamp knob and bezel for 1978–1980.

1978–1980 headlamp switch knobs are chrome plated, with a black inner ring and a chrome-plated center. In 1981 and 1982, knobs are made from glossy black plastic with a thin chrome ring. The center of the knob is black with a symbol for headlamps in white. All 1978–1982 headlamp knobs have a black plastic bezel on the dash. The word "LIGHTS" appears in the bezel in white letters.

All 1978–1982 Corvettes have air-conditioning vents on both sides of the dash, toward the lower, outboard corner. The black plastic vent mechanisms swivel to change the direction of airflow. A grouping of movable slats also controls the direction of airflow. The slats are made from black plastic and have chrome edges.

On non-air-conditioned cars, the vents on either side of the dash allow outside air to enter the passenger compartment. Controls for these vents are positioned underneath the dash.

A small black T-handle pull mechanism beneath the driver-side dash on the left side releases the hood latch. The handle is black, with the words "HOOD RELEASE" painted in white block letters across its face. The hood release cable is in a smooth black plastic sheathing.

The trip odometer reset knob for all 1978–1982 cars is in the lower left area of the speedometer lens. This square knob is made from glossy black plastic.

The headlamp door override switch is mounted beneath the plastic fill panel underneath the steering column. It is a flat black plastic pull-type switch.

Steering Wheel and Steering Column

All 1978 and 1979 cars equipped with a standard steering column have a four-spoke steering wheel. It is completely covered in molded vinyl that matches interior color. Those 1978 and '79 cars equipped with the optional tilt-telescopic steering column, and all 1980–1982 cars, utilize a three-spoke steering wheel. The spokes for this wheel are brushed stainless steel, and the rim is covered with leather dyed to match interior color.

The standard steering column and optional tilt-telescoping column in 1978–1982 are painted to match the interior color in a semi-gloss finish. The column-mounted ignition switch is chrome plated. A notch in the switch aligns with the word "LOCK," which is cast into the column housing when the switch is in the locked position. All 1978–1982 columns have a key release lever located slightly forward of and below the ignition switch.

The tilt-telescoping column has a thick locking ring below the steering wheel to control the telescoping function. The ring is painted to match the rest of the column. Twisting

All 1978–1982 steering columns were painted to match interior color with a semi-gloss finish.

An original, unrestored 1979 interior in rarely seen Corvette Dark Green. Color-keyed carpeted floor mats were part of the ZX2 convenience group option package. A three-spoke leather-covered steering wheel was installed in all 1978–1979 Corvettes equipped with the optional tilt-telescopic steering column and in all 1980–1982s. Those 1978–1979s with a standard column got a vinyl-covered, four-spoke steering wheel.

When optional cruise control was purchased in 1978–1982, the controls were incorporated into a switch on the turn signal lever.

The curved white arrow on the knob of this windshield wiper/washer switch makes it correct for 1978–1979 Corvettes with intermittent wipers (part of the ZX2 convenience group option package) and for all 1980–1982s. Those 1978–1979s that did not have intermittent wipers used the same switch with a plain knob. In 1981–1982, the switch bezel is color keyed to the interior.

the lever on the ring releases the locking mechanism and allows the column to telescope.

A lever similar to but shorter than the turn signal lever controls the tilt function of the optional tilt-telescopic steering column. The tilt lever is located between the turn signal lever and the dash. All columns have a black plastic four-way flasher switch mounted on the right side. This switch consists of a pushbutton inside of sleeve. The sleeve has the word "HAZARD" written on it in white letters in two locations. For all years, a stalk with turn signal, headlight dimmer, and windshield wiper/washer controls is mounted into the steering column.

In 1978 and 1979, intermittent wipers were part of the ZX2 "convenience group" option package. The knob for the windshield wiper/washer switch is plain black plastic on cars that are not equipped with intermittent wipers. On those 1978 and 1979 cars equipped with intermittent wipers and on all 1980–1982 cars, the knob has a white arc and arrow. In 1978–1980 the wiper switch bezel is black, and in 1981–1982 it is the same color as the interior.

With the exception of the 1982 collector editions, all 1978–1982 models use a textured metal horn button painted to match the interior. The collector edition uses a horn button covered with leather dyed to match interior color. A crossed-flag emblem is in the center of the button. Some early 1978s might have been fitted with an unpainted, brushed-aluminum horn button. Some of these were installed in 1977 Corvettes, but Chevrolet recalled them because strong reflections from their surfaces posed a potential safety hazard. It's not clear whether any were installed in 1978s prior to the recall.

Interior Windshield Moldings, Sun Visors, and Rearview Mirror

Three pieces of vinyl-covered molding matched to the interior color cover the inside of the windshield frame for all 1978–1982 Corvettes. The two side pieces are each held on by one chrome-plated Phillips-head screw at the top and two chrome-plated Phillips-head screws on the vertical section. The top piece of molding is retained by chrome-plated recess-head Phillips screws fitted with countersunk washers.

Sun visors are covered with padded soft vinyl. The pattern of the vinyl used for the sun visors matches the

Roof trim panels were color matched to the interior. The difference in shade from one surface to the next is typical. Glass T-tops were an extra cost option.

Windshield garnish molding, trim panels beneath roof panels, and roof surround panels are all color keyed to the interior.

pattern in the vinyl used for seat covers. Each sun visor is held to the windshield frame with chrome-plated recess-head Phillips screws. Sun visor mounts allow the visors to swivel toward the side windows.

In 1978–1980 Corvettes and those 1981 cars assembled in St. Louis, a sleeve describing operation of the turn signal and headlamp dimmer switches, ignition key removal procedure, and proper adjustment procedures for the optional dual sport mirrors slides over the driver-side sun visor. Another sleeve describing proper adjustment procedures for glass T-tops slides over the passenger-side sun visor in those cars equipped with glass tops.

Those 1978 and early 1979 cars equipped with the convenience group option (option ZX2) have a vanity mirror mounted to the passenger-side sun visor. Late 1979 and all 1980–1982 Corvettes have a vanity mirror on the passenger-side sun visor. Beginning in late 1979, the driver-side sun visor mount allows the visor to telescope in and out for a greater range of adjustment.

All 1978–1982 Corvettes have a 10-inch-wide interior day/night rearview mirror mounted directly onto the upper windshield. All mirrors are in a black grained plastic housing. The day/night lever is black plastic as well, with horizontal ribs to enhance grip.

The mirror is fastened to a small mounting pad by means of an Allen screw. The pad is adhered to the windshield with special glue. The mirror's mounting arm is usually flat black, though some cars have a dull silver arm.

Instruments and Radio

Both the speedometer and tachometer in all 1978–1982 Corvettes have flat black faces and white numerals. A secondary scale on the speedometer face indicates kilometers per hour. This scale is blue in 1978 and in those 1979s assembled through approximately July 1979. It is yellow in subsequent 1979s and in all 1980–1982 cars. Corvettes built for export to Canada and elsewhere had a kilometers-per-hour scale in white numerals around the outer edge of the

This is a rare export-only speedometer in a 1978. The car was sold new in Canada, so the speedometer's primary speed scale reads in kilometers per hour rather than miles per hour.

The 1982 speedometer is marked in increments of five miles per hour. Inner numbers indicate kilometers per hour. The tachometer redline for 1978–1979 L48 and 1978 L82 cars with air conditioning is 5,300. The redline is 5,600 in 1978 L82s without air conditioning and all 1979 L82s. Those 1980s with L82s have a 6,000-rpm redline, while all other 1980–1982s have a 5,300-rpm redline.

An original speedometer and tachometer in an unrestored 1979. All 1978 and most 1979 speedometers read to 145 miles per hour, with blue numbers for an inner kilometers-per-hour scale. But late in 1979, intermittently after serial number 44,598 and probably without exception after serial number 48,940, the 85-miles-per-hour speedometer shown here was used. In 1982 speed markings were in increments of 10 miles per hour.

All 1978–1982 center stack instruments utilized white pointers and numerals on a black background. Cars not equipped with an optional "electronically tuned receiver" stereo had a clock in the lower left. Cars with an ETR stereo, which had an integral clock, featured an oil temperature gauge in the lower left.

speedometer and a smaller miles-per-hour scale with blue or yellow numerals closer to the middle.

All 1978 and most '79 cars are fitted with speedometers reaching 140 miles per hour. Those 1979s assembled after approximately July 1979 and all 1980–1982 cars have speedometers to 85 miles per hour. These speedometers have white numerals, with the exception of those indicating 55 miles per hour. That designation is orange. Beginning in 1982, speedometers read in increments of 5 miles per hour instead of the previously used increments of 10 miles per hour.

In 1978 and 1979, cumulative and trip odometer drums are black, with white numerals in all positions except tenths, which are yellow with black numerals. In 1980–1982 the trip odometer drums are yellow, with black numerals in all positions except tenths, which are white with black numerals.

Tachometer redlines vary according to the engine and, at times, whether the car is equipped with air conditioning. In 1978 cars equipped with an L48 engine or an L82 engine and air conditioning have a 5,300-rpm redline. Cars equipped

with an L82 engine but without air conditioning have a 5,600-rpm redline. In 1979 L48s have a 5,300-rpm redline, and all L82s have a 5,600-rpm redline. In 1980 LG4s and L48s have a 5,300-rpm redline, and L82s have a 6,000-rpm redline. In 1981 and 1982, the only available engine got a 5,300-rpm redline.

The center console instrument cluster housing is semi-gloss black. All secondary gauges have a flat black background, white numerals, and straight white needles. The only exception is the clock, which has a red second hand in conjunction with white hour and minute hands.

Those 1981–1982s fitted with an optional electronically tuned receiver (ETR) do not have a clock, since a clock is included in the ETR radio's display. An oil temperature gauge is substituted for the clock in the center instrument cluster.

The last year Corvettes came standard without a radio was 1978. Four different radios were offered that year as extra cost options. These included an AM/FM monaural, an AM/FM stereo, an AM/FM stereo with eight-track player,

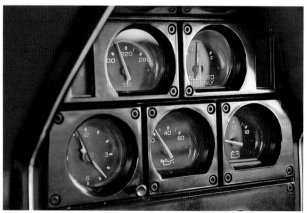

Original center stack instruments in an unrestored 1979.

A correct 1978–1982 AM/FM stereo with correct 1978–1979 black-accented chrome knobs.

This is 1980 option UM2, an AM/FM stereo radio with an eight-track player. All components shown, including the knobs and bezels, are correct for the year.

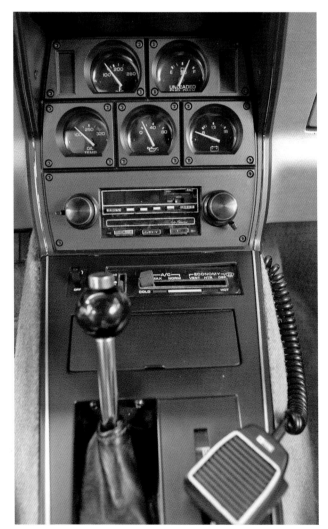

From 1978-82 an AM/FM stereo with integral CB radio was offered as an extra cost option. A total of 19,183 Corvettes came with a CB radio over the option's five model year lifespan.

and an AM/FM stereo with CB. In 1979 the monaural radio became standard equipment. For additional cost, it could be replaced in 1979 and 1980 with a stereo, a stereo with a CB, a stereo with an eight-track, or a stereo with a cassette player. In 1981 the optional radio selection was expanded to include ETRs and combinations of stereo reception, a CB, and a cassette or eight-track player. In 1982 the eight-track could no longer be had in combination with the CB.

All non-ETR radios have a small slide bar above the dial that changes reception between AM and FM. With these radios, a small stereo indicator light comes on when an FM signal is received.

Center Console, Shifter, and Park Brake

All 1978–1982 center consoles have carpeted sides that match the remainder of the car's carpeting. With the exception of the 1982 collector editions, all cars have a console trim plate painted semi-gloss black and accented by a chrome stripe around the outside perimeter. On the collector edition, the console trim plate is painted dark bronze.

All 1978–1982 park brake consoles are made from a flexible, molded vinyl material in the same color as the interior. The park brake lever has a slightly textured, molded black vinyl handle. The lever is chrome plated, as is the bezel around the release button. The button is molded from gloss black plastic.

In cars with manual transmission, the shift pattern is indicated next to the shifter. The shift pattern area is semi-gloss

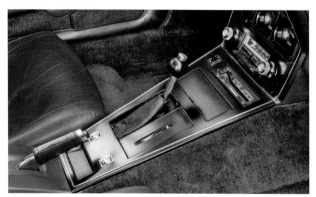

The center console area in an original, unrestored 1979.

This is the correct 1978–1982 park brake lever, with a black molded vinyl grip, a chrome collar, and a gloss black plastic release button.

This 1981 center console area is typical of 1978–1982, except for the 1982 collector edition. The shifter boot is leather for both automatic and manual transmission cars. The rocker switch and a small joystick between the power window switches controlled option DG7, the electric sport mirrors.

black, and the letters and numbers are white. The shifter boot for manual transmission cars is made from black leather and has a sewn seam toward the passenger side of the car.

Manual shifters have a chrome-plated shaft and a threaded-on black chrome ball. A chrome plated T-handle integral to the shaft controls the reverse lockout.

On those Corvettes equipped with automatic transmission, the shift pattern is also next to the shifter. A white pointer in a plastic, lighted band with white painted letters is used to indicate shifter position. Like their manual counterparts, automatic shifters are surrounded by a black leather boot, with a sewn seam facing the passenger side. Automatic shifters are made from a chrome shaft topped by a black plastic ball. The ball has a chrome spring-loaded button in the top to release the detent and allow the shifter to be moved.

All 1978–1982 Corvettes use a similar heater/air-conditioning control assembly. It has two horizontal sliding levers, one to control function and another to control temperature. A separate toggle switch is mounted in the left side of the control unit to regulate blower fan speed. The switch in 1978 and 1979 air-conditioned cars has four positions. In non-air-conditioned cars, it has three positions. In 1980–1982 air conditioning was standard. Therefore only the four-position switch is used.

All 1978–1982 cars have an ashtray inset into the console below the heater/air-conditioning control unit. The ashtray door is semi-gloss black in all cars except the 1982 collector edition. It slides back and forth with slight resistance. The ashtray door is dark bronze in the collector editions. The small tab inside the ashtray has a round hole.

All cars are equipped with a cigarette lighter. The lighter has a gloss black plastic knob with a white circle and ridges around the outer portion. The lighter's element for all years is usually stamped "78 CASCO 12V."

On those 1978–1982 Corvettes equipped with the optional rear window defogger, a control switch is mounted on the left side of the heater/air-conditioning control unit. In 1978 and 1979, the switch has a black handle and black bezel with white letters. When the defogger is on, the indicator light is green. In late 1980 through 1982, the rear window defogger switch is modified slightly, so its bezel is below the surface of the console rather than above it as before. The indicator light is amber, and the bezel has a symbol to represent a heating element.

Rear Storage Compartments and Their Contents

All 1978 and the great majority of 1979 cars feature three enclosed storage compartments behind the seats. In 1980–1982 two enclosed storage compartments are behind the seats. During the last few weeks of 1979 production in September 1979, some cars were fitted with two enclosed storage compartments as in 1980–1982.

The lids for the rear storage compartments found in all 1978–1982 cars are made from molded black fiberglass. All lids are covered with carpet that matches the interior carpet. Each lid is surrounded by a molded plastic border that is painted to match interior color. The entire assembly of lids is also surrounded by a color-matched molded plastic border. With the three-door assembly used in 1978 and most of 1979, the plastic trim around each door is held on with glue. With the two-door assembly used from very late 1979 through 1982, the trim is retained by rivets.

With both the three- and two-door assemblies, the doors are held to their hinges by black-phosphate-plated hex-head bolts with integral flat washers. The hinges attach to the assembly's frame with rivets. The frame attaches to the car's body with chrome-plated or black-oxide-plated Phillips oval-head screws fitted with integral washers.

Each lid latches with a spring-loaded mechanism. Each lid has a chrome button to release its latch. Three-door

The passenger-side rear storage compartment door had these three decals affixed in 1982. Chevrolet began installing thin limit cables at the outer edge of the door during the 1980 model year.

As illustrated by this 1979 example, spare tire and jack usage decals were applied to the underside of the passenger-side storage compartment door.

assemblies use a metal lift handle painted to match interior color on each door. Two-compartment door assemblies use a color-matched plastic handle on each door.

Beginning in mid-1980, thin black plastic-coated cables are attached to the outer edges of both doors and to the compartment frame. The cables prevent the doors from opening far enough to damage the hinges or hinge areas.

With both the two- and three-door assemblies, the compartment behind the passenger's seat is equipped with a lock in the push-button release. The key for the storage compartment lid lock is the same as the keys for the antitheft alarm, spare tire storage compartment, and doors.

In 1978 and 1979, a sticker with jacking instructions is on the underside of the passenger-side compartment lid. In 1980–1982 a sticker pertaining to the aluminum wheels is under the lid on those cars equipped with aluminum wheels. Those 1981 and 1982 cars equipped with standard suspension and automatic transmission were built with a fiberglass rear leaf spring, and these have a sticker under the lid with information about the spring. The 1982 collector edition has a sticker describing the proper procedure for hubcap removal on the underside of the lid.

The compartment directly behind the driver's seat holds the vehicle's battery. It has a thin foam seal around the perimeter of the door opening to help keep battery fumes from entering the passenger compartment.

All 1978–1982 Corvettes use a side-terminal Delco battery. In 1978–1980 two different batteries were used. Both are called Delco Freedom. The standard battery is model 87-5. The optional heavy-duty battery is model 89-5. Delco Freedom batteries used in 1978–1980 have two large raised squares in the top. One of the squares contains the "Delco Eye," a small circle of glass utilized to indicate battery condition. The top of the Delco Freedom battery is blue, and the sides are white. A caution label is affixed to the top,

and the words "Delco Freedom Battery" are written across the top. Beginning in 1981, Delco Freedom II replaces Delco Freedom. The Delco Freedom II used in 1981 and 1982 Corvettes is model number 695. It looks essentially the same as the Delco Freedom battery it replaced, until late 1982, when the top goes from blue to black.

All 1978–1982 battery cables are side-terminal style and have a red positive end and a black negative end. The positive cable terminal has a plus sign molded in, and the negative terminal has a minus sign. The cables are both covered with black insulation with the words "COPPER CLAD ALUMINUM" written in white block letters. The cables are retained with $\frac{5}{16}$-inch hex-head bolts.

With the three-door assembly used in 1978 and most of 1979, the passenger-side storage compartment contains a removable insert. The insert, which is like a squared-off bucket, is made from grayish black fiberboard and measures about five inches deep. The inside has a material called flock. It consists of small strands of black fiber and resembles velvet.

The fiberboard insert contains a small brown paper envelope containing license plate screws. This bag is marked "UNIT NUMBER 3875313" across the top, "LICENSE ATTACHING" on one side, and "REAR PLATE PARTS" on the other side.

The center storage compartment found in three-door assemblies used in 1978 and most of 1979 has black flocking like the passenger-side insert tray. A light is not used in this compartment.

With the two-door assembly used in very late 1979 through 1982, the passenger-side storage compartment contains a removable tray made from smooth black plastic. The plastic says "MADE IN CANADA" and the part number, 14007098.

For all 1978–1982 cars, the insert in the passenger-side rear storage compartment lifts out to reveal an additional storage area beneath. A jack and jack handle are mounted to the bottom of the compartment (to the car's floor panel)

A 1981 passenger-side rear storage compartment. A jack and lug wrench are secured underneath the black plastic tray.

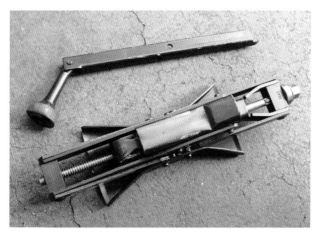

All 1978–1982 Corvettes came with a scissor-type jack and a lug nut wrench secured in the passenger-side storage compartment. The jack was stamped with a four-character manufacturing date code near the nut used to extend and close it. The first number represents the year, the next character is a letter denoting the month, and the third and fourth numbers reveal the day. In this example, "2E27" indicates that this jack was made on May 27, 1982.

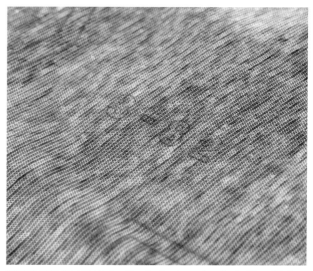

All 1978–1982 Corvettes came with protective storage bags for the T-tops. The bags were made from black vinyl with a cloth interior. A date code stamping is normally found on the lining. This example was made in March 1982.

with a black spring that latches onto a black hook riveted to the floor.

All jacks are painted gloss or semi-gloss black and contain a date code stamping. For 1978 cars, the date code stamping is on the head of one of the rivets on the jack's base. The code contains three numbers, the first indicating the year and the subsequent two indicating the week of production. For example, a 1978 jack with the code "811" was made the 11th week of 1978.

Beginning in 1979 and continuing through 1982, both the location and designation for the jack's date code change. Rather than on a rivet head, the code in 1979 and later cars is stamped into the crossmember at the end where the jack is cranked. The date code begins with a number denoting the year. This is followed by a letter denoting the month, with "A" representing January, "B" representing February, and so on. The code ends with two numbers denoting the day of the month. For example, a jack with a date code of "1E17" was manufactured May 17, 1981.

All jack handles are painted gloss or semi-gloss black and include a pivoting ¾-inch boxed hex wrench on the end for removing and installing lug nuts. A thick rubber ring is fitted around the hex wrench end to prevent rattling.

All 1978–1982 Corvettes have two storage bags to hold the T-tops when they are removed. These bags are made from a vinyl material and are usually black. The bags in some cars are very dark green rather than black.

Most T-top storage bags have a date code stamped inside in ink. Typical date stampings contain a month and year designation. For example, bags manufactured in October 1979 read "10-79." In addition to the date stamping, bags may also contain a logo stamping representing the manufacturer. The most common logo seen is "TEX."

All bags have a flap that closes over the opening and is retained by three chrome-plated snaps.

All 1978–1982 cars have adjustable T-top hold-down straps. Tops are held by a single harness with a Y configuration. It attaches to the rear bulkhead in the luggage area and extends to a chrome-plated anchor attached to the front bulkhead between the seats. Most cars have straps dyed to match interior color, though on occasion black straps are seen in cars that don't have black interiors.

All 1978–1982 Corvettes have molded vinyl trim mounted to the underside of the T-tops. The vinyl is the same color as the interior. A dome light is found in the center of the interior roof trim.

1978–1982 MECHANICAL
Engine Blocks

The engine block casting number for all 1978–1982 engines is located on the top rear driver side of the block, on the flange that mates to the transmission bell housing.

Most 1978 Corvettes utilize a block with casting number 3970010. Some '78s use a block with casting number 376450 or 460703. All 1980 Corvettes equipped with a 350 engine use either a number-3970010 or number-14010207 block. Those 1980 cars equipped with an LG4 305 engine use a number-4715111 block. All 1981 and 1982 Corvettes use a number-14010207 block.

Engine block casting dates for all 1978–1982 Corvettes are located on the top rear passenger side of the block, on the flange that mates to the transmission bell housing. The engine block casting date consists of a letter for the month, one or two numbers for the day, and one number for the year. For example, a number-3970010 block cast on June 12, 1978, would have a casting date of "F 12 8."

All 1980 Corvettes delivered new in California came with option LG4, a 305-cid V-8 rated at 180 horsepower. All other 1980 Corvettes came with either the base 350-cid, 190-horsepower L48 or the optional 350-cid, 230-horsepower L82 engine. This 1980 L48 engine compartment is completely original.

The crowded 1978–1982 engine compartment makes it difficult to see the engine stamping, which is located in a pad at the front passenger side, adjacent to where the water pump mounts. In this 1982 example, "V" indicates where the engine was assembled, the V-8 Engine Plant in Flint, Michigan. The number "0603" is the assembly date, June 3. "ZBA" is the engine suffix code, which represents a 1982 350 cid coupled to an automatic transmission.

All 1978–1982 engines contain two distinct stampings on a machined pad on the top of the passenger side between the cylinder head and the water pump. One stamping is commonly referred to as the assembly stamping. The other is commonly called the VIN derivative stamping.

While the great majority of 1978–1982 cars have the VIN derivative stamping on the machined pad described above, a small number of cars have it on the side of the block, just above and toward the rear of the oil filter mount. This area of the block is not machined and therefore retains a rough cast texture.

The assembly stamping begins with the prefix letter "V" to indicate the Flint engine assembly plant. Following the prefix letter are four numbers indicating the month and day of assembly. After the numbers indicating the assembly date are three suffix letters denoting the particular engine. This suffix code is often referred to as the engine broadcast code or simply the engine code. (Refer to Appendix C for engine suffix codes.)

To illustrate what a typical engine assembly stamping looks like, consider the following 1981 combination: a base 350/190-horsepower engine built on April 5 and coupled to a four-speed transmission. The assembly stamping for such an engine would read "V0405ZAM."

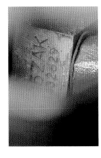

The engine assembly date, suffix code, and VIN derivative were stamped into a pad at the front passenger side of the engine, immediately adjacent to the water pump mount area. It is very difficult to see the stamping because the AIR pump and various other components block it. In this partial view of a 1980 stamping, the "ZAK" suffix indicates that the engine is a 350 cid rated at 190 horsepower and coupled to an automatic transmission. The lower numbers, "32629," are the final five characters in the car's VIN.

The engine assembly date, suffix code, and VIN derivative were stamped into a pad at the front passenger side of the engine immediately adjacent to the water pump mount area. In this 1979 stamping, the "V" represents the Flint V-8 engine plant, "0807" reveals that the engine was assembled on August 7, and the "ZAH" suffix tells us that the engine is a 350 cid rated at 195 horsepower and coupled to an automatic transmission. The lower number sequence, "19S451564," is the car's VIN derivative. The "1" represents Chevrolet Division, "9" is for model year 1979, "S" is for the St. Louis Corvette Assembly Plant, "4" represents the Corvette model, and "51,564" is the serial number of the specific car this engine was originally installed into.

Always remember that the engine assembly date must come after the engine block casting date (you can't assemble an engine before the block is cast), and both the casting date and assembly date must precede the final assembly date of the car (you can't final assemble a car before the engine has been cast and assembled). The great majority of engines were cast and assembled a few weeks prior to the car's assembly date. Some engines were cast and/or assembled months prior to installation, however. Six months is generally accepted as the outer limit between an engine assembly or casting date and the final assembly date of the car.

The VIN derivative stamping, as the name implies, contains a portion or derivative of the car's vehicle identification number. For all 1978 Corvettes except pace cars, the VIN derivative stamping begins with "18S4." The "1" designates the Chevrolet car line, the "8" is for model year 1978, "S" is for St. Louis (where all '78 Corvettes were assembled), and "4" is thought to be a placeholder. The VIN derivative for all 1978 pace cars begins with "18S9."

The VIN derivative for all 1979 Corvettes begins with "19S4." For all 1980 cars, it begins with "1AS4." For 1981s built in St. Louis, it begins with "1BS4," and for '81s built in Bowling Green, it begins with "1B51." For all 1982 Corvettes, the derivative begins with "1C51."

For all 1978–1982 Corvettes, the first four characters of the VIN derivative are followed by the final five characters of the particular car's VIN or serial number. For example, the VIN derivative stamping in the engine for the 9,411th 1978 built would read "18S409411."

All 1978–1982 engine blocks are cast iron. All 1978–1981 and most '82 engines are painted GM Corporate Blue. Beginning in approximately August 1982, engine color was changed to black.

Engines were originally painted before exhaust manifolds were installed. Therefore coverage on the sides of the block behind the manifolds is good. The engine stamp pad and timing tab on the timing chain cover were normally covered up when the engine was painted and therefore they usually appear unpainted.

Cylinder Heads

As with engine blocks, all 1978–1982 cylinder heads have both a casting number and a casting date. As with blocks and other cast parts, the cylinder head casting date typically has a letter to indicate the month, one or two numbers to indicate the day of the month, and one number to indicate the year. (Refer to Appendix G for cylinder head casting numbers.)

All 1978–1982 engines utilize cast-iron cylinder heads. All cylinder heads and head bolts are painted engine color, which is a medium blue. This particular shade of blue was used on all GM engines of the era and is commonly called Corporate Blue.

Intake Manifolds

All 1978 and 1979 base engines use a cast-iron intake manifold, while 1978 and '79 L82 engines use an aluminum intake. All 1980–1982 engines, including base engines, L82s, LG4 California 305s, and '82 cross-fire injection engines, use an aluminum intake manifold.

As with engine blocks and cylinder heads, intake manifolds contain casting numbers and casting dates. As with other cast engine parts, the casting date consists of a letter designating the month, one or two numbers designating the day of the month, and a number denoting the year.

Casting numbers and casting dates for all cast-iron intake manifolds are on the top surface. Casting numbers for aluminum intakes are on the top surface, but casting dates are on the underside. (Refer to Appendix H for intake manifold casting numbers.)

Cast-iron intake manifolds are painted engine color. Aluminum intake manifolds are painted dull silver. All 1978–1982 Corvette engines utilize an aluminum thermostat housing that is painted the same color as the intake manifold.

In 1978–1981 each intake manifold bolt gets a flat washer, unless it also holds on a bracket. Intake bolts that also retain

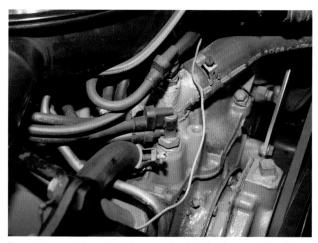

Front intake manifold area details in an unrestored 1979 with a base L48 engine. Note the engine paint overspray on the thermal vacuum switch, use of tower-style hose clamps, and various markings on the hoses.

brackets typically do not have washers. In 1982 intake bolts have a washer-style head and do not use an additional washer.

All 1978–1982 engines use side intake manifold gaskets made from a metal core covered with a fiber composition. No gaskets are used on the ends of the intake. Instead, a light reddish RTV sealant is used on the ends.

Engine lifting brackets are attached to the engines in all 1978–1982 Corvettes. The brackets are painted engine color if a cast-iron intake manifold is utilized and silver if an aluminum intake is used. All engines have one bracket attached to the first and second intake manifold bolt from the front on the driver side. A second bracket is attached to the rear of the intake on the passenger side with one bolt.

Distributor and Ignition Coil

All 1978–1982 cars use a Delco HEI distributor and an electronic tachometer. All HEI distributors have a part number and date code stamped directly into the aluminum housing. These stampings are on the driver side when the distributor is correctly installed in the car. (Refer to Appendix K for distributor part numbers.)

The distributor date code, which represents the day the distributor was assembled, consists of a number representing the year, a letter representing the month, and one or two numbers representing the day of the month. For distributor date codes, the letter "A" represents January, "B" represents February, and so on. As is typical of stamped-in date codes, the letter "I" is skipped, so "J" represents September. The date code on a distributor assembled on January 12, 1979, for example, would read, "9 A 12."

While most distributors were made several weeks before the engine was assembled, it is entirely possible that several months can separate the two. As with most other components, six months is the generally accepted maximum.

All distributors are fitted with a vacuum advance unit. Vacuum advances have part numbers stamped into them in the bracket that mounts the vacuum canister to the distributor.

All 1978–1982 Corvettes use a black Delco Remy distributor cap. The ignition coil is integral to the distributor cap on all cars. It is manufactured by Delco and is black. It says "DELCO REMY" and "MADE IN THE USA" on the top. Also, the word "LATCH" appears on the top twice. A white sticker with a black UPC bar code is present on some coils.

Ignition Shielding

All 1978–1982 Corvettes equipped with a radio are outfitted with ignition shielding. The top shield, which goes over the distributor, is made from black plastic. It has a grainy texture on the outside and an aluminum foil liner on the inside. The shield is unchanged from 1978 to 1981. It is very similar for 1982, except it was shortened on the passenger side.

In addition to the top ignition shield, all radio-equipped cars also have side shielding, V-shaped lower shielding, and spark plug shields. These pieces are steel plated with flash chrome. The quality of the plating is not very good.

The chrome-plated side shielding and V-shaped sections of shielding encapsulate the spark plug wires. The V-shaped shielding runs from the bottom of the vertical shields to the area beneath the spark plugs. The spark plug shields cover only the rear two spark plugs on either side of the engine. The passenger-side spark plug shield used on 1978–1980 L82 engines has a hole for passage of the wire to the temperature sending unit.

The spark plug shields are retained to cadmium-plated brackets with chrome-plated wing bolts or silver-cadmium-plated hex-head bolts. The brackets are silver cadmium plated and may have "FPM" stamped in to represent the manufacturer.

All engines also have a silver-cadmium-plated spark plug heat shield on the right side of the engine only. The heat shield is retained to the engine block by means of a single silver-cadmium-plated indented hex-head bolt.

Spark Plug Wires

All 1978–1982 Corvettes use 8mm spark plug wires manufactured by Packard Electric. The wires are gray, with black boots at both ends.

All spark plug wires are ink stamped every few inches with the words "PACKARD T V R SUPPRESSION," or, on later cars, "PACKARD DELCORE ELECTRONIC SUPPRESSION." In addition, all wires are stamped with a date code. The date code indicates the quarter and the year of manufacture. For example, wires labeled "3Q-81" were made in the third quarter of 1981.

Original ignition wires were 8mm suppression manufactured by Delco Remy. The code "2 Q 80" ink stamped along the length of the wire indicates that it was made in the second quarter of 1980.

Passenger-side carburetor details from a 1980 L48. Note the many differences in component finishes and the part number sticker on the electric choke.

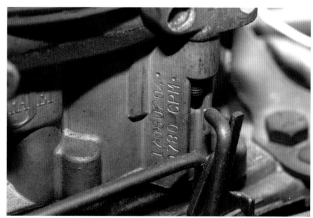

All Rochester Quadrajets installed in 1978–1982 Corvettes had identifying information stamped into the main body on the driver side. Part number "17080204" indicates that this carburetor is for a 1980 L48 coupled to an automatic transmission. The number "0780" denotes that the carburetor was made on the 78th day of 1980. "CPM" is believed to represent the specific assembly plant where the carburetor was manufactured.

All 1978–1981 Corvettes came with a Rochester Quadrajet four-barrel carburetor. This completely original example is on a 1980 L48 engine.

Carburetors and Throttle Body Injection

All 1978–1981 Corvettes have a Rochester Quadrajet carburetor. Carter was at times contracted to manufacture Rochester Quadrajet carburetors for General Motors, and the Carter-built Quadrajets are almost identical to the Rochester-built ones. Carter-built Quadrajets are identified as being manufactured by Carter and may use Carter's system of date coding rather than Rochester's system. (Refer to Appendix J for carburetor numbers.)

Rochester-built Quadrajets contain an alphanumeric sequence stamped into a flat, vertical area of the main body on the rear of the driver side. Either the full seven-digit GM part number or the final five digits of the part number are stamped in. Several letters, which identify the specific plant where the carburetor was made, may be stamped here as well. Finally, four numbers denoting the date of manufacture are also stamped in to this area.

Rochester utilized the Julian calendar for date coding its carburetors. With this system of dating, the first three numbers represent the day of the year, and the final number is the last digit of the year. For example, the Julian date code for a carburetor made on January 1, 1978, would read "0018." The first three digits, "001," represent the first day of the year. The final digit, "8," represents 1978.

With the possible exception of some later units, Carter-built Quadrajets generally don't use a Julian calendar date coding system. Instead, they use a single letter and a single number. The letter denotes the month, with "A" indicating January, "B" indicating February, and so on. The letter "I" is not used, so September is represented by "J." The number in the date code for Carter-built Quadrajets is the last digit for the year of manufacture. So a date code of "D9" indicates the carburetor was made in April 1979.

All carburetors are plated gold dichromate. Plating tends to be rather dark and uniform in color. All carburetors have an insulator separating them from the intake manifold.

In 1982 only, Corvettes use a throttle body injection system instead of a carburetor. Each throttle body injection unit is stamped with a model number but not a date code. The model number is stamped into a vertical area on the flange adjacent to a rear mounting bolt.

Air Cleaner

All 1978–1981 Corvettes are equipped with an air cleaner that is closed to the engine compartment. It receives fresh air from ducting and a plenum assembly on top of the fan shroud.

For 1978 base engine cars, the housing has a single snorkel pointing toward the front of the car, with a slight offset to the driver side. The snorkel is connected to a black molded plastic plenum on top of the fan shroud by means of a duct. The duct is made from black paper over coiled wire and has an accordion shape. It is retained at each end by means of a built-in clamp that snaps into position. Later service replacement ducts are made from plastic instead of paper.

Removal of the air cleaner assemblies reveals many hidden details in this completely original 1982 cross-fire-injection engine compartment.

A factory original 1979 L48 engine compartment. The dual-snorkel air cleaner was previously used only on optional L82 engines, but in 1979–1982, it was used on the base engine as well.

All 1978–1981 Corvette air cleaner bases had some variation of this decal on the driver side. This original example is from a very late 1979 L48 engine.

The snorkel has a vacuum motor that opens to permit the flow of warmed air from a metallic tube connected to the driver-side exhaust manifold. The vacuum motor is painted semi-gloss black and has the words "AUTO THERMAC" embossed on the top.

The air cleaner housing in 1978s equipped with an L-82 engine, and on all 1979–1981 cars, has two forward-facing snorkels. Both snorkels are connected to a molded plenum.

It is similar to the plenum on base engine cars, but it has two connection points.

The air cleaner housing utilized in 1978–1981 is painted gloss black. The air cleaner lid in 1978–1980 is also painted gloss black, but in 1981 it is chrome plated. There are no decals on the lids, but there is a decal on the side of the housings. The sticker utilized on early 1978s reads "KEEP YOUR GM CAR ALL GM." Later '78s and subsequent cars use a sticker that says "KEEP YOUR GM VEHICLE ALL GM."

In addition to the above admonition, the air cleaner sticker contains logos for AC, GM, and Delco, various part numbers and codes, and the replacement filter number. The sticker is white with red and blue lettering.

Original 1978–1981 air filter elements, unlike later replacements, have a fine wire screen around the outside in a vertical (not diagonal) pattern. The horizontal and vertical wire forms rectangles, with the longer measurement running vertically when the element is installed.

All 1978–1981 Corvettes use an AC A348C air cleaner element. The element says "BEST WAY TO PROTECT YOUR ENGINE REPLACE WITH AC TYPE 348C" in white along the horizontal perimeter.

All 1982 Corvettes utilize a unique air cleaner assembly for the cross-fire injection system. It mounts diagonally across both throttle body injection units. The top of the assembly has

All 1982 Corvette engines were fitted with cross-fire injection. All components and finishes shown here are factory correct.

Exhaust heat riser tube and AIR plumbing details on a 1980 L48 engine. The tower clamp securing the hose to the AIR pipe is stamped "1/80" (January 1980).

a black wrinkle finish and a "Cross-Fire Injection" emblem. Metal knobs that are painted black retain the air cleaner assembly cover. Inside the main air cleaner housing are two smaller air cleaners for the two throttle body injectors. The covers of these air cleaners are painted semi-gloss black and use AC A824C paper filter elements.

The cross-fire injection air cleaner housing has a thermostatic vacuum motor assembly in the intake snorkel.

The snorkel is linked to the exhaust manifold by a gloss black metal heat riser tube. An unpainted aluminum PVC tube extends from a black rubber grommet in the passenger-side valve cover toward the PVC filter in the air cleaner housing. The tube connects to the filter with a short length of black rubber hose.

Valve Covers

All 1978–1980 base engines, as well as the 1980 California-only LG4 engines, are fitted with stamped-steel valve covers painted engine color. These are held on with hex-head bolts and metal tabs that are also painted engine color.

Two metal wire retention clips are spot welded to the passenger-side cover. This cover also has a crankcase vent intake hole that gets a black rubber grommet. A tube inserts into the grommet and connects to the air cleaner base.

On base engine cars, two metal wire retention clips are spot welded to the driver-side cover. This cover also has a PCV valve inserted into a hole fitted with a rubber grommet. A hose connects the PCV valve to the carburetor. The driver-side cover also has a provision for the oil filler cap.

All 1978–1980 optional L82 engines utilize cast-aluminum valve covers with longitudinal ribs. The covers are painted semi-gloss black, except for the top edges of the fins, which were natural aluminum. All 1981 and 1982 cars are equipped with the same covers, but they are made from cast

An original, unrestored 1978 L82 engine compartment.

magnesium rather than aluminum. The magnesium covers are painted semi-gloss black, and the top edges of the fins are painted silver.

As with the painted steel covers, a vent hose connects the passenger-side alloy valve cover to the air cleaner base, and a PCV valve is in the driver-side valve cover. Alloy valve covers are retained by silver-cadmium-plated, indented hex-head bolts. These bolts frequently have an "M" in the head.

Passenger- and driver-side alloy valve covers are both made from the same mold. The only difference is that the driver-side cover has a hole for the oil fill cap. The passenger-side cover does not. On the passenger side, where the hole would go, is a rigid disc with the crossed-flag emblem glued on. The passenger-side cover has a hole toward the rear that's fitted with a black rubber grommet. A long black-phosphate-plated steel tube inserts into the grommet and connects to the rear of the air cleaner housing.

Alloy valve covers used on 1978–1980 L82 engines and all 1981 and 1982 engines have chrome-plated twist-in oil fill caps on the driver side. A large "S" for Stant, the manufacturer of the caps, is stamped into the center rivet.

Painted steel valve covers use a steel twist-on oil fill cap in the driver-side valve cover. In 1978 a large "S" for Stant is stamped into the domed center rivet of the cap. In 1979 and 1980, the design of the cap used in painted steel valve covers changes. Instead of a round, domed head, the center rivet is crushed in such a way that four distinct quadrants are formed. This cap has "ENGINE OIL FILL" and "AC FC 2" stamped in around the center rivet. All engine oil fill caps used in conjunction with steel valve covers are painted engine color.

Exhaust Manifolds

All 1978–1980 exhaust manifolds, except those utilized on 1980 LG4 305 California engines, are cast iron. Exhaust manifolds used on LG4 engines, as well as all 1981 and 1982 engines, are tubular stainless steel. All cast-iron exhaust manifolds contain a casting number, which is normally on the side facing away from the engine, and a casting date, which is normally on the side facing the engine. (Refer to Appendix I for exhaust manifold casting numbers.)

Stainless-steel tubular exhaust manifolds used on 1980 LG4 and all 1980–1981 engines are stamped with a part number. Left-side manifolds are stamped "GM 14037671-W," and right-side manifolds are stamped "GM 14037672-W."

Exhaust manifolds were not yet installed when engines were originally painted, so they show no signs of overspray. This applies to both cast-iron and tubular stainless-steel manifolds.

Cast-iron exhaust manifolds use ⁹⁄₁₆-inch hex-head bolts in all positions except the forward-most passenger-side spot. That spot has a stud with an integral nut. The integral nut tightens the stud and retains the manifold, while the protruding portion of the stud is used to fasten the air-conditioning compressor bracket.

Exhaust manifold bolts typically have two concentric rings on their heads. The front two bolts and rear two bolts on both sides of the engine get French locks, with one of the two tabs bent over to prevent the bolts from loosening. The heads on bolts for tubular stainless-steel exhaust manifolds have six lines that radiate out from a small circle in the center. Exhaust manifolds do not use a gasket where they mount to the cylinder head.

Starter Motor

All 1978–1982 Corvettes use a Delco Remy starter motor. Automatic-transmission-equipped cars utilize starters with aluminum noses, while starters for manual-transmission-equipped cars have cast-iron noses. Some motor housings and cast-iron noses are painted semi-gloss black, while others are unpainted. Aluminum noses are unpainted.

The starter's part number and assembly date are stamped into the side of the motor housing. The date code contains a number representing the last digit of the year and a letter denoting the month, with "A" representing January, "B" representing February, and so on. As is typical of stamped-in date codes, the letter "I" is skipped, so September is represented by "J." One or two numbers indicating the day follow the letter denoting the month. For example, a date code of "2B10" indicates that the starter was made on February 10, 1982. (Refer to Appendix N for starter motor part numbers.)

Starter solenoids have a black or brown Bakelite cover for the electrical connections. Solenoid housings may be painted semi-gloss black or be silver cadmium plated.

Starters use a stamped-steel brace to support the forward end (the end facing the front of the car when the starter is installed). The brace mounts to a stud on the starter's end plate and to a threaded boss in the engine block. The brace is painted semi-gloss black.

All 1978–1982 Corvettes came with a Delco Remy starter motor. A part number and manufacturing date code were stamped into each motor's case. The part number "1998241" indicates that this motor is correct for a 1982 Corvette. The date code, "2F 2," reveals that it was made on February 2, 1982.

Every starter has a heat shield to protect it from exhaust system heat. The shield is rectangular and is painted semi-gloss black. The shield attaches to the solenoid screws with barrel nuts.

A black-phosphate-plated spring steel clip is snapped over the starter motor solenoid. This clip holds the wires going to the solenoid in place, so they don't burn against the exhaust manifold.

Oil Filter

All 1978–1982 engines utilize an AC Delco PF-25 spin-on oil filter. Filters are painted dark blue, with a dark blue sticker bearing the AC and GM logos. The sticker has a white border and white lettering and contains the part number 6438261. Original stickers do not say "DURAGUARD," as do the stickers on current AC Delco PF-25 filters.

Alternator, Power Steering Pump, and Fuel Pump

All engines are fitted with a Delco Remy alternator mounted on the driver side. Alternator housings are made from cast aluminum and are not painted or coated with anything.

In 1978 and 1979, the front half of the alternator housing has the unit's part number, amperage rating, and assembly date code stamped in. The date code contains a number for the year and a letter for the month, with "A" representing January, "B" representing February, and so on. As is typical of stamped-in date codes, the letter "I" is skipped, so September is represented by "J." The letter denoting the month is followed by one or two numbers for the day. For example, an alternator stamped "8F22" was assembled on June 22, 1978.

Beginning in 1980 and continuing through 1982, a different alternator is used. With this new design, the assembly date code is different. The first character is either a number or a letter to represent the month. The numbers

Later 1980 and all 1981–1982 alternators had the part number, date code, and other information stamped into the front face of the drive-end housing. The first character of the date code is a number from one through nine, representing January through September, or the letter "O," "N," or "D" for October, November, or December. The next two numbers denote the day, and the final number is the last digit of the year. This example, from a late 1980, shows part number "1101075." The manufacture date is "6050," which translates to June 5, 1980.

one through nine represent January through September, the letter "O" represents October, the letter "N" represents November, and the letter "D" represents December. The first character is followed by two numerals that denote the day of the month. The final numeral is the last digit of the year. So a date code stamping of "5292" indicates that the alternator was manufactured on May 29, 1982. (Refer to Appendix M for alternator part numbers.)

The alternator pulley is made from zinc-plated, stamped steel. Some earlier L82 engines have alternator pulleys machined from solid material. The lower alternator bracket on all cars is cast metal painted semi-gloss black. The upper bracket is stamped steel painted semi-gloss black.

Most 1978–1982 alternators are ink stamped with a one- or two-letter code called a broadcast code. Commonly seen codes are "LP," "WP," and "RK."

Power Steering Pump and Fuel Pump

All 1978–1982 Corvettes are equipped with power steering. The system uses a power steering pump painted semi-gloss black, with a neck that is the same diameter from top to bottom. All pumps have a semi-gloss black, stamped-steel belt guard bolted to the body. A small white and blue sticker reading "NOTICE DO NOT PRY ON RESERVOIR" and the broadcast code "BX" is on the pump housing.

Power steering pump pulleys on all cars are machined from steel stock and feature a raised edge in the front to aid removal with a puller. All pulleys are painted semi-gloss black. All pumps mount to the engine with a stamped-steel support painted semi-gloss black.

All 1978–1981 Corvettes use an AC brand fuel pump. The pump usually has "AC" cast into the top or side of the upper housing and a five-character part number stamped into the underside of the mounting flange. Pumps have a

All 1978–1982 Corvettes came with a Delco Remy alternator mounted on the driver side of the engine. A part number, amp rating, and date code were stamped into the alternator housing. In this example, the part number is "1100908." The "9C20" date codes translates to March 20, 1979.

1978–1982

187

natural, dull silver cast-aluminum body with a gold-iridite-plated lower cover. The part number for all 1978–1981 pumps is 41240.

In 1982 the mechanical, engine- mounted fuel pump is replaced with an electric unit mounted inside the fuel tank. The opening in the fuel pump mount area of the engine block is closed with a block-off plate. The block-off plate is held with hex-head bolts and a stud that goes in the forward upper position. The stud retains a small clip that holds the fuel line.

Corvettes in 1978–1981 did not use an external fuel filter. They have a small filtration device inside the carburetor at the point where the fuel line enters. In 1982 an external fuel filter is used. It is spliced into the fuel line and is mounted inside the passenger-side frame rail below the forward portion of the passenger-side door.

Water Pump, Engine Fan, and Fan Clutch

All 1978–1982 Corvettes use a cast-iron water pump with a boss on top. The boss is drilled and tapped. The tapped hole is closed with a square-head plug. A daub of yellow paint is frequently seen on this plug.

The snout on all water pumps has reinforcing ribs that are part of the casting. Pumps usually have casting number 330818 in the housing, but this is obscured when the pulley is installed. All water pump housings have a cast-in date code. The first character of the code is a letter denoting the month, with "A" representing January, "B" representing February, and so on. The second character is one or two numbers denoting the day. This is followed by a single number denoting the year.

Most water pump pulleys are painted semi-gloss black, though some originals have a black phosphate finish. In 1978 and 1979 cars equipped with an air injection reactor (AIR) pump, the water pump pulley that drives the pump has "3991425BX" stamped in. Cars not equipped with AIR use a water pump pulley with "3991423BW" stamped in. In 1980 the water pump pulley that drives the AIR pump is stamped "188072DE." In 1981 and 1982, this same pulley is stamped "14023158CW."

All 1978–1982 Corvettes use a thermostatically controlled, viscous coupled fan clutch. The clutch uses a metallic coil on the front face as a thermostat. The clutch body is aluminum, while the shaft and mounting flange are steel. Most fan clutches are unpainted, though some are painted dull aluminum.

Original clutches usually have a date code stamped in the flange that goes against the water pump pulley. Clutches (as well as water pump pulleys) are retained by studs and nuts that thread into the pump's front hub. The mounting flange on the clutch has holes rather than slots for the studs to pass through.

All 1978–1982 Corvettes use a cooling fan that is painted gloss black and mounted to the fan clutch with hex-head bolts. Those 1978 and 1979 cars equipped with a base engine but not air conditioning use a five-blade engine cooling fan that is 17.5 inches in diameter. Those 1978 and

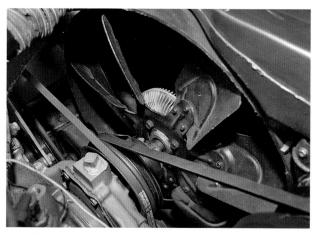

Three different engine fans were used in 1978–1982. The 18.5-inch, seven-blade design shown here was used on base engine cars with air conditioning, cars with a heavy-duty radiator/heavy-duty cooling, and all 1980s with LG4. All L82-equipped cars and all 1981–1982s without heavy-duty cooling got an 18.5-inch, five-blade fan. Base engine 1978–1979s without air conditioning were fitted with a 17.5-inch, five-blade fan.

1979 cars equipped with a base engine and air conditioning, and 1980–1982 cars equipped with air conditioning, heavy-duty cooling, or the optional LG4 California 305-cubic-inch engine, use a seven-blade fan that is 18.5 inches in diameter. All 1978–1980 cars equipped with an L82 engine, as well as all 1981 and 1982 cars not equipped with air conditioning, use a five-blade fan that is 18.5 inches in diameter.

Those 1979 and 1980 cars equipped an with L82 engine and air conditioning have an electric engine cooling fan in addition to the regular cooling fan. It is mounted on the engine side of the radiator with brackets painted semi-gloss black that attach to the fan shroud. The electric fan motor is painted gloss black. The fan is made from black plastic.

Radiator, Hoses, and Related Parts

All 1978–1982 Corvettes use a copper radiator. Radiators were manufactured by Harrison and have that name debossed in the passenger side radiator tank. In addition, a stamped-steel tag containing a two-letter broadcast code and a part number is attached to the passenger side of the radiator. All radiators are painted semi-gloss to gloss black.

All cars use a black or dark gray plastic fan shroud. Shrouds in 1979 and 1980 cars equipped with air conditioning and an L82 engine have an opening at the bottom. This opening has a hinged door that opens when additional cooling is required. A sticker that reads "CAUTION FAN" is on the top of the shroud. Cars equipped with an auxiliary electric cooling fan have a second copy of the sticker toward the bottom of the shroud.

All 1978–1982 cars use a white plastic coolant recovery tank. The tank is mounted underneath the passenger-side fender. It has a black plastic cap with a blue, white, and black sticker on top. The sticker says "NOTICE" in white letters

These 1980 L48 engine compartment details show correct molded foam rubber seals atop the radiator support shrouding and engine air intake duct.

Radiator area details in an unrestored 1979. The shroud is unpainted black fiberglass-reinforced plastic. Contoured foam seals the gaps between the shroud and radiator and between the radiator and hood. Note the use of a tower-style clamp on the upper radiator hose. Worm-style clamps are the norm for radiator hoses, but it's believed that the tower clamp was factory installed in this one-owner, low-mileage, unrestored car.

Front engine compartment details from a 1982. Note subtle variations in component finishes in this original, unrestored example.

This is the correct radiator cap for 1978–1982. The cap is stainless steel, and the rivet in the center is brass. Some 1978 owner's manuals specify an RC-36 radiator cap. Other owner's manuals specify an RC-27 cap, but it is believed that all 1978–1982 Corvettes came with the RC-33 cap. When correctly installed, the cap's arrows align with the overflow tube.

and "ENGINE COOLANT ONLY" in black letters. All coolant recovery tanks are fitted with a black overflow hose. The hose is marked "3/8" and has various other numbers as well as letters written in yellow ink.

All 1978–1982 Corvettes use an RC-33 radiator cap rated at 15 psi and installed directly on the radiator. RC-33 caps contain the AC logo in a circle. They also contain the words "DO NOT OPEN, CHECK LEVEL IN BOTTLE, CLOSED SYSTEM, ALIGN ARROW & VENT TUBE." Some owner's manuals specify the use of an RC-27 cap, but it is believed that only RC-33 caps were installed on the assembly line.

All radiator and heater hoses are molded black rubber. Stamped on radiator hoses in white ink are a part number, the GM logo, and several letters that are believed to be manufacturer's codes. In addition, a colored line usually runs the length of the hose.

Heater hoses usually contain a GM logo in white ink. They sometimes have the letters "DL" or "U" stamped on them also. Most original hoses have three or four thin ridges running lengthwise.

All cars use stainless-steel worm drive clamps for the radiator hoses. All applications use size-28 clamps. Most cars use SURE-TITE brand clamps, though at least one other supplier originally provided clamps to the factory. Original SURE-TITE clamps have "SURE-TITE" in italics stamped into the band along the circumference. In addition, "WITTEK MFG. CO. CHI. U.S.A." is stamped into the worm screw's housing. Radiator clamps do not have date codes stamped in, as some heater hoses do.

Most cars use stainless-steel worm drive clamps for the heater hoses. On occasion, however, tower-style clamps are used for heater hoses. Tower-style clamps are much more likely to be seen on earlier 1978–1982 cars than on later ones.

The ⅝-inch heater hoses use 1¹⁄₁₆-inch clamps. This size typically has a galvanized finish and contains the size, the words "WITTEK MFG. CO. CHICAGO U.S.A.," and a date code stamped into the band. The first number of the date code denotes the quarter, and the following two numbers indicate the year.

The ¾-inch heater hose uses 1¼-inch clamps. These clamps have a cadmium dichromate finish that results in a translucent goldish tint, as opposed to the smaller clamps' dull silver color. The 1¼-inch clamps contain the manufacturer's logo and size designation but do not have a date code. Instead, they have the letters "DCM" stamped into the band.

Brake Master Cylinder and Related Components

All master cylinders are manufactured by Delco and contain the casting number 5460346 and the Delco split circle logo on the inboard side. In addition to the casting number, each master contains a two-letter application code stamped in on a flat surface by the front brake line fitting. Master cylinders in early 1978 cars utilize the code "DM." Later 1978 and all 1979–1982 cars use the code "YC."

In addition to the two-letter application code, a Julian date code is stamped in the flat, machined area adjacent to where the front brake line attaches. The date code typically contains a number indicating the year, followed by three numbers denoting the day of the year. For example, a stamping of "9214" represents the 214th day of 1979.

The entire master cylinder is semi-gloss black, except for machined areas, which are natural. No 1978–1982 masters are fitted with bleeder screws. For all master cylinders, two steel wire bails hold the cover on. A small vinyl sticker with two letters is folded around one of the bail wires. This sticker is white, with the two-letter application code in red. Beginning in 1981, a second sticker is applied to the outboard side of the master cylinder. This sticker is white with black letters and a black bar code.

All master cylinders use a stamped-steel, cadmium-dichromate-plated cover and a rubber gasket. The cover has two domes connected by a small ridge. "WARNING CLEAN FILLER CAP BEFORE REMOVING" and "USE ONLY DOT 3 FLUID FROM A SEALED CONTAINER" are stamped into the cover.

All 1978–1982 Corvettes are equipped with power brakes. Power brake boosters are cadmium dichromate plated.

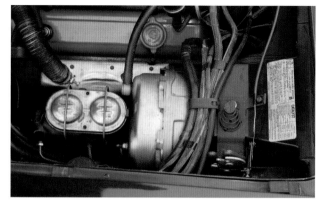
Details of a brake master cylinder and booster and a driver-side firewall in an unrestored 1979. Note the use of black vinyl tape to hold the vacuum hoses together.

Power boosters have a broadcast code as well as a Julian date code stamped in on top. For 1978 Corvettes, the broadcast code is "YB." For 1979 and 1980 cars, the code is "RL." For 1980–1982 cars, the code is "NR." Besides being stamped into the top of the power booster, the two-letter broadcast code and Julian date code are also found on a white sticker affixed to the front of the unit.

The Julian date code stamped into the power booster contains a number corresponding to the final number of the year and then three numbers denoting the day of the year. For example, a booster stamped "1168" was manufactured on the 168th day of 1981.

Air-Conditioning and Heating System Components

All 1978–1982 Corvettes use a Delco Air R-4 radial-style air-conditioning compressor. It is painted semi-gloss black and has a yellow, black, and silver foil sticker on top of the housing. The sticker contains, among other things, the compressor's model number and a date code. The date code contains two numbers for the month, two numbers for the day, one number for the year, and one number for the shift. For example, a date code of "031922" translates to March 19, 1982, second shift.

All 1978 and 1979 Corvettes use a number-1131078 air-conditioning compressor. All 1980–1982 Corvettes use a number-1131198 compressor.

An unpainted, dark gray fiberglass housing covers the evaporator. The housing has a blue and silver Harrison foil sticker, as well as a fan relay. The relay cover is zinc or cadmium plated and does not have any words stamped in it.

Most Corvettes with air conditioning have a vacuum-actuated valve spliced into the heater hose. When the air conditioning is on, this valve shuts off the flow of engine coolant to the heater core.

The blower motors for both air-conditioned and non-air-conditioned cars are painted semi-gloss to gloss black. Motors on air-conditioned cars have a rubber tube that extends from the motor housing to the evaporator housing. Motors on

An original master cylinder cap in a 1979. All 1979–1982 caps were the same.

Most 1978–1979 and all 1980–1982 Corvettes came with air conditioning. This is an original Delco Air compressor from 1978. The compressor, part number 1131078, was used in 1978–1979, but very late 1979s, after serial number 50,000, were assembled with compressor number 1131076. All 1980–1982s used compressor number 1131198. The six numbers printed next to "CODE NO." are a manufacturing date code, with the first two numbers representing the month, the next two numbers indicating the day, the fifth number being the last digit of the year, and the sixth number revealing the shift. In this example, "040681" tells us that this compressor was made on April 6, 1978, during the first shift.

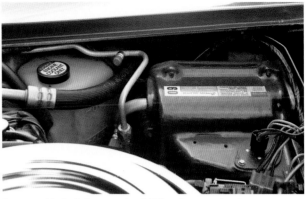

Passenger-side details in an unrestored 1981 engine compartment.

non-air-conditioned cars do not have this tube. Motors have a part number and date code stamped into their mounting flanges. The date code contains one or two numbers to denote the month and two numbers to indicate the year.

Windshield Wiper Motor and Related Components

The wiper motor for all 1978–1982 Corvettes uses an unpainted cast-aluminum housing and transmission case. A black plastic cover goes over the wiper motor transmission assembly. A silver-colored foil sticker containing the motor's part number and date of manufacture is on the motor housing.

In early 1978, the wiper motor is part number 5044814. Later 1978 and all 1979–1982 cars use a number 5044907 wiper motor. (Refer to Appendix P for wiper motor part numbers.)

Date codes for wiper motors use the Julian calendar. One, two, or three numbers indicate the day of the year. This is followed by a single number denoting the year.

The windshield washer pump utilized in 1978–1982 is mounted at the base of the fluid reservoir. The motor for the pump is contained in a silver-cadmium-plated metal housing, and the pump has a white plastic covering.

The windshield washer fluid reservoir is mounted toward the rear of the driver's inner wheelwell. The reservoir is rigid white plastic and does not have fluid level marks. The tank does have "5045644 ASM" and "4961311" in its side in 1978–1981, however. In 1982 these number change to "14047109 ASM" and "22020937." In all years, a long fill neck inserts in the reservoir and extends up slightly below the fender lip. The name "DONLEE" and the part number "344810" appear on the long fill neck.

Air Injection Reactor System and other Emissions Components

In 1978 and 1979, an AIR system is included with all cars equipped with an L82, option NB2 (California emissions), or option NA6 (high-altitude emissions). All 1980–1982

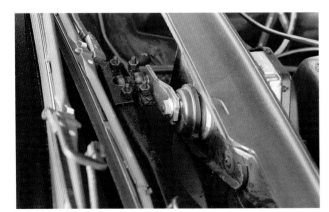

The windshield wiper area was typically rather roughly finished. The wiper motor, transmission, and arms were all installed after the firewall and wiper area were painted black, so none of these parts should have black overspray.

All 1978–1982 Corvettes came with an AIR system. This photo shows passenger-side details of a 1981 AIR pump.

This illustrates the correct factory finishes for the various parts of a 1978 air injection reactor pump. The lower pump bracket was on the engine when the engine was painted. Thus the bracket is engine color.

Driver-side details of an AIR pump in a 1982. Dayco, Gates, and Goodyear were all OEM belt suppliers for 1978–1982 Corvettes. The AIR pump belt shown here is original, with GM, the part number, the manufacturer's logo, and other information ink stamped on the outer surface.

Corvettes are equipped with an AIR system. The AIR system includes two tube assemblies that thread into the exhaust manifolds. In 1978–1980 the system is connected to the driver-side manifold with four tubes (one to each manifold runner) and to the passenger-side manifold with two tubes (one to the front runner and one to the rear runner).

In 1978 and early 1979, the AIR tube assemblies are black cadmium plated. The tubes in later '79s and all 1980–1982 cars are cadmium dichromate plated. The AIR pump body is die-cast aluminum and natural in color. A rough-textured, sand-cast plate, painted semi-gloss black, covers the back of the pump. In 1978–1980 this plate bears casting number 7817872. In 1981 and 1982 it bears casting number 7836920.

All pumps contain a centrifugal filter behind the pulley. This filter, which looks more like a fan, is made from black plastic with rounded fins. All 1978 and 1979 Corvettes use a steel spacer between the front pump pulley and the centrifugal filter. The spacer is zinc or silver cadmium plated. In 1980–1982 the spacer is unplated aluminum.

For all years, the front pump pulley is gray phosphate plated or painted semi-gloss black. Pulleys do not have a stamped-in part number. Most pumps are date coded, though the date can be difficult to see with the pump installed. It is stamped into a boss on the rear underside of the body. The sequence may begin with a letter to indicate the assembly plant or specific line. Then one or three numbers indicate the day of the year on the Julian calendar. Earlier dates (prior to the 100th day) may start with two zeros or may not. For example, a pump assembled on the fifth day of the year may be stamped "005" or simply "5." A fourth (or second) number follows to denote the last digit of the year. This is followed by a number indicating the shift and a letter indicating the model of the pump.

In 1978 most diverter valve bodies are metal, while afterward they are molded plastic. The diaphragm cover and check valves are cadmium dichromate. The diverter valve muffler is plated gray phosphate. The diverter valve part number is stamped into the valve below the muffler. Check valves have a part number stamped into the center ridge.

An air injection reactor pump on a 1980 L48 engine. Note all the different surface treatments on the pump's parts and the use of both worm screw and tower-style hose clamps.

Details of a 1982 air injection reactor pump. Note the use of both worm screw and tower-style hose clamps and the use of metric bolts.

Hoses connecting the various parts of the AIR system are molded black, and most hose clamps are tower style. Clamps have a galvanized finish and contain the size, the words "WITTEK MFG. CO. CHICAGO U.S.A.," and a date code stamped into the band. The first number of the date code denotes the quarter, and the following two numbers indicate the year.

All 1978–1982 Corvettes are fitted with an evaporative control system. This system includes a black carbon-filled canister mounted to the lower left-side inner wheelwell.

All 1978–1982 Corvettes have a positive crankcase ventilation (PCV) valve in the left-side valve cover. The PCV valve has a part number stamped into it. In 1978–1980 Corvettes equipped with an L48 or LG4 engine, and in all 1981 cars, the valve is number CV774C. In those 1978–1980 Corvettes equipped with an L82 engine, the valve is part number CV775C. In all 1982 cars, the valve is part number CV853C.

Many but not all 1978–1982 Corvettes have a transmission-controlled spark (TCS) system. This system includes a thermal vacuum switch mounted on the side of the thermostat housing.

All 1978–1982 Corvettes are equipped with an early fuel evaporation (EFE) system. With this system, a vacuum-actuated valve is mounted to the passenger-side exhaust manifold. A thermal vacuum switch mounted in the thermostat housing controls the valve.

All 1978–1980 Corvettes equipped with air conditioning and an automatic transmission have an antidiesel idle solenoid mounted with a bracket to the carburetor base. The bracket is cadmium dichromate plated, and the solenoid housing is silver cadmium plated.

All 1978–1982 Corvettes are fitted with an exhaust gas recirculation (EGR) system. The heart of the system is an EGR valve mounted on the passenger side of the intake manifold. The EGR valve is manufactured by Rochester Products Division, and that company's logo is stamped into the valve's housing.

The EGR valve housing is cadmium dichromate plated. The lower portion of the valve is unpainted and unplated cast iron. A part number, date code, and broadcast code are stamped into the valve housing. The date code typically consists of five numbers. The first three represent the day of the year, the fourth is the last digit of the year, and the fifth is the shift during which that valve was made. For example, a date code of 15192 indicates the valve was made the 151st day of 1979 during the second shift.

Beginning with 1980, Corvettes equipped with LG4 engines, and continuing in all 1981 and 1982 cars, computer command control (CCC) system is installed. An electronic control module (ECM) mounted in the battery compartment behind the driver's seat controls this system. The ECM is fed data from various devices in different parts of the car. These devices include a manifold absolute pressure (MAP) sensor, an

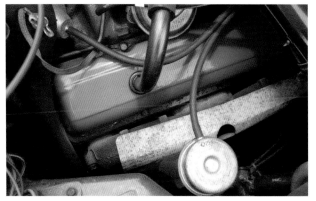

All 1978–1982 Corvettes came with an early fuel evaporation (EFE) system. The EFE actuator was mounted to the rear of the passenger-side exhaust manifold. It is plated with silver cadmium and has the date of manufacture stamped in black ink. The first number of the date code represents the last digit of the year, the letter represents the month, and the final two numbers represent the day. The date code of "9H29" in this 1979 translates to August 20, 1979.

All 1978–1982 Corvettes came with an exhaust gas recirculation (EGR) valve mounted on the passenger side of the intake manifold. The specific valve used depended on which emissions system was required. This Rochester Products valve on an L48-equipped 1979 bears part number "17057427" and date code "19391." The date code uses the Julian calendar, so the first three numbers represent the day of the year, the fourth number is the final digit of the year, and the fifth number indicates the shift. The date code on this EGR valve tells us it was made on the 193rd day of 1979 during the first shift.

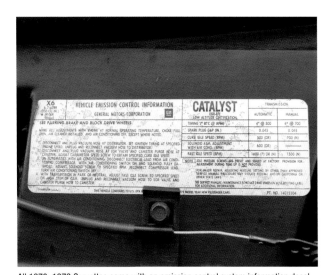

All 1978–1979 Corvettes came with an emission control system information decal on the driver-side firewall, adjacent to the hood latch. The specific label used varied in accord with several factors, including which engine the car came with, whether it was destined to be delivered new in California, and whether it came with option NA6, high-altitude emission equipment. This example is in a non-California, non-NA6 1979 fitted with the base L48 engine.

oxygen sensor, a vehicle speed sensor (VSS), a throttle position sensor (TPS), and an electronic spark timing (EST) sensor.

All 1978–1982 Corvettes have one or two emission system and tune-up information labels. In 1978–1979 a decal is on the left upper area of the firewall, behind the power brake booster and adjacent to the hood latch. In 1979 an additional decal detailing emission system hose routing is on the underside of the hood in the upper driver-side corner. In 1980–1982 a decal with information and a hose routing diagram is on the underside of the hood in the upper driver-side corner.

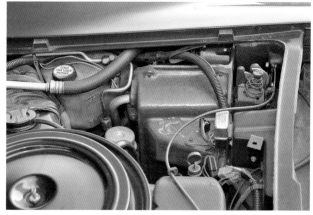

Driver-side engine compartment details in an unrestored 1979. Note subtle variations in component finishes, use of plastic sheathing to house wires, and placement of rubber bumpers in the hood channel.

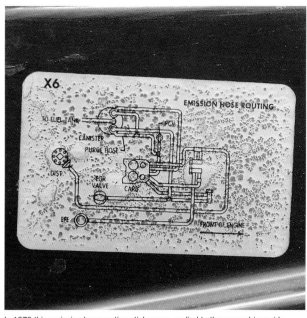

In 1979 this emission hose routing sticker was applied to the upper driver-side corner on the underside of the hood.

Passenger-side firewall details in unrestored 1980 L48 engine compartment.

Wire and hose routing details on the driver side of an unrestored 1979. The engine compartment was painted black before wiring, hoses, and their brackets were installed, so these should show no signs of overspray.

Original hood insulation held in place by correct steel spring clips and disc retainers. Hood strikers, bolts, and shims are typically unpainted, except in 1978 limited edition pace car replicas, where they are usually painted semi-gloss black.

Engine Compartment, Wiring, Horns, and Related Components

The firewall, underside of the hood, and engine compartment side of the inner wheelwells are painted semi-gloss black. The wheel side of the front and rear inner wheelwells are also painted semi-gloss black, though coverage is usually sparse. In addition, the rear areas of the wheelwells normally have some undercoating.

In all cars wire harnesses and adjacent hoses are bundled together in a row, so rather than forming a circle, they are flat. The harnesses and hoses are held to each other with black plastic tie wraps.

All vacuum hose is color coded with an ink stripe that runs the length of the hose. Larger hoses have a green, red, or yellow stripe, while smaller hoses usually have a white stripe.

In 1978 and 1979, the underside of the hood is fitted with a fiberglass insulation mat. It is held on with six metal spring clips. No insulation is used under the hood for 1980–1982 cars.

In 1982 only, the underside of the hood is fitted with a hood louver control system. This system allows additional fresh air to enter the engine's induction system when engine coolant is hot and the throttle is at or near its fully open position.

All 1978–1982 Corvettes are fitted with an electric oil pressure gauge. A gold-iridite-plated metal sending unit is threaded into the engine block above the oil filter.

Dual horns are standard for all years. They are mounted behind the front grille area. From 1978 through mid-1981, horns are mounted inboard of the headlight assemblies. In late 1981 and all 1982 cars, they are mounted farther apart on the outboard sides of the headlights.

Horns have the last three digits of the part number and a manufacturing date code stamped into flat areas near the sound opening. In 1978 and 1979, the low note horn is part number 9000144, and the high note horn is part number 9000143. In 1980 and early 1981, the low note horn is the same, but the high note horn is changed to part number 9000192. In late 1981 and all 1982, the low note horn is part number 9000176, and the high note horn is part number 9000203.

The date code in each horn contains a number denoting the year, a letter denoting the month (with "A" representing January, "B" representing February, and so on), and another number indicating the week. For example, a horn stamped "0F2" was made the second week of June 1980. Each horn is attached to a mounting bracket, and the whole assembly is painted semi-gloss black.

Hood hinges are silver cadmium plated and usually have both body color and underhood black overspray. Hinges are usually fastened by black-phosphate-plated, indented hex-head bolts. The hood support is silver cadmium plated. It has two hinged sections that fold as the hood is lowered. The hood latches are black phosphate plated and mount with

There was only one engine installed in Corvettes in 1981, a 350 cid rated at 190 horsepower. This was the first time since 1955 that an optional engine was not available for Corvettes. With the exception of the aftermarket alarm horn and related wiring mounted in front of the master cylinder, this 1981 engine compartment is original and unrestored.

Details of a 1978 passenger-side firewall. This car is unrestored, and everything shown here is factory correct.

An original L82 engine compartment in a 1978 Limited Edition Corvette Pace Car replica. Though popular with collectors, the signatures on the air cleaner lid of former Corvette chief engineers Dave McClellan and David Hill are not factory correct and were added after the car was built.

Passenger-side hood latch details in an unrestored 1979. Note that all components shown were installed after the firewall was painted black. Therefore they remain unpainted.

Details of a 1978 L82 passenger-side engine. Note the wide variety of plating and paint finishes on the components.

black-phosphate-plated hardware. The driver-side male latch has the hood release cable attached with a brass barrel cable stop. A hex bolt locks the stop to the cable. The cable is inside a smooth black plastic sheath.

Another cable connects the two female latches mounted to the underside of the hood. This cable is inside a black nylon sheath. Its ends are secured to the latches with small clevis pins fitted with flat washers and cotter pins. The cable is secured to the distributor ignition shield with two clips.

1978–1982 CHASSIS
Chassis

All 1978–1982 Corvette chassis are painted semi-gloss black. Chassis for automatic-transmission-equipped cars have a removable, bolt-on center crossmember, while standard-transmission-equipped cars have a welded-on center crossmember. Cars with automatic transmissions do not have a clutch cross shaft tower welded on top of the chassis behind the left front wheel as standard transmission cars do.

In 1978 and 1979, the chassis crossmember that supports the rear differential is made from steel painted semi-gloss black. In 1980–1982 this crossmember is made from unpainted aluminum.

A pair of one-inch high chassis part number sequences is painted in white or yellow on the chassis with a stencil. One sequence is the part number from A. O. Smith (the company that fabricated the chassis for GM). The other sequence is the Chevrolet part number. These part numbers are usually found on the passenger side of the chassis, behind the front wheel. A manufacturing date code is stenciled on the rail as

There are a lot of subtle variations in the finishes of 1978–1982 chassis components. The 1982 chassis parts shown here are original and unrestored, with the exception of the sway bar end links and engine oil filter.

control arms, the area surrounding the ball joint is unpainted. This is more prevalent on later cars.

Control arm cross shafts are painted semi-gloss black on some cars and unpainted on others. Cars with painted cross shafts typically have control arm bushing retention washers and bolts that are also painted semi-gloss black. Cars with unpainted cross shafts typically have retention washers that are gray phosphate plated and bolts that are black phosphate plated.

Front coil springs are natural in finish and sometimes have an irregular bluish cast from the manufacturing process. A green paper sticker contains two black letters indicating the spring's broadcast code (application), as well as a black GM part number.

Front shock absorbers are manufactured by Delco. They are painted semi-gloss black and have the words "DELCO

well. The date contains one or two numbers representing the month, one or two numbers indicating the day, and two numbers denoting the year.

Most 1978–1982 Corvettes have the serial number stamped into their chassis in two locations. It is typically found in the left-side rail, slightly forward of the number-four body mount bracket. It is also typically found on the left-side rear kickup above the wheel area, slightly forward of the number-three body mount bracket.

Steel shims are frequently utilized at body mount points to make up for irregularities in fit. If present, shims are usually taped to the body mount bracket with 1½-inch-wide masking tape. The number of shims needed at each body mount bracket is typically written on the chassis adjacent to the bracket with green, yellow, or white grease crayon. Unlike earlier cars, this number is usually an actual number rather than slash marks. All 1978–1982 body mount cushions are made from molded black rubber.

Front Suspension

Upper and lower front control arms are painted semi-gloss to gloss black. Ball joints are installed after the arms are painted and are therefore not painted. Crushed steel rivets (not bolts) hold ball joints on and are also natural in finish. On some

A 1982 rear chassis. The driver-side muffler is original and displays the GM logo, the part number, and the manufacture date code. The "W" represents Walker, the manufacturer, and "4-82" indicates that the muffler was made in April 1982.

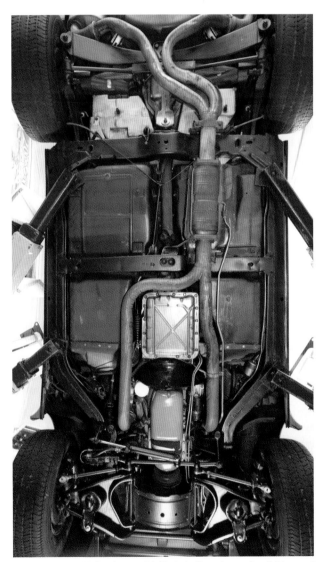

This unrestored 1982 chassis accurately illustrates the various surface finishes used when the cars were initially built.

REMY DAYTON OHIO U.S.A. PLIACELL" and a date code stamped in around the bottom. The Julian date code contains three numbers indicating the day and two numbers denoting the year. In addition, the shock has a small paper sticker with a two-letter broadcast code on the side.

The front upper shock mount rubber bushings are unpainted black rubber. The top upper bushing is larger in diameter than the bottom upper bushing, and the upper shock washer is gray phosphate plated. The front lower shock mount rubber bushings and both rear shock mount bushings are integral and are therefore painted along with the shock.

All 1978–1982 Corvettes utilize a front stabilizer bar. Cars with standard suspension use a 0.875-inch bar, while cars with optional FE7 suspension utilize a 1.12-inch bar. Some cars have a stabilizer bar painted semi-gloss black, while others have a natural, unpainted bar.

Bushings mounting the front stabilizer bar to the chassis, as well as bushings in the end links, are unpainted black rubber. Stamped-steel brackets painted semi-gloss black hold the bar to the chassis. End link bolts are zinc plated 5/16-24 SAE fine thread and usually have the manufacturer's logo "UB" or "WB" on their heads. End link spacers are zinc plated, have a split seam, and typically have a "K" or a "C" stamped in.

Steering Box and Steering Linkage

All 1978–1982 Corvettes use a cast steering gear that is either natural in color or painted semi-gloss black. The box cover is cast aluminum and is retained by three black-oxide-plated hex-head bolts. The letters "WZ" are usually stamped on the box in yellow ink. A five-character date code is cast into the side of the box next to the manufacturer's logo. The first three digits represent the day of the year, and the last two digits represent the year. For example, a date code of "19381" indicates that the box was cast on the 193rd day of 1981.

A forged pitman arm links the steering box to the relay rod. The pitman arm is natural in color and is often seen with a daub of blue or green paint. The steering relay rod and idler arm are typically natural finish. Both parts are forged and tend to have a bluish gray tint. Original idler arms do not have grease fittings.

Tie rod ends are natural finish and also typically have a bluish gray color cast. Daubs of yellow paint are often seen on tie rod ends. Tie rod end sleeves are painted semi-gloss black. Tie rod end clamps have two reinforcing ridges around their circumference and are sometimes painted semi-gloss black and sometimes left unpainted.

The power steering control valve and hydraulic cylinder are painted semi-gloss black. The nut and washers retaining the hydraulic cylinder's ram to the frame bracket are zinc plated. The frame bracket may be painted semi-gloss black or unpainted. Original power steering hoses typically have longitudinal ridges around the entire circumference, while later replacements don't.

The steering box in an unrestored 1978. Note the partially legible two-letter broadcast code stamped on the steering box in yellow ink.

Rear Suspension

All 1978–1980 Corvettes and all '81 cars with four-speed manual transmission that are equipped with standard suspension utilize a nine-leaf steel rear spring. In 1978 and 1979, there are no retaining bands on the rear spring. Beginning in 1980, a retaining band is used around the lower six leaves of the spring. The standard nine-leaf steel springs used in all 1978–1980 cars, and in all '81 cars equipped with a four-speed, are painted light gray and have black plastic liners between the leaves. Since the liners were installed when the springs were painted, they too are painted light gray.

Those 1981 Corvettes equipped with automatic transmission and standard suspension, and all '82 cars equipped with standard suspension, utilize a mono-leaf fiberglass rear spring. This spring is dark gray.

Those 1978 and 1979 cars equipped with optional FE7 suspension utilize a six-leaf steel spring. Those 1980–1982 Corvettes equipped with FE7 suspension use a nine-leaf steel spring. Both configurations of the FE7 rear spring are painted light gray. Unlike the standard steel spring, however, the black plastic liners used in the FE7 spring are not painted.

The center rear spring mount bracket is painted semi-gloss black. The four bolts retaining the spring to the differential typically have the manufacturer's logo "WB" on their heads and are either black phosphate or zinc plated. The outer spring bolts and nuts are usually black phosphate plated. The washers are typically natural.

The six-leaf FE7 rear spring used in 1978 and 1979 is 2¼ inches wide, while the standard suspension rear spring is 2½ inches wide. To compensate for the decreased width, FE7 springs mount to the bottom of the differential cover with two spacers, one in front and the other in back.

Rear trailing arms are painted semi-gloss to gloss black. Rear wheel bearing carriers (also called spindle supports) are painted semi-gloss black and have a part number and date code cast in. The date code has a letter representing the month (with "A" for January, "B" for February, and so on), one or two numbers for the day, and one number for the final digit of the year. The date code for a rear bearing carrier made on April 18, 1980, for example, would read "D 18 0."

All 1978–1982 cars equipped with FE7 suspension have a rear stabilizer bar. The bar is ⁹⁄₁₆-inch diameter and may be painted semi-gloss black or be unpainted. It mounts to the chassis with stamped-steel brackets painted semi-gloss black. Each end of the bar has a link bracket painted semi-gloss black that attaches to a bracket bolted to the trailing arm. The brackets on the trailing arms have plating that is sometimes called pickling. This type of plating results in a brownish olive color. These brackets attach to the trailing arm via bolts that thread into small, unpainted steel plates that slip into the rear of the arms.

Rear camber adjustment rods (also called strut rods) are usually natural and often have a bluish gray tint. Some rods are painted semi-gloss black or are partially painted during the undercarriage "blackout" process. All 1978–1982 cars have rods with 1¾-inch outside diameter ends.

The outboard ends of the camber adjustment rods are held to the rear wheel bearing carriers with forged L-shaped pins that also serve as lower mounts for the rear shock absorbers. These pins, which are sometimes called rear shock brackets, contain raised part numbers.

The inboard ends of the camber adjustment rods attach to a bracket with special bolts painted semi-gloss black. The bolts have integral off-center washers. When rotated, they move the rods in or out and thus allow for rear wheel camber adjustment. The camber adjustment bolts are usually silver cadmium plated, though they may be black phosphate plated instead.

Rear wheel toe adjustment is set with the use of shims placed on either side of the trailing arms where they mount to the chassis. The adjusting shims are rectangular pieces of unpainted steel in varying thicknesses. The shims have a slot in one end that slips over the trailing arm mount bolt. The other ends of the shims are rotated upward, so their holes align with corresponding holes in the chassis. A long cotter pin passes through the stacks of shims on both sides of the trailing arm and through the hole in the chassis.

Rear axle shafts (often called half shafts) are made from forged ends welded to extruded steel tubes. The axle shafts are natural, with the tube being shiny silver and the ends being a dull gray. U-joints do not have grease fittings and do have raised part numbers on the body. They are natural and tend to have that faint bluish tint that is characteristic of forged parts. The outboard axle shaft U-joints are pressed into a flange that is natural in color. The flange is held to the rear wheel bearing carrier by four bolts that are usually black phosphate plated. The bolts are prevented from turning out by two pairs of French locks, the tabs of which are bent over to contact the bolt heads. The French locks are zinc plated and typically have only one of the two tabs adjacent to each bolt bent over.

Front Wheel Assemblies

Front spindles and steering knuckles are natural and tend to have a bluish tint to their gray color. In addition, the lower portions of the spindles are frequently seen with orange or white paint, as though the bottoms of the spindles were dipped into it.

Original front brake backing plates are zinc plated and then chromate dipped. This results in varying finishes, ranging from gold with a faint rainbow of other colors throughout to a dull silver with only a trace of yellowish chromate coloring. Well-preserved original backing plates typically appear dull silver, probably because the chromate dip deteriorates over time.

Front brake caliper support brackets are plated silver cadmium or cadmium dichromate, which results in a translucent gold color with varying degrees of other colors present in a rainbowlike pattern.

Front brake calipers are painted semi-gloss black and frequently have daubs of blue or white paint on the side. Painting is done before the caliper halves are machined. Therefore machined surfaces are unpainted. Bleeder screws are zinc plated and remain unpainted.

Caliper hoses are black rubber with gold-iridite-plated end hardware. Federally mandated DOT specifi-cations are written on the hose in red ink. In addition, a red longitudinal stripe on the hose makes it easier to see if it is twisted. Original hoses typically have raised longitudinal ridges around the entire circumference, while later replace-ments are typically smooth.

Front brake rotors are natural in finish. The front wheel bearing carrier (also called a hub) is riveted to the rotor disc.

Rear Wheel Assemblies

As with the fronts, original rear brake backing plates are zinc plated and then chromate dipped. This results in varying finishes, ranging from gold with a faint rainbow of other colors throughout to a dull silver with only a trace of yellowish chromate coloring. Well-preserved original backing plates typically appear dull silver, probably because the chromate dip deteriorates over time.

Rear brake caliper support brackets are natural and hence a dull gray. On occasion they are painted flat to semi-flat black.

Rear brake calipers are painted semi-gloss black and frequently have daubs of blue or white paint on the side. Painting is done before the caliper halves are machined. Therefore machined surfaces are unpainted. Bleeder screws are zinc plated and remain unpainted.

Rear brake rotors are natural in finish. They are riveted to the rear spindle, which is pressed into the rear wheel bearing carrier. The rivets are drilled out to allow for servicing of the park brake assembly or the rear wheel bearings. The wheel lug nuts retain the rotor in the absence of the rivets.

Transmission

The automatic-transmission-equipped 1978–1981 Corvettes utilize a Turbo Hydra-Matic 350. All 1982 cars equipped with an automatic use a Turbo Hydra-Matic 700-R4. For both transmissions, the main case and the tail housing are cast aluminum with a natural finish.

The identification code for the Turbo 350 transmission is stamped in a vertical surface on the passenger side. This code has six characters. The first is a letter that denotes the manufacturing plant. The second is a number representing the year. The third is a letter denoting the month. The fourth and fifth are numbers representing the day of the month. The final letter is either a "D" for day shift or an "N" for night shift. The letters designating the month of manufacture are as follows: "A" is January, "B" is February, "C" is March, "D" is April, "E" is May, "H" is June, "K" is July, "M" is August, "P" is September, "R" is October, "S" is November, and "T" is December.

In addition to the above-described production code, each Turbo 350 transmission also contains the final eight digits of the serial number of the car it was originally installed into. This sequence is stamped into the case on the driver-side flange adjacent to the oil pan.

The Turbo Hydra-Matic 700-R4 used in 1982 is a four-speed overdrive automatic. It contains a transmission code stamping on the passenger-side oil pan rail. The code begins with the number "9" to indicate the 1982 model year. This if followed by the letters "YA," which represent the application code. Next come three numbers that denote the day the transmission was built. The final character is either a "D" or an "N" to indicate either the day or night shift.

Four-speed manual transmissions used in all 1978–1981 Corvettes are Borg Warner Super T-10 units. With Borg Warner four-speeds, the car's serial number derivative, as well as the production code and assembly date, is stamped into the main case on the driver-side flange adjacent to where the tail housing attaches.

In the production code, the first letter is "W" to indicate Borg Warner. The next letter indicates the month of production, with "A" representing January, "B" representing February, and so on to "L," which represents December. The month code is followed by one or two numbers denoting the day. Next comes a single number to indicate the year. The last number indicates whether the transmission is a close- or wide-ratio unit.

For example, a code of "WG2791" translates to a Borg Warner four-speed built on July 27, 1979. The final "1" indicates that it is a wide-ratio unit.

Differential and Driveshaft

All 1978–1982 Corvettes are equipped with a Posi-Traction limited-slip differential. In 1978 and 1979, the differential case and cover are both natural-colored steel castings and as such are a dull silvery gray. In 1980–1982 the differential case and cover are both natural-colored aluminum castings.

A plastic triangular tag is attached to the differential by means of the oil fill plug. The tag is red, with white lettering that says "USE LIMITED SLIP DIFF. LUBRICANT ONLY" or "LIMITED SLIP LUBE ONLY."

Front input and side output yokes are forgings that are natural in color. Because they are forged, they have a somewhat smoother surface than the case and cover. They tend to have a slight bluish tint to their dull gray color.

Differential cases and covers both have casting numbers and a casting date that includes a letter for the month (with "A" representing January, "B" representing February, and so on), one or two numbers indicating the day of the month, and one number indicating the last digit of the year.

In addition to the casting date, all cases have a stamped-in production code. The production code is on the bottom rear edge of the case, adjacent to where it meets the cover. The differential production code typically begins with two letters to indicate the gear ratio. A single letter denoting the assembly plant usually follows this. Then come one, two, or three numbers representing the day the unit was assembled. After this is a single letter indicating the source for the Posi-Traction unit (not necessarily the company that assembled the differential). The final number in the sequence represents the assembly shift that built the unit. (Refer to Appendix E for differential gear ratio codes.)

The transmission and differential are connected by a driveshaft made from extruded steel tubing welded at each end to a forged universal joint coupling. As with the axle shafts, the driveshaft is natural in color. The center tube portion is bright silver, with longitudinal extrusion lines sometimes visible, and the ends are a dull silvery gray, with a slight bluish hue at times.

A part number stenciled on the driveshaft tube in yellow or white paint is sometimes seen. One or two green circumferential stripes on the tube and daubs of variously colored paint on the forged ends are sometimes seen as well.

Exhaust System

All 1978–1982 Corvettes use an undercar, carbon steel exhaust system manufactured by Walker for Chevrolet. In 1978 cars equipped with an L48 engine use two-inch pipes throughout the system. Those 1978s equipped with an L82 and all 1979–1982 cars use 2-inch pipes from the manifolds to a junction where they join and then 2½-inch pipes for the remainder of the system.

All 1978–1982 Corvettes are equipped with a catalytic converter in the exhaust system. The housing of the converter is made from galvanized steel. A pressed-in round steel plug closes the hole in the underside of the converter that allows it to be filled with the catalyst material. A galvanized steel heat shield is fitted between the converter and the floor. All 1978–1981 converters look the same. The 1982 converters are somewhat longer and narrower than their predecessors. In 1981 and 1982, a pipe from the AIR system is connected to the converter.

Mufflers are galvanized on the exterior and typically have an embossed "W" to represent the manufacturer. In addition, an embossed part number and date code are usually found on each muffler. The date code includes a number for the month and two numbers for the year.

Muffler part numbers for 1978 Corvettes equipped with L48 engines are 458963 for the driver side and 458964 for the passenger side. Muffler part numbers for 1979 Corvettes equipped with L48 engines are 476875 for the driver side and 476876 for the passenger side.

For 1978 and 1979 cars with L82 engines, the muffler part numbers are 473035 for the driver side and 473036 for the passenger side. For 1980 Corvettes, the driver-side muffler is number 14011289, and the passenger-side muffler is number 14011290. For 1981 Corvettes, the driver-side muffler is number 14033965, and the passenger-side muffler is number 14033965. Later 1981 and all '82 cars use muffler number 14033701 on the driver side and muffler number 14033702 on the passenger side.

This extraordinarily original, one-owner 1979 has traveled only a little over 24,000 miles since it was new.

Fuel Lines, Brake Lines, and Miscellaneous Chassis and Underbody Components

All 1978–1982 fuel lines run along, and at times through, the right-side chassis rail. All cars have two fuel lines. One supplies fuel from the tank to the carburetor. The other is a return line.

In addition to the two fuel lines on the right side of the chassis, all cars have a vapor return line on the left side of the chassis. This line is part of the evaporative emission control system.

Fuel lines are galvanized carbon steel. Black rubber fuel hose connects the lines to the tank and the fuel pump. Zinc-chromate-plated spring clamps are usually used to secure the hose to its line.

Brake lines are galvanized carbon steel. Brake line end fittings are brass. Fittings at the master cylinder are often seen with red or blue dye, which was probably used to denote the two different sizes of fittings. In addition, daubs of yellow paint are sometimes seen on the fittings at junction blocks.

Various heat shields are affixed to the underside of the body to help insulate the passenger compartment from engine and exhaust system heat. A sheet steel shield, which is gray phosphate plated, is mounted on the lower vertical area of the firewall on both sides.

All cars are fitted with transmission tunnel insulation. A semi-rigid foil-wrapped blanket in the shape of the tunnel is fastened above the transmission with clips riveted to the underbody.

A variety of steel plates are fastened to the underbody to mount components in the passenger compartment. These components include the battery, seats, jack hold-down clips, and so on. All these plates are painted semi-gloss black and are retained by unpainted aluminum rivets.

Though they are now decades old, C3 Corvettes remain excellent driving cars. They perform as well as or better than many newer sports cars.

Appendices

PRODUCTION TOTALS & VEHICLE IDENTIFICATION NUMBERS

PRODUCTION TOTALS

Year	Coupes	Convertibles	Regular production coupes	Indy pace car replicas	Collector edition	Total
1968	9,936	18,630				28,566
1969	22,129	16,633				38,762
1970	10,668	6,648				17,316
1971	14,680	7,121				21,801
1972	20,496	6,508				27,004
1973	25,521	4,943				30,464
1974	32,028	5,474				37,502
1975	33,836	4,629				38,465
1976	46,567					
1977	49,213					
1978			40,274	6,502		
1979	53,807					
1980	40,614					
1981	40,606					
1982			18,648		6,759	

VEHICLE IDENTIFICATION NUMBERS

1968	194378S400001–194378S428566
1969	194379S700001–194379S738762
1970	194370S400001–194370S417316
1971	194371S100001–194371S121801
1972	1Z37K2S500001–1Z37K2S527004
1973	1Z37J3S400001–1Z37J3S434464
1974	1Z37J4S400001–1Z37J4S437502
1975	1Z37J5S400001–1Z37J5S438465
1976	1Z37L6S400001–1Z37L6S446558
1977	1Z37L7S400001–1Z37L7S449213
1978	1Z87L8S400001–1Z87L8S440274
1978 Indy pace cars	1Z87L8S900001–1Z87L8S906502
1979	1Z8789S400001–1Z8789S453807
1980	1Z878AS400001–1Z878AS440614
1981 St. Louis assembly plant	1G1AY8764BS400001–1G1AY8764BS431611
1981 Bowling Green assembly plant	1G1AY8764B5100001–1G1AY8764B5108995
1982	1G1AY8786C5100001–1G1AY8786C5125407
1968–1971	The fourth character is a "6" for convertibles.
1972–1975	The third character is a "6" for convertibles.
1970–1980	The fifth character indicates what engine was originally installed into the car:
1972	"K" indicates base engine; "L" indicates LT-1; "W" indicates 454.
1973–1974	"J" indicates base engine; "T" indicates L82; "Z" indicates 454.
1975	"J" indicates base engine; "T" indicates L82.
1976–1977	"L" indicates base engine; "X" indicates L82.
1978	"L" indicates base engine; "4" indicates L82.
1979	"8" indicates base engine; "4" indicates L82.
1980	"8" indicates base engine; "L" indicates L82; "H" indicates LG4 305-cid California engine.

OPTION PRODUCTION QUANTITIES AND PRICES

1968

Code	Description	Qty	Price
19437	Corvette sport coupe	9,936	$4,663.00
19467	Corvette convertible	18,630	$4,320.00
A01	Tinted glass	17,635	$15.80
A02	Tinted windshield	5,509	$10.55
A31	Power windows	7,065	$57.95
A82	Head restraints	3,197	$42.15
A85	Custom shoulder harness	350	$26.35
C07	Auxiliary hardtop	8,735	$231.75
C08	Auxiliary hardtop vinyl covering	3,050	$52.70
C50	Rear window defroster	693	$31.60
C60	Air conditioning	5,664	$412.90
F41	Special performance suspension	1,758	$36.90
G81	Posi-Traction rear axle	27,008	$46.35
J50	Vacuum power brakes	9,559	$42.15
J56	Heavy-duty brakes	81	$384.45
K66	Transistor ignition	5,457	$73.75
L30	327/300-horsepower engine	5,875	base engine
L36	427/390-horsepower engine	7,717	$200.15
L68	427/400-horsepower engine	1,932	$305.50
L71	427/435-horsepower engine	2,898	$437.10
L79	327/350-horsepower engine	9,440	$105.35
L88	427/430-horsepower engine	80	$947.90
L89	427/435-horsepower engine with aluminum cylinder heads	624	$805.75
M20	Four-speed wide-ratio manual transmission	10,760	$184.35
M21	Four-speed close-ratio manual transmission	12,337	$184.35
M22	Four-speed heavy-duty manual transmission	80	$263.30
M40	Turbo Hydra-Matic transmission	5,063	$226.45
N11	Off-road exhaust	4,695	$36.90
N36	Telescopic steering column	6,477	$42.15
N40	Power steering	12,364	$94.80
PT6	F70-15 red stripe tires	11,686	$31.30
PT7	F70-15 white stripe tires	9,692	$31.30
PO1	Wheel trim covers	8,971	$57.95
UA6	Horn alarm system	388	$26.35
U15	Speed warning indicator	3,453	$10.55
U69	AM-FM radio	27,920	$172.75
U79	Stereo equipment	3,311	$278.10
–	Leather interior trim	2,429	$79.00

1969

Code	Description	Qty	Price
19437	Corvette sport coupe	22,129	$4,763.00
19467	Corvette convertible	16,633	$4,420.00
A01	Tinted glass	31,270	$16.90
A31	Power windows	9,816	$63.20
A82	Head restraints	38,762	$17.95
A85	Custom shoulder harness	600	$42.15
C07	Auxiliary hardtop	7,878	$252.80
C08	Auxiliary hardtop vinyl trim	3,266	$57.95
C50	Rear window defroster	2,485	$32.65
C60	Air conditioning	11,859	$428.70
F41	Special performance suspension	1,661	$36.90
G81	Posi-Traction rear axle	36,965	$46.35
J50	Vacuum power brakes	16,876	$42.15
J56	Heavy-duty brakes	115	$384.45
K05	Engine block heater	824	$10.55
K66	Transistor ignition	5,702	$81.10
L36	427/390-horsepower engine	10,531	$221.20
L46	350/350-horsepower engine	12,846	$131.65
L68	427/400-horsepower engine	2,072	$326.55
L71	427/435-horsepower engine	2,722	$437.10
L88	427/430-horsepower engine	116	$1,032.15
L89	427/435-horsepower engine with aluminum cylinder heads	390	$832.05
MA6	Heavy-duty clutch	102	–
M20	Four-speed wide-ratio manual transmission	16,507	$184.80
M21	Four-speed close-ratio manual transmission	13,741	$184.80
M22	Four-speed heavy-duty manual transmission	101	$290.40
M40	Turbo Hydra-Matic transmission	8,161	$221.80

(M40 Turbo Hydra-Matic automatic with L71, L88, or L89 engine option costs $290.40)

Code	Description	Qty	Price
N14	Side-mounted exhaust	4,355	$147.45
N37	Tilt-telescopic steering column	10,325	$84.30
N40	Power steering	22,866	$105.35
PT6	F70-15 red stripe tires	5,210	$31.30
PT7	F70-15 white stripe tires	21,379	$31.30
PU9	F70-15 white-lettered tires	2,398	$33.15
PO2	Deluxe wheel trim covers	8,073	$57.95
UA6	Horn alarm system	12,436	$26.35
U15	Speed warning indicator	3,561	$11.60
U69	AM-FM radio	37,985	$172.75
U79	Stereo equipment	4,114	$278.10
ZL1	Special aluminum 427 engine	2	$3,000
ZQ3	350/300-horsepower engine	10,083	base engine
–	Leather interior trim	3,729	$79.00

1970

Code	Description	Qty	Price
19437	Corvette sport coupe	10,668	$5,192.00
19467	Corvette convertible	6,648	$4,849.00
A31	Power windows	4,813	$63.20
A85	Custom shoulder harness	475	$42.15
C07	Auxiliary hardtop	2,556	$273.85
C08	Auxiliary hardtop vinyl trim	832	$63.20
C50	Rear window defroster	1,281	$36.90
C60	Air conditioning	6,659	$447.65
G81	Optional Posi-Traction axle ratio	2,862	$12.65
J50	Vacuum power brakes	8,984	$47.40
L46	350/350-horsepower engine	4,910	$158.00
LS5	454/390-horsepower engine	4,473	$289.65
LT1	350/370-horsepower engine	1,287	$447.60
M21	Four-speed close-ratio manual transmission	4,383	no charge
M22	Four-speed heavy-duty manual transmission	25	$95.00
M40	Turbo Hydra-Matic transmission	5,102	no charge
NA9	California emissions equipment	–	$36.90
N37	Tilt-telescopic steering column	5,803	$84.30
N40	Power steering	11,907	$105.35
PT7	F70-15 white stripe nylon tires	6,589	$31.30
PU9	F70-15 white-letter nylon tires	7,985	$33.15
PO2	Deluxe wheel trim covers	3,467	$57.95
T60	Heavy-duty battery	165	$15.80
UA6	Horn alarm system	6,727	$31.60
U69	AM-FM radio	16,991	$172.75
U79	Stereo equipment	2,462	$278.10
ZR1	Special purpose 350 engine package*	25	$968.95
ZQ3	350/300-horsepower engine	6,646	base engine
ZW4	Four-speed wide-ratio manual transmission	7,806	no charge
–	Leather interior trim	3,191	$158.00

*Option ZR1 is a road racing package with an LT1 engine, stiffer front and rear springs, heavy-duty shock absorbers, a special Harrison aluminum radiator (part number 3007436), an M22 Four-speed transmission, and a heavy-duty brake package. The brake package includes twin pin front calipers, an extra support for each front caliper, a proportioning valve, and metallic brake pads. N40 power steering, A31 power windows, PO2 wheel covers, a C50 rear window defroster, and C60 air conditioning could not be ordered with the ZR1 package.

1971

Code	Description	Qty	Price
19437	Corvette sport coupe	14,680	$5,496.00
19467	Corvette convertible	7,120	$5,259.00
A31	Power windows	6,192	$79.00
A85	Custom shoulder harness	677	$42.00
C07	Auxiliary hardtop	2,619	$274.00
C08	Auxiliary hardtop vinyl trim	832	$63.00
C50	Rear window defroster	1,598	$42.00

Code	Description	Qty	Price
C60	Air conditioning	11,481	$459.00
J50	Vacuum power brakes	13,558	$47.00
LS5	454/365-horsepower engine	5,079	$295.00
LS6	454/425-horsepower engine	188	$1,221.00
LT1	350/330-horsepower engine	1,949	$483.00
M21	Four-speed close-ratio manual transmission	2,387	no charge
M22	Four-speed heavy-duty manual transmission	130	$100.00
M40	Turbo Hydra-Matic transmission (with small-block engine $100.00 extra when car is equipped with LS5 or LS6 engine)	10,060	no charge
N37	Tilt-telescopic steering column	8,130	$84.30
N40	Power steering	17,904	$115.90
PT7	F70-15 white stripe nylon tires	6,711	$28.00
PU9	F70-15 white-letter nylon tires	12,449	$42.00
P02	Deluxe wheel trim covers	3,007	$63.00
T60	Heavy-duty battery	1,455	$15.80
U69	AM-FM radio	21,509	$178.00
U79	Stereo equipment	3,431	$283.00
ZQ1	Rear axle selection	2,395	$13.00
ZQ3	350/300-horsepower engine	14,547	base engine
ZR1	350/330-horsepower engine, special*	8	$1,010.00
ZR2	454/425-horsepower engine, special*	12	$1,747.00
ZW4	Four-speed wide-ratio manual transmission	9,224	no charge
–	Leather interior trim	2,602	$158.00

*Options ZR1 and ZR2 are both road racing packages. The ZR1 package includes an LT1 engine, and the ZR2 package includes an LS6 engine. Both packages also include stiffer front and rear springs, heavy-duty shock absorbers, a special Harrison aluminum radiator (part number 3007436), and a heavy-duty brake package. The brake package includes twin pin front calipers, an extra support for each front caliper, a proportioning valve, and metallic brake pads. N40 power steering, A31 power windows, PO2 wheel covers, the C50 rear window defroster, and C60 air conditioning could not be ordered with the ZR1 package. The ZR1 package could be ordered only with an M22 Four-speed transmission, while the ZR2 could be ordered with either an M22 or an M40 automatic.

1972

Code	Description	Qty	Price
19437	Corvette sport coupe	20,496	$5,533.00
19467	Corvette convertible	6,508	$5,296.00
AV3	Three-point seat belts	17,693	–
A31	Power windows	9,495	$85.35
A85	Deluxe shoulder harness	749	$42.15
C05	Folding top color	6,507	standard
C07	Auxiliary hardtop	2,646	$273.85
C08	Auxiliary hardtop vinyl trim	811	$158.00
C50	Rear window defroster	2,221	$42.15
C60	Air conditioning	17,011	$464.50
F41	Special suspension (included with ZR1 option package)	20	
GS4	3.70 axle type A	985	no charge
GV3	3.08 axle type B	15,845	no charge
GV4	3.36 axle type A	8,676	no charge
GV5	3.36 axle type B	466	no charge
GV7	3.55 axle type B	670	no charge
GV8	4.11 axle type B	356	no charge
J50	Vacuum power brakes	18,770	$47.40
J56	Heavy-duty brakes (included with ZR1 option package)	20	
K19	Air injection reactor	3,912	no charge
LS5	454/270-horsepower engine	3,913	$294.90
LT1	350/255-horsepower engine	1,741	$483.45
M21	Four-speed close-ratio manual transmission	1,638	no charge
M22	Four-speed heavy-duty manual transmission (included with ZR1 option package)	20	
M40	Turbo Hydra-Matic transmission (no charge with small-block engine; $100.35 extra when car is equipped with LS5 engine)	14,543	
NB2	Exhaust emission control	1,766	no charge
N37	Tilt-telescopic steering column	12,992	$84.30
N40	Power steering	23,794	$115.90

Code	Description	Qty	Price
PT1	F70-15 blackwall tires	3,716	no charge
PT7	F70-15 white stripe nylon tires	6,666	$30.35
PU9	F70-15 white-letter nylon tires	16,623	$43.65
P02	Deluxe wheel trim covers	3,593	$63.20
T60	Heavy-duty battery	2,969	$15.80
UL5	Radio delete	292	no charge
U69	AM-FM radio	26,669	$178.00
U79	Stereo equipment	5,832	$283.35
VJ9	Exhaust emission label	1,968	no charge
V78	Certificate of compliance delete*	64	no charge
YE2	Special axle ratio	1	$12.65
YF5	California emissions	1,967	$15.80
YF6	Delete California emissions	1,805	no charge
ZP2	Color and trim override	654	no charge
ZP3	Special paint	48	no charge
ZQ1	Rear axle selection	1,986	$12.65
ZQ3	350/200-horsepower engine	21,352	base engine
ZR1	350/255-horsepower engine, special**	20	$1,010.05
ZR5	Three-point shoulder belts	2	no charge
ZR7	Factory delivery	16	no charge
ZV1	Statement of origin	135	no charge
ZW4	Four-speed wide-ratio manual transmission	10,804	no charge
ZX1	Export preparation	290	price unknown
ZY5	Export tire tax	8	price unknown
ZY6	Taxable tax status	246	price unknown
ZY7	Nontaxable tax status	133	price unknown
Z49	Canadian base equipment	1,234	price unknown

*For those cars exported outside the United States, option V78 deleted the certificate of compliance sticker required by federal law.

**Option ZR1 is a road racing package that includes an LT1 engine, stiffer front and rear springs, heavy-duty shock absorbers, a special Harrison aluminum radiator (part number 3007436), an M22 four-speed transmission, and a heavy-duty brake package. The brake package includes twin pin front calipers, an extra support for each front caliper, a proportioning valve, and metallic brake pads. N40 power steering, A31 power windows, PO2 wheel covers, the C50 rear window defroster, and C60 air conditioning could not be ordered with the ZR1 package. In 1972 (but not in 1970 or 1971) ZR1-equipped cars do not have a fan shroud.

1973

Code	Description	Qty	Price
1YZ37	Corvette sport coupe	25,521	$5,561.50
1YZ67	Corvette convertible	4,943	$5,398.50
A31	Power windows	14,024	$83.00
A85	Deluxe shoulder harness	788	$41.00
C07	Auxiliary hardtop	1,328	$267.00
C08	Auxiliary hardtop vinyl trim	323	$62.00
C50	Rear window defroster	4,412	$41.00
C60	Air conditioning	21,578	$452.00
J50	Vacuum power brakes	24,168	$46.00
LS4	454/275-horsepower engine	4,412	$250.00
L48	350/190-horsepower engine	20,342	standard
L82	350/250-horsepower engine	5,710	$299.00
M20	Standard four-speed manual transmission	8,833	no charge
M21	Four-speed close-ratio manual transmission	3,704	no charge
M40	Turbo Hydra-Matic transmission (with small-block engine; $97.00 extra when car is equipped with LS4 or L82 engine)	17,927	no charge
N37	Tilt-telescopic steering column	17,949	$82.00
N40	Power steering	27,872	$113.00
P02	Deluxe wheel trim covers	1,739	$62.00
QRM	GR70-15 white stripe radial tires	19,903	$32.00
QRN	GR70-15 blackwall radial tires	6,020	no charge
QRZ	GR70-15 white-letter radial tires	4,541	$45.00
T60	Heavy-duty battery	4,912	$15.00

U58	AM-FM stereo radio	12,482	$276.00
U69	AM-FM radio	17,598	$173.00
UF1	Map lite	8,186	$5.00
UL5	Radio delete	384	no charge
YF5	California emissions	3,008	$15.00
YJ8	Aluminum wheels	4	$175.00
–	Rear axle ratio selection	1,791	$12.00
–	Custom interior with leather trim	13,434	$154.00

1974

1YZ37	Corvette sport coupe	32,028	$6,001.50
1YZ67	Corvette convertible	5,474	$5,765.50
A31	Power windows	23,940	$86.00
A85	Deluxe shoulder harness	618	$41.00
C07	Auxiliary hardtop	2,612	$267.00
C08	Auxiliary hardtop with vinyl trim	367	$329.00
C50	Rear window defroster	9,322	$43.00
C60	Air conditioning	29,397	$467.00
FE7	Gymkhana suspension	1,905	$7.00
J50	Vacuum power brakes	33,306	$49.00
LS4	454/270-horsepower engine	3,494	$250.00
L48	350/195-horsepower engine	27,318	standard
L82	350/250-horsepower engine	6,690	$299.00
M20	Standard four-speed manual transmission	8,862	no charge
M21	Four-speed close-ratio manual transmission	3,494	no charge
M40	Turbo Hydra-Matic transmission	25,146	
	(no charge with small-block engine earlier in year; $97.00 extra when car is equipped with LS4 or L82 engine. Later in year, charge increased to $103.00.)		
N37	Tilt-telescopic steering column	27,700	$82.00
N41	Power steering	35,944	$117.00
QRM	GR70-15 white stripe radial tires	9,140	$32.00
QRN	GR70-15 Blackwall radial tires	4,260	no charge
QRZ	GR70-15 white-letter radial tires	24,102	$45.00
U05	Dual horns	5,258	$4.00
T60	Heavy-duty battery	4,912	$15.00
U58	AM-FM stereo radio	19,581	$276.00
U69	AM-FM radio	17,374	$173.00
UA1	Heavy-duty battery	9,169	$15.00
UF1	Map lite	16,101	$5.00
UL5	Radio delete	547	no charge
YF5	California emissions	–	$20.00
Z07	Off-road suspension and brakes*	47	$400.00
–	Rear axle ratio selection	1,219	$12.00
–	Custom interior with leather trim	19,959	$154.00

*Z07 off-road suspension and brakes is an option package available with LS4 and L82 only. It includes stiffer front and rear springs, heavy-duty shock absorbers, twin pin front calipers, an extra support for each front caliper, a proportioning valve, and metallic brake pads.

1975

1YZ37	Corvette sport coupe	33,836	$6,810.10
1YZ67	Corvette convertible	4,629	$6,550.10
A31	Power windows	28,745	$93.00
A85	Deluxe shoulder harness	646	$41.00
C07	Auxiliary hardtop	2,407	$267.00
C08	Auxiliary hardtop with vinyl trim	279	$350.00
C50	Rear window defroster	13,760	$46.00
C60	Air conditioning	31,914	$490.00
FE7	Gymkhana suspension	3,194	$7.00
J50	Vacuum power brakes	35,842	$50.00
L48	350/165-horsepower engine	36,093	standard
L82	350/205-horsepower engine	2,372	$336.00
M20	Standard four-speed manual transmission	8,935	no charge
M21	Four-speed close-ratio manual transmission (available with L82 only)	1,057	no charge
M40	Turbo Hydra-Matic transmission	28,473	
	(no charge with L48 engine; $120.00 extra when car is equipped with L82 engine)		
N37	Tilt-telescopic steering column	31,830	$82.00

N41	Power steering	37,591	$129.00
QRM	GR70-15 white stripe radial tires	5,233	$35.00
QRN	GR70-15 blackwall radial tires	2,825	no charge
QRZ	GR70-15 white-letter radial tires	30,407	$48.00
U05	Dual horns	22,011	$4.00
U58	AM-FM stereo radio	24,701	$284.00
U69	AM-FM radio	12,902	$178.00
UA1	Heavy-duty battery	16,778	$15.00
UF1	Map lite	21,676	$5.00
UL5	Radio delete	862	no charge
YF5	California emissions	3,037	$20.00
Z07	Off-road suspension and brakes*	144	$400.00
–	Rear axle ratio selection	1,969	$12.00
–	Custom interior with leather trim	–	$154.00

*Z07 off-road suspension and brakes is an option package available with L82 only. It includes stiffer front and rear springs, heavy-duty shock absorbers, twin pin front calipers, an extra support for each front caliper, a proportioning valve, and metallic brake pads.

1976

1YZ37	Corvette sport coupe	46,558	$7,604.85
A31	Power windows	38,700	$107.00
C49	Rear window defroster	24,960	$78.00
C60	Air conditioning	40,787	$523.00
FE7	Gymkhana suspension	5,368	$35.00
J50	Vacuum power brakes	46,558	$59.00
L48	350/180-horsepower engine	40,838	standard
L82	350/210-horsepower engine	5,720	$481.00
M20	Standard four-speed manual transmission	7,845	no charge
M21	Four-speed close-ratio manual transmission (available with L82 only)	2,088	no charge
M40	Turbo Hydra-Matic transmission	36,625	
	(no charge with base L48 engine; $134.00 extra when car is equipped with L82 engine)		
N37	Tilt-telescopic steering column	41,797	$95.00
N41	Power steering	46,385	$151.00
QRM	GR70-15 white stripe radial tires	3,992	$37.00
QRN	GR70-15 blackwall radial tires	2,643	no charge
QRZ	GR70-15 white-letter radial tires	39,923	$51.00
U58	AM-FM stereo radio	34,272	$281.00
U69	AM-FM radio	11,083	$187.00
UA1	Heavy-duty battery	25,909	$16.00
UF1	Map lite	35,361	$10.00
UL5	Radio delete	1,203	no charge
YF5	California emissions	3,527	$50.00
YJ8	Aluminum wheels	6,253	$299.00
–	Rear axle ratio selection	1,371	$13.00
–	Custom interior with leather trim	–	$164.00

1977

1YZ37	Corvette sport coupe	49,213	$8,647.65
A31	Power windows	44,341	$116.00
B32	Floor mats	36,763	$22.00
C49	Electro-Clear rear defogger	30,411	$84.00
C60	Air conditioning	45,249	$553.00
D35	Sport mirrors	20,206	$36.00
FE7	Gymkhana suspension	7,269	$38.00
G95	Rear axle ratio selection	972	$14.00
K30	Cruise-Master speed control	29,161	$88.00
L48	350/180-horsepower engine	43,065	standard
L82	350/210-horsepower engine	6,148	$495.00
M20	Standard four-speed manual transmission	5,922	no charge
M21	Four-speed close-ratio manual transmission (available with L82 only)	2,060	no charge
M40	Turbo Hydra-Matic transmission	41,231	
	(no charge with base L48 engine; $146.00 extra when car is equipped with L82 engine)		
NA6	High-altitude emissions	–	$22.00
N37	Tilt-telescopic steering column	46,487	$165.00
QRN	GR70-15 blackwall radial tires	2,986	no charge

205

QRZ	GR70-15 white-letter radial tires	46,227	$57.00
U58	AM-FM stereo radio	18,483	$281.00
U69	AM-FM radio	4,700	$187.00
UM2	AM-FM stereo with eight-track	24,603	$414.00
UA1	Heavy-duty battery	32,882	$17.00
UL5	Radio delete	1,427	no charge
Y54	Luggage and roof carrier	–	$73.00
YF5	California emissions	–	$70.00
YJ8	Aluminum wheels	12,646	$321.00
ZN1	Trailer package	289	$83.00
ZX2	Convenience package	40,872	$22.00

1978

1YZ87	Corvette sport coupe	40,274	$9,351.89
A31	Power windows	39,931	$130.00
AU3	Power door locks	12,187	$120.00
BZ2	25th-anniversary paint	15,283	$399.00
CC1	Removable glass roof panels	972	$349.00
C49	Electro-Clear rear defogger	30,912	$95.00
C60	Air conditioning	37,638	$605.00
D35	Sport mirrors	38,405	$40.00
FE7	Gymkhana suspension	12,590	$41.00
G95	Rear axle ratio selection	382	$15.00
K30	Cruise-Master speed control	31,608	$99.00
L48	350/185-horsepower engine	34,037	standard
L82	350/220-horsepower engine	12,739	$525.00
M20	Standard four-speed manual transmission	4,777	no charge
M21	Four-speed close-ratio manual transmission (available with L82 only)	3,385	no charge
M38	Turbo Hydra-Matic transmission	38,614	no charge
NA6	High-altitude emissions	–	$33.00
N37	Tilt-telescopic steering column	37,858	$175.00
QBS	P255/60R15 white-letter radial tires	18,296	$216.00
QGQ	P225/70R15 blackwall radial tires	2,277	no charge
QGR	P225/70R15 white-letter radial tires	26,203	$51.00
U58	AM-FM stereo radio	10,189	$286.00
U69	AM-FM radio	2,057	$199.00
U75	Power antenna	23,069	$49.00
U81	Dual rear speakers	12,340	$49.00
UM2	AM-FM stereo with eight-track	20,899	$419.00
UP6	AM-FM stereo with CB	7,138	$638.00
UA1	Heavy-duty battery	28,243	$18.00
YF5	California emissions	–	$70.00
YJ8	Aluminum wheels	28,008	$340.00
ZN1	Trailer package	972	$89.00
ZX2	Convenience group	37,222	$84.00
Z78	Limited edition pace car	6,502	$13,653.21

1979

1YZ87	Corvette sport coupe	53,807	$10,220.23
A31	Power windows	20,631	$141.00
AU3	Power door locks	9,054	$131.00
CC1	Removable glass roof panels	14,480	$365.00
C49	Electro-Clear rear defogger	41,587	$102.00
C60	Air conditioning	47,136	$635.00
D35	Sport mirrors	48,211	$45.00
D80	Front and rear spoilers	6,853	$265.00
F51	Heavy-duty shock absorbers	2,164	$33.00
FE7	Gymkhana suspension	12,321	$49.00
G95	Rear axle ratio selection	428	$19.00
K30	Cruise-Master speed control	34,445	$113.00
L48	350/195-horsepower engine	39,291	standard
L82	350/225-horsepower engine	14,516	$565.00
M20	Standard four-speed manual transmission	8,291	no charge
M21	Four-speed close-ratio manual transmission (available with L82 only)	4,062	no charge
M38	Turbo Hydra-Matic transmission	41,454	no charge
NA6	High-altitude emissions	–	$35.00
N37	Tilt-telescopic steering column	47,463	$190.00
N90	Aluminum wheels	33,741	$380.00
QBS	P255/60R15 white-letter radial tires	17,920	$226.20

QGQ	P225/70R15 blackwall radial tires	6,284	no charge
QGR	P225/70R15 white-letter radial tires	29,603	$55.00
U58	AM-FM stereo radio	9,256	$90.00
U69	AM-FM radio	6,523	$199.00
U75	Power antenna	35,730	$52.00
U81	Dual rear speakers	37,754	$52.00
UM2	AM-FM stereo with eight-track	21,435	$228.00
UN3	AM-FM stereo with cassette	12,110	$234.00
UP6	AM-FM stereo with CB	4,483	$439.00
UA1	Heavy-duty battery	3,405	$21.00
YF5	California emissions	–	$83.00
ZN1	Trailer package	1,001	$98.00
ZQ2	Power windows and door locks	28,465	$272.00
ZX2	Convenience group	41,530	$94.00

1980

1YZ87	Corvette sport coupe	40,614	$13,140.24
AU3	Power door locks	32,692	$140.00
CC1	Removable glass roof panels	19,695	$391.00
C49	Electro-Clear rear defogger	36,589	$109.00
F51	Heavy-duty shock absorbers	1,695	$35.00
FE7	Gymkhana suspension	9,907	$55.00
K30	Cruise-Master speed control	30,821	$123.00
L48	350/195-horsepower engine	32,324	standard
L82	350/225-horsepower engine	5,069	$595.00
M18	Four-speed manual transmission	5,726	no charge
M33	Turbo Hydra-Matic transmission (California)	–	no charge
MV4	Turbo Hydra-Matic transmission	34,838	no charge
N90	Aluminum wheels	34,128	$407.00
QGQ	P225/70R15 blackwall radial tires	1,266	no charge
QGR	P225/70R15 white-letter radial tires	26,208	$62.00
QXH	P255/60R15 white-letter radial tires	13,140	$426.16
U58	AM-FM stereo radio	6,138	$46.00
U69	AM-FM radio	985	no charge
U75	Power antenna	32,863	$56.00
U81	Dual rear speakers	36,650	$52.00
UA1	Heavy-duty battery	1,337	$22.00
UL5	Radio delete (credit)	201	-$126.00
UM2	AM-FM stereo with eight-track	15,708	$155.00
UN3	AM-FM stereo with cassette	15,148	$168.00
UP6	AM-FM stereo with CB	2,434	$391.00
V54	Roof panel carrier	3,755	$125.00
YF5	California emissions	3,221	$250.00
ZN1	Trailer package	796	$105.00

1981

1YY87	Corvette sport coupe	40,606	$16,258.52
AU3	Power door locks	36,322	$145.00
A42	Power driver seat	29,200	$183.00
CC1	Removable glass roof panels	20,095	$414.00
C49	Electro-Clear rear defogger	36,893	$119.00
D84	Custom two-tone exterior paint	5,352	$399.00
DG7	Electric sport mirrors	13,567	$117.00
F51	Heavy-duty shock absorbers	1,128	$37.00
FE7	Gymkhana suspension	7,803	$57.00
G92	Performance axle ratio	2,400	$20.00
K35	Cruise control	32,522	$155.00
L81	350/190-horsepower engine	40,606	standard
M18	Four-speed manual transmission	5,757	no charge
MX3	Turbo Hydra-Matic transmission	34,849	no charge
N90	Aluminum wheels	36,485	$428.00
QGQ	P225/70R15 blackwall radial tires	663	no charge
QGR	P225/70R15 white-letter radial tires	21,939	$72.00
QXH	P255/60R15 white-letter radial tires	18,004	$491.92
U58	AM-FM stereo radio	5,145	$95.00
U69	AM-FM radio	851	no charge
U75	Power antenna	32,903	$55.00
UL5	Radio delete (credit)	315	-$118.00
UM4	AM-FM stereo ETR radio with eight-track	8,262	$386.00
UM5	AM-FM stereo ETR radio with eight-track and CB	792	$712.00
UM6	AM-FM stereo ETR radio with cassette	22,892	$423.00

UN5	AM-FM stereo ETR radio with cassette and CB	2,349	$750.00
V54	Roof panel carrier	3,303	$135.00
YF5	California emissions	4,951	$46.00
ZN1	Trailer package	916	$110.00

1982

1YY87	Corvette sport coupe	18,648	$18,290.07
1YY07	Collector edition hatchback	6,759	$22,537.59
AG9	Power driver seat	22,585	$197.00
AU3	Power door locks	23,936	$155.00
CC1	Removable glass roof panels	14,763	$443.00
C49	Electro-Clear rear defogger	16,886	$129.00
D84	Custom two-tone exterior paint	4,871	$428.00
DG7	Electric sport mirrors	20,301	$125.00
FE7	Gymkhana suspension	5,457	$61.00
K35	Cruise control	24,313	$165.00
L83	350/200-horsepower engine	25,407	standard
MD8	Turbo Hydra-Matic transmission	25,407	no charge
N90	Aluminum wheels	16,844	$458.00
QGQ	P225/70R15 blackwall radial tires	405	no charge
QGR	P225/70R15 white-letter radial tires	5,932	$80.00
QXH	P255/60R15 white-letter radial tires	19,070	$542.52
U58	AM-FM stereo radio	1,533	$101.00
U75	Power antenna	15,557	$60.00
UL5	Radio delete (credit)	150	-$124.00
UM4	AM-FM stereo ETR radio with eight-track	923	$386.00
UM6	AM-FM stereo ETR radio with cassette	20,355	$423.00
UN5	AM-FM stereo ETR radio with cassette and CB ($695.00 with collector edition hatchback)	1,987	$755.00
V08	Heavy-duty cooling	6,006	$57.00
V54	Roof panel carrier	1,992	$144.00
YF5	California emissions	4,951	$46.00

ENGINE CODES

1968 HE   **327/300 base engine with Rochester Q-Jet and manual transmission**

HO	327/300	base engine with Rochester Q-Jet and automatic transmission
HP	327/300	base engine with Rochester Q-Jet, a/c, p/s, and manual transmission
HT	327/350	L79 with Rochester Q-Jet, special camshaft, and four-speed
IL	427/390	L36 with Rochester Q-Jet, hydraulic lifters and four-speed
IQ	427/390	L36 with Rochester Q-Jet, hydraulic lifters, and automatic
IM	427/400	L68 with Holley 3x2 carburetors, hydraulic lifters, and four-speed
IO	427/400	L68 with Holley 3x2 carburetors, hydraulic lifters, and automatic
IR	427/435	L71 with Holley 3x2 carburetors, mechanical lifters, and four-speed
IU	427/435	L89 with Holley 3x2 carburetors, mechanical lifters, aluminum cylinder heads, and four-speed
IT	427/430	L88 heavy-duty engine with Holley four-barrel, mechanical lifters, and M22 four-speed

1969 HY   **350/300 base engine with Rochester Q-Jet and manual transmission**

HZ	350/300	base engine with Rochester Q-Jet and automatic transmission
HW	350/350	L46 with Rochester Q-Jet, special camshaft, and four-speed
HX	350/350	L46 with Rochester Q-Jet, special camshaft, a/c, and four-speed
GD	350/350	L46 with Rochester Q-Jet, special camshaft, a/c, K66, and four-speed
LM	427/390	L36 with Rochester Q-Jet, hydraulic lifters, and four-speed
LL	427/390	L36 with Rochester Q-Jet, hydraulic lifters, and automatic
LQ	427/400	L68 with Holley 3x2 carburetors, hydraulic lifters, and four-speed
LN	427/400	L68 with Holley 3x2 carburetors, hydraulic lifters, and automatic
LO	427/430	L88 heavy-duty engine with Holley four-barrel, mechanical lifters, and M22 four-speed
LV	427/430	L88 heavy-duty engine with Holley four-barrel, mechanical lifters, and automatic
LR	427/435	L71 with Holley 3x2 carburetors, mechanical lifters, and four-speed
LX	427/435	L71 with Holley 3x2 carburetors, mechanical lifters, and automatic
LP	427/435	L89 with Holley 3x2 carburetors, mechanical lifters, aluminum cylinder heads, and four-speed
LW	427/435	L89 with Holley 3x2 carburetors, mechanical lifters, aluminum cylinder heads, and automatic
LT	427/435	L71 with Holley 3x2 carburetors, mechanical lifters, MA6, and four-speed
LU	427/435	L89 with Holley 3x2 carburetors, mechanical lifters, aluminum cylinder heads, MA6, and four-speed
ME	427/430	ZL1 performance package, aluminum block, heavy-duty engine with Holley four-barrel, mechanical lifters, and M22
MG	427/430	ZL1 performance package, aluminum block, heavy-duty engine with Holley four-barrel, mechanical lifters, and automatic
MH	427/390	L36 with Rochester Q-Jet, hydraulic lifters, K66, and four-speed

1970

CTL	350/300	base engine with Rochester Q-Jet and four-speed (earlier base engine code)
CTD	350/300	base engine with Rochester Q-Jet and four-speed (later base engine code)
CTM	350/300	base engine with Rochester Q-Jet and automatic transmission (earlier base engine code)
CTG	350/300	base engine with Rochester Q-Jet and automatic transmission (later base engine code)
CTN	350/350	L46 with Rochester Q-Jet, special camshaft, and four-speed (earlier L46 code)
CTH	350/350	L46 with Rochester Q-Jet, special camshaft, and four-speed (later L46 code)
CTO	350/350	L46 with Rochester Q-Jet, special camshaft, a/c, and four-speed (earlier L46 code)
CTJ	350/350	L46 with Rochester Q-Jet, special camshaft, a/c, and four-speed (later L46 code)
CTP	350/350	L46 with Rochester Q-Jet, special camshaft, a/c, and four-speed
CTQ	350/350	L46 with Rochester Q-Jet, special camshaft, a/c, K66, and four-speed
CTU	350/370	LT1 with Holley four-barrel, mechanical lifters, K66, and four-speed (earlier LT1 code)
CTK	350/370	LT1 with Holley four-barrel, mechanical lifters, K66, and four-speed (later LT1 code)
CTV	350/370	ZR1 performance package, LT1 engine, and M22
CZU	454/390	LS5 with Rochester Q-Jet, hydraulic lifters, and four-speed
CGW	454/390	LS5 with Rochester Q-Jet, hydraulic lifters, and automatic
CRI	454/390	LS5 with Rochester Q-Jet, hydraulic lifters, K66, and four-speed
CRJ	454/390	LS5 with Rochester Q-Jet, hydraulic lifters, K66, and automatic

1971

CJL	350/270	base engine with Rochester Q-Jet and four-speed
CGT	350/270	base engine with Rochester Q-Jet and automatic transmission (earlier base engine code)
CJK	350/270	base engine with Rochester Q-Jet and automatic transmission (later base engine code)
CGZ	350/330	LT1 with Holley four-barrel, mechanical lifters, and four-speed
CGY	350/330	ZR1 performance package, LT1 engine, and M22

CPH 454/365 LS5 with Rochester Q-Jet, hydraulic lifters, and four-speed
CPJ 454/365 LS5 with Rochester Q-Jet, hydraulic lifters, and automatic
CPW 454/425 LS6 with Holley four-barrel, mechanical lifters, aluminum cylinder heads, and M22 four-speed
CPX 454/425 LS6 with Holley four-barrel, mechanical lifters, aluminum cylinder heads, and automatic

1972
CKW 350/200 base engine with Rochester Q-Jet and four-speed
CDH 350/200 base engine with Rochester Q-Jet, NB2, and four-speed
CKX 350/200 base engine with Rochester Q-Jet and automatic
CDJ 350/200 base engine with Rochester Q-Jet, NB2, and automatic
CKY 350/255 LT1 with Holley four-barrel, mechanical lifters, and four-speed
CRT 350/255 LT1 with Holley four-barrel, mechanical lifters, K19, and four-speed
CKZ 350/255 ZR1 performance package, LT1 engine, and M22
CPH 454/270 LS5 with Rochester Q-Jet, hydraulic lifters, and four-speed
CPJ 454/270 LS5 with Rochester Q-Jet, hydraulic lifters, and automatic
CSR 454/270 LS5 with Rochester Q-Jet, hydraulic lifters, K19, and four-speed
CSS 454/270 LS5 with Rochester Q-Jet, hydraulic lifters, K19, and automatic

1973
CKZ 350/190 L48 with four-speed
CLA 350/190 L48 with automatic
CLB 350/190 L48 with four-speed (California)
CLC 350/190 L48 with automatic (California)
CLD 350/250 L82 with four-speed
CLH 350/250 L82 with automatic (California)
CLR 350/250 L82 with four-speed
CLS 350/250 L82 with four-speed (California)
CWM 454/275 LS4 with four-speed
CWR 454/275 LS4 with automatic
CWS 454/275 LS4 with automatic (California)
CWT 454/275 LS4 with four-speed (California)

1974
CKZ 350/195 L48 with four-speed
CLA 350/195 L48 with automatic
CLB 350/195 L48 with four-speed (California)
CLC 350/195 L48 with automatic (California)
CLD 350/250 L82 with automatic (federal and some California)
CLH 350/250 L82 with automatic (California)
CLR 350/250 L82 with four-speed (federal and some California)
CLS 350/250 L82 with four-speed (California)
CWM 454/270 LS4 with four-speed (federal and some California)
CWR 454/270 LS4 with automatic
CWS 454/270 LS4 with automatic (California)
CWT 454/270 LS4 with four-speed (California)

1975
CHA 350/165 L48 with four-speed (federal)
CHB 350/165 L48 with automatic (federal)
CHC 350/205 L82 with four-speed (federal)
CHR 350/205 L82 with automatic (federal and California)
CHU 350/165 L48 with four-speed (federal)
CHZ 350/165 L48 with automatic (federal)
CKC 350/205 L82 with automatic (federal)
CRJ 350/165 L48 with four-speed (federal)
CRK 350/165 L48 with automatic (federal)
CRL 350/205 L82 with four-speed (federal)
CRM 350/205 L82 with automatic (federal)
CUA 350/165 L48 with four-speed (federal)
CUB 350/165 L48 with four-speed (federal)

CUD 350/205 L82 with four-speed (federal)
CUT 350/205 L82 with four-speed (federal)

1976
CHC 350/210 L82 with four-speed (federal)
CKC 350/210 L82 with Turbo-Hydra-Matic 400 (federal)
CKW 350/180 L48 with four-speed (federal)
CKX 350/180 L48 with Turbo-Hydra-Matic 350 (federal)
CLM (unverified usage)
CLR (unverified usage)
CLS 350/180 L48 with Turbo-Hydra-Matic 350 (California)

1977
CHD 350/180 L48 with Turbo-Hydra-Matic 350 (California)
CKD 350/180 L48 with Turbo-Hydra-Matic 350 (high altitude)
CKZ 350/180 L48 with four-speed (federal)
CLA 350/180 L48 with Turbo-Hydra-Matic 350 (federal)
CLB 350/180 L48 with Turbo-Hydra-Matic 350 (high altitude; used in early production)
CLC 350/180 L48 with Turbo-Hydra-Matic 350 (California; used in early production)
CLD 350/210 L82 with four-speed (federal)
CLF 350/210 L82 with Turbo-Hydra-Matic 400 (federal)

1978
CHW 350/185 L48 with four-speed (federal)
CLM 350/185 L48 with Turbo-Hydra-Matic 350 (federal)
CLR 350/175 L48 with Turbo-Hydra-Matic 350 (California)
CLS 350/175 L48 with Turbo-Hydra-Matic 350 (high altitude)
CMR 350/220 L82 with four-speed (federal)
CMS 350/220 L82 with Turbo-Hydra-Matic 350 (federal)
CUT 350/185 L48 with Turbo-Hydra-Matic 350 (federal)

1979
ZAA 350/195 L48 with four-speed (federal; early)
ZAB 350/195 L48 with Turbo-Hydra-Matic 350 (federal; early)
ZAC 350/195 L48 with Turbo-Hydra-Matic 350 (California; early)
ZAD 350/195 L48 with Turbo-Hydra-Matic 350 (high altitude)
ZAF 350/195 L48 with four-speed (federal)
ZAH 350/195 L48 with Turbo-Hydra-Matic 350 (federal)
ZAJ 350/195 L48 with Turbo-Hydra-Matic 350 (California)
ZBA 350/225 L82 with four-speed (federal)
ZBB 350/225 L82 with Turbo-Hydra-Matic 350 (federal)

1980
ZAK 350/190 L48 with Turbo-Hydra-Matic 350 (federal)
ZAM 350/190 L48 with four-speed (federal)
ZBC 350/230 L82 engine with Turbo-Hydra-Matic 350 (federal)
ZBD 350/230 L82 engine with four-speed (federal)
ZCA 305/180 LG4 with Turbo-Hydra-Matic 350 (California)

1981
ZDA 350/190 L81 with four-speed (federal)
ZDB 350/190 L81 with Turbo-Hydra-Matic 350 (California)
ZDC 350/190 L81 with four-speed (California)
ZDD 350/190 L81 with Turbo-Hydra-Matic 350 (federal)

1982
ZBA 350/200 L83 with Turbo-Hydra-Matic 700-R4 (federal)
ZBC 350/200 L83 with Turbo-Hydra-Matic 700-R4 (California; early)
ZBN 350/200 L83 with Turbo-Hydra-Matic 700-R4 (California)

TRANSMISSION CODES

1968
S	Saginaw three-speed
P	Muncie four-speed
K	Turbo Hydra-Matic 400 with 327 engine
L	Turbo Hydra-Matic 400 with 427 engine

1969
S	Saginaw three-speed
P	Muncie four-speed
A	M20 Muncie four-speed with wide gear ratio
B	M21 Muncie four-speed with close gear ratio
C	M22 Muncie heavy-duty four-speed with close-gear ratio
K	Turbo Hydra-Matic 400 with 350 engine
L	Turbo Hydra-Matic 400 with hydraulic lifter 427 engine
Y	Turbo Hydra-Matic 400 with mechanical lifter 427 engine

1970
P	Muncie four-speed
A	M20 Muncie four-speed with wide gear ratio
B	M21 Muncie four-speed with close gear ratio
C	M22 Muncie heavy-duty four-speed with close gear ratio
K	Turbo Hydra-Matic 400 with 350 engine
S	Turbo Hydra-Matic 400 with 454 engine

1971
P	Muncie four-speed
A	M20 Muncie four-speed with wide gear ratio
B	M21 Muncie four-speed with close gear ratio
C	M22 Muncie heavy-duty four-speed with close gear ratio
K	Turbo Hydra-Matic 400 with 350 engine
S	Turbo Hydra-Matic 400 with LS5 454 engine
Y	Turbo Hydra-Matic 400 with LS6 454 engine

1972
P	Muncie four-speed
A	M20 Muncie four-speed with wide gear ratio
B	M21 Muncie four-speed with close gear ratio
C	M22 Muncie heavy-duty four-speed with close gear ratio
K	Turbo Hydra-Matic 400 with 350 engine
S	Turbo Hydra-Matic 400 with 454 engine

1973
P	Muncie four-speed
A	M20 Muncie four-speed with wide gear ratio
B	M21 Muncie four-speed with close gear ratio
CK	Turbo Hydra-Matic 400 with L48 350 engine
CY	Turbo Hydra-Matic 400 with L82 350 engine
CS	Turbo Hydra-Matic 400 with 454 engine

1974
P	Muncie four-speed
A	M20 Muncie four-speed with wide gear ratio
B	M21 Muncie four-speed with close gear ratio
W	Warner four-speed
CK	Turbo Hydra-Matic 400 with L48 350 engine
CZ	Turbo Hydra-Matic 400 with L82 350 engine
CS	Turbo Hydra-Matic 400 with 454 engine

1975
W	Warner four-speed
CK	Turbo Hydra-Matic 400 with L48 350 engine
CZ	Turbo Hydra-Matic 400 with L82 350 engine

1976
W	Warner four-speed
AM	Turbo Hydra-Matic 350 with L48 350 engine
XH	Turbo Hydra-Matic 350 with L48 350 engine
CZ	Turbo Hydra-Matic 400 with L82 350 engine

1977
W	Warner four-speed
AM	Turbo Hydra-Matic 350 with L48 350 engine
CB	Turbo Hydra-Matic 400 with L82 350 engine

1978
S6	Warner four-speed, wide ratio (2.85:1 first gear)
ZU	Warner four-speed, wide ratio (2.64:1 first gear)
ZW	Warner four-speed, close ratio (2.43:1 first gear)
5WB	Turbo Hydra-Matic 350
5TL	Turbo Hydra-Matic 350

1979
UH	Warner four-speed, wide ratio (2.64:1 first gear)
UK	Warner four-speed, close ratio (2.43:1 first gear)
TB	Turbo Hydra-Matic 350
WB	Turbo Hydra-Matic 350

1980
ZJ	Warner four-speed, wide ratio (2.88:1 first gear)
JC	Turbo Hydra-Matic 350 with LG4 305 engine
TW	Turbo Hydra-Matic 350 with 35o engine

1981
CC	Warner four-speed, wide ratio (2.88:1 first gear)
8JD	Turbo Hydra-Matic 350

1982
YA	Turbo Hydra-Matic 700-R4

DIFFERENTIAL CODES

1968 and 1969s Manufactured through approximately August 1969

Code	Ratio	Type
AK	3.36:1	standard non-Posi-Traction with 327 and 350
AL	3.08:1	Posi-Traction with 327 and 350
AM	3.36:1	Posi-Traction with 327 and 350
AN	3.55:1	Posi-Traction with 327 and 350
AO	3.70:1	Posi-Traction with 327 and 350
AP	4.11:1	Posi-Traction with 327 and 350
AS	3.70:1	standard non-Posi-Traction with 327 and 350
AT	3.08:1	heavy-duty Posi-Traction with 427
AU	3.36:1	heavy-duty Posi-Traction with 427
AV	3.08:1	Posi-Traction with 427
AW	3.08:1	heavy-duty Posi-Traction with 427
AY	2.73:1	heavy-duty Posi-Traction with 427 and automatic
AZ	3.55:1	heavy-duty Posi-Traction with 427
FA	3.70:1	heavy-duty Posi-Traction with 427
FB	4.11:1	heavy-duty Posi-Traction with 427
FC	4.56:1	heavy-duty Posi-Traction with 427

1969s Manufactured after approximately August 1969 and 1970

Code	Ratio	Type
CAK	3.36:1	standard non-Posi-Traction with 350
CAL	3.08:1	standard non-Posi-Traction with 350
CAM	3.36:1	Posi-Traction with 350
CAN	3.55:1	standard non-Posi-Traction with 350
CAO	3.70:1	Posi-Traction with 350
CAP	4.11:1	standard non-Posi-Traction with 350
CAS	3.70:1	standard non-Posi-Traction with 350
CAT	3.08:1	heavy-duty Posi-Traction with 454
CAU	3.36:1	heavy-duty Posi-Traction with 454
CAV	3.08:1	standard non-Posi-Traction with 454
CAW	3.08:1	standard non-Posi-Traction with 454
CAX	3.36:1	heavy-duty Posi-Traction with 454
CAY	2.73:1	heavy-duty Posi-Traction with 454 and automatic
CAZ	3.55:1	heavy-duty Posi-Traction with 454
CFA	3.70:1	Posi-Traction with 454
CFB	4.11:1	heavy-duty Posi-Traction with 454
CFC	4.56:1	heavy-duty Posi-Traction with 454
CLR	3.36:1	standard non-Posi-Traction with 454

1971

Code	Ratio	Type
AA	3.55:1	Posi-Traction
AB	3.70:1	Posi-Traction
AC	4.11:1	Posi-Traction
AD	4.56:1	Posi-Traction
AW	3.08:1	Posi-Traction
AX	3.36:1	Posi-Traction
LR	3.36:1	Posi-Traction

1972

Code	Ratio	Type
AA	3.55:1	Posi-Traction
AB	3.70:1	Posi-Traction
AC	4.11:1	Posi-Traction
AX	3.36:1	Posi-Traction
LR	3.36:1	Posi-Traction

1973 and 1974

Code	Ratio	Type
AA	3.55:1	Posi-Traction
AB	3.70:1	Posi-Traction
AC	4.11:1	Posi-Traction
AW	3.08:1	Posi-Traction
AX	3.36:1	Posi-Traction
LR	3.36:1	Posi-Traction

1975

Code	Ratio	Type
AA	3.55:1	Posi-Traction
AB	3.70:1	Posi-Traction
AC	4.11:1	Posi-Traction
AY	2.73:1	Posi-Traction
AW	3.08:1	Posi-Traction
AX	3.36:1	Posi-Traction
LR	3.36:1	Posi-Traction

1976 and 1977

Code	Ratio	Type
OA	3.08:1	Posi-Traction
OD	3.36:1	Posi-Traction
LR	3.36:1	Posi-Traction
OB	3.55:1	Posi-Traction
OC	3.70:1	Posi-Traction

1978

Code	Ratio	Type
OK	3.08:1	Posi-Traction
OM	3.36:1	Posi-Traction
OH	3.55:1	Posi-Traction
OJ	3.70:1	Posi-Traction

1979

Code	Ratio	Type
OM	3.36:1	Posi-Traction
OH	3.55:1	Posi-Traction
OJ	3.70:1	Posi-Traction

1980

Code	Ratio	Type
OF	3.07:1	Posi-Traction
OH	3.07:1	Posi-Traction

1981

Code	Ratio	Type
OJ	2.87:1	Posi-Traction with automatic
OK	2.72:1	Posi-Traction with four-speed

1982

Code	Ratio	Type
OA	2.72:1	Posi-Traction with standard wheels
OF	2.87:1	Posi-Traction with aluminum wheels

ENGINE BLOCK CASTING NUMBERS

Casting number 1968	Description	
3914460	early 327/300	
3914678	327	
3916321	early 427	
3935439	late 427	

1969

Casting number	Description
3932386	very early 350
3932388	possible 350 usage
3956618	mid-year 350
3970010	late 350
3935439	early 427
3955270	early 427
3963512	late 427
3946052	ZL1 aluminum block

1970 and 1971

Casting number	Description
3970010	350
3963512	454

1972–1974

Casting number	Description
3970010	350
3970014	late 1972 and early 1973 350
3999289	454

1975–1977

Casting number	Description
3970010	350

1978

Casting number	Description
3970010	350
376450	350
460703	350

1979

Casting number	Description
3970010	350
14016379	late 350

1980

Casting number	Description
3970010	350
14010207	350
4715111	LG4 California 305

1981 and 1982

Casting number	Description
14010207	350

CYLINDER HEAD CASTING NUMBERS

Casting Number	Description
1968	
3917291	327/300 and 327/350
3917292	327/350
3917215	427/390 and 427/400
3919840	427/435
3919842	aluminum L89 427/435 and L88 427/430
1969	
3927186	350/300 and 350/350
3927187	350/350
3947041	350/300
3931063	427/390 and 427/400
3919840	427/435
3919842	aluminum L89 427/435
3946074	aluminum ZL1 427/430 and L88 427/430
1970	
3927186	350/300, 350/350, and 350/370
3927187	350/350
3973414	350/370
3964290	454

Casting Number	Description
1971	
3973487	350
3993820	454/365
3994026	LS6 454/425
3946074	LS6 454/425
1972	
3998993	350/200
3998916	350/255
3973487(x)	later 350/200 and 350/255
3999241	454
1973	
3998993	L48 350
333881	L48 350
333882	L48 350
330545	L82 350
353049	454

Casting Number	Description
1974	
333881	L48 350
333882	L48 350
333882	L82 350
336781	454
1975 and 1976	
333882	350
1977	
376450	L48 350
333882	L48 350 and L82 350
1978–1982	
462624	350
14914416	1980 LG4 California 305

INTAKE MANIFOLD CASTING NUMBERS

Casting Number	Description
1968	
3919803	327, cast iron
3919849	427/390, aluminum
3919850	early 427/400, aluminum
3937795	late 427/400, aluminum
3885069	L88 427/430, aluminum (possible usage)
3933198	L88 427/430, aluminum (possible usage)
3919852	early 427/435, aluminum
3937797	late 427/435, aluminum
1969	
3927184	350, cast iron
3947801	427/390, aluminum
3937795	427/400, aluminum
3937797	427/435, aluminum
3933198	L88 427/430 and ZL1 427/430, aluminum
1970	
3965577	350/300 and 350/350, cast iron
3972110	LT1 350/370, aluminum
3955287	454/390, aluminum
3969802	454/390, aluminum
1971	
3973469	350/270, cast iron
3959594	LT1 350/330, aluminum
3955287	454/365, cast iron
3967474	LS6 454/425, aluminum
3963569	LS6 454/425, aluminum
1972	
6263751	350/200, cast iron
3959594	LT1 350/255, aluminum
6263753	454/270, cast iron

Casting Number	Description
1973	
3997770	L48 350/190, cast iron
3997771	L48 350/190 and L82 350/250, cast iron
353015454, cast iron	
1974	
340261	L48 350/195 and L82 350/250, cast iron
353015	454, cast iron
336789	454, cast iron
1975–1977	
346249	350, cast iron
1978	
346249	L48 350, cast iron
458520	L82 350, aluminum
1979	
14007376	L48 350, cast iron
14014433	late L48 350, cast iron
458520	early L82 350, aluminum
14007378	late L82 350, aluminum
1980	
14014432	L48 350, L82 350, and LG4 305, aluminum
1981	
14033058	L81 350, aluminum
1982	
14031372	L83 350, aluminum

EXHAUST MANIFOLD CASTING NUMBERS

Left-side casting number	Right-side casting number	Description
1968		
3872765	3872778	327
3880827	3880828	427
1969		
3872765	3932461	350
3880827	3880828	427
1970		
3846559	3932465	early 350/300 and 350/350
3846559	3989036	late 350/300 and 350/350
3872765	3932461	LT1 350/370
3969869	3880828	454
1971		
3846559	3989036	350/270
3872765	3932461	LT1 350/330
3880869	3880828	LS5 454/365 and LS6 454/425
3969869	3880828	LS5 454/365 and LS6 454/425

1972		
3932461	3989036	early 350/200
3932461	3932461	late 350/200 and LT1 350/255
386711	386711	LT1 350/255
3969869	3880828	454
1973–1974		
3932461	3932461	350
3969869	3880828	454
1975–1979		
3932461	3932461	350
1980		
3932461	3932461	L48 350/190 and L82 350/230
14037671-W	14037672-W	LG4 305 (tubular stainless steel)
1981–1982		
14037671-W	14037672-W	350 (tubular stainless steel)

CARBURETORS AND CROSS-FIRE INJECTION PART NUMBERS

Description	Manufacturer number	Chevrolet number
1968		
327/300, four-speed	Rochester MV4	7028207
327/300, automatic	Rochester MV4	7028208
327/350, four-speed	Rochester MV4	7028219
427/390, four-speed	Rochester MV4	7028209
427/390, automatic	Rochester MV4	7028216
early 427/400, four-speed, center	Holley R4055A	3925517
late 427/400, four-speed, center	Holley R4055-1A	3940929
427/400, four-speed, ends	Holley R3659A	3902353
early 427/400, automatic, center	Holley R4056A	3902516
late 427/400, automatic, center	Holley R4055-1A	3940930
427/400, automatic, ends	Holley R3659A	3902353
early L71 and L89 427/435, center	Holley R4055A	3925517
late L71 and L89 427/435, center	Holley R4055-1A	3940929
L71 and L89 427/435, ends	Holley R3659A	3902353
L88 427/430	Holley R4054A	3925519
1969		
350/300, four-speed	Rochester MV4	7029203
350/300, automatic	Rochester MV4	7029202
350/350, four-speed	Rochester MV4	7029207
427/390, four-speed	Rochester MV4	7029215
427/390, automatic	Rochester MV4	7029204
427/400, four-speed, center	Holley R4055-1A	3940929
427/400, four-speed, ends	Holley R3659A	3902353
427/400, automatic, center	Holley R4055-1A	3940930
427/400, automatic, ends	Holley R3659A	3902353
L71 and L89 427/435, center	Holley R4055-1A	3940929
L71 and L89 427/435, ends	Holley R3659A	3902353
L88 427/430	Holley R4054A	3925519
1970		
early 350/300, four-speed	Rochester MV4	7040203
late 350/300, four-speed	Rochester MV4	7040213
early 350/300, automatic	Rochester MV4	7040202
late 350/300, automatic	Rochester MV4	7040212
early 350/300, four-speed with ECS	Rochester MV4	7040503
late 350/300, four-speed with ECS	Rochester MV4	7040513
350/300, automatic with ECS	Rochester MV4	7040502
350/350, four-speed	Rochester MV4	7029207
350/350, four-speed with ECS	Rochester MV4	7029507
LT1 350/370, four-speed	Holley R4555A	3972121
LT1 350/370, four-speed with ECS	Holley R4489A	3972123
454/390, four-speed	Rochester MV4	7040205
454/390, automatic	Rochester MV4	7040204
454/390, four-speed with ECS	Rochester MV4	7040505
454/390, automatic with ECS	Rochester MV4	7040504
1971		
350/270, four-speed	Rochester MV4	7040213
350/270, automatic	Rochester MV4	7040212
LT1 350/330, four-speed	Holley R4801A	3989021
454/365, four-speed	Rochester MV4	7040205
454/365, automatic	Rochester MV4	7040204
LS6 454/425, four-speed	Holley R4803A	3986195
LS6 454/425, automatic	Holley R 4802A	3986196
1972		
350/200, four-speed	Rochester MV4	7042203
350/200, four-speed with NB2	Rochester MV4	7042903
350/200, automatic	Rochester MV4	7042202
350/200, automatic with NB2	Rochester MV4	7042902
LT1 350/255, four-speed	Holley R6239A	3999263
454, four-speed	Rochester MV4	7042217
454, automatic	Rochester MV4	7042216
1973		
350/190, four-speed	Rochester MV4	7043203
350/190, automatic	Rochester MV4	7043202
350/250, four-speed	Rochester MV4	7043213
350/250, automatic	Rochester MV4	7043212
454, four-speed	Rochester MV4	7043201
454, automatic	Rochester MV4	7043200

1974

350/195, four-speed	Rochester MV4	7044207
350/195, automatic	Rochester MV4	7044206
350/250, four-speed	Rochester MV4	7044211
350/250, automatic (California)	Rochester MV4	7044506
350/250, four-speed (California)	Rochester MV4	7044507
350/250, automatic	Rochester MV4	7044210
454, four-speed	Rochester MV4	7044221
454, automatic	Rochester MV4	7044225
454, automatic (California)	Rochester MV4	7044505

1975

350/165, four-speed	Rochester M4MC	7045223
350/165, automatic	Rochester M4MC	7045222
350/205, four-speed	Rochester M4MC	7045211
350/205, automatic	Rochester M4MC	7045210

1976

350/180, four-speed	Rochester M4MC	17056207
350/180, automatic	Rochester M4MC	17056208
350/180, four-speed (California)	Rochester M4MC	17056507
350/180, automatic (California)	Rochester M4MC	17056506
350/210, four-speed	Rochester M4MC	17056211
350/210, automatic	Rochester M4MC	17056210
350/210, automatic with a/c	Rochester M4MC	17056506

1977

350/180, four-speed	Rochester M4MC	17057203
350/180, automatic	Rochester M4MC	17057202
350/180, automatic with a/c	Rochester M4MC	17057204
350/180, automatic (California)	Rochester M4MC	17057502
350/180, auto, a/c (California)	Rochester M4MC	17057504
350/180, automatic and NA6	Rochester M4MC	17057582
350/180, automatic, a/c and NA6	Rochester M4MC	17057584
350/210, four-speed	Rochester M4MC	17057211
350/210, automatic	Rochester M4MC	17057210
350/210, automatic with a/c	Rochester M4MC	17057228
350/210, automatic (California)	Rochester M4MC	17057510

1978

350/185, four-speed	Rochester M4MC	17058203
350/185, automatic	Rochester M4MC	17058202
early 350/180, automatic with a/c	Rochester M4MC	17058204
late 350/180, automatic with a/c	Rochester M4MC	17058206
350/175, automatic (California)	Rochester M4MC	17058502
350/175, auto, a/c (California)	Rochester M4MC	17058504
350/175, automatic and NA6	Rochester M4MC	17058582
350/175, automatic, a/c and NA6	Rochester M4MC	17058584
350/220, four-speed	Rochester M4MC	17058211
350/220, automatic	Rochester M4MC	17058210
350/220, automatic with a/c	Rochester M4MC	17058228

1979

350/195, four-speed	Rochester M4MC	17059203
350/195, automatic	Rochester M4MC	17059217
350/195, automatic	Rochester M4MC	17059202
350/195, automatic (California)	Rochester M4MC	17059502
350/195, automatic with a/c	Rochester M4MC	17059216
350/195, automatic, a/c (California)	Rochester M4MC	17059504
350/195, automatic, a/c (California)	Rochester M4MC	17059507
350/195, automatic and NA6	Rochester M4MC	17059582
350/195, automatic, a/c, and NA6	Rochester M4MC	17059584
350/225, four-speed	Rochester M4MC	17059211
350/225, automatic	Rochester M4MC	17059210
350/225, automatic with a/c	Rochester M4MC	17059228

1980

350/190, four-speed	Rochester M4ME	17080207
350/190, automatic	Rochester M4ME	17080204
350/180, automatic (California)	Rochester E4ME	17080504
350/180, automatic (California)	Rochester E4ME	17080517
350/230, four-speed	Rochester M4ME	–
350/230, automatic	Rochester M4ME	17080228

1981

350/190, four-speed	Rochester E4ME	17081217
350/190, automatic (California)	Rochester E4ME	17081218
350/190, automatic	Rochester E4ME	17081228

1982

Cross-fire injection front	Rochester 400	17082053
Cross-fire injection rear	Rochester 400	17082052

DISTRIBUTOR PART NUMBERS

Part Number	Description
1968	
1111194	327/300
1111293	427/390 and 427/400
1111294	427/390 and 427/400 with K66
1111295	L88 427/430 with K66
1111296	L71 and L89 427/435 with K66
1111438	327/350
1111441	early 327/350 with K66
1111475	late 327/350 with K66
1969	
1111490	350/300
1111491	350/350 with K66
1111493	350/350
1111926	427/390 and 427/400

Part Number	Description
1111927	L88 427/430 with K66
1111928	L71 and L89 427/435 with K66
1111954	427/390 and 427/400 with K66
1970	
1111490	early 350/300
1112020	late 350/300
1111491	LT1 350/370 with K66
1111493	early 350/350
1112021	late 350/350
1111464	454/390
1971	
1112050	350/270
1112038	LT1 350/330 with K66
1111493	early 350/350

1112051	454/365
1112053	LS6 454/425 with automatic and K66
1112076	LS6 454/425 with four-speed and K66

1972

1112050	350/200
1112101	LT1 350/255 with K66
1112051	454/270

1973

1112098	350/190
1112130	L82 350/250 with four-speed
1112150	L82 350/250 with automatic
1112051	454/270

1974

1112247	L48 350/195
1112544	L48 350/195 with four-speed and YF5
1112850	L48 350/195 with four-speed and YF5
1112851	L48 350/195 with automatic and YF5
1112150	L82 350/250 with four-speed
1112853	L82 350/250 with automatic
1112526	454/270
1112114	454/270

1975

1112888	L48 350/165
1112880	L48 350/165 with YF5
1112883	early L82 350/205
1112979	late L82 350/205

1976

1112888	L48 350/180
1112905	L48 350/180 with automatic and YF5
1103200	L82 350/210 with four-speed
1112979	L82 350/210 with automatic

1977

1103246	L48 350/180
1103248	L48 350/180 with automatic and YF5
1103256	L82 350/210

1978

1103337	L48 350/185 with four-speed
1103353	L48 350/185 with automatic
1103285	L48 350/175 with YF5
1103291	L82 350/220

1979

1103302	L48 350/195 with four-speed
1103353	L48 350/195 with automatic
1103285	L48 350/195 with YF5
1103291	L82 350/225

1980

1103287	L48 350/190 with four-speed
1103352	L48 350/190 with automatic
1103353 emissions	L48 350/190 with automatic and high-altitude
1103285	L48 305/180 with automatic and YF5
1103291	L82 350/230 with four-speed
1103435	L82 350/230 with automatic

1981

1103443	L81 350/190

1982

1103479	L83 350/200

IGNITION COIL PART NUMBERS

Part Number	Description
1968	
1115270	327/300 and 327/350 with standard ignition
1115207	early 327/350 with K66
1115272	327/350 with K66
1115287	427/390 and 427/400 with standard ignition
1115263	427 with K66
1969	
1115270	350 with standard ignition
1115272	350 with K66
1115287	427/390 and 427/400 with standard ignition
1115263	427 with K66
1970	
1115270	350/300 and 350/350 with standard ignition
1115272	350/350, 350/370, and 454/390 with K66
1115287	454/390 with standard ignition

1971	
1115270	350/270 with standard ignition
1115272	350/330 with K66
1115287	454/365 with standard ignition
1115263	454/425 with K66
1972–1974	
1115270	350
1115287	454

ALTERNATOR PART NUMBERS

Part Number	Description
1968	
1100693	37 amp, all cars without K66 or C60
1100696	42 amp, all engines with K66
1100750	61 amp, all cars with C60
1969	
1100859	42 amp, all 350s without K66 or C60
1100833	42 amp, all 427s without K66 or C60
1100825	61 amp, all cars with C60 or K66
1100884	61 amp, 350/300 with C60
1100882	61 amp, L88 and L89 with K66
1970	
1100901	42 amp, 350/300 without C60
1100900	42 amp, 350/350 and 454/390 without C60
1100884	61 amp, 350/370 and all cars with C60
1971	
1100950	42 amp, 350/330 and 350/270 without C60
1100543	42 amp, 454/425 and 454/365 without C60
1100544	61 amp, all cars with C60
1972	
1100950	42 amp, 350/330 and 350/200 without C60
1100543	42 amp, 454/270 without C60
1100544	61 amp, all cars with C60
1973	
1100950	42 amp, L48 and L82 without C60, and LS4 without N40
1102353	42 amp, LS4 with N40
1100544	61 amp, all cars with C60
1974	
1102394	37 amp, L48 (possible usage)
1100950	42 amp, L48 and L82 without C60, and LS4 without N40
1102353	42 amp, LS4 with N40
1100544	61 amp, all cars with C60 or UA1
1975	
1102483	37 amp, early L48 (possible usage)
1102394	37 amp, later L48 (possible usage)
1100950	42 amp, L48 and early L82 without C60
1102484	42 amp, later L82

Part Number	Description
1100544	61 amp, early cars with C60
1100597	61 amp, early cars with UA1
1102474	61 amp, later cars with C60
1102480	61 amp, later cars with UA1
1976	
1102484	42 amp, all cars without C60
1102474	61 amp, all cars with C60
1977	
1102394	37 amp, L48 (possible usage)
1102484	42 amp, L48 and L82 without C60
1102474	61 amp, early cars with C60 or C49
1102909	63 amp mid-production with C60 or C49
1102908	63 amp, later cars with C60 or C49
1978	
1102394	37 amp, L48 (possible usage)
1102484	42 amp, L48 and L82 without C60
1102908	63 amp, all cars with C60 or C49
1979	
1102394	37 amp, L48 (possible usage)
1102484	42 amp, L48 and L82 without C60
1102474	61 amp, all cars with C60 but without C49 and UA1
1102908	63 amp, all cars with C60 or C49
1101041	70 amp, all cars with C60 and C49 or UA1
1980	
1102474	61 amp, early cars with C60 but without C49 and UA1
1103122	63 amp, mid-production cars with C60 but without C49 and UA1
1103103	63 amp, late cars with C60 but without C49 and UA1
1101041	70 amp, early cars with C60 and C49 or UA1
1101075	70 amp, late cars with C60 and C49 or UA1
1981	
1103103	63 amp, all cars with C60 but without C49
1101075	70 amp, all cars with C60 and C49
1982	
1103103	63 amp, all coupes with C60 but without C49
1103091	63 amp, all coupes with C60 but without C49 (possible usage)
1101071	70 amp, all hatchbacks and coupes with C60 and C49 (possible usage)
1101075	70 amp, all hatchbacks and coupes with C60 and C49

STARTER MOTOR PART NUMBERS

Part Number	Description
1968	
1108361	327 with manual
1108338	327 with automatic
1107365	all 427 except L88
1108351	early L88 with M22 four-speed
1108400	later L88 with M22 four-speed
1969	
1108361	early 350 with manual
1108338	350 with manual
1108427	350 with automatic

Part Number	Description
1107365	early 427 (possible usage)
1108351	427 with M22 four-speed
1108400	427 except L88 with M22 four-speed
1970	
1108338	350 with four-speed
1108381	ZR1 with M22 four-speed
1108418	350 with four-speed (possible usage)
1108430	350 with automatic
1108400	454 with four-speed
1108429	454 with automatic

APPENDIX N

1971
1108338	early 350 with four-speed
1108418	later 350 with four-speed
1108381	ZR1 with M22 four-speed
1108430	350 with automatic
1108400	454 with four-speed
1108429	454 with automatic

1972
1108418	350 with four-speed
1108381	ZR1 with M22 four-speed
1108430	350 with automatic
1108400	454 with four-speed
1108429	454 with automatic

1973–1974
1108418	350 with four-speed
1108430	350 with automatic
1108400	454 with four-speed
1108429	454 with automatic

1975
1108418	early 350 with four-speed
1108430	early 350 with automatic
1108775	later 350 with four-speed
1108776	later 350 with automatic

1976
1108775	350 with four-speed
1108776	350 with automatic

1977
1108775	early 350 with four-speed
1109052	350 with automatic
1109059	later 350 with four-speed

1978
1109052	early 350 with automatic
1109059	early 350 with four-speed
1109065	later 350 with automatic
1109067	later 350 with four-speed

1979
1109065	early 350 with automatic
1109067	350 with four-speed
1998217	later 350 with automatic

1980
1109059	350 with four-speed
1998222	350 with automatic (possible usage)
1998225	350 with four-speed (possible usage)
1998217	350 with automatic

1981
1109067	350 with four-speed
1998217	350 with automatic

1982
1998241	350 with automatic

APPENDIX O

HORN AND HORN RELAY PART NUMBERS

Year	Low-note part number	High-note part number	Relay number
1968 (early)	9000245	9000246	1115837
1968 (late)	9000245	9000246	1115862
1969 (early)	9000245	9000246	1115862
1969 (late)	9000245	9000246	1115890
1970	9000245	9000246	1115890
1971	9000245	–	1115889
1972	9000032	–	3996283
1973	9000032	–	3996283
1974 (early)	9000032	–	329820
1974 (late)	9000049	9000038	344813
1975 (early)	9000049	9000038	344813
1975 (late)	9000033	9000106	344813
1976	9000144	9000143	344813
1977	9000144	9000143	344813
1978	9000144	9000143	344813
1979	9000144	9000143	344813
1980	9000144	9000192	344813
1981	9000144	9000192	25505674
1982	9000176	9000203	25505674

APPENDIX P

WINDSCREEN WIPER MOTOR NUMBERS

Year	Part number
1968	5044683
1969	5044731
1970	7044758
1971	7044758
1972	5044780
1973	5044784
1974	5044811
1975	5044814
1976	5044814
1977	5044814
1978	5044814 (standard)
1978	5044907 (pulse)
1979	5044814 (standard)
1979	5044907 (pulse)
1980	5044907
1981	5044907
1982	5044907

AIR-CONDITIONING COMPRESSOR PART NUMBERS

Year	Part number
all 1968 and early 1969 small-block	5910645
1969 small-block	5910741
1969 big-block	5910740
1970 small-block	5910741
1970 big-block	5910740
early 1971 small-block	5910741
late 1971 small-block	5910778
1971 big-block	5910740
1972 small-block	1131002
1972 big-block	5910797
1973 small-block	1131002
1973 big-block	5910797
1974 small-block	5910741
1974 big-block	5910740
1975	5910741
1976 A-6 axial type	5910741
1976 R-4 radial type	1131078
1977	1131078
1978	1131078
1979	1131078
1980	1131198
1981	1131198
1982	1131198

GLASS DATE CODES

All 1968–1982 Corvette glass was manufactured by Libby Owens Ford (LOF). The date code contains a letter for the month and a second letter for the year.

LOF month code		LOF calendar year code	
January	N	13	Z
February	X	14	X
March	L	15	V
April	G	16	T
May	J	17	N
June	I	18	Y
July	U	19	U
August	T	20	L
September	A	21	I
October	Y	22	C
November	C	23	G
December	V	24	J
		25	A
		26	Z
		27	X
		28	V

BODY BUILD DATE CODES

1968

A	August 1967
B	September 1967
C	October 1967
D	November 1967
E	December 1967
F	January 1968
G	February 1968
H	March 1968
I	April 1968
J	May 1968
K	June 1968
L	July 1968
M	August 1968

1969

A	August 1968
B	September 1968
C	October 1968
D	November 1968
E	December 1968
F	January 1969
G	February 1969
H	March 1969
I	April 1969
J	May 1969
K	June 1969
L	July 1969
M	August 1969
N	September 1969
O	October 1969
P	November 1969
Q	December 1969

1970

A	January 1970
B	February 1970
C	March 1970
D	April 1970
E	May 1970
F	June 1970
G	July 1970

1971

A	August 1970
B	September 1970
C	October 1970
D	November 1970
E	December 1970
F	January 1971
G	February 1971
H	March 1971
I	April 1971
J	May 1971
K	June 1971
L	July 1971

1972

A	August 1971
B	September 1971
C	October 1971
D	November 1971
E	December 1971
F	January 1972
G	February 1972
H	March 1972
I	April 1972
J	May 1972
K	June 1972
L	July 1972

1973

A	August 1972
B	September 1972
C	October 1972
D	November 1972
E	December 1972
F	January 1973
G	February 1973
H	March 1973
I	April 1973
J	May 1973
K	June 1973
L	July 1973

1974

A	August 1973
B	September 1973
C	October 1973
D	November 1973
E	December 1973
F	January 1974
G	February 1974
H	March 1974
I	April 1974
J	May 1974
K	June 1974
L	July 1974
M	August 1974
N	September 1974

1975

A	October 1974
B	November 1974
C	December 1974
D	January 1975
E	February 1975
F	March 1975
G	April 1975
H	May 1975
I	June 1975
J	July 1975

1976

A	August 1975
B	September 1975
C	October 1975
D	November 1975
E	December 1975
F	January 1976
G	February 1976
H	March 1976
I	April 1976
J	May 1976
K	June 1976
L	July 1976
M	August 1976

1977

A	August 1976
B	September 1976
C	October 1976
D	November 1976
E	December 1976
F	January 1977
G	February 1977
H	March 1977
I	April 1977
J	May 1977
K	June 1977
L	July 1977
M	August 1977

1978

A	September 1977
B	October 1977
C	November 1977
D	December 1977
E	January 1978
F	February 1978
G	March 1978
H	April 1978
I	May 1978
J	June 1978
K	July 1978
L	August 1978

1979

A	August 1978
B	September 1978
C	October 1978
D	November 1978
E	December 1978
F	January 1979
G	February 1979
H	March 1979
I	April 1979
J	May 1979
K	June 1979
L	July 1979
M	August 1979
N	September 1979

1980

A	October 1979
B	November 1979
C	December 1979
D	January 1980
E	February 1980
F	March 1980
G	April 1980
H	May 1980
I	June 1980
J	July 1980
K	August 1980

1981 (cars assembled in St. Louis)

A	August 1980
B	September 1980
C	October 1980
D	November 1980
E	December 1980
F	January 1981
G	February 1981
H	March 1981
I	April 1981
J	May 1981
K	June 1981
L	July 1981

1981 (cars assembled in Bowling Green)

B05	May 1981
B06	June 1981
B07	July 1981
B08	August 1981
B09	September 1981
B10	October 1981

1982

C10	October 1981
C11	November 1981
C12	December 1981
C01	January 1982
C02	February 1982
C03	March 1982
C04	April 1982
C05	May 1982
C06	June 1982
C07	July 1982
C08	August 1982
C09	September 1982
C10	October 1982

EXTERIOR PAINT COLOR CODES, INTERIOR TRIM COLOR CODES, AND AVAILABLE COMBINATIONS

1968 Interior color/trim codes

STD	black vinyl
402	black leather
407	red vinyl
408	red leather
414	medium blue vinyl
415	medium blue leather
411	dark blue vinyl
425	dark orange vinyl
426	dark orange leather
435	tobacco vinyl
436	tobacco leather
442	gunmetal vinyl

1968 Exterior color codes and available trim combinations

900	Tuxedo Black (available with all interior colors)
421	Polar White (available with all interior colors)
974	Rally Red (STD, 402, 407, 408)
415	LeMans Blue (STD, 402, 414, 415, 411)
978	International Blue (STD, 402, 414, 415, 411)
983	British Green (STD, 402) 984
984	Safari Yellow (STD, 402)
52	Silverstone Silver (STD, 402, 442)
988	Cordovan Maroon (STD, 402)
26	Corvette Bronze (STD, 402, 425, 426, 435, 436)

1969 Interior color/trim codes

STD	black vinyl
ZQ4	black vinyl
402	black leather
407	red vinyl
408	red leather
411	bright blue vinyl
67	bright blue leather

427 green vinyl
428 green leather
420 saddle vinyl
421 saddle leather
416 gunmetal vinyl
417 gunmetal leather

1969 Exterior color codes and available trim combinations
900 Tuxedo Black (available with all interior colors)
422 Can-Am White (available with all interior colors)
974 Monza Red (STD, ZQ4, 402, 407, 408, 420, 421)
976 LeMans Blue (STD, ZQ4, 402, 411, 412)
980 Riverside Gold (STD, ZQ4, 402, 420, 421)
983 Fathom Green (STD, ZQ4, 402, 427, 428, 420, 421)
984 Daytona Yellow (STD, ZQ4, 402)
986 Cortez Silver (available with all interior colors)
988 Burgundy (STD, ZQ4, 402, 420, 421)
990 Monaco Orange (STD, ZQ4, 402)

1970 Interior color/trim codes
400 black vinyl
403 black leather
407 red vinyl
411 blue vinyl
422 green vinyl
418 saddle vinyl
424 saddle leather
414 brown vinyl

1970 Exterior color codes and available trim combinations
972 Classic White (available with all interior colors)
974 Monza Red (400, 403, 407, 418, 424, 414)
423 Marlboro Maroon (400, 403, 418, 424, 414)
976 Mulsanne Blue (400, 403, 411)
979 Bridgehampton Blue (400, 403, 411)
982 Donnybrooke Green (400, 402, 422, 418, 424, 414)
984 Daytona Yellow (400, 403, 422)
986 Cortez Silver (available with all interior colors)
992 Laguna Gray (available with all interior colors)
27 Corvette Bronze (400, 403)

1971 Interior color/trim codes
400 black vinyl
403 black leather
407 red vinyl
412 dark blue vinyl
423 dark green vinyl
417 saddle vinyl
420 saddle leather

1971 Exterior color codes and available trim combinations
905 Nevada Silver (400, 403, 407, 412, 423)
912 Sunflower Yellow (400, 403, 423, 417, 420)
972 Classic White (available with all interior colors)
973 Mille Miglia Red (400, 403, 407)
976 Mulsanne Blue (400, 403, 412)
979 Bridgehampton Blue (400, 403, 412)
983 Brands Hatch Green (400, 403, 423)
987 Ontario Orange (400, 403, 423, 417, 420)
988 Steel Cities Gray (400, 403, 417, 420)
??? War Bonnet Yellow (400, 403, 423, 417, 420)

1972 Interior color/trim codes
400 black vinyl
404 black leather
407 red vinyl
412 blue vinyl
417 saddle vinyl
421 saddle leather

1972 Exterior color codes and available trim combinations
924 Pewter Silver (available with all interior colors)
912 Sunflower Yellow (400, 404, 417, 421)
972 Classic White (available with all interior colors)
973 Mille Miglia Red (400, 404, 407, 417, 421)
945 Bryar Blue (400, 404)
979 Targa Blue (400, 404, 412)
946 Elkhart Green (400, 404, 421, 417)
987 Ontario Orange (400, 404, 417, 421)
988 Steel Cities Gray (400, 404, 407, 417, 421)
76 War Bonnet Yellow (400, 404, 417, 420)

1973 Interior color/trim codes
400 black vinyl
404 black leather
425 dark red vinyl
413 dark blue vinyl
415 medium saddle vinyl
416 medium saddle leather
418 dark saddle vinyl
422 dark saddle leather

1973 Exterior color codes and available trim combinations
910 Classic White (available with all interior colors)
914 Silver Metallic (available with all interior colors)
976 Mille Miglia Red (available with all interior colors)
922 Medium Blue Metallic (400, 404, 413, 415, 416)
927 Dark Blue Metallic (400, 404, 413, 415, 416, 425)
947 Elkhart Green Metallic (400, 404, 415, 416)
980 Orange Metallic (400, 404, 413, 415, 416, 418, 422)
953 Yellow Metallic (400, 404, 413)
952 Bright Yellow (400, 404, 413, 418, 422)
945 Blue-Green Metallic (400, 404, 415, 416, 418, 422, 425)

1974 Interior color/trim codes
400 black vinyl
404 black leather
425 dark red vinyl
413 dark blue vinyl
415 medium saddle vinyl
416 medium saddle leather
406 silver vinyl
407 silver leather
408 neutral vinyl

1974 Exterior color codes and available trim combinations
910 Classic White (available with all interior colors)
914 Silver Mist Metallic (400, 404, 406, 407, 413, 415, 416, 425)
976 Mille Miglia Red (400, 404, 406, 407, 408, 415, 416, 425)
922 Medium Blue Metallic (400, 404, 406, 407, 413)
948 Dark Green Metallic (400, 404, 406, 407, 408, 415, 416)
980 Orange Metallic (400, 404, 406, 407, 408, 415, 416)
956 Bright Yellow (400, 404, 406, 407, 408, 415, 416)
968 Dark Brown Metallic (400, 404, 406, 407, 408, 415, 416)
917 Corvette Gray Metallic (available with all interior colors)
974 Medium Red Metallic (400, 404, 406, 407, 408, 415, 416, 425)

1975 Interior color/trim codes
19V black vinyl
192 black leather
73V dark red vinyl
732 dark red leather
26V dark blue vinyl
262 dark blue vinyl
65V medium saddle vinyl
652 medium saddle leather
14V silver vinyl
142 silver leather
60V neutral vinyl

1975 Exterior color codes and available trim combinations
10	Classic White (available with all interior colors)
13	Silver Metallic (19V, 192, 73V, 732, 26V, 262, 65V, 652, 14V, 142)
76	Mille Miglia Red (19V, 192, 73V, 732, 60V, 65V, 652, 14V, 142)
22	Bright Blue Metallic (19V, 192, 26V, 262, 14V, 142)
27	Steel Blue Metallic (19V, 192, 26V, 262, 14V, 142)
42	Bright Green Metallic (19V, 192, 65V, 652, 14V, 142, 60V)
70	Orange Flame (19V, 192, 65V, 652, 60V)
56	Bright Yellow (19V, 192, 65V, 652, 60V)
67	Medium Saddle Metallic (19V, 192, 65V, 652, 60V)
74	Dark Red Metallic (19V, 192, 65V, 652, 14V, 142, 60V, 73V, 732)

1976 Interior color/trim codes
19V	black vinyl
192	black leather
71V	dark firethorn vinyl
712	dark firethorn leather
322	blue-green leather
152	smoke gray leather
64V	light buckskin vinyl
642	light buckskin leather
15V	white vinyl
112	white leather
692	dark brown leather

1976 Exterior color codes and available trim combinations
10	Classic White (available with all interior colors)
13	Silver Metallic (19V, 192, 71V, 712, 322, 15V, 112, 152, 64V, 642)
72	Corvette Red (19V, 192, 71V, 712, 64V, 642, 15V, 112, 152)
22	Bright Blue Metallic (19V, 192, 152)
33	Dark Green Metallic (19V, 192, 64V, 642, 15V, 112, 152, 322)
70	Orange Flame (19V, 192, 64V, 642, 692)
56	Bright Yellow (19V, 192, 692)
64	Light Buckskin (15V, 112, 19V, 192, 64V, 642, 692, 71V, 712)
69	Dark Brown Metallic (19V, 192, 64V, 642, 15V, 112, 692)
37	Mahogany Metallic (19V, 192, 71V, 712, 15V, 112, 152, 64V, 642)

1977 Interior color/trim codes
19C	black cloth
192	black leather
72C	medium red cloth
722	medium red leather
15C	smoke gray cloth
152	smoke gray leather
64C	buckskin cloth
642	buckskin leather
112	white leather
27C	dark blue cloth
272	dark blue leather
69C	dark brown cloth
692	dark brown leather

1977 Exterior color codes and available trim combinations
10	Classic White (available with all interior colors)
13	Silver Metallic (112, 19C, 192, 72C, 722, 27C, 272, 15C, 152)
19	Black (112, 19C, 192, 72V, 722, 64C, 642, 15C, 152)
26	Light Blue Metallic (112, 19C, 192, 15C, 152)
28	Dark Blue (112, 19C, 192, 15C, 152, 27C, 272, 64C, 642)
41	Chartreuse (19C, 192)
66	Orange Metallic (19C, 192, 64C, 642, 69C, 692)
52	Corvette Yellow (19C, 192, 69C, 692; code number changed from 52 to 56 midyear)
80	Tan Buckskin (112, 19C, 192, 64C, 642, 69C, 692, 72C, 722)
83	Dark Red (19C, 192, 64C, 642, 15C, 152)
72	Medium Red (112, 19C, 192, 72C, 722, 15C, 152, 64C, 642)

1978 Interior color/trim codes
15C	silver cloth (pace car replica only)
152	silver leather (pace car replica only)
19C	black cloth
192	black leather
72C	medium red cloth
722	medium red leather
76C	saffron cloth
762	saffron leather
59C	light doeskin cloth
592	light doeskin leather
12C	oyster white cloth
122	oyster white leather
29C	dark blue cloth
292	dark blue leather
69C	dark brown cloth
692	dark brown leather

1978 Exterior color codes and available trim combinations
10	Classic White (available with all interior colors)
13	Silver Metallic (12C, 122, 19C, 192, 72C, 722, 29C, 292, 76C, 762)
19	Black (12C, 122, 19C, 192, 72C, 722, 59C, 592, 76C, 762)
52	Yellow (19C, 192, 69C, 692, 12C, 122)
59	Frost Beige (19C, 192, 72C, 722, 29C, 292, 76C, 762, 59C, 592, 69C, 692)
72	Red (19C, 192, 72V, 722, 59C, 592, 12C, 122)
83	Dark Blue Metallic (122, 12C, 19C, 192, 72C, 722, 59C, 592, 29C, 292)
66	Orange Metallic (19C, 192, 64C, 642, 69C, 692)
82	Mahogany Metallic (122, 12C, 19C, 192, 76C, 762, 59C, 592)
89	Dark Brown Metallic (122, 12C, 19C, 192, 59C, 592, 69C, 692)
13U 07M	Silver Anniversary (12C, 122, 19C, 192, 72C, 722, 29C, 292, 76C, 762)
19U 47M	Pace Car Replica (15C, 152)

1979 Interior color/trim codes
192	black leather
722	medium red leather
59C	light doeskin cloth
592	light doeskin leather
12C	oyster white cloth
122	oyster white leather
29C	dark blue cloth
292	dark blue leather
49C	dark green cloth
492	dark green leather

1979 Exterior color codes and available trim combinations
10	Classic White (available with all interior colors)
13	Silver Metallic (12C, 122, 192, 722, 29C, 292, 49C, 492)
19	Black (12C, 122, 192, 722, 59C, 592)
28	Frost Blue (192, 29C, 292, 12C, 122)
52	Yellow (192, 59C, 592, 12C, 122)
58	Dark Green Metallic (192, 59C, 592, 49C, 492, 12C, 122)
59	Frost Beige (192, 722, 29C, 292, 49C, 492, 59C, 592)
68	Hilton Brown Metallic (192, 59C, 592, 12C, 122) (also appears as code 82)
72	Red (192, 722, 59C, 592, 12C, 122)
83	Dark Blue Metallic (122, 12C, 192, 722, 59C, 592, 29C, 292)

1980 Interior color/trim codes
192	black leather
722	medium red leather
59C	light doeskin cloth
592	light doeskin leather
12C	oyster white cloth
122	oyster white leather
29C	dark blue cloth
292	dark blue leather
492	dark green leather
79C	claret cloth
792	claret leather

1980 Exterior color codes and available trim combinations

10	Classic White (available with all interior colors)
13	Silver Metallic (12C, 122, 192, 722, 29C, 292, 79C, 792, 492)
19	Black (12C, 122, 192, 722, 59C, 592)
28	Dark Blue Metallic (192, 722, 59C, 592, 29C, 292, 12C, 122)
52	Yellow (192, 12C, 122)
58	Dark Green Metallic (192, 59C, 592, 492, 12C, 122)
59	Frost Beige (192, 122, 12C, 29C, 292)
47	Hilton Brown Metallic (available with all interior colors)
83	Medium Red (192, 722, 59C, 592, 12C, 122)
76	Dark Claret Metallic (122, 12C, 192, 59C, 592, 79C, 792)

1981 Interior color/trim codes

19C	charcoal cloth
192	charcoal leather
722	medium red leather
64C	camel cloth
642	camel leather
29C	dark blue cloth
292	dark blue leather
152	silver leather
67C	medium cinnabar cloth
672	medium cinnabar leather

1981 Exterior color codes and available trim combinations

06	Mahogany Metallic (64C, 642, 67C, 672)
10	Classic White (19C, 192, 722, 64C, 642, 29C, 292, 67C, 672)
13	Silver Metallic (19C, 192, 722, 152, 29C, 292)
19	Black (19C, 192, 722, 64C, 642, 152, 67C, 672)
24	Bright Blue Metallic (19C, 192, 152, 64C, 642, 29C, 292)
28	Dark Blue Metallic (722, 64C, 642, 29C, 292, 152)
52	Yellow (19C, 192, 64C, 642)
59	Frost Beige (722, 64C, 642, 29C, 292, 67C, 672)
75	Red (19C, 192, 722, 64C, 642, 152)
79	Maroon Metallic (19C, 192, 722, 64C, 642, 152)
84	Charcoal Metallic (19C, 192, 722, 64C, 642, 152)

33/38	Silver/Dark Blue (29C, 292, 152)
33/39	Silver/Charcoal (19C, 192, 152, 67C, 672)
50/74	Beige/Dark Bronze (64C, 642)
80/98	Red/Dark Claret (64C, 642, 152, 67C, 672)

1982 Interior color/trim codes

592	collector edition hatchback silver beige leather
132	silver gray leather
182	charcoal leather
74C	dark red cloth
742	dark red leather
64C	camel cloth
642	camel leather
22C	dark blue cloth
222	dark blue leather
402	silver green leather

1982 Exterior color codes and available trim combinations

10	Classic White (available with all interior colors)
13	Silver Metallic (132, 182, 74C, 742, 22C, 222)
19	Black (132, 182, 74C, 742, 64C, 642, 402)
24	Silver Blue Metallic (132, 182, 64C, 642)
26	Dark Blue Metallic (132, 64C, 642, 22C, 222)
31	Bright Blue Metallic (132, 182, 64C, 642, 22C, 222)
39	Charcoal Metallic (132, 182, 74C, 742)
40	Silver Green Metallic (182, 402)
56	Gold Metallic (132, 64C, 642)
59	Silver Beige Metallic (592)
70	Red (132, 182, 74C, 742, 64C, 642)
99	Dark Claret Metallic (132, 74C, 742, 64C, 642)
13/99	Silver/Dark Claret (132, 74C, 742)
24/26	Silver Blue/Dark Blue (22C, 222)
13/39	Silver/Charcoal (132, 182)
10/13	White/Silver (132, 182)

FINAL MONTHLY SERIAL NUMBERS

1968

September 1967	400905
October 1967	403410
November 1967	405682
December 1967	407922
January 1968	410386
February 1968	412647
March 1968	415000
April 1968	417676
May 1968	420928
June 1968	423978
July 1968	unknown
August 1968	428566

1969

September 1968	703041
October 1968	706272
November 1968	709159
December 1968	711742
January 1969	714695
February 1969	717571
March 1969	720543
April 1969	721315
May 1969	no cars built
June 1969	723374
July 1969	725875
August 1969	728107
September 1969	730963
October 1969	734067
November 1969	736798
December 1969	738762

1970

January 1970	402261
February 1970	405183
March 1970	407977
April 1970	408314
May 1970	410652
June 1970	413829
July 1970	417316

1971

August 1970	101212
September 1970	102226
October 1970	no cars built
November 1970	102675
December 1970	105269
January 1971	108230
February 1971	110886
March 1971	113626
April 1971	115983
May 1971	118223
June 1971	120686
July 1971	121801

1972

August 1971	501344
September 1971	503697
October 1971	506050
November 1971	508406
December 1971	510310
January 1972	512661
February 1972	515020
March 1972	517613
April 1972	519993
May 1972	522611
June 1972	525226
July 1972	527004

1973

August 1972	401138
September 1972	403539
October 1972	406054
November 1972	408696
December 1972	410679
January 1973	413600
February 1973	416301
March 1973	419253
April 1973	421933
May 1973*	428892
June 1973	431731
July 1973	434464

1974

August 1973	401250
September 1973	404111
October 1973	407605
November 1973	410813
December 1973	412830
January 1974	416184
February 1974	419258
March 1974	422367
April 1974	425751
May 1974	429602
June 1974	433257
July 1974	no cars built
August 1974	no cars built
September 1974	437502

1975

October 1974	402385
November 1974	406180
December 1974	409110
January 1975	413159
February 1975	417112
March 1975	420856
April 1975	425228
May 1975	429379
June 1975	433474
July 1975	438465

1976

August 1975	401602
September 1975	405693
October 1975	409982
November 1975	413481
December 1975	416696
January 1976	420568
February 1976	424370
March 1976	428760
April 1976	432805
May 1976	436656
June 1976	440830
July 1976	444767
August 1976	446558

1977

August 1976	402287
September 1976	406337
October 1976	410547
November 1976	414216
December 1976	417551
January 1977	421118
February 1977	424662
March 1977	429041
April 1977	433057
May 1977	437029
June 1977	441233
July 1977	445179
August 1977	449213

1978 Regular Production

September 1977	403186
October 1977	407401
November 1977	411316
December 1977	414695
January 1978	418154
February 1978	422503
March 1978	425280
April 1978	no cars built
May 1978	428833
June 1978	433131
July 1978	436848
August 1978	440274

1978 Pace Car Production

March 1978	901675
April 1978	905766
May 1978	906502

1979

August 1978	400770
September 1978	404612
October 1978	409292
November 1978	413389
December 1978	416891
January 1979	421182
February 1979	425115
March 1979	429500
April 1979	433259
May 1979	437626
June 1979	441770
July 1979	445884
August 1979	450434
September 1979	453807

1980

September 1979	400011
October 1979	404267
November 1979	408343
December 1979	411652
January 1980	416198
February 1980	420057
March 1980	424380
April 1980	427800
May 1980	431152
June 1980	434509
July 1980	438049
August 1980	440614

1981 St. Louis–Assembled Cars

August 1980	400775
September 1980	404136
October 1980	408594
November 1980	412124
December 1980	415234
January 1981	418399
February 1981	421392
March 1981	424742
April 1981	426422
May 1981	428003
June 1981	429775
July 1981	431611

1981 Bowling Green–Assembled Cars

June 1981	100692
July 1981	103155
August 1981	105025
September 1981	106896
October 1981	108995

1982**

October 1981	100515
November 1981	100590
December 1981	102647
January 1982	105004
February 1982	107287
March 1982	110060
April 1982	112598
May 1982	115020
June 1982	117686
July 1982	120227
August 1982	121889
September 1982	124433
October 1982	125408

*The May 1973 production total includes 4,000 serial numbers from 424001 through 428000 that were not utilized.

**Though the final serial number is 25,408, actual 1982 production totaled 25,407. The discrepancy is attributed to the loss of one serial number

Index

Air cleaner,
  1968–1969, 35
  1970–1972, 77
  1973–1977, 130
  1978–1982, 182–185
Air conditioning/heating
  system components,
  1968–1969, 41, 42
  1970–1972, 82
  1973–1977, 138, 139
  1978–1982, 190, 191
Air injection reactor,
  1968–1969, 43, 44
  1970–1972, 84, 85
  1973–1977, 139–141
  1978–1982, 191–194
Air vents,
  1968–1969, 23, 28
  1970–1972, 64, 68
  1973–1977, 112, 118
  1978–1982, 171
Alternator,
  1968–1969, 37, 38
  1970–1972, 79
  1973–1977, 134
  1978–1982, 187
Ashtray,
  1968–1969, 28
  1970–1972, 68
  1973–1977, 119
  1978–1982, 176
Back glass,
  1968–1969, 13
  1970–1972, 55
  1973–1977, 99, 100
  1978–1982, 157, 158
Battery,
  1968–1969, 29, 49
  1970–1972, 68, 69, 92
  1973–1977, 120, 150
  1978–1982, 171, 177, 201
Body fiberglass,
  1968–1969, 8
  1970–1972, 50
  1973–1977, 93
  1978–1982, 151
Body paint,
  1968–1969, 8
  1970–1972, 50
  1973–1977, 93
  1978–1982, 151
Brake lines,
  1968–1969, 49
  1970–1972, 92
  1973–1977, 150
  1978–1982, 201
Brake master cylinder,
  1968–1969, 41
  1970–1972, 81, 82
  1973–1977, 137
  1978–1982, 190
Bumpers, front,
  1968–1969, 8
  1970–1972, 50
  1973–1977, 95
  1978–1982, 151, 154
Bumpers, rear,
  1968–1969, 15, 16
  1970–1972, 57
  1973–1977, 102–104
  1978–1982, 161
Carburetors,
  1968–1969, 34, 35
  1970–1972, 75–77
  1973–1977, 129, 130
  1978–1982, 182
Carpet,
  1968–1969, 22
  1970–1972, 63
  1973–1977, 111, 112
  1978–1982, 170

Center console,
  1968–1969, 26–28
  1970–1972, 67, 68
  1973–1977, 117–119
  1978–1982, 175, 176
Chassis,
  1968–1969, 45, 46
  1970–1972, 87
  1973–1977, 145, 146
  1978–1982, 196, 197
Chassis components,
  1968–1969, 49
  1970–1972, 92
  1973–1977, 150
  1978–1982, 201
Cigarette lighter,
  1968–1969, 28
  1970–1972, 68
  1973–1977, 119
  1978–1982, 176
Convertible top frames,
  1968–1969, 30, 31
  1970–1972, 71
  1973–1977, 123
Convertible tops,
  1968–1969, 16
  1970–1972, 57, 58
  1973–1977, 104
Cylinder heads,
  1968–1969, 32
  1970–1972, 72
  1973–1977, 126
  1978–1982, 180
Dash pad,
  1968–1969, 22
  1970–1972, 63, 64
  1973–1977, 112
  1978–1982, 170, 171
Dash panels,
  1968–1969, 22
  1970–1972, 63, 64
  1973–1977, 112
Differential,
  1968–1969, 48, 49
  1970–1972, 91, 92
  1973–1977, 149, 150
  1978–1982, 200
Distributer,
  1968–1969, 32, 33
  1970–1972, 73, 74
  1973–1977, 127, 128
  1978–1982, 181
Door glass,
  1968–1969, 13
  1970–1972, 55
  1973–1977, 99, 100
  1978–1982, 157, 158
Door handles,
  1968–1969, 13
  1970–1972, 55
  1973–1977, 100
  1978–1982, 158, 159
Door hardware,
  1968–1969, 20, 21
  1970–1972, 62
  1973–1977, 109, 110
  1978–1982, 168, 169
Door jambs,
  1968–1969, 21, 22
  1970–1972, 62, 63
  1973–1977, 110, 111
  1978–1982, 169, 170
Door locks,
  1968–1969, 13
  1970–1972, 55
  1973–1977, 100
  1978–1982, 158, 159
Door panels,
  1968–1969, 20, 21
  1970–1972, 62
  1973–1977, 109, 110

  1978–1982, 168, 169
Door perimeter,
  1968–1969, 21, 22
  1970–1972, 62, 63
  1973–1977, 110, 111
  1978–1982, 169, 170
Driveshaft,
  1968–1969, 48, 49
  1970–1972, 90, 91
  1973–1977, 149, 150
  1978–1982, 200
Early Fuel Evaporation
  (EFE) system,
  1975–1977, 141
  1978–1982, 193
Engine blocks,
  1968–1969, 31, 32
  1970–1972, 71, 72
  1973–1977, 123–126
  1978–1982, 178–180
Engine compartment,
  1968–1969, 44, 45
  1970–1972, 85, 87
  1973–1977, 141, 142
  1978–1982, 195, 196
Engine fan,
  1968–1969, 38, 39
  1970–1972, 79, 80
  1973–1977, 134, 135
  1978–1982, 188
Evaporative control system,
  1971–1972, 85
  1973–1977, 141
  1978–1982, 193
Exhaust, side, optional,
  1968–1969, 14
Exhaust gas recirculation
  (EGR) system,
  1978–1982, 193
Exhaust manifolds,
  1968–1969, 36
  1970–1972, 78
  1973–1977, 133
  1978–1982, 186
Exhaust system,
  1968–1969, 49
  1970–1972, 92
  1973–1977, 150
  1978–1982, 200, 201
Exterior,
  1968–1969, 8–17
  1970–1972, 50–58
  1973–1977, 93–105
  1978–1982, 151–163
Fan clutch,
  1968–1969, 38, 39
  1970–1972, 79, 80
  1973–1977, 134, 135
  1978–1982, 188
Fascia, rear,
  1968–1969, 15, 16
  1970–1972, 57
  1973–1977, 102–104
  1978–1982, 161
Fenders, front,
  1968–1969, 11
  1970–1972, 54
  1973–1977, 97, 98
  1978–1982, 156, 157
Fuel filter,
  1968–1969, 38
  1978–1982, 188
Fuel lines,
  1968–1969, 49
  1970–1972, 92
  1973–1977, 150
  1978–1982, 201
Fuel pump,
  1968–1969, 38
  1970–1972, 79
  1973–1977, 134

  1978–1982, 168, 169
Gas cap,
  1968–1969, 14, 15
  1970–1972, 56
  1973–1977, 102
  1978–1982, 159–161
Gas fill door,
  1968–1969, 14, 15
  1970–1972, 56
  1973–1977, 100–102
  1978–1982, 159–161
Gauges,
  1968–1969, 26
  1970–1972, 66, 85
  1973–1977, 115–117, 141
  1978–1982, 175, 195
Glove box,
  1978–1982, 170, 171
Grille area, front,
  1968–1969, 8, 10
  1970–1972, 50, 52
  1973–1977, 95, 96
  1978–1982, 155, 156
Headlamp bezels,
  1968–1969, 10, 11
  1970–1972, 53, 54
  1973–1977, 97
  1978–1982, 156
Headlamp door, front,
  1978–1982, 156
Headlamp switch,
  1968–1969, 22, 23
  1970–1972, 64
  1973–1977, 112
  1978–1982, 171
Headlamps,
  1968–1969, 10, 11
  1970–1972, 53, 54
  1973–1977, 97
  1978–1982, 156
Heater/air-conditioning control,
  1968–1969, 27, 28
  1970–1972, 68
  1973–1977, 118, 119, 139
  1978–1982, 176
Hood,
  1968–1969, 11, 12
  1970–1972, 54, 55
  1973–1977, 98, 99
  1978–1982, 157
Hood graphics,
  1970–1972, 54
Hood release,
  1968–1969, 23, 24
  1970–1972, 64, 87
  1973–1977, 112, 142
  1978–1982, 171, 196
Hood stripes,
  1970–1972, 54, 55
Horns,
  1968–1969, 25, 34, 45
  1970–1972, 65, 76, 85, 87
  1973–1977, 114, 141, 142
  1978–1982, 172, 195
Hoses,
  1968–1969, 39–41
  1970–1972, 80, 81
  1973–1977, 135–137
  1978–1982, 188–190
Ignition coil,
  1968–1969, 32, 33
  1970–1972, 72, 73
  1973–1977, 127, 128
  1978–1982, 181
Ignition shielding,
  1968–1969, 33, 34
  1970–1972, 74, 75
  1973–1977, 128, 129
  1978–1982, 181
Ignition switch,
  1968–1969, 23

1978–1982, 172
Instruments,
  1968–1969, 25, 26
  1970–1972, 66
  1973–1977, 115–117
  1978–1982, 173–175
Intake manifolds,
  1968–1969, 32
  1970–1972, 72, 73
  1973–1977, 126, 127
  1978–1982, 180, 181
Interior,
  1968–1969, 17–31
  1970–1972, 59–71
  1973–1977, 105–123
  1978–1982, 164–178
Interior switches and controls,
  1968–1969, 22, 23
  1970–1972, 64
  1973–1977, 112, 113
  1978–1982, 171
Jack and jack handle,
  1968–1969, 30
  1970–1972, 69, 70
  1973–1977, 122
  1978–1982, 177, 178
Kick panels,
  1968–1969, 22
  1970–1972, 63
  1973–1977, 111, 112
  1978–1982, 170
Lap and shoulder belts,
  1968–1969, 19, 20
  1970–1972, 61
  1973–1977, 108
  1978–1982, 167, 168
License plate area, front,
  1968–1969, 10
  1970–1972, 52, 53
  1973–1977, 95, 96
  1978–1982, 155, 156
Mechanical systems,
  1968–1969, 31–45
  1970–1972, 71–87
  1973–1977, 123–144
  1978–1982, 178–196
Mirror, door,
  1968–1969, 13
  1970–1972, 55
  1973–1977, 100
  1978–1982, 158, 159
Mirror, rearview,
  1968–1969, 25
  1970–1972, 65, 66
  1973–1977, 114, 115
  1978–1982, 172, 173
Molding, side rocker,
  1968–1969, 14
  1970–1972, 55, 56
  1973–1977, 100
  1978–1982, 159
Oil filter,
  1968–1969, 37
  1970–1972, 78, 79
  1973–1977, 133, 134
  1978–1982, 187
Park brake,
  1968–1969, 26–28
  1970–1972, 67, 68
  1973–1977, 117–119
  1978–1982, 175, 176
Parking lamps,
  1968–1969, 8, 10
  1970–1972, 50, 52
  1973–1977, 95, 96
  1978–1982, 155, 156
Pedals,
  1968–1969, 22
  1970–1972, 63
  1973–1977, 111, 112
  1978–1982, 170
Positive Crankcase
  Ventilation (PCV) valve,
  1968–1969, 36, 43

1970–1972, 77, 85
1973–1977, 131, 132, 141
1978–1982, 185, 186, 193
Power steering pump,
  1968–1969, 38
  1970–1972, 79
  1973–1977, 134
  1978–1982, 187, 188
Quarter trim panels,
  1968–1969, 22
  1970–1972, 63
  1973–1977, 111, 112
  1978–1982, 170
Radiator,
  1968–1969, 39–41
  1970–1972, 80, 81
  1973–1977, 135–137
  1978–1982, 188–190
Radio antenna,
  1968–1969, 14
  1970–1972, 56
  1973–1977, 100
  1978–1982, 159
Radios,
  1968–1969, 25, 26
  1970–1972, 66
  1973–1977, 115–117
  1978–1982, 173–175
Seats,
  1968–1969, 18, 19
  1970–1972, 60, 61
  1973–1977, 106, 108
  1978–1982, 165–167
Shifter,
  1968–1969, 26–28
  1970–1972, 67, 68
  1973–1977, 117–119
  1978–1982, 175, 176
Side-marker lamps,
  1968–1969, 10, 15
  1970–1972, 52
  1973–1977, 96, 104
  1978–1982, 156
Spare tire and wheel,
  1968–1969, 17, 29
  1970–1972, 59, 69
  1973–1977, 105, 120
  1978–1982, 163, 177
Spark plug wires,
  1968–1969, 34
  1970–1972, 75
  1973–1977, 129
  1978–1982, 181
Starter motor,
  1968–1969, 36, 37
  1970–1972, 78
  1973–1977, 133
  1978–1982, 186, 187
Steering box,
  1968–1969, 46
  1970–1972, 88, 89
  1973–1977, 146
  1978–1982, 198
Steering column,
  1968–1969, 23–25
  1970–1972, 64, 65
  1973–1977, 113, 114
  1978–1982, 171, 172
Steering linkage,
  1968–1969, 46
  1970–1972, 88, 89
  1973–1977, 146
  1978–1982, 198
Steering wheel,
  1968–1969, 23–25
  1970–1972, 64, 65
  1973–1977, 113, 114
  1978–1982, 171, 172
Storage compartment, passenger side,
  1968–1969, 29
  1970–1972, 69
  1973–1977, 105, 120
  1978–1982, 177, 178
Storage compartment, rear,

1968–1969, 28–30
1970–1972, 68–70
1973–1977, 120–123
1978–1982, 176–178
Storage tray, rear window,
  1968–1969, 28, 30
  1970–1972, 68, 70, 71
  1973–1977, 120
Sun visors,
  1968–1969, 25
  1970–1972, 65, 66
  1973–1977, 114, 115
  1978–1982, 172, 173
Suspension, front,
  1968–1969, 46
  1970–1972, 87, 88
  1973–1977, 146
  1978–1982, 197, 198
Suspension, rear,
  1968–1969, 46, 47
  1970–1972, 89, 90
  1973–1977, 146, 147
  1978–1982, 198, 199
Taillamps,
  1968–1969, 15, 16
  1970–1972, 57
  1973–1977, 102–104
  1978–1982, 161
Throttle body injection,
  1978–1982, 182
Tires,
  1968–1969, 16, 17
  1970–1972, 58, 58
  1973–1977, 104, 105
  1978–1982, 161–163
Transmission Controlled
  Spark (TCS) system,
  1970–1972, 85
  1973–1977, 141
  1978–1982, 193
Transmission,
  1968–1969, 48
  1970–1972, 90, 91
  1973–1977, 148, 149
  1978–1982, 199, 200
Trim tag,
  1968–1969, 17, 18
  1970–1972, 59, 60
  1973–1977, 105, 106
  1978–1982, 164, 165
T-top,
  1978–1982, 161
T-top storage bags,
  1968–1969, 30
  1970–1972, 70
  1973–1977, 122
  1978–1982, 178
Turn signal levers,
  1968–1969, 24, 25
  1970–1972, 64, 65
  1973–1977, 114
  1978–1982, 164, 172
Underbody components,
  1968–1969, 49
  1970–1972, 92
  1973–1977, 150
  1978–1982, 201
Valance panel, rear,
  1968–1969, 15
  1970–1972, 57
  1973–1977, 102, 103
Valve covers,
  1968–1969, 36
  1970–1972, 77, 78
  1973–1977, 131–133
  1978–1982, 185, 186
Vent grilles, rear deck,
  1968–1969, 14, 15
  1970–1972, 56
  1973–1977, 100–102
Voltage regulator,
  1968–1969, 37, 38
Water pump,
  1968–1969, 38, 39

1970–1972, 79, 80
1973–1977, 134, 135
1978–1982, 188
Wheel assemblies, front,
  1968–1969, 47
  1970–1972, 90
  1973–1977, 147, 148
  1978–1982, 199
Wheel assemblies, rear,
  1968–1969, 47, 48
  1970–1972, 90
  1973–1977, 148
  1978–1982, 199
Wheel covers,
  1968–1969, 16, 17
  1970–1972, 58, 59
  1973–1977, 104, 105
  1978–1982, 161–163
Wheels,
  1968–1969, 16, 17
  1970–1972, 58, 59
  1973–1977, 104, 105
  1978–1982, 161–163
Windows, rear,
  1968–1969, 16, 28
  1970–1972, 58, 68
  1973–1977, 104, 119
  1978–1982, 158, 176
Windows, side,
  1968–1969, 13, 20
  1970–1972, 55, 62
  1973–1977, 99, 109
  1978–1982, 158, 168, 173
Windshield moldings, interior,
  1968–1969, 25
  1970–1972, 65, 66
  1973–1977, 114, 115
  1978–1982, 172, 173
Windshield vent grille,
  1968–1969, 12
  1970–1972, 55
Windshield washer,
  1968–1969, 12, 13
  1973–1977, 99
  1978–1982, 157
Windshield washer fluid reservoir,
  1968–1969, 42
  1970–1972, 84
  1973–1977, 139
  1978–1982, 191
Windshield washer pump,
  1968–1969, 42
  1970–1972, 83, 86
  1973–1977, 139
  1978–1982, 191
Windshield wiper door,
  1968–1969, 12
  1970–1972, 55
Windshield wiper door mechanism,
  1968–1969, 42
  1970–1972, 82–84
Windshield wiper motor,
  1968–1969, 42
  1970–1972, 82–84
  1973–1977, 139
  1978–1982, 191
Windshield wiper/washer control
  switch,
  1968–1969, 25
  1970–1972, 66
  1973–1977, 115
  1978–1982, 172
Windshield wipers,
  1968–1969, 12
  1970–1972, 55
  1973–1977, 99
  1978–1982, 157
Windshields,
  1968–1969, 13
  1970–1972, 55
  1973–1977, 99, 100
  1978–1982, 157, 158